I0796837

Richmond Views the West

MODERN WAR STUDIES

RICHMOND VIEWS THE WEST

Politics and Perceptions in the Confederate Capital

LARRY J. DANIEL

University Press of Kansas

Published by the University Press of Kansas (Lawrence, Kansas 66045), which was organized by the Kansas Board of Regents and is operated and funded by Emporia State University, Fort Hays State University, Kansas State University, Pittsburg State University, the University of Kansas, and Wichita State University.

Library of Congress Cataloging-in-Publication Data
Library of Congress Control Number: 2025016613 (print)
ISBN 9780700640102 (cloth)
ISBN 9780700640119 (ebook)

British Library Cataloguing-in-Publication Data is available.

EU Authorised Representative Details: Easy Access System Europe
Mustamäe tee 50, 10621 Tallinn, Estonia | gpsr.requests@easproject.com
Printed in the United States of America

10 9 8 7 6 5 4 3 2 1

The paper used in this publication is acid free and meets the minimum requirements of the American National Standard for Permanence of Paper for Printed Library Materials Z39.48–1992.

To my grandchildren—
Luke, Will, Caroline, Kennedy, and Barrett

CONTENTS

MAPS AND ILLUSTRATIONS

MAPS

ILLUSTRATIONS

PREFACE

In 2018 the historian Earl J. Hess published an article in which he challenged fellow Civil War authors to break the comfortable molds of strategy, tactics, and generalship and "cast our research nets far, wide, and deep." He argued for pursuing broader and less-explored themes rather than continuing down the well-traveled path of chronicling Civil War battles with little analysis. While Hess was specifically addressing military historians, his broader point struck a chord. It is time to become more creative, expand limited parameters, and, as he wrote, plot a fresh research agenda.[1]

With that in mind, I wrote *Richmond Views the West*, the story of the Heartland and trans-Mississippi and how they were perceived from the seat of power hundreds of miles away. This is not a book about the internal workings of the armies, tactics, and logistics. Indeed, the reader never steps foot on the battlefields of Pea Ridge, Shiloh, Vicksburg, and Atlanta. Rather the story is told exclusively from the vantage of the Confederate capital in Richmond, Virginia. In 1990 Steven Woodworth published his pathbreaking book *Jefferson Davis and His Generals: The Failure of Confederate Command in the West*. The missive concentrated on the Confederate president's relationships with often contentious generals and his strategy as it related to the Heartland. His work, I would argue, has the best biographical vignettes of Confederate generals in the West, written with Woodworth's usual edge and repartee. The story is viewed from the bird's-eye vantage of the historian. The reader thus gets the accurate facts as the story develops.

The subtitle of my book, *Politics and Perceptions in the Confederate Capital*, belies the thesis. The events are told in real time as they unfolded and as they were interpreted by not only Davis but also his cabinet, civil servants, the capital press corps, congressmen, and civilians. In short, my book does not look back but rather ahead. Perceptions, not always reality, were formed by power struggles, often unreliable news accounts, premature or exaggerated military dispatches, and cultural vantages. I have attempted, as much as sources would permit, to take a look inside cabinet meetings, to listen to the gossip in the lobby of the Spotswood Hotel, to hear the rancorous debates of western congressmen, and to understand the capital press in controlling the narrative. Today we would view this as an inside-the-beltway glance, albeit of the Confederate capital. In so doing, the reader gets a better sense of the confusion, urgency, and the time lapses that often occurred before assessments were sorted out. This is not a military book per se but rather a look at how military events shaped politics and perceptions in the center of influence.

The historians Andrew Bledsoe and Andrew Lang concluded that there should be a marriage between "narrow drum-and-trumpet histories" and the more "theoretical war-and-society approaches," which often attempt to "minimize or circumvent military considerations." The integration of these methodologies, they suggest, would result in a "richer understanding of an immensely complicated past." *Richmond Views the West* is an attempt to view the western conflict primarily through the lens of civilian influence and power-wielding.[2]

Virginia authorities strongly lobbied for relocating the original capital of Montgomery, Alabama. The town had its limitations, and despite some balking the decision to relocate was logical and a foregone conclusion. Richmond was only a hundred miles from Washington, D.C., and the primary battlefield in the East would certainly take place between the two cities. With a population of 38,000, the Virginia capital was second only to New Orleans as the largest Southern city, and unquestionably it was the most important industrial center. Indeed, there were only twelve cities in the United States that surpassed Richmond in manufacturing. But it was the aura, political primacy, and symbolism of the Old Dominion that clearly held sway.[3]

Richmonders nonetheless viewed with suspicion the throng of outsiders who converged on their city. There was anxiety over the city's safety, and many shared the suspicion of the blustery Senator Louis Wigfall of Texas, when he asserted that the Cotton States "desired to drag the border States out of the Union, so that the brunt of the war might fall on them, and the Cotton States might escape." The government was nevertheless coming—and with it a flood of civil servants; initially about 1,000 arrived from Montgomery. Provincialism notwithstanding, the city extended a polite, if not totally enthusiastic, welcome.[4]

The move shifted the political balance. The first session of the Provisional Congress comprised delegates from the seven initial seceding states—the so-called Cotton States. With the exceptions of South Carolina, the oversize First Congressional District of Georgia (which included Savannah and the Atlantic Coast), and Florida, all of the delegates initially hailed from the West. President Jefferson Davis and Vice President Alexander Stephens were westerners. If President Abraham Lincoln forged a cabinet of competitors and former opponents, a so-called team of rivals, Davis sought geographical rather than political diversity. Westerners thus filled four of six cabinet posts. With the move to Richmond, the political psychology and clout shifted eastward. The capital press corps would now be centered in Richmond, as would the political power brokers. Virginia would henceforth become the central focus. A "Virginia first" military strategy was soon being proposed. Westerners became jittery. "The Gulf States expect your care, you were elected President of them, not Virginia," an Alabamian bluntly wrote Davis. The Mississippian Jacob Thompson expressed that "the fear [here] is that [the] eye of the Administration is so exclusively fixed upon [Virginia] that we may be neglected & stripped of the means of defense."[5]

Political prestige notwithstanding, the western voting bloc still held the majority in the Confederate Congress (18–8 in the Senate, 75–41 in the House), especially by the end of 1861, the year Missouri and Kentucky delegates were seated—that is, *if* westerners voted in lockstep on issues, which they did not. Voting patterns often fell along antebellum party affiliations. In the election of 1862, several of Davis's staunchest western congressional supporters were defeated, with the winning candidates focusing on peace prospects. It was the enormous size of the West, however, that primarily prevented it from ever becoming a monolith. From the mountains of East Tennessee, to the rolling piney woods of Mississippi, to the prairies of Texas, regional cultures formed, often resulting in clannish thought patterns grounded in geographical isolation and agriculture.

"Geography," wrote Hess, "more than any other factor, made the Civil War in the West unique." The sheer magnitude of the West is difficult to fathom. Texas alone is the size of modern-day Ukraine, and Alabama is the size of England. I have divided the Confederacy into three sections, minus the border states of Missouri and Kentucky. The Eastern Theater includes Virginia, North Carolina, South Carolina, Georgia-1 (a congressional district that encompassed nearly a fifth of the state including Savannah and the coast), and Florida, which together roughly totaled 27 percent of Confederate land size. The Heartland includes Georgia (minus Georgia-1), Alabama, Mississippi, Tennessee, and one-fifth of Louisiana (Louisiana-1 and Louisiana-2, which included Baton Rouge and New Orleans), totaling 26 percent. The trans-Mississippi includes Arkansas, Texas, and two-thirds of Louisiana and represents 47 percent of land size. The Heartland and trans-Mississippi together thus totaled 73 percent of land size, or the equivalent of roughly 90 percent of the size of modern-day France and Germany combined! When the diarist Mary Chesnut, then living in Richmond, heard of the Confederate victory at the Battle of Wilson's Creek, Missouri, she wrote: "Far enough off for us to believe anything we chose." Edward A. Pollard, editor of the *Richmond Examiner*, referred to the Western Theater as "distant and obscure." The clash, therefore, was one not only of military strategies but also of competing cultures.[6]

It must be remembered that the Richmond aristocracy viewed the vast expanse of the West as the frontier. It lacked the stately buildings, bourgeoisie, and snobbish social circles of Richmond. By the time of the Civil War, the city had become a fashion showplace and possessed an exaggerated expression of gentry manners. Northerners visiting the city in prewar days were taken aback by the "high-dressed condition" at all times of the day and, according to one historian, a "certain overarching in social behavior."[7]

Their perception was not totally accurate. When William H. Russell, a London correspondent, visited Memphis during the summer of 1861, he was surprised to see the "extent and size of the edifices public and private." The capitol buildings of Mississippi, Alabama, and Tennessee (all of which still stand) were the equal in beauty and architecture to Virginia's. But there were differences. Memphis and Nashville were surpassed in population by the likes of Portland (Maine), Troy (New York), and Manchester (New Hampshire). Even a westerner, when viewing a Texas cavalry regiment, had to admit that they were "certainly a rough looking set." Thomas Connelly, in his iconic command-level study of the Confederate Army of Tennessee, wrote that, "in the Virginia army, a man of

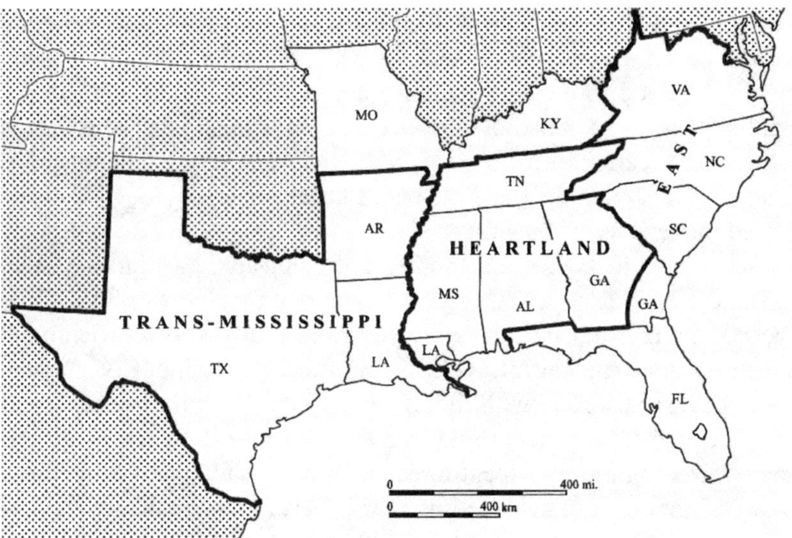

The Confederate West. Map by Mary Lee Eggert.

the coarseness of a Jubal Early was considered something of an oddity. In the Tennessee army, a tobacco-chewing, cursing, hard-drinking general such as Benjamin F. Cheatham was an accepted fact." The same could be said of several crude and obscene western politicians, who were often hypersensitive, drunk, quick-tempered, and violent, such as Louis Wigfall of Texas, John Clark of Missouri, William Yancey of Alabama, Henry S. Foote of Tennessee, and Robert Toombs of Georgia, all of whom were now taking residence in the boarding houses and hotels of the capital.[8]

When the Davises arrived in Richmond, the reception was electric. There were serenades, bouquets, speeches—all were charmed. It was their Palm Sunday; Good Friday would come soon enough. Early on, the First Family of the Confederacy could not help but notice an emerging condescending attitude on the part of "old Richmond." As westerners, the Davises did not seem to measure up to the deeply provincial and clannish standards of the city's elite. It has been suggested that this was due to the fact that they were westerners conducting a war among the milieu of Tidewater society. Their developing cool reception was, according to one historian, "less personal than sectional." Perhaps so, but it quickly turned personal. First Lady Varina Davis especially came under catty criticism. A Confederate senator's wife dismissed her as a "coarse western woman." Mrs. Joseph E. Johnston of Virginia initially referred to the first lady as "a western Belle," but it did not take long for her to substitute "woman" for "Belle." Mrs. Davis would later recall "a certain offishness in their [Richmonders'] manner toward strangers." The president and his wife thus experienced loneliness and viewed themselves as outsiders.[9]

Even when capital citizens momentarily viewed the war in the West, their attention was never far from the enemy at the doorstep. Well over a year and a half passed before the president ventured from Richmond to the Heartland (he never traveled west of the Mississippi River), as he often became absorbed with the minutia of the Virginia front lines. It would be an overstatement to say that the West was Richmond's forgotten war. Much time was spent in capital circles attempting to devise a strategy either to stop the bleeding in the West or to win the war in Virginia before it was lost in the West. Although this is not a thesis-driven book, there are several overarching themes that emerge. Even the most brilliant victories in Virginia could not insulate Richmond from the pain of the disastrous losses in the West, especially Fort Donelson, New Orleans, Vicksburg, and Atlanta. Public opinion in the capital, spurred by biased press reports, often deified certain western generals, such as P. G. T. Beauregard, Sterling Price, and Joseph E. Johnston, whose performance did not justify the public adoration. Indeed, even following the debacle at Fort Donelson, congressional leaders continued to praise the totally inept John Floyd and Gideon Pillow. Additionally, the policy decisions of the Davis administration, notably that of territorial defense and the policy of static defense—defending the rivers from fixed fortifications—forever set the war in the West on a spiraling downward trend from which it never recovered. That policy ultimately cost the South ten divisions, nearly 62,000 troops. Finally, perceptions were often grounded in confusion and lack of clarity. Settled historical issues for modern readers were, at the time, fluid and open to interpretation. No one had a crystal ball.

The military theorist Carl von Clausewitz famously wrote that war was politics by other means. If, as Albert Castel concluded, "the course of the war determines the course of politics," then the reverse must also be true: the course of politics determines the course of the war. Relating the story of the Western Theater as seen from Richmond could not be told without exploring the two sides of that equation. I have, with minor exceptions, limited my focus to western politicians. I do not delve into the formation of the Confederate republic, the antebellum political culture, or the evolution of Confederate nationalism, topics that have been covered in other works.[10]

I have defined the West as both the Heartland and the trans-Mississippi because the cast of characters and strategies were overlapping. Bracketing these two areas together, however, presented a challenge in organizing the material. I have attempted to keep the chapters focused on four sectors—the Appalachian highlands, Heartland, Mississippi Valley, and trans-Mississippi—while keeping the larger narrative in a progressing chronological sequence. Events were obviously occurring simultaneously in all sectors, resulting in some narrative imbrication. In those instances, I did the best I could. As for the photographs, I have attempted to avoid the familiar images of various generals and venture down a path less traveled, concentrating primarily on the western congressional delegation.

A word needs to be said about Thomas Connelly and Archer Jones's provocative book *The Politics of Command: Factions and Ideas in Confederate Strategy*. The authors present the idea of a "western concentration bloc," referring to an informal organization of politicians and generals who generally agreed on the goals of the western theater. But it also served as a power bloc that countered General Robert E. Lee's Virginia-centric strategy. One of these agreements was the preoccupation with the central corridor via Nashville, Chattanooga, and Atlanta into the Lower South. In defining the western concentration bloc, Connelly and Jones outlined four factions, each of which independently held sway, but together they formed an extensive and underrated influence on Confederate strategy. The authors thus posed a question: "Was it possible that the real power base of the Confederacy did not lie in Richmond? Did it instead rest on some intangible line stretching from the Bluegrass through the lower Virginia valley to Columbia and Charleston [P. G. T. Beauregard]?" Without getting into the intricacies, I would simply contend that the power base remained solidly in Richmond—namely, the executive branch—and not by some quasi-connected political and military western bloc.[11]

Whether or not the western concentration bloc was indeed concentrated, or whether its subgroups were accurately defined, the historian Richard McMurry argued that a western power bloc was at least powerful enough to effectively immobilize Davis. The president listened to both sides of the debate—Lee's strategy to concentrate in Virginia, and western lobbying to concentrate in the Heartland. He could never bring himself to make a clear decision. "The two sides of the debate were of about equal strength, and the president, caught between them, was paralyzed. Instead of developing an overall Rebel war plan and making a clear choice, Davis took the politician's easy way out—he tried to please both sides by dividing Confederate resources more or less equally between East and West. As a result, the Confederacy could not ultimately sustain combat in either Virginia or the West." Davis, of course, labored under a fragile nationality.[12]

How the president viewed matters and how Richmond citizens came to their conclusions were two different issues. Every congressman, editor, civil servant, and civilian saw himself/herself as a "bar room general," as a reporter referred to it, every bit as capable as the occupant in the Confederate White House. Dysfunction frequently ruled the day as politicians bickered, plotted, and intrigued.

Not all battles were fought on blood-stained fields. Some conflicts were settled in the halls of congress, in heated cabinet meetings, in newspaper editorial rooms, and in smoke-filled hotel lobbies where politicians and citizen insiders huddled. These conflicts, though hardly glorious, were nonetheless often determinative in setting policy, applying political pressure, and shaping a war narrative. The combatants in this case wore civilian clothes, and their weapons were in the form of inspirational words, political annoyances, emerging alliances, and agonizing judgment calls. Students of the war cannot understand the battles that took place along the banks of the Tennessee River, along the bluffs and backwaters of the Mississippi Delta, or in the red clay and thickets of northern Georgia without understanding the psychology and politics of what was happening hundreds of miles away, seemingly a world away, in Richmond. This is that story.

I wish to particularly thank Timothy B. Smith for reading the manuscript and offering his suggestions. He is a longtime and valued friend and veteran author of the Western Theater. Also, I initially tossed the idea of this book to several members of the Society of Civil War Historians of the Western Theater, notably Richard McMurry and Sam Elliott. Their encouragement served as the impetus for undertaking this project.

1

The Complexities of Neutrality

The clamor on the streets of Richmond in June 1861 represented a curious mixture of excitement and unwelcomed chaos. The locals, who had known one another for years, looked with suspicion upon the stream of office seekers, politicians, and profiteers streaming into the city. Being the new capital of the fledgling Confederacy meant the relocation of numerous departments, each with its own infrastructure. Even at this early date, an estimated 30,000 troops were encamped around the city. Workmen converted the tobacco warehouses in Jefferson Ward to house Yankee prisoners. The city was also in the process of cleaning out the dilapidated row houses and brothels in the rear of the Exchange Hotel. The Custom House, on Bank Street facing Capital Square, housed the Federal court house, post office, and custom office. A room on the second floor was now refitted to become the office of the president, Jefferson Davis. In the yard outside, a huge Confederate flag waved defiantly atop the newly erected fifty-foot flagpole, a visual reminder of where the nation's true power resided. It would be near the end of summer before the permanent Davis residence, the former John Brockenbrough house at Twelfth and Clay, would be ready. The pale gray plaster on the three-story house prompted one wag to say that the residence was not the White House but the "Gray House." Until it was ready, the First Family resided in the Spotswood Hotel.[1]

The western congressional delegation scoured the city for housing. Ultimately one-third of the politicians settled in a half-dozen hotels, including seventeen in the Spotswood and nine in the Exchange, the balance in more than a score of boarding houses. There was some minimal effort to collect into state delegations—four Georgians were at

The Confederate White House on East Clay Street. (Library of Congress)

Mrs. Yerby's on Clay and Leigh—but the majority roomed wherever they were fortunate enough to find space. Alabama Senator William L. Yancey bedded at the home of Mrs. Young, on Marshall and Seventh Streets, while Senators Gustavus Henry of Tennessee and Ed Sparrow of Louisiana lodged at Mrs. Elliott's on Eleventh Street. Georgia Congressman Thomas R. R. Cobb was thrilled when he moved out of his "noisy hotel, with its uncourteous waiters and clerks," into a private residence.[2]

Davis wrote of the "*one party* of the South," but in fact the Confederacy was a political nation that fought about almost everything. If Virginians and South Carolinians held the prestige in the new Confederate Congress, it was their proverbial western stepbrothers who held the votes. Even so, westerners bickered and held grudges. Many had served as the opposition party in the U.S. Congress for so long that they seemingly did not know how to govern in their new setting. For now, however, the disparagements were kept to cliques, private letters, and whisperings. There were bigger issues on the table—beginning with Kentucky.[3]

An anonymous native Kentuckian living in the capital heard disconcerting talk as he walked about. When it came to the Bluegrass State, he admitted that "a general anxiety prevails." In a letter to the *Whig*, "Louisianian" attempted to reassure Richmonders about his home state. Although acknowledging that a majority of the population would vote for the Union Party as opposed to the States' Rights Party, that did not necessarily translate into anti-secessionist sentiment. He explained the inconsistency by saying that only one-fourth of the voters, comprising Germans and transplanted Northerners, were undeniably Lincolnites. One-third of the Union Party, however, naively believed that the United States would continue to permit Kentucky to remain a slave state. Once their delusion had been exposed, they would readily unite with the one-third of the voters who strongly supported secession.[4]

Kentucky, in fact, represented the first major headache for the Confederate War Department. The commonwealth had rejected Abraham Lincoln's call for troops, and the statehouse, in a vote of 69 to 29, had adopted a policy of armed neutrality. A resolution proclaimed that Kentucky should take no part in the current war, and a position of neutrality was adopted, meaning that troops from neither side would be allowed on Kentucky soil.[5]

Davis, being a Kentuckian and having been educated at Transylvania College in Lexington, knew well the state's history. While representing Mississippi in the U.S. Senate, he had strongly resisted the efforts of Kentucky Senator Henry Clay, the "great pacificator" and "Harry of the West." Clay resorted to compromise to avoid secession. He died in 1852, but his successor, John J. Crittenden, had taken up the baton of compromise. From Davis's perspective, compromise meant more concessions on the part of the South. Although Kentucky was a slave state, the population remained deeply divided; Davis had to tread lightly. Even Southern sympathizers, such as Governor Beriah Magoffin, Senator John C. Breckinridge, and Simon Boliver Buckner, commanding the state army, supported neutrality. Davis vowed not to make the first move.[6]

Most Southerners believed that the Bluegrass State would ultimately side with the Confederacy. It was originally part of Virginia, and a vast majority of the population denounced abolitionists. It was reported that former Kentucky governor C. S. Morehead asserted that, in a vote, 99 out of 100 would go for the South. The *Dispatch*, frustrated with the state's nondecision decision, evoked scripture: "Chose ye whom ye will serve. No man can serve two masters." But the issue was complicated. The press (the *Louisville Journal*, *Louisville Democrat*, and *Frankfort Commonwealth*) overwhelmingly favored the Union. If Kentucky sided with the Union, the *Enquirer* declared, the Federal government would arm 50,000 blacks. The *Dispatch* added to the alarmist talk by claiming that 100,000 abolitionists would flood the state within days. The main issue, however, was time. Inevitably one side or the other, either surreptitiously or overtly, would break the neutrality. Every day that a buffer state was in existence represented one more day for the South to build fortifications, seek badly needed arms, and rush reinforcements to the border. Once neutrality was broken, a new, 400-mile front would be opened.[7]

John B. Jones, an editor and popular Southern novelist in more peaceful days and now observant clerk in the War Department, noticed a "large, well-proportioned gentleman" milling around the capital during the latter part of June 1861. Upon inquiry, he discovered that the stranger was Leonidas Polk, the Episcopalian bishop of Louisiana. A *New York Herald* reporter, who would meet him five months later, described Polk as fifty (he was fifty-five), tall, with a Roman nose, sunken mouth, tight lips, frosted hair, and side whiskers. He suggested that a New Yorker might envision an older man wearing a Stetson at the Astor House, add two inches to his height, and sprinkle in a few more gray hairs, then you "will have Leonidas Polk in perfection." Never a deep theologian or intellectual, Polk ascended to the episcopacy at the age of thirty-two primarily because of his wealth and image—he was cousin to former President James K. Polk. A pious man, it was nonetheless rumored that he was given to cursing when he too freely imbibed.[8]

The slaveholding patrician had been in communication with the president concerning the status of Kentucky and the upper Mississippi Valley. A close friend of Davis during their formative days back at West Point, Polk, the "fighting bishop," ask him to "consider me at your service in any way," a veiled implication that he was seeking a commission. He subsequently arrived in Richmond, ostensibly to visit Louisiana troops in his priestly capacity, but there was clearly other business to be discussed. During his week-and-a-half-long stay, the cleric dined with the president and members of the cabinet, held several conversations with General Robert E. Lee, and had "two long & full conversations" with Davis. In writing to his wife on June 10, Polk spoke of his presidential conversations as "the interview"—an interesting choice of words, believing that "it will not be otherwise than producing of good results." Davis was seeking an officer of rank to command operations in the huge Department No. 2 that included the upper Mississippi Valley. It seemed more than coincidental that even then a delegation from New Orleans was in Richmond seeking the appointment of just such an officer. The problem was that Polk had no military experience, having gone into the priesthood upon graduation from the Academy. The president nonetheless offered him department command, choosing his "esteemed friend" over proven talent in the field, adding, "I loved him."[9]

Although the appointment of Polk seemed baffling, even Varina would later recall her husband's "way of taking for granted that everyone agrees with him." Davis's father, Samuel, who embraced him only once and rarely spoke at home, possessed an autocratic and detached persona. At age seven, while living in Mississippi, Samual sent Jefferson back to his birthplace of Kentucky to attend boarding school, where he was the sole Protestant. He was not allowed to say goodbye to his mother; indeed, she was unaware of the decision. He returned home at age ten, but at fourteen he was again sent back, this time to college in Lexington. The man now leading the Confederacy was in many ways his father—aloof and intolerant of disagreement. He typically sought self-effacing relationships. There was something about the president, according to one of his cabinet members, "just an indescribable something," that offended people.[10]

The chief executive actually preferred an even closer friend at Department No. 2: Albert Sidney Johnston. Polk himself had earlier written Davis that "our old friend Gen'l Johnston" should receive theater command. In their Richmond discussions, the president openly talked of Johnston receiving command. Writing to his wife on June 10, Polk admitted: "We want & he [Davis] wants Genl A. S. Johnston badly. He has not yet arrived." Therein lay the problem. Johnston was traveling overland from California, and it would be an unknown number of weeks before he arrived. Matters meanwhile were pressing in Tennessee, and a decision could not wait. Commanding Tennessee state forces was Major General (state rank) Gideon Pillow, a pompous political hack, disliked and distrusted by the president's brother and almost certainly by the president as well. Jones also heard that Pillow was "exceedingly unpopular" with Adjutant General Samuel Cooper. Polk would therefore keep the Tennessean in check. After praying, taking counsel, and feigning surprise at Davis's offer, the bishop accepted the position. He would, in his own words, "fill the gap" for Sidney Johnston. Polk was offered a brigadier's commission, which was soon upgraded to major general. As he descended the steps of the Virginia capital, which now doubled as the Confederate Congress, a gentleman approached Polk and congratulated him on his promotion. The cleric quickly informed him that it was not a promotion, adding: "The highest office on earth is that of a bishop in the church of God." Yet another would address him as "General Polk," only to be corrected: "*Bishop* Polk."[11]

Department No. 2 appeared to be more of an enormous gerrymandered congressional district than it did a cohesive military jurisdiction. It embraced both sides of the Mississippi River north of the Red River in Louisiana. It also included Tennessee west and south of the Tennessee River, a section of Arkansas roughly between Memphis and Little Rock, and a sliver of Alabama north of the Tennessee River from Decatur and Huntsville to Stevenson. What it did not include, at least initially, were the still uncommitted states of Kentucky and Missouri. It would prove an impossibly oversize sector to control, but there was a central advantage. Both the Mississippi and Tennessee Valleys were under unified command. If the rivers had served as a department boundary, then the Federals could simply advance along the seam, leaving Confederate commanders arguing about competing strategies.[12]

News of the appointment soon made its way into the press. Polk's earlier relationship with Davis was never mentioned, only that he had been a "contemporary" at the academy. The *Whig*, straining for some comment, remarked that it had been heard that Polk was "endowed with administrative talent." A desk man was not exactly an exciting endorsement, but it was his former occupation that caught the attention of the people. The thought of a bishop donning a uniform and strapping on a sword became the subject of "much comment" and "even some merriment" on the streets of Richmond. The *Enquirer* admitted that it was "somewhat strange." The readers were assured that Polk and Pillow were "close and bosom friends" who had known one another for twenty years; complete cooperation could be expected. Whether or not it was one of John Jones's government-orchestrated press releases was not known.[13]

For most capital citizens, the West continued as distant in thought as it did in geography. The majority of the residents fixated on the flood of militia companies and refugees marching into Richmond. City officials tended to turn a blind eye toward the flourishing brothel trade. Euphoria prevailed after the victory at Manassas on July 21; western congressmen were elated. Indeed, Congressman Cobb believed the battle to be "one of the most decisive battles in the world."[14]

Civilian authorities nonetheless saw what escaped the attention of the public and even politicians. Barely three weeks into his new command, Polk presented an overly ambitious plan to invade Missouri, a scheme previously proposed by Pillow and rejected by the War Department. Even though the state had not seceded, overzealous Unionists had initiated fighting, which served as sufficient justification for the current move. An offensive along the west side of the Mississippi River would also avoid the sticky issue of Kentucky neutrality. Richmond gave a nod of approval. While Polk maintained his headquarters in Memphis, Pillow proceeded from the Bluff City in a caravan of eight steamboats jammed with 6,000 troops to occupy New Madrid, Missouri. On July 31, Polk confirmed to Secretary of War Leroy Walker that the town had been taken with no resistance. Unfortunately, the expedition was plagued from the start—sickness, insufficient wagons, exaggerated troop returns of Southern forces in Arkansas and Missouri. Panicked Northern papers nonetheless feared the worst, believing that St. Louis was the target. Richmond papers were more than delighted to run the articles. The Confederates now had a supply base for operations into Missouri and could erect fortifications at New Madrid and Island No. 10 upriver to prevent the passage of Union ironclads, known to be under construction at Cairo (Illinois) and St. Louis.[15]

Bombastic press reports notwithstanding, Department No. 2 was in disarray. A Memphis delegation loudly complained to Richmond that Pillow, their favored son, had not been tapped for department command. Congressman David Currin, a Memphian representing Tennessee-11, requested that the subject be revisited. Walker assured Pillow that Polk had been sent to command only Confederate troops, not the state army. It was a distinction without a difference, since Tennessee Governor Isham Harris soon tendered all state troops to the Confederate government, something that Pillow obviously knew was coming. The Tennessean was offered a Confederate commission, not one commensurate with his state rank, but that of a brigadier; he was enraged. It rankled Pillow that he had served in the Mexican–American War, albeit without distinction, while Polk had no field experience. Even the bishop futilely requested that Pillow be granted a major general's commission; it was not going to happen.[16]

Currin continued to receive letters from constituents, which he promptly forwarded to Davis. The most troubling of these came from

Sam Tate, president of the Memphis & Charleston Railroad. "Polk and Pillow are at loggerheads," he warned. "Polk giving a command and Pillow countermanding it by the same messenger. Something must be done and that quickly. Pillow, I learn, is acting on his own hook; will not give up his position as senior general; denied Polk's authority to give him orders."[17]

Missouri Lieutenant Governor Thomas C. Reynolds wrote Davis on August 19 that he considered New Madrid a "dangerous and absurd point of departure for an expedition into Missouri." He had met with Pillow and found him "bent on the project." When warned about the swamps in that portion of the state, the brigadier simply shrugged off the concern, claiming that he "knew all about them." The expedition would have proven "a dead failure" but for the lack of resistance on the part of the Federals.[18]

Unfamiliar with dissent in his role as bishop, Polk became exasperated with a defiant Pillow. He may also have been brooding over the lack of fawning he received in Tennessee. He therefore wrote the president that he did not wish to serve for the duration of the war. Polk never specifically stated that he wished to retire, but Davis, either through another dispatch or reading between the lines, interpreted it as such. Brushing it off, however, the president replied that Department No. 2 would now be expanded to include Arkansas and Missouri. On September 13, he notified Polk, to the bishop's great relief, that Johnston was on the way to command an expanded Department No. 2 that stretched from the Appalachians to the trans-Mississippi. As for Polk's conflict with Pillow, which was known in Richmond, Davis advised the bishop to keep the malcontented brigadier on a short leash. Pillow, meanwhile, was also complaining to Richmond of Polk's "varying views and countermanding orders," which interfered with his operation.[19]

Governor Magoffin was getting nervous. Already the Federal government had semi-breached the neutrality by operating a sizable camp of instruction, Camp Dick Robinson, in eastern Kentucky, where volunteers were mustered, armed, and trained. He now had to worry about encroaching Confederate troops at New Madrid. On August 3, he requested that Davis reaffirm his conviction to honor the neutrality. Unfortunately, the president became deathly ill in August; Jones believed that he might die. The Washington correspondent of the *New York Herald* even reported that he did die! Visitors to the Executive Mansion noticed his flushed appearance. The effect of this ill-timed breakdown was that Davis did not reply to Magoffin until August 28, perhaps creating the suspicion that he was stalling. Davis did offer his reassurance, conditioned on Union activity. His response was released to the Richmond press two weeks later.[20]

Davis, of course, desired to maintain the neutrality, because it de facto favored the Confederacy. As long as there was a buffer state, the South had to worry about only one avenue of invasion into the Heartland: Missouri. Yet this "policy," if it can be called that, was implicit. Precisely what Davis said to Polk during their Richmond meeting was behind closed doors, but regarding the neutrality nothing was put in writing. The president thus left an opening for what was about to occur.

On September 8, eleven days after Davis's reply to Magoffin, the unexpected happened. A panicked Harris telegraphed the War Department that Polk had violated the neutrality by occupying Columbus, Kentucky, on the Mississippi River! "I regard the move as unfortunate, calculated to injure cause in the State," the alarmed governor advised. Polk's subsequent response claimed that the Federals had aggressively taken a position across the river from Columbus with the clear intent of seizing the town, an action seen as a provocation. Using the "plenary power designated to me," he took matters into his own hands and made the first move. Davis composed an order that the occupation was unauthorized and that Polk should immediately withdraw, but he quickly acquiesced. "He [Polk] was ordered by telegraph[] to abandon the town and return to his former position. Then the order was countermanded, and he remains," observed Jones.[21]

Magoffin was apoplectic. The day after Columbus was seized, General Ulysses S. Grant marched his Federal forces into Paducah. The governor wired the bishop-general to immediately withdraw. Convinced that he had stolen a march on the enemy, Polk's response, released by the War Department to the Richmond press, noted that the Federals had forced his hand. Additionally, he argued, the pro-Union state legislature had been using the neutrality as a cover for the operation at Camp Dick Robinson, which had mushroomed to 10,000 troops. In truth, neither side had respected the neutrality. The Confederates had set up recruiting stations and conducted covert raids, and the Confederate Congress had secretly appropriated $1 million for pro-Southern state forces *before* Polk's advance. The occupation of Columbus had been a "military necessity," insisted Polk, one that had been approved by Davis (albeit belatedly, he neglected to add). Buckner pleaded with Davis to order a withdrawal. "I can raise thousands of neutrality Union men to expel the Federals," he asserted. Any troops he would be raising, however, would not be "neutrality Union men" but rather pro-Southern secessionists, meaning that Buckner would be fighting a de facto proxy war for the Confederates. Davis felt that he could not permit the "political elements" to get in the way of "military necessity." In war, however, political policy shaped the military as much as the military affected political practicalities. Nonetheless, Polk agreed to withdraw if the Federals would. Grant refused; the time for bargaining was over. Still naively hoping for a buffer state, Davis remained "deeply anxious" about Kentucky and pleaded for the bishop to walk gently.[22]

The move received broad support in Richmond. "Doubtless they [Polk and Pillow] had intelligence of the enemy's design to occupy Paducah, and [they] determined to break up a pretty little plan of Gen. Grant to invade Tennessee from that direction. He [Grant] has thus been effectively checkmated," reported the *Dispatch*. The *Enquirer* was of a like mind. It was not Polk's intent to violate the neutrality, but it was clear that the Federals had already done so, a move at the very least tolerated by the state legislature. As Polk had written: "Kentucky was fast melting away under the influence of the Lincoln government." Indeed, as he revealed to the president in a letter published in the papers, "I believe, if we could have found a respectable pretext, it would have been better if we had seized this place some months ago," thinking that he had intentionally not expressed to the War Department. Bishops, after all, do not *take* orders; they *give* orders.[23]

The Kentucky legislature immediately signed an alliance with the United States. Morehead was arrested and languished in prison for months. Buckner and Breckinridge escaped to avoid arrest and cast their lot with the Confederacy. The Richmond press expressed their utter contempt for the Kentucky legislature. "This was very cold and selfish[] and very unlike Kentucky," denounced the *Whig*. The *Enquirer* also expressed disdain: "Kentucky, the land of hero's rival, under the influence of demagogues has disgraced herself by acknowledging alliance with the Yankeeized government."[24]

Tennessee Senator Gustavus A. Henry, the long-bearded, fifty-seven-year-old former law-school classmate of the president, although acknowledging Harris's concerns, believed that it would be "ruinous to order him [Polk] back." He believed, as did many, that the pro-Union Kentucky legislature used neutrality as a subterfuge for arming loyalists. Davis's early concerns soon evaporated. When Robertson Topp of Memphis wrote the president an opposing view, Davis shrugged off the criticism by endorsing the letter: "Stupid censure of Genl. Polk for marching into Ky."[25]

By the end of September, reprinted Northern articles claimed that the Mississippi River bristled with Rebel sharpshooters and masked batteries and that Polk's force at Columbus had swelled to 26,000. The War Department knew better; the returns of October showed 16,307 troops at Colombus, with 7,500 more scattered throughout West Tennessee and northern Mississippi, from Fort Henry on the Tennessee River to Island No. 10 and Fort Pillow on the Mississippi River.[26]

Edmund Ruffin, the well-known agriculturalist, planter, political commentator, and fanatical secessionist whose white hair, extending beyond his shoulders, kept him from being a crowd-blender, often resided in Richmond. He kept abreast of the latest news through the press and by frequenting the lobbies of the Spotswood and the Exchange, where politicians and visitors huddled. The buzz was all about Kentucky. "The Reign of Terror has already commenced in Ky," he entered in his diary on September 27. "The [pro-Southern] Louisville Courier has been put down by military order—& Ex-Gov. Morehead & two other secessionist have been seized, carried off, & imprisoned beyond the limits of Ky." A week later he added: "Gov. Magoffin is closely guarded—& one report is that he had already escaped, & is raising the people in opposition to the legislature that is the tool of Yankeedom."[27]

At the War Department, it was becoming increasingly apparent that the ineffectual secretary of war, Leroy Walker, described as a "slow coach" and "a profuse [tobacco] spitter," would be replaced. Davis had never worked well with the Alabamian; any parting would be mutual. The press openly reported that Polk would be chosen as the new secretary of war, but other westerners were mentioned as well, including Harris and Breckinridge. Jones, however, had been noticing the increased visits at the War Department of Judah Benjamin, the secretary of state, and it was quietly being discussed that he aspired to the post. Jones knew that the former New Orleans attorney would unquestionably have a great deal of influence with the president, because he had studied his character and knew how to play to his likes and dislikes. He was correct; Benjamin was given the position, although he was no more of a military

A fervent secessionist, Edmund Ruffin kept abreast of the latest Richmond gossip by loitering in the lobbies of the Exchange and Spotswood Hotels. (Library of Congress)

man than Walker. It mattered not, as Davis needed only an administrative overseer; he would remain the ultimate arbiter of strategy. Although a nonpracticing Jew, perhaps even a nonbeliever, Benjamin encountered a sea of anti-Semitism; many in the capital saw him as no better than a Yankee.[28]

On November 9, thrilling news arrived from the West—a victory! A six-hour battle had been unexpectedly fought at Belmont, Missouri, opposite Columbus, two days earlier. Pillow's 2,500-man outpost had been suddenly attacked by 8,000 bluecoats under Grant. Polk rushed reinforcements across the Mississippi River and forced back the enemy; the Yankee retreat turned into a rout. The Union loss was estimated at 400–500, with Southern casualties reportedly less. Davis immediately telegraphed his thanks to Polk and his troops for their "glorious contribution." That afternoon the *Dispatch* ran an article header: "Great Battle Near Columbus—The Federals Defeated With Heavy Loss." Press accounts continued to run for the next two weeks. The Memphis papers that arrived in the capital began angrily focusing on Pillow and why he had allowed a surprise attack in the first place. The *Whig* added its voice: "To be surprised is one of the gravest faults in the military code. Victory after it scarcely atones for it."[29]

If there was any place in Richmond to learn the latest military and political gossip, it was in the lobbies of the Spotswood and Exchange Hotels. Throughout October and November three Kentuckians—John C. Breckinridge, Humphrey Marshall, and William Preston—all resided at the Exchange as unofficial lobbyists, and it was there that Edmund Ruffin encountered them. The Kentuckians admitted that the "submissionists and Unionists" were in the majority. At the end of October, Ruffin made his way to the Spotswood, where he encountered a second Kentucky delegation. The political pressure was mounting.[30]

Ruffin, on December 6, encountered the Kentucky "Sovereignty Commission" at the Exchange, composed of Preston, Henry C. Burnette, and William E. Simms. They represented an unofficial delegation seeking the commonwealth's admission into the Confederacy. The next day Burnette and Simms made their case before the cabinet. Even though a large proportion of Kentuckians were pro-Southern in sentiment, they would be crushed if not given some assurance of protection beyond military aid. Under current state laws they could be tried for treason. Magoffin, they claimed, had proven useless, "pretending that he was virtually a prisoner." There were whisperings that he had property in the North and that he was afraid of losing it; they simply no longer trusted the man. The admissions proposition was, of course, irregular, but the president was willing to bend the rules and forwarded the case to Congress. There were westerners who opposed the state's admission, such as Alabama Congressman Jabez J. L. Curry. He argued that the

The Spotswood Hotel was ground zero for Richmond political and military gossip. (Library of Congress)

representatives would have no constituency and that "the majority of the people are not in sympathy with us." He was correct, but the failure to admit the state would be a political embarrassment. The secretary of war unartfully said that the Confederacy did not want Kentucky as an ally but as a battleground. Despite qualms on the part of some, the motion was approved. Davis, ignoring the clear evidence, would continue to believe that Kentuckians "by a large majority" sided with the South.[31]

The Kentucky delegation, which would arrive in Richmond in December 1861 and January 1862, comprised mostly lawyers, many of whom had previously served either in the U.S. Congress or the state legislature or had been candidates for such positions; all were avowed secessionists. Simms and Burnette became senators. Due to a unique Confederate law, members of Congress could simultaneously serve in the army; thirty-six senators and representatives would ultimately hold the rank of colonel. Burnette was one of these, his regiment being the 8th Kentucky. He nonetheless relinquished his commission (it was said

Senator William E. Simms of Kentucky. (Library of Congress)

because he could not maneuver his regiment in the field, or so the rumor went in Richmond). An unsympathetic newspaper referred to him as "a big, burly, loud-mouthed fellow who is forever raising points of order." He referred to the flag of the United States as a "Black Republican banner" and Northerners as "Abe Lincoln's dogs." Sporting a diamond-shaped white beard, Simms also had his detractors. Colonel Josiah Gorgas, heading the Ordnance Department, confided in his journal: "What a farce to have 'Senators' from Kentucky, especially such Senators as Simms—a long-lank, unprepossessing man" who would

The chunky, boyish-faced Kentucky Senator Henry C. Burnette hardly looked the role of a power-wielding Confederate congressman. (Library of Congress)

become known in the capital for getting rich off speculating. Horatio Bruce, a Louisville lawyer representing Kentucky-7, would become prominent in the House, as would Eli M. Bruce (no relation), representing Kentucky-9, who was a major player in the pork-packing business. At age seventy, Thomas B. Monroe was one of the oldest members of the Provisional Congress. Beyond giving the commonwealth a congressional delegation, the vote proved largely perfunctory. The Confederacy controlled only that small sector along the Tennessee–Kentucky line. Nonetheless, another star had been added to the national banner.[32]

Thomas Bragg, the newly appointed Confederate attorney general, had a chance to meet with some of the Kentuckians. They insisted that many Unionists would come over to the South if there was a promise that they would be "kindly received," as though such a guarantee could ever be made. Political rhetoric notwithstanding, recruiting in the Bluegrass State remained tepid.[33]

Matters at Columbus meanwhile remained quiet. Polk had recovered from an earlier accidental cannon explosion that had left him seriously injured. That he was not killed had been due only to God, luck, or perhaps bad luck, depending upon the beholder.. As for the long-anticipated attack on the town, Pillow expressed "no apprehension" for its safety. Indeed, according to a Northern item, 10,000 Southern reinforcements were being rushed from Virginia and would arrive in Columbus by Christmas. Maybe it was true, maybe not; capital citizens had no way of knowing. Wharf boats were reportedly being sunk in the Mississippi River channel and a chain was being stretched across the river. Richmonders read a reprinted Memphis article that calmed jittery nerves: "All is quiet at Columbus, Ky."[34]

2

By the Hard Lessons of Adversity

John Jones became increasingly concerned about Missouri throughout June. Even though the state had not yet seceded, fighting had broken out and it quickly turned ugly. He read press accounts of massacres, hangings, bridge burnings, and roving bands of robbers and Jayhawkers wreaking havoc in the western portion of the state. On the seventeenth, Federal forces scattered 1,500 Missouri State Guard at Booneville capturing 60–70, resulting in the loss of the Missouri River in the central portion of the state. Bewildered that the Yankees had been able to ascend the Missouri River, Jones wondered what had become of "the marksmen and deer hunters of Missouri?"[1]

Although 850 travel miles separated Richmond and St. Louis, capital citizens were well aware of the importance of the state. The *Dispatch* reminded its readers that Missouri boasted a larger white population (more than a million) than any Southern state. Rich deposits of copper, iron, zinc, and coal were being mined, and the state had been a leading source of lead for nearly 150 years before the war, the very item needed for small arms ammunition. A Confederate army in St. Louis could menace all of western Illinois and take the Yankee stronghold and shipbuilding facility at Cairo in reverse. But there were problems. St. Louis was largely populated by Germans and Northern-born citizens, and even some slaveholders in the state did not favor secession. The future thus remained in question. Unlike neutral Kentucky, however, Unionist zealots were not content to walk lightly.[2]

Several envoys arrived in Richmond from the trans-Mississippi that June. Christopher Columbus Danley, a distinguished Little Rock newspaper editor who, in younger days, had turned down an appointment to West Point, checked into the Exchange at the southeast corner of Franklin and Fourteenth Streets. He conferred with the president on the twelfth and again on the fourteenth to discuss pressing military matters at the bequest of the Arkansas Military Board. Next arrived Edward C. Cabell, a native of Richmond, graduate of the University of Virginia, former U.S. congressman from Florida, and currently a St. Louis attorney. He was on a secret mission for the governor of Missouri, Claiborne Jackson, seeking Confederate intervention in his state. Davis, aware of political sensitivities, refused on the legal ground that Missouri had not yet seceded. Cabell immediately telegraphed Missouri Lieutenant Governor Thomas C. Reynolds, then in Memphis, to hurry to the capital.[3]

Reynolds, who wore gold-rimmed glasses and sported an inch-long beard beneath his chin, arrived in Richmond on the nineteenth. He and Cabell promptly met with the president and secretary of war. Reynolds was typically a calm and deliberate man who frequently began his sentences with, "Well . . . ," but his 1834 duel with Missouri governor B. Gratz Brown, in which Brown received a leg wound, was common knowledge. Years after the war, Jackson would suffer from dementia and hallucinations. In 1887, he would calmly write his wife a suicide note before walking to the third floor of the Custom House in St. Louis and plunging to his death down the elevator shaft. It was all in the future.[4]

It soon became evident that Reynolds and Governor Jackson were at odds, the former an advocate of Confederate intervention and the latter ostensibly a proponent of peaceful coexistence, up to and including state neutrality. The difference between Jackson and Magoffin in Kentucky was that Jackson, or so he claimed, was actually stalling for time and surreptitiously seeking intervention. Jackson and Thomas L. Snead, along with General Sterling "Old Pap" Price, commanding the state army, thus signed truce negotiations with Major General William S. Harney, the Federal commander in Missouri, while attempting to make a secret deal with Davis. The president knew of the truce, it was openly reported in the Richmond press, and to him it evoked "evidence of vacillation, bordering on bad faith." Davis held up a Jackson proclamation stating that Price would use the state army to drive out any Confederate troops coming into Missouri. Sitting up in his chair while compressing his lips, the president uttered: "Now at the very moment he [Jackson] made this offer [to Harney], you, Mr. Cabell, with a commission from him to me and presenting a request for those Confederate troops to be sent into Missouri, so that had I assented to the request, those troops . . . might have to fight against, instead of with, General Price's army." Jackson, however, had come with his own secret document, this one from Price, who was playing both ends against the middle. While seeking a truce with the Federals, and unbeknownst to Jackson, Price actually sought intervention. Could Davis trust any of these Missourians?[5]

On Friday, July 26, the beardless, narrow-faced Jackson, accompanied by former U.S. senator David Atchison, a longtime Davis friend, checked into the five-story Spotswood Hotel at the corner of Eighth and Main. That evening an expectant crowd gathered in front of the hotel and called upon Jackson to give a speech—he did not disappoint. "I doubt not you want to hear something of Missouri," he began, words greeted with loud cheers. "Well, we have had some little skirmishing there; we have no taste for standing off and looking on, and when we get close to the enemy, we are bound to make him smell our powder." The fighting words were precisely what the crowd longed to hear. He continued: "Ben McCulloch, you all know him," referring to the former neighbor of Davy Crockett, veteran of San Jacinto, Indian fighter, and Texas Ranger, now commanding Confederate forces in Arkansas. "With 8,000 men he came to our assistance with troops from Texas, Arkansas, and Louisiana. One regiment [3rd Louisiana] from the last state was the first and best I ever saw. They came all the way on foot, they came to fight and not to retreat." It was meat to a hungry crowd. He dramatically concluded: "'Give me liberty or give me death' is my motto in this contest," words that were followed by a prolonged thunderous applause. Jackson, the politician, had delivered.[6]

The next day's meeting with Davis did not go as well. His sensitivities offended by the governor's double-dealing, the president viewed him more as an opportunist than a committed secessionist. The issue had nonetheless become moot. Union General Nathaniel Lyon, who superseded Harney, had rejected yet another olive branch extended by Jackson and Price. Davis's suspicions of Jackson nonetheless did not translate into abandoning Missouri. The War Department promptly notified McCulloch to cautiously render assistance, still recognizing that the state had not yet left the Union. Reynolds, who never favored appeasement, issued his own proclamation, printed in the *Whig*, that dissented "in a friendly spirit" from the governor.[7]

While Jackson and Atchison met with the president, a state convention convened back in Missouri; matters did not go as expected. The representatives deposed the governor and the legislature and called for a new state election in November. The way Edmund Ruffin heard the story in Richmond, the state legislators favoring secession had been unable to attend the convention for fear of arrest or violence. "Thus," he told his diary, "the southern & true men being excluded, the remaining submission 'rump' Convention has erected itself into a revolutionary & despotic government."[8]

Jackson returned home and issued a declaration of independence, while Reynolds and Atchison attempted to smooth tensions between the governor and Davis. They assured him that Jackson simply had a case of "constitutional timidity, procrastination[,] and irresolution," but at heart he supported the cause. Sometime in late June or early July (there was no visitor log and the trip went unnoticed by the press), Reynolds and Cabell, the latter having taken up residence in the capital as an unofficial lobbyist, again met with Davis. Once more, it was closed-door. Word leaked out, however, that Reynolds requested a commission to command the Missouri state army. In terms of Confederate intervention, the *Enquirer* cautioned patience, believing that Missouri would eventually join the "sister of states," although conceding that "they have been slow in falling into line."[9]

It did not take long for Lyon's force to move against Price. McCulloch, on June 29, notified the War Department of the stunning news: "Missouri has been crushed and all of her forces are falling back from the Federal troops in the state." Richmond citizens would not learn of the collapse for two weeks, when a Memphis *Appeal* article appeared in the *Dispatch*. Federal forces had poured into the state, and Price's army, ceding the wealthy northern and central sections, including the capital, had fallen back to the Ozarks in the southwestern portion of the state. Readers were assured that the enemy advance would be checked before it reached the Arkansas state line.[10]

Therein lay a problem of the War Department's own making. There were no less than three independent jurisdictions, with little communication among them, each reporting directly to Richmond. McCulloch's command included northwest Arkansas and the Cherokee Nation, with headquarters in Fort Smith. The district of Brigadier General William J. Hardee embraced northeast Arkansas near the Missouri border. Polk, at Department No. 2, commanded the area of Arkansas along the Mississippi River and halfway to Little Rock and now extended to New Madrid, Missouri. The president was warned of the lack of unified objectives and potential bickering. Matters would be resolved with the arrival of Albert Sidney Johnston it was believed, but until then no changes were made.[11]

McCulloch's force of 5,700 Arkansans and Louisiana troops had broken camp at Fort Smith and made a juncture with Price's 9,000 poorly armed Missouri state troops at Cassville, Missouri, on July 29. A slow advance was made against Lyon until August 10, when the Federals made a surprise attack against the Rebel encampment at Oak Hill, as the Richmond papers referred to it, or Wilson's Creek, so named by the Northern papers. According to McCulloch's dispatch of the tenth, Confederate forces scored a decisive victory, losing 1,095 to Lyon's 2,100, with Lyon counted among the slain. By August 15, Ruffin, passing time at the dispatch office on Main Street, began picking up contradictory details of the battle; some Northern accounts claimed victory, others defeat. The reports of a Confederate victory were soon semi-confirmed and became public. "We are rejoicing over a victory at Springfield, Missouri," Judith McGuire wrote, although conceding that she had seen only Northern articles. By the nineteenth, enough confirming reports had been received for the *Whig* to headline "The Great Victory in Missouri." Earlier claims that McCulloch and Price had been killed were discredited. A reprinted Union letter admitted that they had been "badly whipped and cut to pieces," and he feared in the upcoming state vote that "Missouri will go out by a large majority." As for Ruffin, if St. Louis was burned to the ground, it would be "well deserved," as the city was filled with nothing but "foreigners (Germans) or northerners."[12]

Meanwhile, Reynolds continued his bridge-mending efforts between Davis and Jackson, but the president made it clear that he no longer wished to deal directly with the governor. The lieutenant governor insisted that Jackson had learned "by the hard lessons of adversity" and that in the future he would be more careful in taking counsel. Reynolds assured the president that the governor had "taken the final plunge" and now fully embraced secession. Davis nonetheless remained suspicious, and that went for Price as well.[13]

The *Enquirer* of September 16 carried a brief two-day-old article from a St. Louis paper claiming that Price, leading a column of 16,000, was approaching Lexington, Missouri. More accounts had arrived by the twenty-third, declaring that Price had attacked Lexington, but there were no particulars. No Southern accounts arrived, but there were plenty of Federal articles to glean and they were all saying the same thing—the 3,500-man Union garrison at Lexington had been captured. The troops had been marched out to the tune of "Dixie" played by a Rebel band. The Richmond dailies simply added their own headlines—"Glorious Victory at Lexington, Missouri" and "The Triumph in Missouri"—and then ran the Union articles beneath. The *Enquirer* crowed that the 40,000-man Federal army in St. Louis had been outmaneuvered by "the skill of Price and his band of citizen soldiers." Reported battlefield spoils included 3,000 badly needed arms, seven guns, 750 horses, and the great seal of the state of Missouri.[14]

The West had its first hero. The *Whig*, feeding the public appetite, ran an article titled "Major General Sterling Price of Missouri." Price sent his aide, Colonel Thomas L. Snead, to Richmond to discuss the state of affairs and a possible alliance with the Confederacy. Snead also took the opportunity to suggest that Price be given command of all Southern troops in the trans-Mississippi. The capital press joined in the chorus, declaring that the Missourian should be made a major general in the Confederate army. The *Enquirer* described him as over six feet, massively large chin, extremely polished, and strikingly temperate. But there were problems. Old Pap, despite his small triumphs, was a political general who held an exaggerated opinion of his own military prowess. Additionally, the president still clung to his prejudice against the Price–Jackson team due to their initial public appeasement with the Federals, simultaneously attempting to secretly negotiate with Richmond. Cloak-and-dagger was simply not Davis's game. As for John Jones, he feared that the Missouri hero was becoming "too popular, and there is a determination on the part of West Pointers to 'kill him off.' I fear he will gain no more victories."[15] But the Union army in Missouri was *actually* planning to kill off Price faster than any Confederate West Pointers.

By October 25, Arkansas governor H. M. Rector warned Judah Benjamin, now at the War Department, that a large enemy force was approaching the northwest border of Arkansas. Price would be joining McCulloch at or near the state line. McCulloch also warned Richmond that the enemy, 30,000 strong, was slowly advancing. The Missouri

State Guard—"under the control of politicians," the Texan disgustedly wrote—had 13,000 troops, but 4,000–5,000 would be returning home when their enlistments expired. Next came Price's November 10 and December 16 appeals, claiming that 40,000 Federals were within two days' march of him. McCulloch had to reinforce him so that together they could cut their way to the Missouri River. But McCulloch would not be coming. Insisting he had done all he could, McCulloch withdrew his troops into Arkansas and went into winter quarters. Snead would later write that McCulloch saw the Missourians as "nothing but a half-armed mob, led by an ignorant old militia general," which was unquestionably true—and an opinion almost certainly held by Davis as well. As for additional arms for Missouri, Benjamin insisted that he could send muskets only for troops mustered into the Confederate service. The bottom line was that in neither Arkansas nor Richmond were Confederate authorities willing to go out on a limb for Price and Jackson. Feeling abandoned, bitterness began to simmer among the Missourians. Fortunately for Price, the Federal army suddenly withdrew. The State Guard thus went into winter quarters at Osceola, Missouri, on the Osage River.[16]

Despite Price's perilous position, the Northern papers continued to spread panic. The State Guard was reportedly growing. A battalion from Iowa was already in the army, plus two more regiments were on the way from southern Iowa—or so reported. Two of Price's aides had gone into northern Arkansas to recruit, with one mustering 2,000 and the other 1,900. It was believed that Price, with 20,000 troops, had plans to march to the Missouri River and then go into winter quarters. The Richmond public assumed all was going well; insiders knew better.[17]

Politics meanwhile took center stage. Back in the summer, a Missouri convention had deposed the governor and state legislature and called for a popular referendum to settle the issue of secession. Jackson at that time, not waiting for the vote or perhaps fearful of its outcome, declared a declaration of independence. On November 3, the Southern-aligned legislators held a rump convention and declared an ordinance of secession. The Confederate Congress was all too willing to accept the proposal and declared Missouri the twelfth state to join the Confederacy.[18]

The Missouri delegation to the Confederate Congress included two senators and seven representatives. One of the latter, the Virginia-born

Casper W. Bell, a small-town lawyer and newspaper editor, would quickly align with the anti-administration clique. He was countered by the pro-Davis supporter Thomas A. Harris, who was known to be an alcoholic. The recognized leader was Charles W. Vest, then thirty-one, who toward the end of the war would be horsewhipped by an angry woman. Senator Robert L. Y. Peyton, whose half-sister was married to a nephew of Jefferson Davis, was generally uncooperative with the administration. It was the other senator, however, John B. Clark, a brigadier in the Missouri State Guard, who would become an outspoken leader in the anti-administration bloc. As a child, he spent a winter with Indians as a hostage to guarantee a treaty with white settlers. In antebellum days, he challenged Governor Jackson to a duel, but friends worked out a peacemaking arrangement. In a Congress that would have its share of vulgar and unsavory characters, the fifty-nine-year-old Clark, a former U.S. congressman, proved second to none. His Wilson's Creek leg wound and rheumatism had not slowed his drunkenness, gambling, and philandering (he was rumored to have slept with Albert Pike's mistress), all of which would become well-known street talk in Richmond. Even his obituary would one day concede his "stern and rugged character." As a lawyer, he claimed to have defended a hundred men for murder, only one of whom was hanged. In court he would dramatically cry and shed tears, which he used as a ploy to win sympathy. Clark enjoyed talking and always took the lead in conversation. A fellow Confederate senator recalled that he had "a good deal of vanity" and desired to impress people that he was "a man of some importance." This was the Missouri delegation on its way to the capital.[19]

Walking down Ninth Street to the former four-story Virginia Mechanics Institute, previously used as a night school for those training in the mechanical skills and an exhibit hall for various items, one would find the Confederate War Department. A modest brick building, the interior had never been finished. There was no paint or wallpaper on the walls or carpet on the floor. The offices on the first floor housed the secretary of war and the adjutant general. The last, under the direction of Samuel Cooper, employed over eighty clerks who processed literally hundreds of letters, official orders, troop returns, and reports, eight-tenths of which, according to Jones's estimate, were requests for commissions. The Northern-born Cooper had married into a prominent

Senator John B. Clark of Missouri was known throughout Richmond for his vulgarities. (Library of Congress)

Virginia family and had been a close antebellum associate of Davis. He was the senior officer of the Confederacy, outranking even Lee, but he rarely ever wore a uniform. Many dismissed him as a fidgety, red-tape bureaucrat who never voiced an opinion. Later in the war, it was rumored that Davis might replace him, prompting one woman to quip that it would be two years before Cooper realized it. It was no secret that he disdained Walker. The war secretary's office hummed with activity. Those waiting to get an audience lounged about outside, chewing, laughing, talking, or bullying the lone guard.[20]

In the War Office, where the latest rumors swirled, the growing angst between McCulloch and Price was becoming common knowledge. Rather than simply transferring one of them to another department, Davis resorted to placing an officer of rank over both of them. Sidney Johnston was supposed to be that officer, but, preoccupied with Kentucky, he

Samuel Cooper, the Confederate Adjutant General, fidgeted with his shirt collar as though it was too tight. (Library of Congress)

had shown little interest in Arkansas, which alarmed the Arkansas senator Robert W. Johnson. To that end, Davis summoned Colonel Henry "Harry" Heth, a Virginian and West Pointer commanding a regiment in western Virginia. Only thirty-six-years-old, Heth's jet-black hair was already beginning to show slight streaks of gray. "Young man," Davis asked, "how much rank can you stand?" The colonel responded appropriately that he was not the judge of such a question. "I will make you a major general," the president continued, "and send you to the trans-Mississippi; Price and McCulloch are fighting each other over there harder than they are fighting the enemy."[21]

It did not take long for the news to leak to the press, and the bitter feud became public. According to the *Whig* of December 7: "We have heard it alleged," the paper remarked, "that discord exists between McCulloch and Price and that cooperation cannot be expected between them." The paper believed that one or the other should be reassigned but made it clear that it should not be Price. "Price is on his own soil," the editor asserted. As for Heth: "It would be unjust to place him under the disadvantage of superseding a man, who has been credited all of the army that exists in Missouri, and of which he is the idol." The *Dispatch* admitted that rumors were running rampant.[22]

Ruffin gave his blunt assessment. Davis's appointment of Heth was "very unpleasing to his best friends & thorough supporters." Given the dissension between the officers, it was reasonable to place an officer of note over them both, "but not this young colonel, recently but a captain in the U.S.A., & whose only known ground for the designated great promotion & distinction is that he was educated at West Point."[23]

As public and political pressure mounted, Davis's obstinacy became apparent. When the Mississippi congressman Wiley P. Harris expressed his displeasure about Heth, the president could not refrain from making a surly response. "Language was said by Tallyrand to be useful for the concealment of one's thoughts, but in our day it fails to communicate any thought," he vented. "If it had been otherwise, the complaint in relation to Genl. Heth of which you speak could not have been made. If it [Harris's complaint] is designed by calling Heth a 'West Point cadet' merely to object to his education in the science of war, it may pass for what it is worth." "But if it is intended to assert that he is without experience," Davis continued, then his years of service in Missouri and on the frontier "will to those who examine before they censure be a sufficient answer." He ended on a sardonic note, stating that he had long ago learned to dismiss "hasty censure."[24]

The van of the Missouri congressional delegation was in Memphis when they heard of Heth's promotion. Upon arriving in Richmond, five congressmen rushed to get an audience with the president. They warned him of the ruin that would result "if some stranger to our troops" was appointed. Opposing views piqued the chief executive, and his response was, in the words of the congressmen, "firm and even impatient." He alluded to the difficulties between McCulloch and Price and said that he had recently adopted a policy that all major generals should be West Point graduates. Furthermore, he had doubts that Governor Jackson was an avowed secessionist. The appointment would stand. Having gotten nowhere with Davis, the representatives next had a blunt talk with Heth, warning him that the Missouri army would follow no one but Price. Clark and Congressman John R. Cooke subsequently arrived in the capital; they found the president "very much in the same mood."[25]

Congress meanwhile lauded Price's victories. A unanimous vote of thanks was extended to the general for his victories, a move meant as much as a rebuke to Davis as support for the Missourian. Congressmen assured their newly arrived Missouri colleagues that Heth's appointment would not be confirmed in either chamber. The press meanwhile continued its rampage. "We cannot believe that the Administration would be guilty of such reckless imbecility as this change would indicate. . . . The idea of his [Price] being superseded is too preposterous for a moment's consideration." The Nashville *Union & American*, hardly believing the absurd rumors, dismissed it as "a mere sensation in one of the Richmond papers."[26]

A proadministration article attempted to make a rebuttal. The brouhaha had all been a misunderstanding. "We all, Congress, newspapers, and public, have been laboring under a strange misapprehension," declared one response, almost certainly written by an unnamed government source. Heth was appointed to command only Confederate troops in the trans-Mississippi; Price and his State Guard would obviously not be affected. It was becoming the government's stock answer. The administration continued to push hard for all state troops to be tendered into Confederate service. Once done, Heth would supersede Price, denials to the contrary. The second argument was that, if Price received a major general's commission in the Confederate army, he would have to be reassigned, since Missouri troops remained under state control. Davis, of course, had no intention of making Old Pap a major general.[27]

Heth, too, had been reading the newspapers and listening to the open criticism, both from congressmen and on the street. He made an appointment with Benjamin and admitted that he was simply not the person to send. If he went, they "would both unite and fight me," leaving him "between the upper and nether mill stone." Benjamin advised him that, if he turned down the promotion, he could not be a major general; Heth agreed. Davis withdrew the nomination and within days he was made a brigadier and returned to western Virginia.[28]

It now came time for McCulloch to be cast into the political maelstrom. On Saturday night, December 14, the Texan stepped off the train at the Richmond depot. The small, weathered-faced, slightly round-shouldered man checking into the Exchange was far from an uncouth western ruffian; indeed, he appeared more as a planter. He had never completely regained use of his right shoulder after an 1831 duel in which he was hit but never returned fire. Totally opposite in personality to Price, McCulloch was not a backslapper; some saw him as antisocial. Typical of officers in the trans-Mississippi, he never wore military insignias. If he was anything, he was scrappy and not to be trifled with.[29]

J. W. "Deacon" Tucker, a Price newspaper hack, had written an article, carried in the *Whig*, that denounced McCulloch for not assisting Price following Wilson's Creek as well as the administration generally for ignoring the state's needs. The House requested that the president forward all documents relating to the Confederate withdrawal in Missouri. McCulloch, still in Richmond on December 22, fired off a lengthy letter to Benjamin (also printed in the *Whig*) in which he disclaimed responsibility, as he point by point addressed Tucker's accusations. He did not march with Price to Springfield due to a lack of ammunition. McCulloch adamantly insisted that he had given all of the logistical support he could, including the loan of 715 muskets, none of which were ever returned. As to his men "chaffing, like a caged lion, to join the Missourians," it was news to him. He ticked off several complaints against Price, with whom he admitted he had never "been on the most friendly terms personally." The Missouri troops were totally undisciplined; indeed, the cavalry was put to flight after a single cannon shot. He refused to follow the Missourian to Lexington because it would pull him even farther away from his assigned sector, which included northwestern Arkansas and the threat from Kansas. His state troops were returning home, thus leaving him with only 2,500 men. Every time he made a three-year call for Confederate enlistments, the Arkansas Military Board would counter with a one-year call for state troops.[30]

The issue of a commander for the trans-Mississippi continued to be discussed in late December. The cabinet emerged with a name: Major General Braxton Bragg, commanding Confederate forces between Pensacola and Mobile. In his subsequent letter to the general, Benjamin made it clear what the cabinet, and clearly the president, saw as the problem. The Missouri State Guard was "a mere gathering of brave and undisciplined troops." Price had advanced in a move considered "fatal rashness." Yet Bragg was not ordered to report, merely requested to accept the appointment. He politely declined, stating that he found the appointment "not enticing." The realistic prospect of recovering lost ground he believed to be "most gloomy." As for the troops, they had allowed so much license over the past months that they would be worse than raw recruits, who could be properly molded from the start. Besides, the people of Mobile were in a panic and saw him as their only hope. Thomas Bragg, Braxton's brother and the attorney general, noted that literally every general in the Confederacy was discussed.[31]

The year was nearly complete, but time remained for two more angry letters to arrive. Jackson continued his denunciation of the administration for its perceived failure to respond to his state's needs. "Their [Missourians] confidence in the good faith of the Confederate Government has to some extent been shaken," he wrote. With Davis, push would almost inevitably result in pushback. He had no authority to grant Price a Confederate commission over a state army. As far as government assistance to Missouri, he had done everything in his power to render support. "You seem only to remember what others have not done," Davis fired back. "You speak of delay and neglect of Missouri by the authorities in Richmond. Yet, you have not furnished me a single [Confederate] regiment." He again repeated that all Missouri state troops should be promptly tendered to the Confederate States of America. The president's response, though blunt, proved quite accurate. Jackson and Price wished to retain total local control while receiving logistical and financial support from the national government. It remained to be seen who would blink first.[32]

In the final cabinet meeting of 1861, Davis's frustration with Price became evident. "The Missourians have provoked the President a good deal about Price," observed Thomas Bragg. Congress had done its part by appropriating $1 million for the Missouri war effort, but still its troops remained in the militia. Indeed, "they seem to be making no effort to get them into the [Confederate] Service." Davis asserted that all of Price's operations "had been rather useless or worse than useless," save that they had diverted some Federal troops from the Mississippi River. Having been thwarted in his attempt to supersede Price, the issue of an appropriate officer continued to be discussed. With Braxton Bragg out, who could appease both the administration and the Missourians? Thomas Bragg thought that he had a hunch. "I believe Gen'l [Earl] Van Dorn will be sent."[33]

3

Cumberland Plateau—Gateway to the West

Landon C. Haynes, an East Tennessee newspaper editor, would forever be associated with his notorious feud with William G. "Parson" Brownlow, the fiery and uncompromising Knoxville newspaper editor, Methodist preacher, and avowed anti-secessionist. It was whispered that Haynes orchestrated an assassination attempt on Brownlow, but this was never proven. Haynes would also become a Methodist preacher, but he refused to relinquish his war against "unholy Whigs." Each man preferred church charges against the other, resulting in the revocation of Haynes's license to preach. He later went into law and served in the Tennessee state senate. In the current conflict, he was appointed by the state legislature as one of Tennessee's senators to the Confederate Congress. Widely credited for his oratory skills, it was said that he could make an audience "laugh or cry at will."[1]

In early July 1861, Haynes, now a senator, became alarmed over statements made by his old nemesis the Parson, who openly claimed that civil war in East Tennessee was inevitable and that 10,000 Unionists were already armed with shotguns and rifles. Any day he expected to hear that the bridges of the East Tennessee & Virginia Railroad, the vital link to Richmond, had been sabotaged. The senator pleaded for Confederate troops. Thus, while the War Department was besieged with requests for men, arms, and material for Polk's Department No. 2 and Price's state army in Missouri, urgent appeals now came from East Tennessee.[2]

The fiery Senator Landon C. Haynes of Tennessee had little tolerance for East Tennessee Unionists. (National Archives and Records Administration)

Administration officials were concerned about that vital region; they had a right to be. The white population in that portion of the state was actually larger by 25 percent compared to the radically secessionist West Tennessee, and the vast majority of East Tennesseans had voted not to secede. Unquestionably there were Southern nationalists within the thirty counties, but there were simply not enough of them, despite assurances from the *Whig* that recruitment in Confederate regiments was thriving. The mountain "tories" as they were called (many preferred the term "traitors") were defiant. The reason these loyalists held a differing view from Middle and West Tennesseans was not only isolation from an underdeveloped region but also and primarily agriculture. This was not cotton country, and slaves were few. Most mountaineers were small farmers who scraped out a living raising hogs and corn and, by the time of the war, increasingly wheat. In the French Broad Valley alone, tollgate keepers estimated that 150,000 to 175,000 hogs passed through annually, bound for the slaughter pens in North Carolina.[3]

The pro-Southerners did not lack for advocates. They included not only Haynes but also four representatives in the Tennessee congressional caucus, the most outspoken being William G. Swan. Though only forty, the East Tennessee Democrat had established an impressive biography—lawyer, holder of real estate, state attorney general, judge, and former Knoxville mayor. He was also co-owner of the *Knoxville Register*, a vehement counter to Brownlow's *Knoxville Whig*. Swan in fact hated Brownlow every bit as much as Haynes did; indeed, his expressed desire was to this particular parson hang. In July, even before he took his seat in the Confederate Congress, the Knoxville editor made his voice known to Davis. He had recently traveled to Bradley County, Tennessee, along the Tennessee–Georgia line. Word had leaked that a cavalry company had been dispatched to confiscate loyalist firearms. Within twelve hours a thousand Unionists had taken up arms. Such reports were corroborated by a correspondent of the *Dispatch* on location in East Tennessee, who wrote that traitors were busily at work to inaugurate a reign of terror. "[T]reason and rebellion are loudly talked," he reported, and the military would soon be required.[4]

But there was conflicting information. According to the anonymous writer "East Tennessee," who submitted an article in the *Whig*, the only ones advocating violence were "a few broken down politicians of the low order," along with some "quinine black-hearted abolitionists, together with rogues, robbers, and beggars." Davis feared overreacting. Flooding the sector with troops, which were in short supply at any rate, could agitate the tories, and besides, Governor Harris was up for reelection in August. Thus, the administration adopted a conciliatory policy. What Davis did do was to send an officer, namely Brigadier General Felix Zollicoffer, a wealthy former U.S. congressman and, like Haynes and Swan, a newspaper editor. Never in good health, he had also been slightly wounded in an 1852 duel with another editor. Zollicoffer had a limited military background as a lieutenant in the Seminole War, but Harris, out of political necessity, had requested that a Whig be given a commission. Davis knew little about the man, but he appeared popular in Tennessee, and someone of his ilk was needed to rally Southern support in that precarious sector. Some nonetheless grumbled about his contrarian "habits" and that he had never even personally drilled a squad.[5]

Zollicoffer's orders from the War Department were to stop arms smuggling into the region, protect the rail line connecting Richmond and Chattanooga, and crush any insurgency. Upon arriving at his new assignment, the brigadier issued a proclamation appealing for calm. He also let it be known that treason would not be tolerated. He cultivated relationships with some Knoxville Unionists, and Brownlow was allowed to continue publishing. The president also dispatched Albert M. Lea, a West Point graduate who had formerly served as Knoxville city engineer, as an "emissary." According to an East Tennessean whose letter appeared in the *Dispatch*, this was not enough. Home Guard units continued quietly arming, and the sector remained a tinderbox.[6]

Congress was not in a mood to coddle. On August 3 two laws were passed: the Alien Enemies Act and the Sequestration Act. The first declared that anyone refusing to swear allegiance to the Confederate government would be subject to arrest. That in and of itself would not necessarily resolve the issue. In East Tennessee these mountaineers would simply join the Federal army, move to eastern Kentucky outside of Confederate reach, or hide in the mountains, familiar terrain in which they had grown up. It was the second act that had real teeth. All those refusing to submit would have their property confiscated and sold at public action. Although it would take time to enact, ultimately scores, perhaps hundreds, would lose their hard-earned property. True, their cabins did not look like much, but it was all that they had. The *Enquirer* nonetheless declared it "a very just law." Dissidents would experience the harsh consequences of their disloyalty.[7]

As summer gave way, the growing Union concentration at Camp Dick Robinson in eastern Kentucky, which led directly through Cumberland Gap, presented a growing threat. Intelligence arriving at the War Department indicated that 4,000 armed men were present, with another 1,000 at Barboursville and 400–500 recruits coming in daily. With plenty of muskets available, loyalist squads from East Tennessee were reportedly crossing the state line and returning fully armed. Invasion from Kentucky would eventually come, but for now neutrality blocked overt aggressive actions on both sides. Then, on September 7, Cooper, in a rewriting of events, notified Zollicoffer that the neutrality had been breached "by the occupation of Paducah by Federal forces." To the former newspaper editor and current brigadier, such was long overdue. "For weeks," he wrote Governor Magoffin, his response published in the Richmond papers, "I have known that the Federal commander at Hoskin's Crossroads [Camp Dick Robinson] was threatening an invasion of East Tennessee and ruthlessly urging our people to destroy our own [rail] road and bridges." The Federals had constantly been threatening "maneuvering positions." He immediately advanced his troops and occupied Cumberland Gap.[8]

On September 8, the *Whig* gave an update. Zollicoffer was reported to have marched fourteen miles into Kentucky. He might not go farther, the paper asserted, "but Camp Dick Robinson, in Garand County, filled with renegades and Yankees, is right in front of him, some sixty or seventy miles, and we greatly mistake Zollicoffer, if he does not bag that game before he halts." The Northern press meanwhile fretted that Cumberland Gap was being fortified in preparation for a Southern invasion.[9]

When Thomas A. R. Nelson, the clean-shaven, narrow-faced U.S. congressman serving Tennessee-1, attempted to make his way through the lines to get to Washington, D.C., he was captured by Home Guards in Virginia. Escorted to Richmond, he engaged in friendly conversations with the Tennessee delegation. Davis, hesitant to deal with a political prisoner, released him on his word that he would return to East Tennessee and issue a statement in the Knoxville paper appealing to all loyalists to desist from their opposition to Confederate authority. It was either that or face indefinite imprisonment. Nelson agreed, but the subsequent article had little effect.[10]

Back in June 1861, Unionists had gathered at Greenville, Tennessee, to sign a proclamation stating that the mountain counties of the state wished to remain in the Union. They desired peace, but if state authorities chose otherwise, then loyalist troops would be mustered into the Federal army. It was obvious, however, that without Confederate intervention Unionists would become involved. Zollicoffer warned that several thousand tories in southeastern Kentucky were threatening the gaps into Tennessee. Harris pleaded with the War Department for a show of force, stating that "the rebellious spirit of that people" could simply not be tolerated. By mid-September, 8,000 Southern troops had streamed into the area, but the sector was huge and the soft targets were numerous.[11]

The primary concern remained the 240-mile rail line that ran from Bristol, Virginia, to Chattanooga, Tennessee. The track represented a direct lifeline to the West. Although just a single line, the track was owned by two different companies: the East Tennessee & Virginia (139 miles from Bristol to Knoxville), and the East Tennessee & Georgia (110 miles from Knoxville to Chattanooga). Although both lines were bedeviled by problems, it was the East Tennessee & Virginia that proved especially vulnerable. The track was beset with rock slides, rail accidents, and slowdowns due to insufficient rolling stock. By the end of September, the equivalent of 300–400 carloads of blankets and clothing, all bound for Richmond, were stockpiled at Knoxville. To maintain three trains daily each way, Benjamin instructed Colonel Abraham C. Myers, at the Quartermaster Department, for an additional six engines and seventy freight cars. The stock would be taken, either by contract or impressment, from the Western & Atlantic Railroad in North Georgia and the Mobile & Ohio Railroad. It was the only option available, but it promptly brought the ire of Georgia Governor Joseph Brown.[12]

The *Enquirer* was convinced that the surge of Confederate troops would resolve the issue. There was "no longer any serious danger from the tories of East Tennessee." This proved to be wishful thinking. Barely two months had passed when, on November 8, a coordinated insurgent attack was made on several of the railroad's bridges. The damage proved minimal, but the reaction was immediate and heavy-handed. In the dragnet that followed, five bridge-burners were hanged (with the full blessing of the War Department) and scores placed in irons and removed to a prison in Tuscaloosa, Alabama. Frantic letters began to arrive. Senator Haynes reminded Davis that there was much riding on the outcome. If the Southerners were defeated and the railroad seized, there would be violent rebellion in the region. One worried mountaineer, writing to the president, told him that, if the tories were successful, every Southern man would be arrested or murdered in his sleep. Some, such as Alfred G. Graham, editor of the pro-Southern *Jonesboro Union*, advocated for the deportation of all Unionists, meaning a near depopulation of some counties. "By removing the hostile element from our counties we have peace," he wrote Davis, naively thinking that raids could not be conducted across state lines. The *Whig* meanwhile began to ask the question that was on the minds of some: "How do their [Union] correspondents repeat all the conversations heard nightly at the Spotswood [Hotel]? There are bridge burners in our midst."[13]

The East Tennessee lobby was hard at work. Haynes kept Davis apprised of Zollicoffer's perilous situation. J. G. M. Ramsey, a prominent East Tennessee secessionist (but one who recognized that the majority of the local population would never accept separation), pleaded for additional reinforcements. From Huntsville, Alabama, Sam Tate wrote a friend at the Tredegar Iron Works in Richmond to see if he had any influence at the War Department to solicit reinforcements for Zollicoffer. The result of this letter-writing campaign netted only a single newly recruited North Carolina regiment. Ramsey asked Davis for the return of the 3rd Tennessee, then stationed in Virginia. The regiment's presence would stimulate volunteering, "which I am humiliated to say is very low."[14]

Ruffin was hearing the gossip at the Exchange Hotel. Preston privately confided his "grave concerns" about East Tennessee, where he believed Zollicoffer to be seriously threatened by the growing Yankee presence in eastern Kentucky. Davis was also getting nervous. Having sent a political general to command in East Tennessee, he was having second thoughts that a professional should be in charge; he had just the man in mind. He summoned the gaunt, beardless, and weather-faced Brigadier General George Crittenden, then commanding a brigade in Virginia. The Crittenden family had been longtime Davis associates, but George, noted the *Dispatch*, "unlike his father [Kentucky Senator John J. Crittenden] and brother [U.S. Brigadier General Thomas Crittenden], is true to the cause of the South." The president promoted George to major general and sent him to command the two brigades currently in East Tennessee. In extolling his virtues—West Point class of 1842 and breveted in the Mexican–American War—the *Dispatch* omitted the gossip on the streets of the capital that "he is a drunkard." Upon his arrival in Knoxville on December 1, Crittenden immediately became embroiled in the case of Parson Brownlow, believed by many to have been complicit in the recent bridge-burnings. Based on instructions from the War Department, Crittenden granted Brownlow safe passage through Knoxville to Kentucky, but local authorities had him arrested. The finger-pointing began and Crittenden was promptly recalled to the capital. It was made clear, both verbally and in writing, that his authority extended only to Zollicoffer's Brigade, now in southeastern Kentucky, and William Carroll's brigade, then organizing in Knoxville. Colonel Danville Leadbetter would be in charge of railroad defense and sensitive internal issues. Brownlow was subsequently released.[15]

John Baxter, a prominent East Tennessee Unionist and lawyer who had reconciled with Confederate authority, arrived in Richmond in late November. Senator Haynes embraced his secessionist shift, but many remained suspicious of his newfound conversion. Surprisingly, Baxter ran for a seat in the Confederate Congress in September, but he was easily defeated by Judge Swan. Baxter raised eyebrows when he was subsequently retained by some of the accused bridge-burners. The Confederate attorney general, down on his back and taking blue mass and quinine, met with the East Tennessean upon his arrival in the capital. Many East Tennessee tories had been arrested, and Baxter feared the consequences if they were all tried by court-martial. Thomas Bragg gave his assurance that such would not be the case. Benjamin, who joined the conversation, said that only bridge-burners would be dealt with by military trial. The sensitive subject of Brownlow, who was hiding out in the mountains, was also brought up. Baxter asked permission for him to leave Tennessee. Benjamin thought it was advisable and vowed to bring the matter to the president's attention.

The next day, Baxter, along with Bragg and Benjamin, received an audience with Davis. Baxter claimed that he could "tranquilize things" in East Tennessee if the government would give him their confidence and adopt his suggestions. Precisely how he intended to bring this about, beyond his own sense of self-aggrandized magnetism, remained unclear. It mattered not; when it came to East Tennessee, Davis had made up his mind. The loyalists had "abused his confidence" by rejecting his conciliatory policy, and the bridge-burnings were the final straw. Zollicoffer and others had advised him that the time for mild measures had passed. Benjamin joined in by referring to the hostile attitude of the people. Perhaps also, Davis saw through Baxter's poor mountain grammar, which was hard to miss, and realized that this waffler could simply not garnish the confidence of either side. The meeting was over. Within four months, Baxter had again adopted a Unionist stance.[16]

Despite Baxter's swagger that he could mollify the East Tennessee sector, and Swan's statement that the military surge had had the desired effect, not all agreed. One was an anonymous soldier who submitted his views to the *Dispatch*. To think that pacification had come to the hills and coves of East Tennessee "is a great mistake," he warned. "There is much dissatisfaction in every county in East Tennessee." Indeed, at that very moment his unit was engaged with an estimated 1,500 Unionists in

Cocke County. It was clear that the mountain men were not only willing but also quite capable of resisting.[17]

Crittenden did not return to Knoxville until December 15. By that time, Zollicoffer, on his own volition, had left a small garrison at Cumberland Gap and marched fifty miles to the northwest, where he crossed his brigade to the north side of the Cumberland River at Beech Grove, Kentucky. Richmond officials were informed of the move, but given the distances involved (it was a four-day horseback ride from Knoxville to Beech Grove), and their lack of knowledge of the situation, the War Department deferred to Zollicoffer. Crittenden, belatedly informed of the move, prepared to come to his subordinate's aide. Meanwhile, he ordered the brigadier back to the south side of the Cumberland River. It was not until Christmas Eve that Crittenden began his march from Knoxville with William Carroll's Brigade; it would take him ten days to arrive. He discovered, to his shock, that Zollicoffer had in fact *not* recrossed.[18]

Capital citizens were aware, through Northern news articles, that Zollicoffer, reportedly 6,000 strong, had crossed the Cumberland River and had marched toward Somerset, Kentucky. The *Dispatch* of December 31 carried a four-day-old article stating that Crittenden and his staff had departed Knoxville on Christmas night "for a destination unnecessary for us to mention at present." The wilds of Kentucky were nonetheless remote, and Richmonders remained transfixed about the Federal buildup on the Virginia Peninsula and a possible attack on Norfolk. A growing Federal fleet at Hampton Roads also spelled trouble.[19]

The capital prepared for Christmas Day, carrying on the pretense of normalcy. For two weeks the ladies of the city had been purchasing candy and toys for the children, although inflation and the blockade had created spot shortages. "We wonder if Santa Claus will 'be around' tonight?" wondered the *Whig*. "Our belief is that he will surely be here, and [he] will distribute his gifts liberally to all the little folks[] who hang up their stockings."[20]

The balmy springlike weather in Richmond on New Year's Day 1862 belied the date. The generally good public spirit that prevailed in the capital also provided a veil for deeper-brewing problems: a growing anti-administration clique, a press corps that would soon turn hostile, and the vulnerability of the West, which seemed geographically and mentally distant. On this day, however—a day in which the war had not yet turned gruesomely ugly—a surface spirit of contentment prevailed. The president received guests between noon and three o'clock at the open reception in the Executive Mansion, although Varina was indisposed. Hundreds were in attendance to extend New Year's tidings to the president, and the armory band played martial music on the front lawn. It would be the best day of the winter.[21]

Mississippi Congressman James T. Harrison desired nothing more than for Congress to complete its work so that he could return home to Columbus. "I am tired out completely," he disgustedly wrote his wife on January 8. "It seems to be utterly impossible to get a majority of the members to go to work and stick with it. The truth is that most of the members have no objection to playing Congressman. . . . Many of the members go away & come back when they please, taking care to leave others to carry on business." A week later he added: "The Congress has been engaged for the last three weeks on discussing some military bills that ought to have been dispensed of in as many days. We are not through with them yet & no mortal man can make a reasonable guess when we will be."[22]

News from the West continued to be back-page as attention increasingly focused on a Federal expedition, described as "gigantic," forming at Hampton Roads under General Ambrose Burnside. At the War Department, figures of 20,000 bluecoats were batted about in what appeared to be a repeat of the Port Royal, South Carolina, expedition, that resulted in the capture of that position. The Northern papers conveniently provided the names of the schooners, canal boats, and steamers, and although the destination was unknown, Southern military leaders surmised (from the shallow-draft vessels mentioned) that it had to be the North Carolina coast. The citizens of Mobile nonetheless fretted that the target might be them or Pensacola.[23]

Tragedy then struck—not along the coast but in eastern Kentucky. According to a *Louisville Democrat* article dated January 21, Crittenden's Division had suffered a shocking defeat a hundred miles from Knoxville. Details were sketchy, but an apparent surprise attack had been attempted to crush George Thomas's isolated Federal division at a place called Fishing Creek; matters had gone terribly wrong for Crittenden. The article claimed that the Rebels sustained 200 killed and wounded, with Zollicoffer counted among the slain. The remnants of Crittenden's routed division escaped to the south bank of the Cumberland River, with artillery and supplies being abandoned before crossing. A dispatch later that day confirmed a defeat, with the loss of 500 killed and wounded; the entire division was in full retreat. The roads to Knoxville or Nashville were open via Jacksboro or Jamestown.[24]

"We have heard bad news from Kentucky," Thomas Bragg jotted in his diary on January 23. "The President and Sec'y of War keep military matters to themselves—they have been in conference today. I hope they will be able to devise some means to repair the disaster in Kentucky." No official report had arrived by the February 4 cabinet meeting. "The President said it would seem that all but two or three regiments behaved badly—these few did all the fighting—the others ran away as soon as those in front were driven back."[25]

By January 23 the shocking news had hit the Richmond dailies. "We have unpleasant news in Kentucky," reported the *Enquirer*. Although updates were arriving at a pace that could only be described as nerve-wracking, it was clear that a serious defeat had occurred at a village called Somerset. The loss in the Cumberland Plateau represented the first major Confederate defeat in the West. Articles lifted from the St. Louis and Philadelphia papers placed casualties at 275 and characterized Crittenden's shattered forces as "utterly defeated." The *Dispatch* claimed that the Northern accounts were exaggerated, and the *Enquirer*, attempting to put on a best face, suggested that the defeat might prove to be an advantage by awakening apathy. The East Tennessee & Virginia Railroad, the jugular to the West, nonetheless lay dangerously exposed. Scant details trickled in over the next several days, though only through reprinted Northern articles; no government dispatches arrived.[26]

George Bagby, the *Charleston Mercury*'s capital correspondent, was intent on finding out what was taking place behind closed doors. His sources confided: "'Old Jeff's' blood is up, and he intends to repair the disaster in Kentucky at any cost whatever." In the January 31 cabinet meeting, the president openly discussed the turn of events. "The place where troops were most needed now was in East Tennessee," he declared. Reinforcements would soon be on the way.[27]

No additional news had been received by January 24. Bragg frankly did not know precisely how far Crittenden's troops had fled. "He [Leroy Walker] would express no opinion of Gen'l Crittenden until possessed of all the facts. Said the President regarded him [Crittenden] as an able officer." The *Enquirer*, however, was already mentioning the general's old drinking problems "in no very delicate terms." The sleet and hail in the capital throughout the day seemed an appropriate backdrop for the grim news that continued to arrive.[28]

While initial reports claimed that Crittenden's Division was retreating toward Knoxville, an article from a Louisville paper dated January 25 stated that it was instead snaking toward Gainesboro, Tennessee, on the south bank of the Cumberland only seventy-two miles from Nashville! Later Southern accounts substantiated the report. On the night of January 25, a large group of citizens gathered at the St. Charles Hotel, at the corner of Main and Fifteenth, to pay tribute to Zollicoffer, the third Southern general to be lost in the war.[29]

The papers attempted to calm jittery nerves. On January 27, the *Whig* assured its readers that Crittenden's Division was actually at Monticello, Kentucky, only twenty-five miles southwest of Somerset. "The flying frightened fugitives have greatly exaggerated our disaster," the paper asserted. The division had regrouped and resupplied, and the Federals were not pursuing. Updated information in the *Dispatch* confirmed that Crittenden's shattered division had merely paused at Monticello and was now at Gainesboro. If an aggressive Federal commander was to successfully press the Confederates, Nashville could be outflanked. A Confederate column from Knoxville would not be in a position to intercept for fear of being drawn too far from Cumberland Gap and the railroad.[30]

Arriving dispatches continued to portend trouble. Colonel Leadbetter had heard that Crittenden's Division was down to a thousand men; a couple hundred had fled east to Knoxville. The garrison in that city comprised a single regiment and two unarmed battalions, and only a battalion guarded the railroad. The colonel pleaded for an additional two or three regiments. Haynes bluntly wrote the president that nothing but bad roads and natural obstacles prevented the enemy from entering East Tennessee. Congressman John D. C. Atkins had heard from Harris that the Tennessee troops would never rally under Crittenden.[31]

Unsettling rumors now began to circulate. Crittenden, who notoriously had been court-martialed in the Old Army due to alcoholism, had reportedly resumed his old habit. The president, who had appointed him primarily on the basis of long-standing family ties, could hardly believe it, but an investigation was ordered. Indeed, the general, aware of the accusations, requested a Court of Inquiry. "It is already circulated here that he [Crittenden] is very intemperate[] and that it was known when he was appointed. I fear it is too true," Bragg confided in his diary. Several congressmen, hearing from their constituents, notified the War Department that East Tennesseans had lost all confidence in Crittenden. Ramsey wrote of the general's "constant inebriation" and warned that the division was near mutinous. A letter arrived on the president's desk from a citizen in Morristown, Tennessee, denouncing the "Whiskey Barrel General (Crittenden)." Haynes and Swan pleaded with Davis for a new commander. "Let him [i.e., his replacement] be brave, skillful, and sober, sober, sober!" begged the congressman.[32]

The whispers soon became press fodder. A group of Mississippians made its way to Gainesboro to check on friends and relatives in the 15th Mississippi. They subsequently submitted a resolution, published in the *Whig*, exposing the "many rumors." The scandal also included stories of alleged betrayal due to Crittenden's pro-Union father and brother. Acrimony also pointed to Davis for having "selected a known drunkard for a Major General." Congressman Cobb did not mince words. The defeat was "attributable entirely to a drunken, Godless General." Bagby—part reporter, part gossip columnist—mingled with the Tennessee delegation; the congressmen were all too eager to talk. They heard that Zollicoffer opposed the ill-advised offensive at Somerset but had been overruled. Haynes, on the powerful Military Affairs Committee, requested the general's immediate ouster.[33]

As for their part, the president and secretary of war stubbornly resisted the criticism. The final investigation concluded shockingly that the accusations were no more than rumors spread by panicked fugitives and were "without foundation." The inept major general kept his job—at least for now. Nevertheless, Benjamin wrote, the president "thinks it best" to break up the division. In the subsequent reorganization, Crittenden would be leading an expanded command.[34]

During the first week in February, more troubling news arrived from Colonel James E. Rains, commanding at Cumberland Gap, who bypassed Crittenden, being "a great distance from us" and "unable to render any assistance." The late defeat at Somerset had left his command isolated and exposed to attack. One report, perhaps unreliable but nonetheless to be taken seriously, told of 22,000 Yankees headed directly for the Gap. To contest this force, he counted 1,400 troops and a battery; he needed reinforcements and quickly. Fear reigned that East Tennessee would be overrun.[35]

4

The Rise and Fall of Albert Sidney Johnston

On Thursday afternoon, September 5, 1861, in the midst of a warm but steady rain, the Danville train creaked into the Richmond rail depot. Stepping off the passenger car was the highly anticipated Albert Sidney Johnston. It appeared more than coincidental that the *Dispatch* happened to have a reporter present. He described him thus: "He is about six feet high, his face is well sunbrowned by a Southern sun, he wears a mustache, but no whiskers, is well-built, having no superabundant flesh, has a look as one trained to command, and presents a soldierly appearance in every respect." His description stood in stark contrast with a soldier who would see the general several weeks later and described him as "medium sized, portly gentleman of about forty-five [actually he was fifty-eight—L. J. D.], and dressed in civilian clothes & slouch hat & upon first site would not impress a stranger favorably as to anything more than an ordinary citizen." Johnston's receding hairline had left him with only a tuft of hair on the top of his head. He had a square jaw and extended moustache, which he trimmed back prior to the war. Davis was sick in bed when Johnston subsequently called at the Confederate White House. When the president heard the bell ring and the general's footsteps below, he said: "That is Sidney Johnston's step. Bring him to me."[1]

The *Whig* offered the particulars of Johnston's background: a native of Kentucky, graduate of West Point, commander of the army of the Texas Republic (after the bloodshed of the Alamo and San Jacinto), veteran of the Mexican–American War, and colonel of the 2nd United

States Cavalry, he led the 1857 Mormon Expedition and more recently commanded the Department of the Pacific. The *Dispatch* pronounced him as a "star of the first magnitude in the military world." To those who encountered the general, he appeared stern, almost grave. He spoke slowly and was a poor public orator; one of his aides compared him to Moses—"slow of speech." He was known for his "quiet and unassuming manners." The press knew nothing of, or at least failed to report, how this quiet and unassuming man had been left permanently maimed in an 1837 duel and that he had also challenged Sam Houston, the hero of Texas, to a duel. The press knew nothing of his being sued in a failed business venture. Nor was he the reluctant warrior, having advocated for the renewal of fighting with Mexico and with local Indians, thereby incurring bad blood with Houston. Richmonders also did not know that the Mormons had accused him (wrongly) of inciting Indians against them. There was much that capital residents did not know about Albert Sidney Johnston.[2]

Given Davis's prejudice for Johnston, his assignment to Department No. 2 was a fait accompli. Even so, westerners had been clamoring for his appointment. Senator Henry petitioned for Johnston, as did a Memphis citizens committee. Jacob Thompson, former secretary of the interior, hailed his arrival. Even Polk, virtually conceding his own lack of gravitas, lobbied Davis for "our friend" Johnston. The appointment made sense; even the United States Army desired him. Davis already had Joseph E. Johnston and P. G. T. Beauregard, the victors of the Battle of Manassas, to command in Virginia. Sidney Johnston was a Kentuckian by birth and a Texan by choice; he was seen as a westerner. The war appeared to be going well in the West, with small but highly lauded victories of Wilson's Creek, Lexington, and Belmont. In truth, Albert Sidney Johnston was walking into a strategic cauldron.[3]

Upon his arrival at Nashville, Johnston faced his first decision. Should he withdraw Polk, on his left at Columbus, or advance his center into Kentucky? Davis left the matter to him. Now that the Kentucky legislature had aligned with the Union, however, there was no longer any pretense at neutrality. Why withdraw Polk only to have the Federals fill the vacuum? "The troops *will not* be withdrawn," the general telegraphed the president on September 16. He advanced 4,000 troops under Buckner to Bowling Green.[4]

Capital citizens read with delight as reprinted Northern articles declared panic in Kentucky. Confederate troops were reported to be within thirty-six miles of Louisville, with Johnston in the lead. The *New York Times* announced that, unless heavy reinforcements were sent to Kentucky, the Rebels would occupy the entire Ohio Valley and winter in Louisville and Cincinnati. Privately, however, the War Department had concerns. Johnston warned that he did not have half the troops necessary to avert a disaster. Kentuckians were not volunteering in significant numbers; indeed, they appeared "passive, if not apathetic." Johnston ordered Brigadier General Hardee's command in Arkansas to report to Bowling Green. To cover the defenses of Clarksville, Tennessee, he had no choice but to shift 5,000 of Polk's troops to that sector, leaving the bishop with only 11,000 at Columbus. The center corps at Bowling Green, which soon counted 10,000 troops, faced an estimated 20,000 bluecoats (the *Dispatch* placing the number at 30,000). Benjamin sent 3,560 Enfield rifles, which had just arrived through the blockade, but the War Department's resources were stretched thin, especially in Virginia, where 70,000 Confederates faced a wildly exaggerated 200,000.[5]

Jones was one of the few insiders who knew the truth, and the numerical disparity kept him up at night. "The enemy's papers represent that we some 80,000 men in Kentucky, and this lulls us from vigilance and effort in Virginia," he wrote on October 21. "The Secretary of War knows very well that we have not 30,000 troops there, and that we are not likely to have more. We supposed Kentucky would rise. The enemy knows this fact as well as we do; nevertheless, it has been his practice from the beginning to exaggerate our numbers. It lulls us into fanciful security." How many Federals were in Kentucky was anyone's guess. The *Dispatch*, reprinting a Cincinnati article, placed the number at 60,000, with 25,000 more being sent from George McClellan's Army of the Potomac in Virginia, but it could all be disinformation.[6]

Jones also fretted about the Union ironclad fleet known to be under construction in the West. "If they get possession of the Mississippi River, it will be a sad day for the Confederacy," he wrote uneasily. The public nonetheless remained remarkably oblivious to the danger. South of Columbus, Kentucky, the press had written about a fortification under construction by the name of Fort Pillow, but there were no details. In terms of the fortifications on the Tennessee and Cumberland Rivers—Forts Henry and Donelson—the Richmond papers were silent save for a perfunctory mention. The public would have been aghast had it known the true condition, particularly of Fort Henry, the poorly constructed and homely little fort protecting the entire Tennessee Valley.[7]

Despite a lucky win in the Battle of Belmont, Confederate-occupied Kentucky continued to be held by a woefully inadequate force. Johnston's minor sorties were working, at least for the time being. Nonetheless, by December 8 he reported that sickness had whittled down his Bowling Green force to barely 15,000 troops. A skeptical Benjamin pored through the monthly returns. How could Johnston have only 15,000 when his own December 31 return revealed 22,600 present for duty? That number did not include three brigades (one of which numbered 2,500) that failed to file a report. Was Johnston bluffing the War Department as well as the enemy?[8]

Despite the disparity, the reports arriving from the Heartland were far from discouraging. The anticipated advance on Bowling Green by Don Carolos Buell's Army of the Ohio had not materialized. Indeed, an eyewitness from Louisville claimed that a quarter of that army was sick. Rumors from civilians and Yankee deserters spoke of large-scale dissatisfaction among the Federal ranks. The *Cincinnati Gazette* candidly reported that displeasure was openly expressed. The *Cincinnati Commercial* reported that Buell had voiced his concern to Washington that his army remained an "armed mob." Kentuckians continued to give assurances that if a vote was held, without interference from Yankee bayonets, the Confederacy would receive a mandate. Senator Henry had heard from his son, Major John F. Henry of the 4th Tennessee, stationed at Columbus, offering assurances to those who had been "unnecessarily excited" by alarmist press accounts.[9]

So stable did Bowling Green appear that the *Dispatch* began to question Sidney Johnston's strategy. Buell had been checked at Bowling Green, even as Joseph E. Johnston had done with McClellan at Centreville. Indeed, the paper asserted that no attack would be made at Bowling Green and sounded a "forewarning" that reinforcements needed to be sent to Zollicoffer in eastern Kentucky. A Federal offensive against the Virginia & Tennessee Railroad would sever the lifeline to the West. More could be accomplished by concentrating in that sector than by continued massing at Bowling Green. John M. Daniel, the narrow-faced, chin-dimpled editor at the *Examiner*, expressed contempt at the administration's policy of defense. Although never having served in the military, he insisted that Bowling Green and Columbus could both be relieved if an offensive was launched through western Virginia. Richmond would spawn a host of armchair generals.[10]

Johnston continued to plead for more of everything. A January 8,

1862, Bowling Green dispatch, not received for a week, claimed that he had 23,000 troops (as curiously compared to 19,000 a week earlier) opposing Buell's 80,000. He did not expect parity of strength but hoped that his force could be expanded to 50,000. Johnston's task was indeed daunting. He had forty-four understrength infantry regiments to cover a sector 160 miles in length. Neil S. Brown, former Tennessee governor, U.S. congressman, and minister to Russia, also wrote to Benjamin claiming that Buell had 75,000, perhaps 100,000, while "[w]e do not have half that number to oppose them." Johnston, or more likely Harris, had apparently been communicating with politicians. Benjamin pledged to send John Floyd's Virginia brigade, but it had only 2,500 troops. Polk, meanwhile, bypassed department headquarters and informed Davis directly that he faced Grant with 30,000–50,000 men and that Johnston had copped 5,000 of the Columbus garrison for Clarksville.[11]

Davis, however, doubted Johnston's estimate that Buell had 75,000 troops. The figure was based on a stolen document from Federal headquarters in Louisville. A list, published in the *New York Times*, conveniently listed every Union regiment in Kentucky and total army strength. Davis, however, dismissed this intelligence as disinformation. During a January 6, 1862, cabinet meeting, he openly discounted the captured Louisville document and claimed that Buell's strength "could not exceed 45,000 effectives." Benjamin likewise questioned the numbers. John Floyd's brigade would soon be arriving, and in a few more days, it was argued, Johnston should be going on the offensive.[12]

A blast of artic air soon returned to the capital, and by mid-January snow blanketed the streets of Richmond. On the evening of January 14, Colonel St. John Liddell called at the Executive Mansion. A Mississippian from the same county as the president, Liddell remembered him from his childhood, although the two had been formally introduced only six months earlier. The officer bore a letter from Johnston. The general, perhaps playing on his friendship with Davis, requested more men and arms. Already questioning Johnston's numbers, the president's face turned grim as he read the letter. "My God! Why did General Johnston send you to me for arms and reinforcements when he must know that I have neither?" In recalling the scene years later, Liddell remembered Davis as "angry," "abrupt," "impatient," and "not at all cordial." When the Mississippi colonel suggested that troops could be sent by stripping the coast, the atmosphere became testy, bordering on combative. Davis mentioned that he had already come under sharp criticism for sending Floyd's Virginia brigade to Bowling Green. He seemed disinclined to accept Liddell's strategic views of a massive Confederate concentration in Kentucky and dismissed Johnston's self-proclaimed critical situation. As for the synopsis of Southern troop strength, Davis suggested that most of the absent and sick would return to the ranks before active campaigning. He was under tremendous public and political pressures, and no governor was willing to spare men. The next night, at the president's invitation, Liddell dined with the First Family. Davis appeared "quite another man" as he reminisced about West Point days. The colonel, his mind on the mission, could only listen with forced attention. As Liddell was shown to the door at the conclusion of the dinner, Davis remarked: "Tell my friend, General Johnston, that I can do nothing for him." Liddell, exhausted and feeling quite unwell, departed: "I found it quite cold on the streets of Richmond."[13]

Davis spoke the truth given his policy of territorial defense. He remained adamantly—some would say stubbornly—committed to the concept that all territory was of strategic, diplomatic, political, and logistical value. Barely a week before Liddell's arrival, he had written the governor of Mississippi: "I shall much regret if any successful raid be made against the villages of our coast." The policy obviously placated governors, members of Congress, and most civilians. Whether or not it was the correct policy, at least at this stage, was relegated to a crystal ball of opinions.[14]

Jones, at the War Department, believed that a dangerous game was being played. He confided in his diary: "Again the Northern press gave the most extravagant number to our army in Kentucky, some estimates are as high as 150,000. I know, and Mr. Benjamin knows, that Gen. Johnston has not exceeding twenty-nine thousand effective men." He suspicioned that the Federals knew well of Johnston's weakness and were purposely releasing disinformation. By claiming vastly wild Confederate numbers, they were banking that Richmond would not send additional reinforcements. "*Well, no reinforcements are sent*," he disgustedly concluded.[15]

At the cabinet meeting on Friday, January 17, the news from the West proved particularly gloomy. Davis read Polk's recently arrived letter expressing fears that his 10,000 troops were about to be attacked by overwhelming numbers. From Bowling Green, a letter from an officer offered a "not very flattering picture of things." The enemy greatly outnumbered them; Kentuckians appeared to "stand aloof" and were ready to take sides with the enemy should the tide turn in its favor. "Upon the whole," fretted Thomas Bragg, "we have much to apprehend."[16]

The tiff between Polk and Pillow was also discussed. Pillow's resignation was read, although the specific reason remained vague. Two days later Thomas Bragg received a letter from a Judge Nicholson, a Memphis friend of his, who disclosed that the two generals could still "not get along together" but that Pillow's resignation should not be accepted because "he has influence in Tennessee." Judge Nicholson advised transferring him to Johnston in Bowling Green. "I will mention it to the President," Bragg told his diary. As for Davis, the attorney general admitted that he had never "seen him so gloomy." The president's tendency was to become "somewhat irritable when opposed—wants to have his own way."[17]

On January 22, Johnston notified the War Office of the stunning news of Crittenden's defeat at Somerset, Kentucky; the civilian authorities gasped. Unless a blocking force could be sent to Burkesville, Tennessee, a hundred miles east of Nashville, Buell's army would be in a position to pin down Johnston's forces at Bowling Green while the eastern Kentucky column maneuvered to flank Nashville. Johnston wrote that he could not send reinforcements to Crittenden, having already detached 8,000 to Russellville to shore up Polk's right flank. His Bowling Green force faced an estimated 80,000. If any more troops were detached to either of the flanks, the center would become untenable. There were a couple additional raw regiments expected, but they were untrained and susceptible to measles. All available troops must be rushed to Tennessee.[18]

On January 23, a day before the bad news hit the papers, Bragg had gotten wind of a potential Federal overland march to bypass Fort Henry. Some 10,000 bluecoats had occupied Murray, Kentucky, and were marching twenty-two miles south to seize Paris, Tennessee. "I hardly think this can be true—they may endeavor to get below Columbus by a rapid march and break up the Mobile [&] Ohio Rail Road. If they are advancing as stated, they may turn the position at Columbus." A week later, however, a copied article from Memphis headlined: "Predicted Fall of Fort Henry and Subsequent Disaster."[19]

It was no secret in Richmond that Davis had long clashed with forty-four-year-old General P. G. T. Beauregard, the flamboyant, publicity-seeking, and (to the president's mind, at least) highly overrated Louisiana general. His slicked, graying hair, curled at the ears, with a strip of vertical hair extending from the bottom lip to the chin, gave him more the appearance of a French officer. Indeed, he could speak French as well as English. To Davis, he was more than just a nuisance; Beauregard was trouble. He had powerful friends in Congress, including his father-in-law, the former U.S. Senator John Slidell of Louisiana. Despite the general's insistence that he had patriotism, not political ambition, in mind, there was talk that he might seek higher office—perhaps the presidency. By early 1862 there was no pretense of friendship between the two. Beauregard communicated directly with congressmen, rejected attempts at presidential appeasement, argued with Benjamin, quarreled over issues of strategy, and implied in his Manassas after-action report, published in the *Whig*, that Davis had vetoed his plan to capture Washington, D.C. and Baltimore. Precisely how "the Creole Gentleman," as the *Dispatch* referred to him, ended up in Department No. 2 has long been shrouded in closed-door conversations.[20]

Davis was forever silent on the negotiations dealing with the Beauregard transfer. The only one talking was Congressman Roger Pryor, a blustery and violent Virginia fire-eater. He had been one of a party of four men to enter Fort Sumter and demand its surrender back in April 1861. According to the *New York Tribune*, he was "literally dressed to kill, bristling with bowie-knives and revolvers, like a walking arsenal." He impulsively drank what he thought to be a glass of brandy, only to discover that it was poison. He thereupon, according to a surgeon, spent some time in "purgings, pumping, and pukings."[21]

Sometime in late January 1862, Pryor proceeded to Beauregard's headquarters in Centreville, Virginia. He had been approached by the Military Affairs Committee, of which he was a member, and certain congressmen from the Mississippi Valley states to plead with the Louisiana general to go to the West as Sidney Johnston's second-in-command. He would command the Columbus sector, where a major Union offensive was anticipated. The Richmond papers had been sounding ominous warnings to that effect, and Polk desired to resign. Unquestionably the presence of the hero of Manassas would have an electrifying affect in the Heartland, and both he and the president cared deeply for that theater. Two questions would forever persist: Did the congressmen initiate the meeting with Pryor? Or did Davis summon the Virginian, who, enamored by presidential power, then floated the idea to the congressmen?[22]

Pryor related to Beauregard that Johnston had 70,000 troops—40,000 at Bowling Green and 30,000 at Columbus—a figure that he had gotten from Benjamin. It was a lie. The number may have approximated the aggregate present, a figure that for fighting strength was useless, but the secretary of war had in his possession the more accurate present-for-duty return of 31 December 1861, revealing 22,253 at Bowling Green and 20,992 at Columbus, for a total of 43,245. Jones wrote on January 24 that the Northern press had intentionally exaggerated the claims of 150,000 Rebels in Kentucky and Tennessee, when in truth there were not 60,000. Their further estimates of 50,000 Federals could also be dismissed; they probably had three times that number. The clerk predicted that matters were coming to a head: "The shadows of events are crowding thickly upon us, and the events will speak for themselves—and that speedily."[23]

The greater slippery slope for Beauregard was the assurance that the assignment was temporary. Once a western offensive had been completed, he would return to Virginia. Beauregard's friends sensed a setup. Robert Toombs of Georgia warned that the general, once in the West, would never return. By the time he received the warning, the Louisiana general had accepted the position. Perhaps it was ego, of which the Louisiana general had no shortage. Perhaps he privately coveted department command. Perhaps it was a mixture of patriotism and sensing that he could be perceived as the savior of the West. Regardless of the motive, he was headed for Department No. 2: 750 miles distant from Richmond, away from the capital press corps, and out of the president's hair. Jones's diary for January 14 revealed his take on the transfer: "Beauregard has been ordered to the West. I knew that doom was upon him."[24]

The Heartland, at least for now, faded from Richmond's view. Hearing that one of Stonewall Jackson's divisions in Virginia was in an exposed position, Benjamin on January 30 ordered the general to immediately withdraw it to Winchester. The response was swift and unmistakable: Jackson, intolerant of any interference, submitted his resignation. It was more than a tiff or a misunderstanding. The loss of the general, already an icon even by 1862 standards, would have been irreparable. Cooler heads prevailed and Jackson was persuaded to withdraw his resignation.

In the game of power politics, however, there was little doubt who had won. Benjamin, already fighting intense anti-Semitism, now began to endure open gossip. According to Georgia Congressman Thomas R. R. Cobb, Benjamin was a "eunuch" (i.e., impotent) who got married to cover the truth, but the woman told it out. Although never divorced, she later moved to Paris, France, to be with a paramour; capital gossip ran rampant.[25]

As January gave way to February, scant attention was paid in Richmond to a page-three article that came from the West. The dateline read Memphis: "Attack of Fort Henry." Gunboats had opened on the Tennessee River fort, but no damage had been done. The bluecoats were landing troops two miles upriver for an expected attack, but the garrison was in full force, and no apprehensions were expressed. If a crisis appeared to be looming, however, it was not in the West. Burnside's expedition had at last departed Hatteras and was feared to be headed for Roanoke Island on the Upper Outer Banks of North Carolina. If it fell, the backdoor to Norfolk would be open; capital citizens braced. Meanwhile, throughout February 6, Davis prepared his inauguration message, to be read on George Washington's birthday, the twenty-second. It would be the official launch of his six-year presidential term, the swearing-in at Montgomery having been provisional.[26]

On Friday, February 7, a bombshell hit—not from Roanoke Island but Fort Henry. A dispatch from Harris read: "Fort Henry fell yesterday. Memphis & Clarksville Railroad bridge over Tennessee [River] damaged. Lost all the artillery and stores at Henry." Unless Tennessee was hurriedly reinforced, "the injury is irreparable." An article in the *Dispatch* later that day was headlined "Attack Upon Fort Henry," but the information was a day behind that received at the War Department. News of the fort's surrender nonetheless leaked out. Ruffin learned the truth on February 7. Congress was in closed session, so he hurried over to the Exchange Hotel to see what he could learn. "No further particulars. It is a great disaster," he told his diary. Thomas Bragg also expressed concern. "There is a general gloom over the city."[27]

The next day Johnston confirmed the news of the fort's surrender. The enemy's gunboats were even then ascending the Tennessee River, with nothing to stop them short of Florence–Muscle Shoals, Alabama, where the shoals prevented further ascent. Embarrassingly, a number of civilians waved to the ironclads as they passed. Johnston had his mind on more important matters. Operations would soon commence against Fort Donelson on the Cumberland River, only twelve miles by land from Fort Henry. If not bleak enough, it was the balance of the dispatch that sent chills down the backs of administration officials. Johnston believed that Fort Donelson was doomed and would fall even without the enemy's infantry, thereby resulting in the fall of Nashville. In consultation with Beauregard, who was by then on the scene, it was determined to immediately withdraw Johnston's center corps, under Hardee, to the south bank of the Cumberland River, lest it be trapped on the north bank by the Federal navy. On the heels of the destruction of Johnston's right, his center now appeared on the verge of collapse. Officials in Richmond quietly fretted. Could the Bowling Green column get back in time?[28]

Given the catastrophic turn of events, the editorial in the *Dispatch* of February 8 appeared remarkably placid. Fort Henry was never meant to be held against a heavy bombardment, and doubtless the forts would fall to the enemy. As for the destroyed Tennessee River railroad bridge south of the fort, supplies could still be gotten across. Conceding that the Confederates could not stop the Union ironclads, the paper concluded: "[B]ut when he [Grant] marches against us on dry land, then is our opportunity." Perhaps so, but what of the fate of Nashville, which now hung in the balance? As for the loss of Fort Henry, the paper was dismissive: "The loss is not a matter to cause any serious concern."[29]

The press might calm jittery civilian nerves with figments, but Jones knew better: "Fort Henry has fallen. . . . The catalogue of disasters I feared and foretold under the policy by the War Department [i.e., territorial defense][] may be a long and terrible one." The transfer of troops to Tennessee, which had previously been regarded as impossible, now became doable. On February 9, Benjamin notified Johnston that 5,000 troops had been ordered to him from New Orleans; it was not enough. The next day, Harris wired the War Department to send 10,000 muskets, warning "Nashville is in great danger." All the stops were pulled out. Some 3,600 arms, including 1,200 newly arrived Enfield rifles, were rushed to the West—800 to Knoxville, 1,200 to Johnston, and the balance to a scattering of regiments then organizing. A regiment was ordered from Pensacola to Knoxville but was subsequently redirected to Decatur, Alabama, to protect the railroad bridge. One Georgia and three Tennessee regiments then in Virginia were loaded on boxcars for Knoxville. A couple of other newly mustered and totally untrained Tennessee and North Carolina regiments were rushed to plug the East Tennessee breach.[30]

Reports, either officially or through press sources, remained few. On February 10, three-day-old news arrived from Nashville via Mobile stating that 8,000–10,000 reinforcements under Pillow were on their way to Fort Donelson. Reprinted Northern articles filled the news vacuum. A message from General Henry W. Halleck, commanding western Union forces, stated: "Fort Henry is ours. The flag of the Union is re-established on the soil of Tennessee. It will never be removed." The ironclads came to within 300 yards of the fort, and the Rebel infantry was found to have "cut and run." The Union infantry did not reach the scene of action until half an hour after the surrender of the fort. Thomas Bragg heard that the Southerners retreated without a fight. "I fear it is too true," he confided in his diary.[31]

The events unfolding at the Twin Rivers, significant through they were, remained a distant world to Richmond—758 miles distant to be precise. Much closer to home and on the minds of citizens remained Roanoke Island, which not only protected the North Carolina Sound but also was the key to Norfolk and an approach to the Confederate capital. Included among the 2,500-man garrison was the Richmond Blues, a company manned by the some of the city's most prominent families. On the evening of February 9, Cooper received a shocking dispatch from Major General Benjamin Huger at Norfolk: Roanoke Island and its garrison had surrendered to a combined Federal land and naval attack. Captain O. Jennings Wise, former editor of the *Enquirer*, had been mortally wounded. Some 15,000 troops at Norfolk sat idle, but Huger refused to send them and the government did not interfere. The coastal correspondent for the *Dispatch* expressed disgust: "We are apparently more anxious about the positions in Kentucky and Tennessee[] than our own. There is something wrong in all this." The young captain lay in state at the Capitol, and Bagby described for his readers the tearful throng that viewed his body. Thousands braved the snow to attend the funeral at St. James Episcopal Church. For several days, the gloomy outcome of the North Carolina disaster consumed the news cycle.[32]

"No news from Tennessee and [to] the South," Bragg wrote on February 11. "The enemy have I think already cut off all communications south, crossing the Tennessee below Florence [Alabama]. Well—it [is] a long road that has no turning." Reports from Memphis were getting through, but having to come via Mobile, it was a four- to five-day-old story by the time it arrived. The *Dispatch* of February 13 carried a four-day-old article that noted that Federal gunboats had ascended the Tennessee River to Tuscumbia, Alabama, where some warehouses were burned. There was talk of a possible raiding party marching overland to Iuka, Mississippi, in an attempt to break the Memphis & Charleston Railroad.[33]

Something big appeared to be brewing at Fort Donelson, but there were few details. The fortification had reportedly been attacked by a vastly superior force. "We have 15,000 men there to resist, perhaps 75,000! Was ever such mismanagement known? Who is responsible for it? If Donelson falls, what becomes of the ten or twelve thousand men at Bowling Green?" a fearful Jones asked. The fort—"so far as we know," noted the *Examiner* of February 13—still held out, but the current dilemma offered the anti-Davis editor yet another opportunity to harp on the administration's "do nothing policy of defense [that] enabled the United States to organize and precipitate on that point [Fort Donelson] its whole western army. . . . The game we are in is no child's play."[34]

In the cabinet meeting on February 14, a Nashville dispatch of the previous day was discussed. An artillery engagement at Fort Donelson had taken place, but the enemy was held at bay. "We hear nothing [new] today," an anxious Bragg wrote. "Our troops are raw and I fear short of ammunition. If they are not, they *may* sustain themselves. Pillow commands them." Later that night at 10:30 p.m., more news arrived—good news! A Tennessee congressman received a telegram that in the battle of February 13 the Southern troops had emerged victorious. The enemy forces had been repulsed three times with heavy losses, and they had been pursued beyond the trenches. "I hope it may be true, all of it," the attorney general cautiously wrote. "Something was needed to revive the drooping spirits of our people."[35]

When Beauregard returned to Nashville, he took time to write a bitter letter to Pryor. He was sick—both physically (he had had throat surgery before leaving Richmond) and at the true state of affairs, by which now he was painfully aware. The numbers he had been given were patently phony, and Johnston, far from preparing for an offensive, was hanging on by his fingernails. "I am taking the helm when the ship is already on the breakers, and with but few sailors to man it." Depressed, sick, and disgusted, he nonetheless believed that Johnston had done the best he could. The Louisiana general believed that some minor locations must be conceded "or we will lose them all in succession." He trembled at the thought that Fort Donelson might be next. Major General Braxton Bragg, commanding at Pensacola and Mobile, warned Benjamin on February 15 that the Confederate forces were "too much scattered." He argued for an immediate concentration by forfeiting Florida (except Pensacola), Texas, and Missouri. "We must cease our policy of protecting persons and property, by which we are defeated in detail." The Bragg proposal was openly discussed in the cabinet meeting of February 16. In an attempt to undo what his own failed policy had created, Davis ordered Bragg to transport his 7,500-man division to Tennessee. This policy reversal, of course, would not come in time to help Fort Donelson, where a large expeditionary force was fast approaching.[36]

The sun shone through on Sunday, February 16, melting the sleet and snow of the previous day. Ruffin loitered around the telegraph office on Sunday, February 16, anxiously awaiting news from Fort Donelson, but no dispatches arrived. "My anxiety," he jotted in his diary, "(as with others) is intense." Rumors abounded (all false) that Hardee was on his way to Fort Donelson, where Johnston had already arrived, and that Beauregard might also go. "We are in a critical condition—God be with us," the attorney general wrote. The next day, as sleet coated the trees in Richmond, a telegram clicked over the wire confirming the success of the Confederate army in the battle of February 15. Union casualties tallied to 1,240 and 600 captured, with Southern losses of 500. The lines suddenly went dead. The telegraph news agent, a Mr. Pritchard, told Ruffin on February 17 that as late as 1 a.m. attempts had been made to get a dispatch through, with no success. A *New York Herald* item carried in the *Dispatch* of February 18 claimed that Fort Donelson had been invested with an estimated 15,000 Rebels trapped inside and all communications cut. The public was kept on tenterhooks.[37]

Richmond remained in a state of suspense. Midnight approached on February 17 when another telegram arrived from Fort Donelson, this one dated February 16. Thomas Bragg did not see it until he got up the next morning, and by that time it was in the morning paper. "My misgivings were but too true. . . . I have heard nothing but a thousand rumors. There is a general gloom prevailing all the sensible." The shocking news came out the next day. A dispatch arrived from Harris: "Fort Donelson has fallen and Nashville will fall into the hands of the Federals. No stand can be made there. Give me your plans." The news proved stupefying. All of central and eastern Kentucky were now gone, as was a large portion of the Tennessee Valley. Hardee also sent a telegram later that day, but not received until Wednesday, February 19, that his corps was falling back to Nashville. Beauregard, in his sickbed in Jackson, Tennessee, also hurriedly wired that Columbus "must meet the fate of Fort Donelson." He suggested a small garrison of 3,500 (which he believed it should have been in the first place) and the immediate withdrawal of the balance of Polk's Corps. The next day, the Louisiana general received his answer from Richmond: "Evacuation decided upon."[38]

Even before the story hit the capital papers, the calamitous news leaked out and was being openly talked about on the streets. A pall fell across the city. Colonel Howell Cobb, former governor of Georgia and member of the Provisional Congress, happened to be in Richmond on February 18 as his regiment, the 16th Georgia, passed through the city. "The terrible disaster at Fort Donelson is a terrific shock upon weak nerves—and somewhat trying to strong ones. I cannot despair and do not. . . . The extent of the disaster is not yet known," he wrote his wife. That same day, Ruffin admitted: "Fort Donelson has fallen! That naked but all[-]important fact is all that is learned." Benjamin admitted to General Braxton Bragg that "we grope in the dark" and that news of a mass capture came only through the Northern press. The next day Ruffin noted that he knew nothing of the losses except through Yankee accounts, which claimed a staggering 15,000 prisoners, including Johnston, Buckner, and Pillow. Confusion reigned.[39]

The same day, February 19, Davis received a dispatch from Hardee at Nashville: Johnston was falling back to Murfreesboro. The stunning headline on Thursday, February 20, told it all—"Surrender of Fort Donelson." The news had come from numerous Northern papers—Baltimore, Philadelphia, New York, St. Louis, and Cincinnati; all claimed the capture of 15,000 prisoners. "In all Kentucky, and we may say in all the Southwest, the rebels now hold but one position of importance—Columbus; and that is isolated and untenable. The rebels will flee from there, as they have fled from Bowling Green, if our Generals will only permit them to do so." Simon Buckner's surrender note had been published, leaving Richmond officials to wonder why a subordinate officer had signed rather than Pillow and Floyd, who were in command. It later came to light that they had escaped on the last departing boats. Mississippi Congressman Reuben Davis (no relation to the president) took his seat in Congress just as the news broke. "Everything seemed dismal and dreary," he recalled. Word of the disaster was widely known, and officials warned that everyone should expect the worst.[40]

All hope was not lost. The *Dispatch* of February 21 conceded that the fort had fallen, but stories of a capture en masse may have been exaggerated. The only confirmed Southern reports (up to the night of February 13) were that casualties remained light. A representative of the Virginia legislature, attached to Floyd's Brigade, had arrived in Richmond that day; he told of no mass capture. "No news from Donelson—and that is bad news," Jones jotted in his diary on February 21. "Benjamin says he has no definite information. But prisoners taken say that the enemy have been reinforced, and are hurling 80,000 against our 15,000." Davis, still in shock, wrote to his brother that day, mentioning the "recent disasters in Tennessee" and the urgent need to "retrieve our waning fortunes in the West." He simply could not bring himself to believe that so large a force of Confederates had surrendered without a severe battle to cut their way out.[41]

A dispatch, dated Tuesday February 18, arrived in the capital on February 2—there was yet hope. The bulk of the Donelson garrison had escaped and, coupled with Hardee's Corps marching south from Bowling Green, an army of 35,000 was even then assembling for the defense of Nashville. Johnston had "no idea" of surrendering the city. It was a castle in the air. Thomas Bragg heard it whispered that Johnston *would* surrender the city on the agreement that private property would be respected.[42] The *Whig* reported that there had been 1,600 casualties and 12,000 prisoners and that few had escaped. Johnston had evacuated the Tennessee capital, and Hardee's Corps was retreating to an unknown destination. On the afternoon of February 20, Ruffin heard that "Buckner's Corps" had escaped and that even then the troops were arriving in Nashville. No one knew what to believe."[43]

On February 21, the day before the president was scheduled to deliver his Inaugural Address, the anti-Davis Representative Henry Foote predictably took the opportunity to deliver a "characteristic speech" on the House floor on the conduct of the war. Feigning that his words were not aimed at the president, his barbs were leveled primarily at Benjamin.[44]

At the Ordnance Department, Colonel Gorgas wrote what many were thinking: Why were the reinforcements not sent sooner? An additional 10,000 men "would have converted Donelson from an overwhelming disaster to a victory." If Grant had been defeated at Donelson, "as he might easily have been," the tide would have been reversed, sending the Federals reeling back into Kentucky. "Our President is unfortunately no military genius, & could not see the relative value of [the] position. Pensacola was nothing compared to Donelson."[45]

The slow, steady rain on Saturday, February 22, Inauguration Day, set the tone for the recent litany of disasters. Capital Square was black with umbrellas as the pattering of rain almost drowned out the president's voice. A huge canvas had been hastily spread, and as people gathered underneath there were mumblings that the weather portended an evil omen. The president admitted that "the tide for the moment is against us" but gave assurances that the ultimate result would be in their favor. Exhausted and stricken with painful facial neuralgia, Davis nonetheless "seemed self-poised in the midst of disasters, which he acknowledged had befallen us," observed Jones. "And he admitted that there had been errors in our war policy. We had attempted operations on too extensive a scale. . . . I like these candid confessions." Congressman Davis was less hopeful: "Every step taken up to that time had been, as I thought, defeated by tardiness of movement and inadequate preparation." Alexander H. Stephens, the frail, diminutive, and habitually gloomy vice president, was plunged into despair—"The Confederacy is lost," he wept.[46]

Judith McGuire had hoped to go to the inauguration but had been kept away by the wretched weather. She admitted that "[o]ur people are depressed by our recent disasters," but she took comfort in the bravery of the troops. A woman and her daughter in the room next to her had two sons at Fort Donelson, and she did not know their fates. "Poor ole lady!" she lamented. "The telegraph wires in Tennessee are cut and mail communication very uncertain." Robert Kean, a Virginia lawyer and current bureaucrat in the War Department, continued to dismiss accounts of a mass capture, but even he conceded that the road to Nashville was wide open and Columbus was cut off. "The timid will begin to croak, the half-hearted to quail and suggest submission, and the traitorous to agitate," he predicted. Ruffin was still not certain that Nashville had fallen, but he had resolved that at least 12,000–13,000 had been captured at Donelson, and from all accounts Pillow and Floyd had escaped with only 800. He wrote in blunt language: "There seems great disposition to despond[] with many persons."[47]

An attack upon Columbus appeared to be only a matter of time. The *Dispatch* of February 24 carried a Memphis article claiming that Beauregard was prepared to defend the city "at all hazards." The next day, however, Ruffin noted secretly: "It is whispered, from earlier information not published, that Gen. Beauregard has announced the necessity of evacuating Columbus." On March 2, Polk telegrammed Benjamin:

An 1865 photo of the Washington Monument, Capital Square, Richmond, where Jefferson Davis delivered his Inaugural Address in a drenching rain in February 1862. (Library of Congress)

"The work is done. Columbus gone." As usual, it was the Northern press that broke the story.[48]

Congressman Davis caught up with Benjamin one day and inquired about reinforcements to Tennessee. It would not be necessary, the secretary told him. Recognition of the Confederacy by Great Britain within the next ninety days was a virtual certainty, and at that time the war would come to an end. The United States, of course, would claim all occupied territory. "But what of Kentucky and Tennessee?" the congressman asked. Benjamin's answer proved shocking: "We shall hold from the Memphis [&] Charleston [Rail] Road south, and the Northern states can keep what is north of that line." Was the administration actually

Judah Benjamin was viciously denounced by congressmen as "Judas Iscariot Benjamin" and the "Jewish puppeteer." (Library of Congress)

considering that, as long as the western Cotton States were retained, it would be willing to write off the Upper South? If this was actually the case, said the congressman, then by all means there should be an immediate cessation of hostilities to avoid further bloodshed.[49]

Benjamin's astonishing admission—perhaps nothing more than ideas floated within administration circles—proved moot; British recognition would not be forthcoming. Back in November 1861, a United States ship had stopped the mail packet *Trent* bound for the Bahamas and seized two Confederate emissaries aboard—James Mason and John Slidell, bound for France and Britain. The incident enraged the British (although they had been doing the same thing for decades) and created a diplomatic crisis for the United States. For weeks the Confederacy held out high hopes for British recognition; it was not to be. Abraham Lincoln accepted a face-saving gesture, and the incident was diffused. Mason subsequently wrote that the news of the capture of Fort Donelson had had "an unfortunate effect" in Great Britain. Yet some in the administration remained remarkably delusional.[50]

News had still not arrived from Nashville. Jones anticipated the city's inevitable fall, although "no one seems to anticipate such a calamity," he divulged on February 25. The next day, confirmation arrived of the evacuation of the city. The description in the press, related by a veteran of Fort Donelson, told of the panic in the Tennessee capital that he compared to the Federal rout at Manassas. Fleeing families clogged the roads to the south, and the railroad depot was filled to capacity. The otherwise anonymous "R. H. G." expressed disgust at hundreds of cowardly men who were among the refugees. The story sent chills throughout Richmond. Did such a fate await the national capital?[51]

Over at the Ordnance Department, the Northern-born but Southern-married Colonel Gorgas was also reading the news. He had cast his lot with the South, despite the fact that he detested Southern heat. The art-loving officer, unquestionably the most efficient bureaucrat in the capital, could also be prickly. The loss of Nashville, which he considered "a shameful chapter," brought out his testy side. Johnston "should have insisted on the defense of the city & asked to remove the women and children." It would be the opening salvo in a litany of recriminations that was to follow.[52]

Tuesday, March 4, was a national Day of Fast. The Reverand Mr. Leftwich at the Third Presbyterian Church, at Twenty-fifth and Broad, preached from the text of 1 Peter 5:6: "Humble yourselves under the mighty hand of God, that he may exalt you in due time." The pastor spoke directly to the losses in Tennessee and Kentucky. The reason for the setbacks was theological in nature. The nation must be purged of its sins—vainglorious pride of ancestry, the want of missionary spirit, and profanity. He urged the congregation to repent, else they would be deserving of their fate. Editor Daniel chose to blame Davis rather than God for the turn of events: "When we find our President standing in a corner telling his beads, and relying on a miracle to save the country, instead of mounting his horse, and putting forth every power of the Government to defeat the enemy, the effect is depressing in the extreme."

5

The Demagogues of Congress

The increasing vehemence of the capital press had become a sore point in the cabinet even before the disasters in Tennessee. Daniel's *Enquirer* assailed the administration almost daily. Thomas Bragg thought that the paper had a tendency to be "mischievous and injurious." He also noticed that its articles seemed always to be appearing in the *New York Herald* and other Northern papers. As the extent of the February catastrophes began to be absorbed, the full fury of the press was unleashed. "Shall the cause fail because Mr. Davis is incompetent? Tennessee under Sidney Johnston[] is likely lost. Mr. Davis retains him." The president was denounced as being "motionless as a clod" and "cold as ice."[1]

Conversely, some westerners, grasping for straws, pleaded with the chief executive to come to the West and personally take command. "For God's sake come!" a panicked Charles Ready of Murfreesboro wrote. He believed that Johnston's demoralized army, which even then was slogging through his town, could be saved only by Davis's presence. A petition signed by fourteen Memphis citizens described the population as "generally desponding." Congressman Eli M. Bruce of Kentucky wrote from Atlanta in early March that Johnston had inexcusably lost 12,000 men and the Mississippi Valley. If Davis could not personally come to salvage the crisis, then he must give immediate command to Beauregard, Bragg, or Breckinridge. The message was clear: anyone but Johnston.[2]

On March 8, a Saturday, both Tennessee senators and eight of eleven congressmen, unable to hide their indignation, paid a visit to the Confederate White House. Davis received the unsolicited callers, almost certainly knowing why they were there. Senator Henry, the namesake of

Fort Henry and someone who had earlier petitioned for the appointment of Johnston, now turned on the erstwhile local favorite. The group stated bluntly that Tennesseans had lost confidence in Johnston's leadership. "This may be all wrong, foolishly wrong; but the stubborn fact remains that his command has lost confidence" in him. The general needed to be replaced, although they left naming his successor to the prerogative of the president. They had essentially asked Davis to do precisely what he never, under any circumstances, would be willing to do: give up on his revered friend. "If Sidney Johnston is not a general, the Confederacy has none to give you," he curtly replied. The conversation was over.[3]

Congressman Davis of Mississippi described the Tennessee delegation as "wild with rage." They would "listen to no reason" and went about making the most "savage denunciations" of Johnston. Davis hoped for cooler heads to prevail, but he was familiar with Henry Foote, one of the ringleaders. Although acknowledging him as "the best stump speaker then living," he was also aware of his dark side.[4]

Foote could be charming, but by nature he was sarcastic, impulsive, and abrasive. His temper got him into trouble on more than one occasion; he had engaged in four duels and was wounded in three of them, one of which left him with a limp leg for life. The politics of ultimatum had long been a Southern tactic in antebellum Congress, but in 1850 Foote took it to a new level. He made a veiled threat on the floor of the United States Senate that if he did not get his way on the issue of California statehood, and in the time frame demanded, he would "break up the House" by sparking a melee. He had also engaged in three fistfights, one with Jefferson Davis himself. The fray occurred in 1847 when the two men, both serving as Mississippi senators at the time, got into a fight over "squatter sovereignty." Davis believed that the Missouri Compromise should be extended to the Pacific Ocean, while Foote advocated for having the residents of the affected states and territories vote. The words became heated and a brawl ensued, Davis later claiming that he "whipped him until I was pulled off." In 1853 Foote ran for governor of Mississippi against his old antagonist. He won (barely) by portraying his states' rights opponent as a secessionist. As sectional tensions increased over the years, however, Foote's unionist position became a liability. He moved to California and later to Nashville.

When Tennessee seceded, the opportunist Foote reversed his former position and was subsequently elected to the Confederate Congress representing Tennessee-5, which included Nashville. His new position

Congressman Henry S. Foote of Tennessee, archenemy of the Davis administration. (Library of Congress)

gave him a platform to continue his venomous opposition to Davis. He became arguably the most despised member in the House, with one newspaper labeling him as "a great bag of gas." A U.S. congressman commented that Foote's lengthy diatribes were in "Greek, Latin, the Bible, Shakespeare, Vattel, and heaven knows what else." When Foote entered the Confederate Congress, even the *New York Times* noted that he had not "changed his habits one wit by going to Richmond." Even Foote's wife, Rachael, got caught up in the acrimony. She wrote that Varina Davis "dresses badly, in no taste. She is not much liked here, and she is said to control 'Jeffie' as she calls her husband. She has several children. She takes little notice of them, they go about with their clothes tossed on in any way and every style."[5]

Unfortunately, Davis's western congressional opposition extended beyond the Tennessee delegation. Casper Bell of Missouri, now a disciple of Foote, became an obstructionist. Thomas Cobb, the clean-shaven, dark-haired, slaveholding congressman representing Georgia-9, had become increasingly irritated with "Davis and his toadies." The colonel-congressman, an evangelical by choice and a pessimist by nature, became embittered when he was passed over for promotion. He believed that the president reneged on his agreement to expand his unit, Cobb's Legion, into a brigade. He "deliberately violated his agreement with me," he barked, declaring Davis a "monomaniac" on the subject of West Point. He further denounced him as "an obstinate fool" and by February 1862 admitted that he was "now recognized as being a part of the opposition." As for Benjamin, the anti-Semite congressman vilified the secretary of war as "a dirty dog."[6]

Cobb believed that Congress would have deposed Davis but for his weak and inept successor, the "selfish demagogue" Alexander Stephens. The vice president was also beginning to distance himself from Davis. He nonetheless was unwilling to go along with a call to impeach the president and make Robert Toombs of Georgia or Gideon Pillow, the coward of Fort Donelson, dictator. Stephens continued his contemptuous view of the legislature. "This is a very poor Congress," he confided. He saw only a few qualified men in the House, and not more than two or three in the Senate, with Thomas Semmes of Louisiana and Clement Clay of Alabama counted among the last.[7]

Opposition in the House paled to the growing western opposition in the Senate, beginning with Louis T. Wigfall of Texas. The Texan's violent past seems to have moderated by the time of the war. He had previously chalked up several duels, near duels, and a murder (the other man drawing on him first). He admitted that his past nearly ruined his law practice, and he had given up "wine, women & cards," or at least women and cards; he remained a notorious alcoholic while in Richmond. Cobb disgustedly wrote that the senator "is half drunk all the time and bullies about everywhere." Wigfall actually began the war as a pro-Davis advocate, even serving as a presidential aide; this did not last long. Some of the dissention was stoked by Charlotte Wigfall, the senator's wife, who found it impossible to keep her opinions to herself; some of the talk got back to the Davises. Louis Wigfall, often fueled with alcohol, also found it difficult to keep his own counsel. He reportedly made a speech about the president in front of a hotel; again, it got back to Davis. There were attempts at reconciliation, but in the end the senator from Texas remained mostly hostile.[8]

Davis also discovered that longtime friends could turn on him. William L. Yancey of Alabama had the reputation of being one of the best orators in the South, but he could not remember people's names, and his introverted nature was well-known. Nonetheless, he began the war as a Davis supporter, famously introducing him to a Montgomery crowd: "The man and his hour have met." It was widely rumored that he would be offered a cabinet post, but he was instead sent on a diplomatic mission to England, a rather odd assignment for a fire-eater and a man often lacking in personal diplomacy. He eventually became bored with the position, ran for a seat in the Senate, and began his tenure in March 1862. Over time, he would turn on Davis, calling him "conceited, wrong-headed, wranglesome, and obstinate."[9]

Alabama's other senator, Clement C. Clay, had been a longtime Davis friend dating to their days in the Senate. During a time of grave illness, it had been Clay who helped nurse Davis back to health, sometimes spending all night at his bedside. But for his frail health, he would have been offered a cabinet post. He nonetheless could be peevish, and he had his frustrations with his friend. "He is a strange compound which I cannot analyze," he wrote. "He will not ask or receive counsel, and, indeed, seems predisposed to go exactly the way his friends advise him not to go." For the most part, however, Clay remained a faithful friend and ally.[10]

Following the recent Tennessee disasters, Clay received a letter from a constituent, Lieutenant Colonel Edward D. Tracey, serving with the 19th Alabama in Johnston's retreating army. He reported that the troops remained in a "sad state of disorganization" and were still recovering from the "terrible shock" of the fall of Fort Donelson and the loss of Nashville. The officer added that "many are hesitating in their hearts between God and Baal, & most are far below which would lead them to prefer a wilderness & a desert, to homes polluted by invaders." Pleading for help, Tracey concluded that "nobody [in Richmond] seems alive to its [the Tennessee Valley's] vast importance & few know where it is."[11]

The press, meanwhile, continued its disparaging comments. "The knowledge of a disease is necessary to a cure. Our president has lost the confidence of the country," snipped the *Whig*. It denounced Yankees and Jews, who constituted a large proportion of the administration, an obvious attack on Samuel Cooper and Gorgas in the former and Benjamin and Myers in the latter. The *Examiner* evaluated that Davis's Inaugural Address threw "no light on the real condition of the country," and it dismissed his cabinet as "mere clerks." The *Enquirer* called for a complete investigation of the Donelson disaster. George Bagby, in addition to being the capital reporter for the Charleston *Mercury*, also wrote a quarterly editorial in the *Southern Literary Messenger*, a sophisticated Richmond magazine founded by Edgar Allan Poe. He pulled no punches in his anti-administration rhetoric. During the dark days of winter, with the defeats at Mill Springs, Roanoke Island, and the Twin Rivers, the public anxiously awaited a sentence of cheer and defiance from the president. "But that sentence never came. The people were left to themselves. Their ruler lifted up a piteous, beautiful, appropriate prayer in his Inaugural, and then in his message tried to throw the blame, if blame there were, upon the shoulders of Congress." The scene soon shifted from the press to the halls of Congress.[12]

On Wednesday, February 26, as the gavel pounded in the opening session of the Senate, a shaken Davis had a statement read by his secretary. Although admitting recent defeats, the president still entertained hope that the reported losses at Fort Donelson had been greatly exaggerated. His delusion would simply not permit him to accept that so large a force could have surrendered. He nonetheless painfully, and perhaps half-heartedly, conceded that his policy of territorial defense had overextended the resources of the Confederacy. He nonetheless later related to an Alabama judge that the policy would have been successful *if* the government had received the arms that it had every reason to expect.[13]

Thomas Jefferson Foster represented Alabama-1 in Congress, which included his huge landholdings in Courtland. The 27th Alabama, the regiment that he had raised and subsequently served as the original colonel, had been captured at Fort Donelson; he wanted answers. On Wednesday, February 27, he made a motion on the floor of the House that a committee be appointed to investigate the disasters at Fort Henry and Fort Donelson. He specifically desired to know if other forts had been constructed and, if so, why they had not been not completed. The motion easily passed. A five-person committee of western congressmen was named, with Davis archenemy Henry Foote as chairman.[14]

The Virginia state capital doubled as the home of the Confederate Congress. (Library of Congress)

"Accounts from Tennessee are by no means favorable, the people of Nashville have no spirit—and in East Tennessee the Union men are quite defiant," Thomas Bragg noted in his journal on February 27. On March 3, Johnston's army was reportedly at Huntsville. The attorney general wrote despondently: "Tenn. will be overrun and abandoned. This is bad but there is no help for it." The next day the remains of Crittenden's Division linked up at Huntsville with 3,500 troops—all that remained of a division that six weeks earlier counted 6,000. "The State [Tennessee] is gone—the people will submit—such are the indications." Other reports arrived that were "not being creditable to Nashville."[15]

Writing to Benjamin on March 4, Johnston disclosed that his army was on the road to Decatur, Alabama. He would be at the telegraph office at Fayetteville, Tennessee, the next day. The administration faced mounting pressure. There was still no official report of the Donelson defeat, and congressmen were beginning to get impatient. Pillow, in a self-serving attempt to get ahead of the narrative, had submitted his after-action report to the press. Johnston's and Floyd's reports were urgently needed.[16]

It became increasingly obvious to Davis how he could protect his favorite general and himself simultaneously. There was ample evidence to point the finger at Floyd and Pillow, the inept generals commanding at Donelson, both of whom had unceremoniously managed to escape the surrender. Buttressing the president's case was a letter received from Captain Charles Wickliffe of the 7th Kentucky claiming that "the army could easily have been saved." Such comments, coupled with Pillow's self-serving report, proved sufficient to have them both removed from command on March 11. Unfortunately, many in the capital—misinformed politicians, the press, and citizens alike—rallied behind the generals, who had fought "until it was futile," heroically managing to save 5,000 of the garrison. The *Dispatch* insisted that the only charge leveled at the generals was that they did not remain to receive the surrender. "But this, in the eyes of the public, is the most venial of all offenses." Regarding Pillow, the paper pronounced him a "bold, daring, dashing officer," comparing him to Marshal Ney under Napoleon! Senator Henry petitioned to have both officers returned to duty.[17]

It was some weeks before the Fort Donelson investigative committee gave its preliminary findings, stating that a "mass of testimony was yet to be taken." The report clarified that it was merely a factfinding commission and that the removal of Floyd and Pillow from command was the sole purview of the president. There seemed little doubt, however, that three of the five members (Ethlebert Barksdale of Mississippi, Thomas Hanley of Arkansas, and Thomas Foster of Alabama) strongly disagreed with a minority report submitted by Foote of Tennessee and Horatio Bruce of Kentucky purporting that Johnston had given his consent to surrender the fort. The majority believed that Johnston's March 18 response, boasting of the gallantry of Floyd and Pillow, had been misconstrued to mean that he agreed with their decision. Indeed, in the same letter Johnston had written that "events show that the investment was not as complete as the information of the scouts led them to believe." Additionally, Johnston's February 14 dispatch clearly stated that, if "he [Floyd] lost the fort, to get his forces back to Nashville." Therein lay the gray area—the fort at the time was not lost.

The report also took issue with Floyd's after-action report, claiming that he had withdrawn his Virginia brigade to cut his way through the enemy lines. The congressmen questioned how one brigade could accomplish what the entire army had failed to do. Floyd also said that his Virginia brigade did not entirely escape, while some units, such as the 300 troops of the 20th Mississippi, managed to get out. The investigation proved that the 300 troops in question were not, in fact, even at Fort Donelson but were on furlough or in hospitals. Of the Mississippians actually present in the battle, all were captured. Foote and Bruce nonetheless desired to have their minority report placed on the record, which attempted to vindicate Floyd and Pillow and essentially blame the loss of the garrison on Johnston. The minority report could be accepted only by unanimous consent, and Barksdale quickly objected. The report was nonetheless filed.[18]

A brutally cold wind blew through Richmond on Friday, March 7, although little snow remained. Colonel Liddell was back in the capital on a mission that he dreaded: presenting Johnston's after-action report. He met with Davis, who again appeared to be "in a very unpleasant humor." In a clear attempt to divert culpability from both Johnston and the administration, the president placed the Twin Rivers debacle squarely on the shoulders of Floyd and Pillow. It was apparent to Liddell that Davis had given way to "fits of vindictive prejudice." The president nonetheless supported Johnston, whom the colonel privately thought had mismanaged the retreat. Before leaving the capital, Liddell met with Senator Ed Sparrow of Louisiana. The subject of Benjamin came up; both held him in low esteem.[19]

While visiting in Richmond, Liddell read that the Confederate ironclad CSS *Virginia* (formerly USS *Merrimack*) had destroyed two Union ships and ran aground three others at Hampton Roads. It had been a long time since there was anything to cheer about. The next day, March 9. the Federal ironclad USS *Monitor* offered battle. Although the *Dispatch* heralded "The Wonderful Naval Victory," the *Merrimack* had been neutralized and the blockade remained in effect. Davis nonetheless interpreted the event to mean that Norfolk and the Peninsula were now secure; perhaps troops could be shifted to Joe Johnston's army, known to be withdrawing from Centreville, Virginia.[20]

If there were shaky glimmers of hope in Virginia, the news from the West remained depressingly grim. The press reported Johnston's army as still retreating to Decatur, while Polk's Corps had abandoned Columbus and withdrawn to Island No. 10. A March 6 article in the *Dispatch* declared that 20,000 Federals were two days out from New Madrid, Missouri, just south of Island No.10, in an obvious intent to take the position in reverse. A dispatch from Johnston also arrived that day admitting that there had been many desertions among the Tennessee troops. He would be shifting Hardee's Corps west toward the Mississippi Valley, stating that Beauregard had been urging him to hurry on. The enemy at Nashville had swelled to 25,000, with more on the way.[21]

Virginia Clay, wife of the Alabama senator, could no longer bring herself to enjoy the social life in the capital; news from her mother in Huntsville played on her mind. Thousands of Confederate sick had flooded the city and were being sheltered in houses and windblown shanties with only a blanket to comfort them. Rumors abounded that the president would be in town on the night of March 2. Citizens lined up at the depot until 2 a.m. to get a glimpse, but like so many other rumors it turned out to be false. Not long afterward, Mrs. Clay received the dreaded news that the Yankees occupied Huntsville and that their house had been ransacked.[22]

Reading Pillow's Fort Donelson report in the paper, Ruffin disgustedly concluded: "We cannot learn anything near the main facts." On one issue, however, he had made up his mind: "But it seems to me that nothing can excuse Gen. A. S. Johnston for not having reinforced the army at Fort Donelson from the larger army at Bowling Green, which retreated to Ten. during the very time. I hold Johnston as condemnable for this, & almost as inefficient, as Gen. Huger in permitting the loss of Roanoke Island & its whole army."[23]

When the House met in session on March 10, it did not take long for the sparks to fly. Tennessean David Currin, representing Tennessee-11, introduced a resolution to expand the Fort Donelson investigation to include the Quartermaster Department. He was "not given to idle rumors," but the huge abandonment of supplies in Nashville clearly pointed to mismanagement. Foote rose in support of the resolution, but James Moore of Kentucky sounded a note of caution. If the resolution was to be debated, then the House should go into closed session. Shouts of "No! No!" greeted the suggestion. Robert Hilton of Florida, the forty-one-year-old widowed lawyer and Tallahassee newspaper editor, opposed the resolution on the ground that the War Department, not Congress, was the proper channel to investigate such matters. Foote was "mortified and surprised" at such a thought.

John Atkins, a lawyer who much preferred farming and politics, represented Tennessee-10, a West Tennessee district. He had been lieutenant colonel of the 5th Tennessee in Polk's Corps before taking his seat in Congress. He did not mince words; General Johnston should be

Congressman John D. Atkins of Tennessee furiously opposed General Albert Sidney Johnston following the loss of Fort Donelson. (Library of Congress)

included in any investigation. Johnston well knew, or at least should have known, that when the Tennessee River and Cumberland River gauges rose that the gunboats would be allowed easy passage. "But Johnston had but one idea—a single Idea—to make a stand at Bowling Green. It was his great idea." He had heard that Johnston was a Davis favorite, and he regretted having a differing view, but Tennesseans had lost all confidence in the general.

Congressman Moore of Kentucky defended the native son. It was only of late that Johnston had 25,000 men to oppose the enemy's 100,000, a ridiculously exaggerated number that was silently accepted. If he had fought a battle at Nashville, that beautiful city would have been left in ashes. He knew that a half-dozen steamers had been in the city for six months but that only five men had been repairing them. Besides, why did the people of Nashville themselves not fortify their city? Foote gave an angry response. Johnston had called for 1,000–1,500 slaves to construct the Nashville fortifications and that they had been provided, an assertion that was patently false. There was literally not a shotgun left in the city, yet a Richmond journalist dared to question why women and children did not fight. Why should they fight when Pillow and Floyd were "flying fast." Moore stood to make it clear that Foote's remarks had no reference to his comment.[24]

Congressman Peter Gray of Texas, Johnston's adopted state, came to his defense, claiming that judgments were premature. "If the people of Tennessee based their bravery upon the popularity of their leader, they were not the gallant people who he had hoped." Gray expressed his continued support of Johnston and suggested that his patriotism should not be in question. Atkins said that Johnston's patriotism was never in question. He then openly revealed that the Tennessee delegation had gone to the president and asked for the general's removal. He regretted that he was forced to speak so plainly. William Swan of Knoxville had not signed the petition, but he wanted it on the record that he was not a Johnston apologist. Reuben Davis, who briefly served under Johnston at Bowling Green, insisted that the general had done the best he could with the resources at his disposal. The problem was not him but rather failed government policy. Thereafter, the Mississippi congressman would later recall, no one with the administration would have any interaction with him. The question was finally called with the yeas voting fifty-two and the nays twenty-three; the investigation had now broadened to include Johnston.[25]

"Great complaints of the misconduct of Gen. A. S. Johnston, which have even reached congress. I hope he may be superseded," Ruffin defiantly wrote. Thomas Bragg was also hearing the talk. "Tennesseans (i.e., congressmen) complain bitterly of Gen'l [Johnston] and the abandonment of Ten. as they term it, they seem to fear the Union element in that state, which is no doubt very strong."[26]

The troubling turn of affairs in the West began to take a toll on Davis. In the March 7 cabinet meeting, Bragg noticed that the president appeared depressed. In the cabinet meeting on March 19, Davis's hallmark personality traits—combative when challenged and impatient with disagreement—became evident. He "lost his temper," became "annoyed," and appeared "distressed" that he was "met with denunciation instead of support." He feared "all is lost—Our people are dispirited & losing confidence." The president sent Johnston a warm but pointed letter. He had "not been a little disturbed" by the attacks on the general, which had proven "painful to me" and "injurious to us both." He assured the embattled general that his confidence in him had never wavered and that he had "made for you such defense as friendship prompted" and that "many years of acquaintance justified." Yet Davis urgently needed something to answer the critics and mount a defense.[27]

Conflicting accounts as to the actual number of prisoners captured at Fort Donelson lingered for weeks. The Northern press reported 16,000, but the *Dispatch* assured its readers that the actual number was "but a fraction" of that figure. Nonetheless, the *Appeal*, in an article reprinted in the *Dispatch*, placed Southern losses at 1,600 killed and wounded and 12,000 captured, with Union losses at 4,000. The *Whig* placed the prisoner count at 7,000, a figure that gave only slight solace to Judith McGuire, as she lamented that even that was "too many!" As late as March 19, Ruffin expressed frustration: "Though several official reports have been published, we are still ignorant of the amount of the loss, & of that of the enemy at Fort Donelson."[28]

William Boyce, a Davis-hating congressman from South Carolina, despaired at the turn of events. "Things are in a very gloomy state," he wrote on March 17. "Is not Kentucky gone? Is not Missouri gone? And is Tennessee not slipping from our grasp?" Instead of advancing, Davis chose to pause the armies at the Kentucky and Missouri borders. From the outset, he never "thought [Davis] was the man." He was "puffed up with his own conceit" and "looks upon independent opinion as an attack on him. Common sense he considers treason." Believing that "we will be Davis-ized into nothing," he concluded: "[M]y spirits are down to zero."[29]

That same day, the bitter debate in Congress continued. Foote once again lambasted Benjamin. The House select committee to study the Fort Donelson defeat had presented thirteen questions for Johnston; the War Department "utterly disregarded them." The Nashville congressman made a motion to censure Benjamin; the debate turned heated. Burgess Gaither of North Carolina and John Wilcox of Texas stood to oppose the "unwarranted attacks of the gentleman from Tennessee." Foote angrily replied that, if the secretary of war was offended by his remarks, then "it was but feeble to what he might expect." He nonetheless withdrew his motion.

William Boyce, a bitter anti-Davis South Carolina congressman, became depressed that the West was "slipping from our grasp." (Library of Congress)

Two days later, Foote introduced a House motion that the officers and men, including the generals in the Fort Donelson battle, receive the thanks of the Congress for their gallant conduct. The proposal, made even before the select committee had completed its investigation, raised a howl. John W. Crockett of Kentucky replied that the resolution was tantamount to saying: "We doubt whether you deserve a vote or not, but we will give it to you anyway." Alabamian E. S. Dargan, the former mayor of Mobile known for his piercing calls of "Mr. Ch*eer*-man," questioned why the boats that carried Floyd and his Virginians to safety were not sent back for more troops. James Pugh of Alabama likewise considered the motion premature. Sensing the increased hostility, Foote withdrew his motion.

Wilcox of Texas took the floor to strongly defend both Floyd and Pillow and suggested that they had been relieved of command only because the War Department was "too apt to yield to biting criticism of certain gentlemen." He expressed confidence that both officers would ultimately be vindicated. Foote immediately stood to retort that the comment was apparently aimed at him, suggesting that the Texas congressman was more bitter than effective, which caused some laughter. He then took the opportunity to once again go on a tear against Johnston. There was no living man who could defend him given the facts developed to date. His failure to protect Nashville and the destruction of a massive amount of stores begged for a full investigation. Wilcox, a strong Davis supporter, attempted to clarify that there was no opposition between him and the president. He supposed that Floyd and Pillow were relieved due to "opinions advanced by a portion of the press" and "in deference to the public opinion." As for Foote, Wilcox claimed that the gentleman from Tennessee always seemed to have something to say "that will make the hairs stand upon your head, but that it never comes!" He then related the story of the blasphemer who left the tailboard of his wagon down only to find all of the contents missing. He cried out: "I cannot do justice to the subject," which evoked laughter. Wilcox had hoped that Foote would be "free from the clouds [that] had previously depressed him," but it seemed that he was once again on a familiar subject: the conduct of General Johnston. He again evoked laughter by expressing hope that within thirty days "his conscience would smite him for his criticisms of Albert Sidney Johnston." Muscoe Garnett from Virginia stood to lament "this woeful waste of time;" the House proceeded to other business.[30]

Much of the outcry continued to be targeted at Benjamin, denounced by Foote as a "fiendish character" and the "Jewish puppeteer." Cobb of Georgia echoed the sentiments. "A grander rascal than this Jew Benjamin[] I do not believe lives in the Confederacy." He is a "mean low sycophantic dodging Jew." In a rare move to both appease his critics and remove a favorite target of the opposition, Davis transferred Benjamin from the War Department to head the State Department, replacing R. M. T. Hunter, who had taken a seat in the Senate. The *Examiner* disgustedly remarked that the "representation of the Synagogue is not diminished." Replacing Benjamin would be George W. Randolph, the

In his brief tenure as secretary of war, George W. Randolph packed the War Department with Virginia-centric bureaucrats, many of whom were related to him. (Library of Congress)

quiet-spoken Virginia lawyer who was not a brigadier general. As the only member of the cabinet with any military experience (albeit that was minor), he garnered respect within army circles. He was widely accepted by the western congressional delegation; even Foote was uncharacteristically supportive.[31]

As with all of Davis's selections, however, there were problems. Randolph was sickly, suffering from what ultimately was diagnosed as chronic tuberculosis. There was some talk that Benjamin may have been behind the selection, hoping to be able to manipulate him. If such was the case, it did not work. Some dismissed him as "merely a *clerk*, an underling." That comment, though stinging, had a ring of truth. Davis relegated only minor administrative matters to him, continuing to see himself as the South's war manager. Being a West Point graduate and former U.S. secretary of war, had led Davis to an aggrandized view of his own military genius. Additionally, unlike Lincoln, Davis had familiarity with most of the top officers and had decades-long relationships with some, including George Crittenden and Sidney Johnston, both of whom were now under scrutiny.[32]

In the midst of western congressional infighting, a name began to increasingly gain gravitas in the capital: Robert E. Lee. The West Point graduate, veteran of the Mexican–American War, and current commander of Virginia state forces was held in high esteem by virtually all in the Old Army, Davis included, although the two had never been close at the academy. Unfortunately, Joseph E. Johnston, then commanding the Confederate army in northern Virginia, had always held an angst against Lee that resulted in a strained relationship. In early March, the president requested that Congress create the position of "Commanding General of the Confederate States." Surprisingly, a congressional attempt was made to bypass presidential/civilian control and give Lee total military authority, thereby cutting Davis out of the loop. Seeing himself as the commander in chief, the president quickly vetoed the legislation. This raised a "perfect storm," according to one congressman, but the subsequent attempt to override the veto found little favor. Davis then simply assigned Lee to his new position as military adviser without a title, meaning that no new office was created and congressional approval was unnecessary. Bagby gave his nod of approval to both Lee and Randolph. "They are men, not quills."[33]

The biggest change at the War Department was Randolph's infusion of twenty-five cultural elites and technocrats, 68 percent of whom were related to the secretary by blood or marriage. Randolph did this to ensure a sense of personal loyalty, but it would also ensure no diversity of thought. Department clerk John Jones looked with disgust upon such aristocratic nepotism. The pending question was how this stacking of Virginia-centric thinking, which would long outlast Randolph's tenure, would influence western decision-making.[34]

A batch of five-day-old Memphis papers arrived on March 6 detailing the latest news from the West; the situation appeared dire. A large enemy force was in the vicinity of Cumberland Gap, hindered only by rain and snow. Frequent Union gunboat sorties had been made up the Tennessee River as far as Florence, Alabama. Reports of the evacuation of Columbus were premature, but a Union army 50,000 strong was eight miles from the city and marching south in an apparent attempt to take the town in reverse. Everywhere, it seemed, the Federals appeared to be on the move.[35]

Although a bevy of discredited western generals continued to consume the public's attention, there was one officer who was beginning to grab the headlines: Colonel Nathan Bedford Forrest. Even though not a professionally trained soldier, being a semiliterate Memphis slave trader, he was destined to become a legend. At his funeral in 1877, old citizens described him as a "terror." Before the war was over, many a bluecoat would learn this firsthand. Forrest and his Tennessee cavalry regiment famously cut their way out of Fort Donelson and ruthlessly restored order among the mob during the evacuation of Nashville, killing five rioters who dared to get in their way. On March 19, eleven Mississippi and Tennessee congressmen requested his promotion to brigadier. The commission came several months later, but Forrest had caught the attention of those in the capital; it would not be the last time.[36]

On Wednesday, March 26, thirty-one-year-old Captain Thomas M. Jack, Yale graduate, Galveston attorney, and aide and personal associate to Sidney Johnston, arrived in the capital to present the general's updated response. Quite unlike the reception described by Liddell two and a half weeks earlier, the captain characterized the chief executive as courteous, even kind. "How is your General—my friend General Johnston?" Davis queried. The Johnston letter (written over a three-day period) was part after-action report and part personal missive. His scouts estimated Don Carolos Buell's army at 50,000, marching from Nashville to Columbia. The "army" at Decatur was 20,000 (actually 17,000), with the addition of Crittenden's defeated East Tennessee division, which had finally limped in. It was Johnston's intent to join up with Beauregard's West Tennessee column (Polk's two divisions), plus the two divisions from the Gulf Coast, at Corinth and strike a blow before the two Federal armies could unite.[37]

As for Fort Donelson, Johnston admitted that the "blow was most disastrous" and "almost without remedy." He reinforced the position as best he could with his limited resources, but he had made it clear to Floyd that, if the fort could not hold, then his force should retreat to

Nashville. It is possible that this could have been done, but the facts of the investigation were not fully known. As for the personal attacks leveled at him, he gave a stoic response: "The test of merit in my profession with the people is success. It is a hard rule, but I think it right." Johnston also forwarded answers to about half the thirteen questions posed by Foote's select committee, stating that he would complete the questionnaire when he was not so overwhelmed with work. Davis took the opportunity to write a return letter reassuring his friend: "My confidence in you has never wavered and I hope the public will soon give me credit for judgment rather than to continue to arraign me for obstinacy."[38]

Precisely what the Yankees were up to in Tennessee remained anyone's guess. A consensus was beginning to emerge, at least among reporters, that Grant's army at Pittsburg Landing, Tennessee, and Buell's army marching from Murfreesboro, would unite to attack either Corinth or somewhere between that place and Florence to disrupt communications on the Memphis & Charleston Railroad. Only administration insiders knew just how dire the situation remained. Hearing that Grant's army had encamped at Savannah, Tennessee, on the Tennessee River raised the concern of Thomas Bragg: "This is a bold movement and shows that they are confident of beating us with ease." Chattanooga was virtually defenseless, and some reports (false, at it developed) indicated that Grant's army was already on the march. At the March 14 cabinet meeting, Davis even talked about the possibility of his going to Tennessee and joining Johnston's army.[39]

The gloom of winter failed to thaw as spring approached. Both Johnstons were retreating—the increasingly quarrelsome Joseph to within fifty miles of Richmond and Sidney to Corinth, where he hoped to reverse the desperate situation in Department No. 2, where everything seemed to be going wrong. Matters were fast coming to a head, if not in Virginia the certainly in the West, where waning fortunes simply had to be reversed. As March ended, Davis assured Johnston that "the future will be brighter." The capital anxiously awaited updates.[40]

On April 5, Davis received a two-day-old dispatch from Johnston in Corinth: "General Buell is in motion, 30,000 strong from Columbia by Clifton to Savannah; Mitchell behind him with 10,000, Confederate forces, 40,000, ordered forward to offer battle near Pittsburg [Landing]. Hope engagement before Buell can form juncture." The army would be advancing in four corps, an odd structure given that two of the four "corps" were actually division-size. The chief executive promptly responded: "I hope you will also be able to close with the enemy before his columns unite. I anticipate victory."[41]

Rumors about a great western battle swirled throughout the capital the next day, but there were no details. Davis exhibited great anxiety, privately relating to Varina: "I know Johnston, and if alive either good or bad would have been communicated at once." At some point on the seventh, probably in the morning, a fateful telegram arrived at Cooper's office:

> Battle-Field of Shiloh, Miss., April 6
>
> this morning attacked the enemy in strong position, and after a severe battle of ten hours, thanks to the Almighty, gained a complete victory, driving the enemy from every position. Loss on both sides heavy, including our commander-in-chief, General A. S. Johnston, who fell gallantly leading his troops into the thickest of the fight.
>
> G. T. Beauregard
> General Commanding[42]

Dispatches from several sources now began furiously clicking over the wires, the first coming via Mobile. "Glorious news from the West!" hailed the morning *Whig*. Johnston had attacked Grant's army, capturing eight batteries and many prisoners. "The enemy are in full retreat and the Confederates are in hot pursuit. . . . We expect to capture the larger portion of the entire army." The *Dispatch* echoed "reliable information" that the Federal army would be destroyed or captured. Later that day a dispatch arrived from William Preston—Johnston's brother-in-law and aide—confirming the all-too-stunning truth: Albert Sidney Johnston was dead. In the Adjutant General's Office, John Withers noted that "Richmond is elate[d] today" of the news of a battle in Tennessee "in which we were completely victorious," although he conceded that the loss of Johnston had "cast a gloom over the great victory." Judith McGuire wrote similarly: "Our victory at Shiloh complete, but General Albert Sidney Johnston was killed. The nation mourns him as one of our most accomplished officers. . . . It is an overwhelming loss to the Western army[] and the whole country." The *Whig* related some of the grisly details of the general's passing—one of his legs was torn by a shell and a bullet struck him in the chest. The news for Senator Henry and his wife hit much closer to home. Their twenty-four-year-old son, Major John F. Henry of the 4th Tennessee, fell mortally wounded. His body was removed to the family plot in Clarksville, where he was buried in Greenwood Cemetery.[43]

Dr. John Lansing Burrows, minister of the First Baptist Church on Broad Street, was a fixture in the city. Many sessions of the Confederate Congress had been opened by his prayers. On Monday afternoon of April 7, he held a special service to give thanks to the Almighty for the great victory in Tennessee. The text of his sermon seemed most appropriate—1 Samuel 3:21: "The Lord appeared again, in Shiloh." Much of the sermon was spent in reflecting the "sad depression" caused by the losses of Fort Henry and Fort Donelson. People at the time posed a question: "What has driven Him [God] from us?" Burrows answered the question by stating that it was God's way of humbling the Southern people and driving them back to the true source of strength and success. But God had not forsaken them. "The most cheering association of all that connects itself with this victory is, that God has revealed Himself as our shield and defense. 'THE LORD appeared again, in Shiloh."[44]

There were no less than eleven Southern correspondents at Shiloh, including Felix G. De Fontaine of the *Dispatch*. The capital dailies reprinted vivid accounts from western papers, including those from Memphis, New Orleans, Mobile, Atlanta, and Savannah. In the last, Peter W. Alexander, arguably the premier journalist in the South, offered an early accurate report of what occurred during the battle. Grant had been reinforced by Buell's army on Monday, April 7, driving Beauregard, now in command, back to Corinth. The Federals quickly called off the chase. Losses on both sides were severe, and not all of the immense captures from the first day's battle could be salvaged. De Fontaine corrected an earlier account of Johnston's death, noting that a bullet had struck an artery in his leg and the general bled out within twenty minutes. Earl Van Dorn's army from Arkansas was on the way to Corinth, as were regiments from Chattanooga. Grant had 40,000 men in the field on Sunday, 5,000 more on Monday; Buell brought an additional 15,000. Total Yankee casualties eclipsed 21,000. Colonel Gorgas did not know what to think of the Shiloh reports, as both sides seemed to play loose with the numbers. "Our loss was probably 5000, while the enemy lost a few thousand more." His estimate was off by half.[45]

The miserable weather on April 7 continued the next day with a mix of snow and rain. At noon the Senate took up a House resolution declaring that the "thanks of Congress are eminently due, and are hereby cordially tendered, to Gen. Gustave T. Beauregard[] and the officers and troops under his command." Profound sorrow was expressed over the death of Johnston, which "obscures our joy with a shade of sadness." Several senators, including Haynes of Tennessee and Clark of Missouri, wondered if the resolution might not be premature. No one opposed an expression of gratitude, but reports had not yet been filed. Senator Henry then interrupted to announce that Johnston might not be dead! He had just received a telegram from a gentleman from Kentucky claiming that Johnston had been only badly wounded. George Davis of North Carolina wondered how that could be, since the original news had been received from the general's own adjutant. Wigfall reminded the assembly that, following the Battle of Pea Ridge, Van Dorn had sent notification of the death of Brigadier General Louis Hébert, only to have to retract the statement later. "In the excitement of the battlefield, nothing can be known of positive certainty." The resolution was tabled.[46]

Confirmation was received later that afternoon. In a joint session of congress, the president, through a spokesman, announced what by that time everyone knew: "[I]t has pleased Almighty God to crown the Confederate arms with a glorious victory over our invaders." Although admitting that details remained "few and incomplete," he relayed the basic facts as he knew them, stating that at last account the enemy was "endeavoring to effect a retreat." In terms of Johnston, "the last lingering hope has disappeared, and it is but too true that General Albert Sidney Johnston is no more." A bullet had penetrated an artery in his leg, causing him to bleed out in a matter of minutes. The message then got personal: "My long and close friendship with this departed chieftain and patriot forbid me to trust myself in giving vent to the feeling which this intelligence has evoked." His only solace was that "[t]he last sound he heard was their [troops'] shout of triumph."[47]

John Wilcox introduced a resolution acknowledging the great national loss and, out of respect, that Congress should adjourn the next day, April 9. Even that simple gesture met a challenge. John Perkins of Louisiana, while agreeing with the sentiment, believed that there was simply too much business to suspend for a day. Foote, one of the general's most outspoken critics, perhaps hoping to deflect censure from his past comments, now incredibly and hypocritically requested that Wilcox withdraw his motion, claiming: "We cannot feel but deeply saddened at the loss of the gallant Johnston." The motion passed.[48]

Acrimony was now heaped on the Tennessee delegation for its vociferous criticism of the fallen hero. Senator Haynes, who had led the delegation to oust the general, took the floor and openly admitted his mistake. Thomas Bragg took pen in hand: "It is thought that he [Johnston] fell victim to the assaults of the demagogues in & out of Congress for the loss of Fort Donelson to the enemy. . . . The reaction has already commenced, and the denunciation[s] of Foote and his confederates are now loud and bitter." Daniel, the unrepentant editor of the *Examiner*, while begrudgingly acknowledging that Shiloh was a victory, albeit not as significant as Manassas, gave credit to Beauregard; Johnston was never mentioned. As for Foote, he avoided the issue, never mentioning it in either of two books that he wrote during the postwar years.[49]

Albert Sidney Johnston was now the seventh general to be killed in the war, five of them in western battles. Thomas DeLeon remembered that the former public clamor was quickly brushed aside and replaced with "universal acclaim to canonize him." Indeed, an erroneous perception prevailed in the capital that the press had goaded the general to strike prematurely. Ruffin expressed remorse over his previous condemnation: "I regret & heartily repent that I, in common with the public in general, had blamed & harshly denounced, Gen. Johnston for not having succored & saved Fort Donelson. . . . There appears in today's paper [April 9] the only vindication of his conduct which he had uttered. . . . He & Pres. Davis were old and warm friends." It was now reported that Johnston did not have 50,000–60,000 but rather 30,000, of which 16,000 were sent to Fort Donelson, leaving him but 14,000 to confront Buell's 80,000. Pillow and Floyd did not call for further reinforcements, surmised Ruffin, "to divide the glory[] for themselves."[50]

A *Whig* editorial, specifically targeting its longtime political rival the *Enquirer*, denounced the "very bitter and unjust reproaches" that had been hurled at Johnston. His last days were "dogged with defamatory criticism." Information was now forthcoming that Johnston had time and again requested reinforcements but that his pleas went unheeded. If the reinforcements that had been rushed to Donelson from the Gulf Coast had been sent in the fall of 1861 rather than in the winter of 1862, the results might have been very different—assuming of course that the troops had been used correctly. The *Enquirer* gave a quick response claiming that the *Whig* offered "excuses, if it does not justify, the late circumstances of Gen. A. S. Johnston by those who at present heap flowers upon his grave." True, the president and the cabinet were not infallible, "but neither is the *Whig*."[51]

The streets still had a thin layer of snow from the previous night on Wednesday, April 9. The president invited Thomas Bragg to dine with him; it would be his last day on the job, he having resigned to return home to North Carolina. Following the "very plain dinner," the subject of the West came up. The latest report from Tennessee was "not so favorable." Grant had been heavily reinforced; Beauregard had been forced to retreat to Corinth, unable to salvage all of the captured artillery and ammunition. Bragg worried over what would come next. To fall back south of Corinth meant that Memphis would have to be abandoned, "which will not do"; he anticipated another great battle any day.[52]

Press accounts nonetheless continued to crow the great victory along the Tennessee River. Nearly 3,000 prisoners had been taken, and only the enemy gunboats prevented a larger triumph. Beauregard declared that he had only 38,000 troops on the battlefield and that Southerners "could whip the Federals three[-]to[-]one in a fair fight." The hyperbole seemingly had no end, including reports that eighty guns were captured and that Buell had been killed. Although the Confederates had retreated to Corinth, the *Dispatch* did not believe that the Federals would "hazard an engagement with the victorious Beauregard." Particularly encouraging was the conclusion that the victory would "change the face of things in Europe."[53]

Slowly the reality that Shiloh had not in fact been a triumph became apparent to Ruffin, yet he continued to ignore Yankee claims of a great victory. Even Northern papers placed their casualties at a horrendous 15,000–20,000. "May we have more such defeats!" he chuckled. Although dismissing the "outrageously and ludicrously exaggerated" Federal accounts, he feared that this would be the narrative reprinted in London, thereby winning the propaganda war for the enemy. Thomas Bragg was slowly perceiving that the "great victory at Corinth [Shiloh] grows small. Instead [of] 80 pieces of artillery we have 14—and 3000 instead of double that number of prisoners. . . . Such are the 'reliable' accounts we get."[54]

Mournful Richmond citizens read accounts of Johnston's funeral, held in New Orleans five days after the battle. His body lay in state at City Hall for two days, his sword at his side. Present with him was his son William Preston Johnston, although the general's wife remained in

California. Long lines solemnly passed the flower-draped casket. His personal staff, including his brother-in-law William Preston, stood loyally with him to the end. Louisiana Governor Thomas O. Moore and other dignitaries stood in silence. The casket was temporarily interred at St. Louis Cemetery in the family tomb of New Orleans Mayor John Monroe until it could be removed to Texas.[55]

An unanticipated outcome of the general's death was the addition of his son William to the presidential staff. It so happened that the thirty-one-year-old officer was in Richmond after the funeral, recuperating from pneumonia and typhoid, the effects of which would remain with him for the duration of his life. He was assigned as a presidential aide and promoted to colonel. The appointment was clearly a sentimental one for Davis. The sickly, bookish, Yale-educated lawyer-turned-soldier was, as one historian phrased it, "the last remaining tangible presence of his dead father." In fact, the colonel, although devoted to his father, lived apart from him almost his entire life. The enfeebled officer held the president in awe, and Davis reciprocated with admiration and affection. At the president's request, he dined almost every evening with the First Family, and he would be invited to take up residence on the third floor of the Executive Mansion. The young officer remained the final connection to his dear friend, and Davis expressed to him: "I cannot think calmly of your Father. I cannot speak or write of him without immotion." The chief executive frequently confided in William, and the young colonel's analysis and prejudices, especially as they related to western matters, would be significant. To his wife, Rosa, however, the young Johnston downplayed his influence, claiming that "delicacy and common sense" caused him to remain silent. Once in the president's orbit, however, he did not remain silent.[56]

6

To Defend Both the City and the Valley

Officials at the War Department held their breaths. Despite the losses at the Twin Rivers, the Mississippi Valley continued to hold—at least for now. Nevertheless, Sidney Johnston's center was reeling back to Decatur, Alabama, thereby exposing his left, now under Beauregard. The *Whig* reasoned that the Federals were attempting to flank the Creole general, causing him to "fall down the [Mississippi] River." Reinforcements, according to the *Dispatch*, were being rushed to the Mississippi Valley, but even a military novice like John Jones could see that Columbus, Kentucky, could now be taken in reverse. Indeed, on February 27 he heard that the town was to be evacuated. "Beauregard sees that it is untenable with Forts Henry and Donelson in possession of the enemy. He will not be caught in a trap as that. But he is erecting a battery at Island No. 10 that will give the Yankees trouble. I hope it may stay the catalogue of disasters."[1]

All the heavy guns at Columbus were safely removed to Island No. 10 and New Madrid, a few miles downriver on the west bank in Missouri. Beauregard considered the position impregnable, and the *Dispatch* assured civilians that the Mississippi Valley was safe. Island No. 10 was "the real key" and "a perfect Gibraltar," words that had been said of Columbus. Yet even the most heavily fortified positions could always be outflanked or invested. At least Edmund Ruffin was coming to that conclusion: "I should think that we had had enough of risking armies in fortifications in reach of the enemy's naval forces."[2]

It soon became clear that the Federals saw New Madrid as the softer target. By March 3, John Pope's 20,000-man Federal army was reportedly two days out. On March 19, news arrived in Richmond that New Madrid had fallen six days earlier. The garrison had escaped, but the artillery had to be abandoned. The *Enquirer* downplayed the event, noting that the position was of little strategic value, but communications to Island No. 10 had clearly been severed. Reports soon leaked out that Major General John P. McCown had made a feeble defense; Davis was livid. There were also accusations of McCown's drinking habits. Representative Foote had heard from his son, Captain Henry S. Foote, aide to McCown, that rumors of the general's drunkenness were patently false, initiated by a jealous brother "who I am told drinks freely." Davis nonetheless expressed indignation over the "cowardly conduct" of the general.[3]

The Union navy now began a siege to reduce the island and Tennessee shore batteries. While official dispatches remained sparse, press "telegraphics" from Memphis and New Orleans correspondents arrived almost daily throughout late March and into April. Civilians War Department officials read the updates at the same time. According to the *Whig* of April 1, over 3,000 13-inch shells had struck the island, but there had been little damage to the parapets and none to the magazines and heavy guns. It was reported that the Federals were actively engaged cutting a canal through the backwaters on the Missouri side so their transports could circumvent the island batteries. Their efforts would prove unsuccessful, or so it was believed, due to the large cypress trees and thickly tangled roots. Thomas Bragg nonetheless could not help but express begrudging amazement: "What energy they display! This, with the great means that they have, enable them to accomplish wonders."[4]

On April 11, a congressman received a disturbing dispatch claiming that Island No. 10 had been abandoned. The news was kept in private circles. Nearly a week later a Richmond citizen received a letter from a friend in Memphis claiming that the island garrison had indeed surrendered. The public did not receive confirmation for ten days, and that came through the Northern press. Another "Gibraltar" was gone; capital citizens expressed shock. Sally Brock admitted that the loss was "a terrible blow." Precisely how many prisoners were taken depended on the account—7,000 by Northern tally, 2,000 by Southern, with 1,000 escaping. The loss in heavy artillery proved staggering, the Federal accounts claiming seventy guns. The *Dispatch* expressed contempt: "We were utterly assured the place was impregnable[] and that the enemy would never pass it. Two day's after Beauregard's reassuring dispatch the island fell with its garrison. . . . We are utterly disgusted." Senator Williamson Oldham believed that, to any "reasonably thinking man," the administration's policy of static defense was flawed.[5]

In his *Southern Literary Messenger* editorial, George Bagby could not maintain his rage. "We have been whipped in almost every engagement since last Fall." While he listed Roanoke Island and Kernstown, Virginia, on the eastern portion of the ledger, the western renumeration was pointedly longer: Mill Springs, Fort Henry, Fort Donelson, the fall of Nashville, New Madrid, Pea Ridge, and now Island No. 10. John Withers, in the Adjutant General's Office, remained remarkably disinterested in the recent western affairs. He chose instead to concentrate on the miserable weather, adding that there had been "no military news of consequence."[6]

Fort Pillow was abandoned on June 4, and reports reached the capital that Memphis was in a state of panic. The *Whig* concluded that "the Government has no further use for Memphis." The first report of what now seemed predictable did not arrive until June 14. A brief naval battle had been fought at Memphis on June 6, and the Confederate fleet had either been destroyed or scuttled. The entire upper Mississippi Valley was now in enemy hands.[7]

With the fall of Fort Henry, War Department officials belatedly rushed reinforcements from the Gulf Coast to Tennessee. Braxton Bragg was ordered to leave a "weak garrison" at Pensacola and an "effective garrison" at Mobile and proceed to Tennessee with his division. By the end of February 1862, Major General Mansfield Lovell, commanding Department No. 1, had also sent eight regiments, two batteries, 500 arms, and a million cartridges, prompting him to caution Richmond: "People [in New Orleans] are beginning to complain." When Louisiana Governor Thomas Moore notified the administration that he had some ninety-day troops, he was told to send them on, thereby adding two more regiments and two batteries. The reinforcements arrived in time to fight at Shiloh, where they sustained severe losses. New Orleans regiments alone suffered 678 casualties.[8]

Stripping the Gulf Coast of troops was a gamble, but it was one Davis had to take. In a word, the Upper South was being overrun. That did not mean that the Gulf Coast was secure; it was not. Back in December

1861, the Federals, in brigade strength, had landed on Ship Island, a barren strip of land off the Mississippi coast, sixty miles from New Orleans and forty miles from Mobile. The landing, according to reprinted New York articles, was the forerunner of a huge, 30,000-man expedition to be led by Benjamin Butler, which would attack either Mobile or New Orleans, most likely the former. Nonetheless, in mid-January 1862, activity appeared "very quiet."[9]

The issue of the Butler expedition came up in the January 6 cabinet meeting. Lovell, it was reported, remained unconcerned, believing that New Orleans was safe from a land assault. He suspicioned that the intended target was Mobile. As for Bragg, he remained preoccupied with Pensacola. Benjamin therefore desired old Brigadier General Daniel Ruggles, a Northerner from Massachusetts who had cast his lot with the South and was then serving in Pensacola, to command at Mobile, but Davis leaned toward letting Bragg retain command. In the midst of the discussion, it came out that there was "not entire harmony" between Bragg and Lovell. From the outset Bragg felt that Ruggles should have been given command of Department No. 1. In truth, the matter went deeper. Bragg, being from Louisiana and commander of the state forces, was incensed that he had not been selected to command at New Orleans. He was also jealous of Beauregard, who received a commission that predated his, a move that he considered (wrongly) to be a slight from Davis. Furthermore, Bragg had offered Lovell a position in the state army, which he declined. Bragg simply did not like the man. "I fear therefore the thing will not work well if an attack is made in the direction of Mobile," Thomas Bragg jotted in his journal. "However, Gen'l B. [Bragg] has his hands full now without enlarging his command." Meanwhile, on February 1, a rumor swirled in the capital that New Orleans had surrendered! It turned out to be nothing more than a Northern newspaper rumor.[10]

New Orleans was the largest city in the Confederacy, with 150,000 inhabitants, and represented the commercial and financial center of the Deep South. It is doubtful that anyone in the administration, or for that matter in the Confederate Congress, knew the precise statistics. If they did, they would have understood that the South's connection to Britain lay in that port. In 1860, 68 percent of the cotton exports and 72 percent of the grain exports were bound for that nation. Matters in New Orleans had been quiet; Ruffin suspected that the government knew more than it was telling.[11]

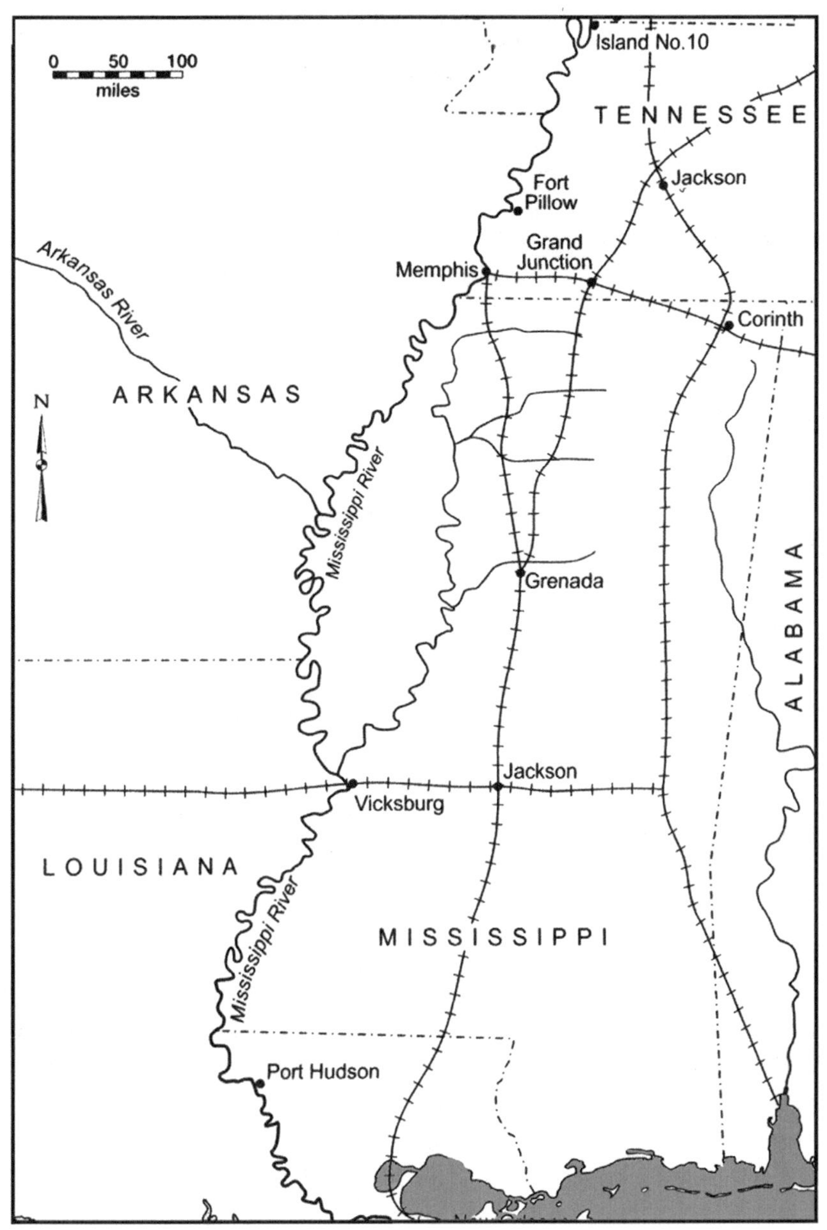

The Mississippi Valley. Map by Mary Lee Eggert.

As the Butler expeditionary fleet began to swell in size, panic spread along the Gulf Coast. Still suspecting that the target was Mobile, the *Dispatch* offered reassurances. If an amphibious landing was made somewhere along the Mississippi Coast, the terrain between there and Mobile would be nearly impassable, cut by bayous, swamps, tangled thickets, and rivers. Brigadier General Samuel "Sam" Jones, commanding at Mobile, was nonetheless growing nervous. He had only 1,000 armed men (mostly militia) and 500 unarmed men. If the target was Pensacola, he had 3,500 men, half of them unarmed, with no field artillery. Unless the government could quickly increase the Mobile garrison to 5,000, the city would be "in imminent danger of falling." Alabama Governor John Gill Shorter made a case for Pensacola. It may not be important to us, he wrote the War Department, but it was to the enemy. From that position, the Federals could launch an overland expedition into central Alabama. The position needed 5,000 well-armed men immediately. Everywhere the demands were immediate, the resources limited.[12]

Lovell advised Richmond that he had declared martial law in New Orleans due to the "heterogeneous elements" and "an excitable population." The New Orleans press could no longer publish military news, meaning that no updates were received in Richmond. From the middle of March to the end of the month, the only reprinted articles from New Orleans related to the fact that there would be no Mardi Gras that year and the near completion of a luxurious four-story theater with a sixty-one-foot stage.[13]

Butler's expeditionary force finally committed—not toward Mobile but New Orleans! On March 22, during the news blackout, a dispatch from Lovell suddenly clicked over the wires: "Seven vessels of the enemy inside the mouth of the river [Mississippi]." Five days later he warned: "The enemy is in large force at the mouth of the river." The department commander now pleaded for arms to repel a possible amphibious assault. Some 1,880 arms, purchased by the state of Louisiana, had come through the blockade in Florida, but the shipment had been copped by Governor John Milton, who refused to release them. Governor Moore notified Benjamin: "I am greatly annoyed." Lovell candidly advised that, without the arms, the city would be in a "precarious condition." On April 10, Lovell appealed for 5,000 arms; none were sent.[14]

Facing two simultaneous assaults, and with pressure mounting, the president had to make an anguished decision. He gambled that Fort Jackson and Fort St. Phillip at New Orleans could defeat the formidable, but wooden, Federal fleet under Admiral David Farragut. Indeed, he considered the southern threat a probable feint. Thus, on April 10, with the entire Gulf Coast on edge, he wired five governors, including those of Mississippi, Alabama, and Louisiana, that Beauregard at Corinth needed still more men: "The necessity is imminent." In addition, he ordered CSS *Louisiana*, an ironclad under construction at New Orleans, to proceed upriver to Island No. 10 to confront the Union ironclad fleet upriver. Lovell had informed the War Department that the city defenses included 310 heavy guns—surely enough to repel the enemy fleet. "The purpose is to defend [both] the city and the valley," Davis wrote. It made logical sense, but Moore was furious; panic spread in New Orleans.[15]

"We hear nothing from New Orleans," Thomas Bragg wrote on April 15. Later that day a dispatch arrived indicating that trouble loomed. The enemy fleet had grown to forty vessels, and the Union mortars were shelling Fort Jackson and Fort St. Phillip. John Withers heard muted talk in the Adjutant General's Office on April 18 that the forts had fallen; nerves were on edge. The first time the news became public was in the *Whig* issue of April 23. By that time the forts had been under fire for a week and a half. Davis telegraphed Moore: "In painful anxiety await further intelligence." The next day, April 24, Thomas Bragg noted that the "Richmond papers say the *Louisiana* left N. Orleans a week or more since, whether up or down the river is not known," virtually admitting that even insiders were dependent on the press for updates. A jarring dispatch arrived from Lovell later that day: "The enemy has passed our forts." Two days later the warships had dropped anchor at New Orleans and the mayor had surrendered the city.[16]

The War Department suppressed the story for two days. As Richmond churches began letting out on Sunday, April 28, news of a "momentous disaster" suddenly began to stir. So breathtaking was the chatter that Ruffin, initially at least, dismissed it as ridiculous. Within hours he caved to reality. "It is too true. New Orleans is in possession of the enemy, & without resistance! The Yankee power has struck a most heavy blow & obtained a great triumph." Helen Keary, the president's niece, happened to be in the capital when the news broke. Writing to her parents in Mississippi, she described the scene there: "Oh, what a blow the fall of New Orleans was! It liked to have set us all crazy here. Everyone looks depressed, and the cause of the Confederacy seems drooping and sinking; but if God is with us, who can be against us?" To add insult to injury, the letter was intercepted and reprinted in several Northern papers. Judith McGuire observed that the city was "shrouded in [a] gloom" that made "chicken-hearted men and women despondent."

Thomas Bragg was "thunder struck" when he read the morning paper. "Tis strange and yet I fear it is all too true," he wrote. "If New Orleans has fallen our cause is lost."[17]

Given that McClellan's army was now a scant four days' march from Richmond, there were those who could focus only on the enemy at the gate. The bureaucrats Jones and Withers simply ignored the loss of New Orleans in their journals. Even Jules de St. Martin, brother-in-law of Judah Benjamin and himself a transplanted New Orleans resident, stoically shrugged his shoulders. Gorgas nonetheless remained defiant: "The evacuation of N. Orleans by Lovell is a shameful chapter in our history. He should have insisted upon the defense of the city & asked for 48 hours to remove the women & children."[18]

Back in his prewar days, when Davis had served as secretary of war in Washington, he knew of the monumental amount of work that had been expended on the forts of the lower Mississippi. It seemed incomprehensible that a wooden fleet could make it past such formidable masonry fortifications. He had assured Lovell that the city would be "defended from above," meaning the upper Mississippi Valley. Secretary of the Navy Stephen Mallory had long been an easy target for political sniping, especially from Foote, and there were now renewed attacks. "The hour is dark and gloomy," the secretary privately wrote. "The destruction of the Navy was a sad blow and has affected us bitterly, bitterly, bitterly!"[19]

The *Enquirer* attempted to paint a best face. Although admitting that the news was a "heavy blow," this was mitigated by the fact that "we were anticipating it." No one was in a mood to believe obvious newspaper lies. Senator Yancey, visiting in Montgomery in early May, learned firsthand that the people of central Alabama were absolutely *not* anticipating it. The loss of the city, he wrote the president, "has created a profound impression upon the public's mind here," resulting in "some depression."[20]

Word soon reached the capital that Butler, now commanding the Federal occupation force, had issued several perceived tyrannical proclamations, the most egregious of which being the notorious "woman's order." The intent was to prevent the most militant of the New Orleans ladies from uttering their verbal abuse and overt snubbing of Union soldiers. The May 15 order declared that any woman who persisted in this conduct would be "treated as a woman of the town, plying her avocation." The threat stopped the offenses and no arrests were ever made, but Butler had earned a reputation as a tyrant and a monster.

Senator Yancey denounced the "cowardly and barbarous treatment of our people."[21]

Increasingly, Britain and France distanced themselves from a collapsing Confederacy, most of which was occurring in the West. A reprinted article from the *London Times* expressed that the South was simply outmatched. The *Manchester Guardian*, while denouncing the barbaric treatment of the people of New Orleans, concluded that the time for British intervention "has not yet come, if indeed it ever will." The *Dublin Freeman* revealed little sympathy over the reports of harsh civilian treatment. "Perhaps a city like New Orleans, famed for its rowdies, should for a time be placed under restraint. All the vengeance of the South is concentrated in that city of half-breeds." The loss of New Orleans also postponed if not ended the hope of a French intervention under Napoleon III.[22]

It was becoming increasingly evident to some in the capital that fortifications, even masonry ones, could usually not stop the Union navy and that ultimate victory could be achieved only from concentration in the center. The military answer was nonetheless not the political answer, and Davis was not about to perfunctorily defend the rivers and ports. He remained undeterred and continued to insist that control of the Mississippi River, or at least what was left of it, was paramount to avoid "dismemberment." As for now, the loss of New Orleans was a shocking blow; recriminations were forthcoming.[23]

The administration was in crisis mode. The reaction over the fall of New Orleans was predictable and immediate. The *Enquirer* furiously screamed: "The Confederacy had been piled with emphatic and continued assurances from New Orleans, that the defenses of the city were complete and impregnable. . . . And yet New Orleans has fallen!" Increasingly the focus became not strategy but personalities, especially Lovell and Mallory. Few in the capital knew much about the brown-haired, bulbous-nosed forty-year-old Lovell. In New Orleans they knew him as a "showy horseman" who sat in the saddle "straight as a spear." Indeed, the idlers down at the wharf used to love to see him pass on the steamboat deck without dismounting. What Richmonders did know was not always accurate. He was not born in Boston but in Washington D.C., and his parents did not die and leave him orphaned at an early age. Nonetheless, his prewar Northern associations and late commitment to the Confederacy raised suspicions that "he is a Yankee" and an "eleventh hour convert." Scurrilous rumors floated relating to his pro-Union speeches in New York. Interestingly, the capital press defended him, but the whisperings continued. Ruffin admitted that there were "dark suspicions . . . even of treason," and Jones expressed disgust that "a Mass. man" had commanded the department.[24]

Lovell heard through a Richmond friend (possibly his former West Point classmate Gustavus Smith) that the popular tide had turned against him and of Davis's contentment not to contradict the narrative. Lovell wrote directly to the president; he received no response. As for his request for a court of inquiry to tell his side of the story, it was repeatedly delayed. Already an article had appeared in the *New Orleans Delta*, reprinted in the *Whig*, that laid blame for the loss of the city at the doorstep of the administration. If Lovell could deflect some of the public ire, then Davis was quite content to let it happen. He took satisfaction in writing his brother: "Gen. Lovell arrived here yesterday [May 21] but he is [so] universally odious that his ability [influence] is lessened."[25]

Congress, which was not in session the day New Orleans fell, did not reconvene until August 1862. By that time matters had dramatically altered. Robert E. Lee had replaced the wounded Joseph E. Johnston and had defeated McClellan in fierce fighting on the Peninsula. Casualties had been frightful, but once again the capital felt secure. Under Lee's leadership the war would take a dramatic turn that no one could have foreseen. At the time, however, there were critics. Jones noted: "Lee does not follow up his blows on the whipped enemy, and some sage critics censure him for it." Criticism aside, had the outcome been otherwise, the war would have been over. On the first day of the new session, Davis announced to Congress: "The vast army which threatened the capital of the Confederacy has been defeated." But there was always the West. A recurring theme was thus developed: Could the war in Virginia be won faster than the war in the West was being lost?[26]

Even though the loss of New Orleans was complex, outraged congressmen were looking for a single person to blame—and they had one in Mallory. In the House, Foote related the story of a party of a dozen young women and a dozen young men. That evening the women were heard talking through a thin wall. "I do love Mr. Thompson," said one. "He is such a fool!" Laughter erupted in the chamber. The president and his advisers love Mallory, he continued, because "he is such a fool." On August 27 Foote called for a vote of no confidence on the secretary, but the matter was tabled. There were also rumblings in the Senate. Semmes of Louisiana had heard that the ironclad *Louisiana* might have had a significant impact on the battle but for mismanagement. Some were claiming negligence on the part of the navy secretary, although they admitted that they had only accusations, not facts. A joint committee was proposed to investigate the matter. Wigfall believed the proposal to be nothing more than a fishing expedition. Albert Brown of Mississippi took to the floor to say that the president was "not an idiot." Davis had seen the confidential reports, and if there had been mismanagement he would not have retained Mallory. It was rather oddly concluded to investigate the Navy Department but not its head.[27]

Lovell took his 3,000 infantry and 1,000 heavy artillerists north to Vicksburg, Mississippi. The Confederates in the West were retreating so fast that it led to command confusion. Beauregard in the north believed that he had jurisdiction over Jackson and Vicksburg, whereas Lovell insisted that he was in command. The War Department had to quickly redefine department lines along the33rd Parallel, giving Lovell jurisdiction. By May 18, the advance of Farragut's fleet had arrived at Vicksburg. The demand for the surrender of the city was promptly rejected. Davis liked what he read: "The people of Vicksburg and Grand Gulf have shown more spirit than those of New Orleans," he wrote Varina. The two Vicksburg papers were getting through to the capital, but even so news remained sporadic. Federal warships periodically shelled the city, but damage remained slight, at least through the reports of early June.[28]

"We are more successful in Virginia than elsewhere," observed Judith McGuire. "The whole Mississippi Valley, except Vicksburg and its environs, is now in the hands of the enemy and that place must surrender." With the fall of Fort Pillow and the surrender of Memphis, the evacuation of Vicksburg seemed inevitable. But Vicksburg held![29]

Davis, disappointed by Earl Van Dorn's performance in the trans-Mississippi, decided to place him in command of the Department of Southern Mississippi and East Louisiana, to supersede Lovell. Despite the president's assurance that the reassignment was "from no want of confidence," the news undoubtedly rankled the Mississippian. He no longer held an independent command and was answerable to the commander of the Army of the Mississippi, then at Tupelo. He arrived in Vicksburg on June 21 and immediately telegraphed Davis that twenty-seven Union transports with an estimated 10,000 troops had ascended the Mississippi River and would arrive by the night of June 27. It appeared that a land assault was imminent.[30]

The Federals were well aware that the Southerners had an ironclad vessel, CSS *Arkansas*, under construction on the Yazoo River, a tributary that emptied into the Mississippi north of Vicksburg. Indeed, a lifted Northern news article even gave the dimensions of the vessel and noted that the armor was made of railroad bar iron. "It is believed that the Yankees will attempt to capture the ram Arkansas if they lose half their fleet in doing so," noted the *Dispatch*. Before any beachhead could be attempted, the issue of the *Arkansas* had to be decided.[31]

As infantry reinforcements rushed to Vicksburg, Richmond officials anxiously awaited the status of the *Arkansas*. On July 15, a dispatch from Van Dorn arrived on the desk of the president. *Arkansas* had made a successful run past twelve or thirteen enemy gunboats, running two ashore (attempting to keep from sinking) and seriously damaging many others. The ironclad would have to undergo repairs on her riddled smokestack and "Then Ho! for New Orleans!" Beginning July 17 and extending for two weeks, the public learned the details. At a time when good news was sorely needed from the West, it came as a godsend. Judith McGuire jubilantly wrote in her diary: "Our large gunboat, *Arkansas*, ran into the Federal fleet of twelve or thirteen gun-boats and rams, and [it] overcame them completely. Vicksburg stands the bombardment with unflinching gallantry."[32]

The ironclad was now moored at the Vicksburg wharf. On July 22, the Federal fleet shelled the city and its batteries until after dark. Two days later a run was made once more past the Confederate defenses in a desperate attempt to destroy *Arkansas*. Van Dorn fired off a dispatch to Davis: "An attack made this morning by two ironclad rams to sink *Arkansas*. The failure [was] so complete it was almost ridiculous." Both Farragut's fleet and the Upper Squadron soon departed; the first siege of Vicksburg had ended in victory. "Vicksburg has triumphantly withstood the shelling of the enemy's fleet of gun-boats," Jones ecstatically entered in his journal. "This proves that New Orleans might have been successfully defended and could have been held to this day by Gen. Lovell. So, West Point is not always the best criterion of one's fitness to command." There was much left unsaid in his statement, not the least of which was that Van Dorn *was* West Point. It mattered not; perceptions were not always grounded in the facts.[33]

7

Hubris

Back in December 1861, when Davis nominated Harry Heth to command the newly organized Department of the Trans-Mississippi, the opposition had been fierce. Davis appeared more than willing to fight it out, but Heth was not and he withdrew his name. The newly seated Missouri congressional delegation was fast becoming the grain of sand that irritated. A major general was needed who would be acceptable both to the president and to the annoying Missourians. Braxton Bragg, the desired candidate, had politely declined.

Davis settled on a longtime Mississippi friend, the five-foot, five-inch, dapper Major General Earl "Buck" Van Dorn, then commanding a division in Virginia. He had graduated West Point (barely) and had experience in the Mexican–American War and later in fighting Comanches on the Texas frontier, where he received two serious arrow wounds. He had experience in the trans-Mississippi; more important, he was "entirely acceptable" to the Missouri delegation, which had finally conceded that their beloved Price would not be tapped. Van Dorn's name had previously been discussed in the cabinet and passed over, but precisely what was said will never be known. Perhaps it was because of his limited command experience. Perhaps his reputation of being rash and a hothead had given the president pause. "He craved glory beyond everything," General Dabney Maury would later write of him. There was also the issue of gossip. It was an open secret that he had fathered three children with a mistress, all three taking the Van Dorn name. Nonetheless, the trans-Mississippi was a mess, and someone had to be sent to supersede the quarreling McCulloch and Price. Van Dorn received his orders to report to his new command and departed the capital on

Thursday, January 16, 1862. He desired to see his wife before he departed, but Davis and Benjamin instructed him to "hurry off," as "great events were hanging off the times."[1]

Thomas Bragg revealed some uneasiness as he wrote in his diary on the evening of January 16, 1862. "He [Van Dorn] will have to create his Army and there is some doubt whether he can do it." He was well aware of the "bad feeling here among the Missouri delegation in Congress. They complain that their state has been neglected—talk of superseding Price etc. Everything has been explained to them by the President, but it does not satisfy them." Within weeks of Van Dorn's arrival in Arkansas, word reached Richmond of a great victory. Thomas Bragg expressed skepticism. "We have often heard so before," he dismissively wrote on March 3, "and I put little confidence in the news." The report turned out to be false.[2]

Shortly thereafter, March 12, contradictory rumors again became "rife on the streets." George Bagby heard that Van Dorn and Price had been "horribly whipped." There were other dispatches and telegrams to Arkansas congressmen that told a different outcome. The sketchy details related that a two-day battle had been fought between Van Dorn and Union General Samuel R. Curtis, with 30,000 men on each side. The poorly armed Southerners had "fought like devils," and Van Dorn had been left in possession of the battlefield. Brigadier Generals McCulloch and James M. McIntosh had been killed. "In official circles this is regarded as a victory, and it is believed that the next news will announce it as a fact," the *Dispatch* confidently related. Bragg wanted to believe the good news but admitted that "we hear many things from that quarter which turn out to be untrue." A week later, a six-day-old Memphis article told the truth: Van Dorn's army had in fact been driven back in the Battle of Pea Ridge along the Arkansas–Missouri border, although the general defiantly (and disingenuously) boasted that "he is not whipped." Republished Yankee accounts begged to differ, but the details and numbers remained clouded. Van Dorn's after-action report, published in the press on April 19, claimed that he had 14,000 troops opposing 17,000–24,000. He sustained 800 casualties, compared to the Federal's 2,000. Borrowing from a line in *Pilgrim's Progress*, Thomas Cooper DeLeon—"Cooper" he liked to be called—remembered that the news of Pea Ridge resulted in a "slough of despond." Nonetheless, Gorgas concluded that the battle was "indecisive but by no means discreditable to us." Congressman Vest received a letter from a Price soldier stating candidly that Van Dorn simply underestimated the size of the enemy.[3]

Following Pea Ridge, Van Dorn withdrew his army to Van Buren, Arkansas, on the Arkansas–Cherokee Territory line. He planned on moving due east to Jacksonport, Arkansas, and then north to Pocahontas, Arkansas, near the Missouri border. From there he intended to march the seventy miles or so to New Madrid and operate in the rear of John Pope's army, then besieging that place. At least that is what the newspapers in early April claimed. The only problem is that events were moving faster than arriving reports. Before Van Dorn had completed his cross-state trek, New Madrid had fallen. Sidney Johnston redirected him to Memphis and subsequently to Corinth, something that Davis knew on March 25 but the that public did not learn until April 12.[4]

The arrival of the Army of the West in Corinth meant that all of Missouri and northern Arkansas to within thirty-five miles of Little Rock was now occupied by Curtis's army. Indeed, it was only logistics that prevented the bluecoats from marching into the state capital. Governor Rector had been forced to flee, and the Arkansas congressional delegation was on a rampage. Four of the five members of the powerful Senate Military Affairs Committee were from the trans-Mississippi—Sparrow of Louisiana, Johnson of Arkansas, Wigfall of Texas, and Peyton of Missouri. Only Henry from Tennessee came from the Heartland. The Arkansas congressmen requested that a new commander be sent to a reorganized and enlarged Department of the Trans-Mississippi. They preferred Bragg or Price, but a return of Van Dorn was totally unacceptable. Rector also accused the administration of abandoning the state and hinted that Arkansas might secede from the Confederacy. An alarmed Davis wrote Van Dorn that he should reassure Rector that the Army of the West had been only temporarily transferred to meet an emergency and it would be returned as soon as possible.[5]

Van Dorn and Beauregard recommended, and the War Department subsequently approved, a new commander, the recently promoted Major General Thomas C. Hindman. Precisely how much Davis, or for that matter anyone in the War Department, knew about Hindman, beyond the fact that he was an Arkansas political general is not known. The diminutive (five-foot, one-inch), overbearing hothead had served as a U.S. congressman, where a colleague commented that he seemed "perpetually anxious to have a duel." He had enemies, both personal and political, which led him to be wounded in an 1856 street fight. He had the bullet removed from his chest without the use of anesthetic and while chomping a cigar. His father-in-law detested him and did everything in his power to prevent the wedding. Hindman fractured his leg in an 1858 storm, and thereafter his left leg was shorter and he walked with a limp. Known as an accomplished orator and a meticulous dresser, he lunged at a political opponent who once dared to refer to him as "my sweet-scented individual." During the Battle of Shiloh, while riding his horse at a dead run and "whopping like a Comanche," the Arkansan received a broken hip when his horse was killed. His fellow officers in the current conflict knew him as a dangerous conniver, someone who was not to be trifled with, but also as a ferocious fighter and an officer of some talent.[6]

In an amazing episode of organizational skill, Hindman by June had concentrated an army of 18,000 infantry, 6,000 cavalry, and forty-four guns at Little Rock and Pine Bluff. He went on the offensive against Curtis, who retreated down the White River to the safety of the Federal gunboats. In early July, the *Dispatch* reported that the Arkansas general was on the verge of cutting off the Federal retreat to Helena, sixty miles south of Memphis—"his [Curtis's] capture is considered certain." Indeed, the capital press reported that 8,000 prisoners had been bagged. "Delightful if true," wrote a thrilled Judith McGuire, who conceded the next day that the news was in fact *not* true. A later article told that, due to a shortage of ammunition, Hindman had been forced to let the Federals escape. This led the *Whig* to publish a satirical article claiming that Van Dorn had bagged Curtis and Hindman had bagged him again, Sidney Johnston had bagged Grant, and Braxton Bragg had bagged Buell. "Cotton bagging, linen bagging and leather bagging will do, but this eternal paper bagging won't do."[7]

Despite Hindman's brief but extraordinary performance, Davis had concerns. There had been complaints about his draconian enforcement of the conscription law, and one of his subordinates, Brigadier General Albert Pike, commanding in the Indian Territory, had written Davis denouncing Hindman as "an Arkansas politician" whose only desire was to advance his political aspirations after the war by saving his state. Pike also complained that 2,000 arms earmarked for his Indians had been commandeered by Hindman for his troops. Arkansas Congressman Grandison D. Royston was also making rumblings in the House regarding some of Hindman's tactics. Even so, the root of the matter came down to Davis's prejudice for West Pointers. Hindman's commission as major general had been a political expediency. A professional was needed to oversee matters. In June 1862, Davis appointed Major General John "Prince John" Magruder from the Army of Northern Virginia. Known as the "aristocrat of aristocrats" in the Old Army, the Virginian, who spoke with a slight lisp, had performed well early in the Peninsula Campaign, although an unsubstantiated charge of drunkenness in the latter part of the campaign would later have to be investigated. He would be the third trans-Mississippi commander within six months.[8]

Davis never consulted with his cabinet about military appointments, a policy that Stephen Mallory found frustrating. He believed that Price would have been the better choice for the trans-Mississippi because he had the support of the people and Magruder "is a stranger." He conceded, however, that Price would most likely have been preoccupied with Missouri to the exclusion of the balance of the other states. "[T]he president doubtless takes the largest view of the subject; & I know he does all for the best." Van Dorn got wind of the appointment and advised Davis to wait, "as it would have a bad effect." Price was on his way to the capital, and Van Dorn strongly advocated for the Missourian. Davis's mind was made up: Magruder would be sent. But he never made it. While in route, he was recalled to answer the charges of alcoholism during the Battle of Malvern Hill. Magruder protested to the president, claiming that the Missouri congressmen wanted him. Davis bluntly told him that it was only because he had promised to give deference to Price. "They care nothing for you, General. It is Price they wish for."[9]

Davis quickly found a replacement—Theophilus H. Holmes, an old family friend and, like so many other western appointees, a weak West Pointer who had washed out in a small command. A gaunt, disheveled old man, nicknamed "Granny" by his men, he was extremely deaf, but according to Senator Oldham "that was the least objectionable of his deficiencies." He was indecisive, and all in all "he did not know what to do." The general begged the president not to send him to an even larger department, but he was too reticent to quarrel with the final decision—just the type of general that Davis desired. He did not arrive at Little Rock until August 1862, at which time he again fruitlessly pleaded to be relieved; he was instead promoted to lieutenant general. For the fourth time (Heth, Hindman, Magruder, Holmes) Davis had intentionally bypassed Price for department command. Senator Clark expressed outrage, and Price once again considered resigning. In unfiltered disgust, Clark wrote the general that, protestations to the contrary, "everyone knows" how "indifferent" and "unfriendly" the president was toward the plight of Missouri. No one was "so odious as President Davis, while no one is so popular as yourself." Yet he encouraged him not to resign; work remained to be done.[10]

From outward public appearance, matters appeared to be progressing in the trans-Mississippi. The Northern news reported that "[t]he whole country of the White River [Arkansas] is reported to be in arms." Representative Vest assured capital citizens that, from official and newspaper sources, "the people are rising up all over the State." Jones at the War Department had heard the same reports. "From Texas, West Louisiana, and Arkansas, we shall soon have tidings. The clans are gathering, and 20,000 more, half mounted on hardy horses, will soon be marching for the prairie country of the enemy."[11]

Governor Moore nonetheless expressed irritation that Louisiana had been divided into two districts, neither with a headquarters within the state. It would take him several weeks to communicate with Hindman in Little Rock. He was more than perturbed with the Confederate White House; he was angry. "This persistent neglect is incomprehensible," he wrote Davis, reminding him that he had not had a response from him in two months. If Moore wanted a Louisiana district, he would get one. Brigadier General Richard Taylor, who had been commanding a brigade in Virginia, had become seriously ill during the Peninsula Campaign, suffering from arthritis that eventually progressed to paralysis in his lower extremities, with accompanying severe headaches. Despite his chronic health problems and the fact that the pious Stonewall Jackson was dismayed at his profuse cursing, Taylor was a good officer. He also happened to be the son of former President Zachary Taylor and brother-in-law to Davis. He had been recuperating in Richmond for a month and was now in need of a command. Taylor was thus promoted to major general and sent to a newly organized Louisiana district, with headquarters in Alexandria.[12]

There was actually more to the transfer than simply placating the hysterical Louisiana governor; Taylor was on a covert mission. Although Randolph had stacked the War Department with Virginians, there was a notable exception. He came under the influence of three former members of the Louisiana Washington Artillery (5th Company), all of whom had fought at Shiloh. Thomas L. Bayne, a young New Orleans lawyer and son-in-law of Gorgas, was assigned to the Ordnance Department, while Joseph Denegre and Stephen Chalaron, a New Orleans commission merchant and an accountant respectively, had been transferred to the War Department. Together they piqued Randolph's interest in an overly ambitious plan to retake New Orleans. The secretary of war in turn collaborated with Davis to form an incomplete strategy. The military element would comprise troops from Mobile, Texas, Jackson (Mississippi), and the new Louisiana recruits to be raised and trained by Taylor. They would work in conjunction with a fifth column made up of unscrupulous merchants and mercenaries. So secret was the mission that it was only verbally related to Taylor. Major General Ruggles in Jackson, unaware of the plan, devised a similar strategy and transmitted it over the telegraph wire in an uncoded message. Ruggles also sent a messenger to Richmond. Randolph politely related that he should mind his own business.[13]

Sterling Price had long been a press and congressional favorite, much to the chagrin of the administration. The *Whig* of January 10, 1862, noted that "the accomplished chief of the War Department [Benjamin], who takes all the New Orleans newspapers," could not have missed a stinging editorial in the *Bee*. "It appears that the men who direct the conduct of the war have disapproved Gen. Price's aggressive spirit (*esprit d'initiations*)[] and are afraid that the success of his plans might derange the deep-laid combinations of that famous policy of inaction which he so sorely affected every patriot," declared the paper. Governor John Pettus also made a plea for Price. He could do more than anyone in the field to raise troops in Arkansas and Missouri. He remained "a popular idol," and his leadership was sorely needed after "a long train of disasters."[14]

Nine days later, on June 19, Price arrived in the capital. It was the first time Richmond citizens had actually seen the proclaimed hero of the trans-Mississippi. The *Whig* headlined: "The Washington of the West is now in Richmond—All hail!" The Richmond correspondent for the *Charleston Courier* described him as a six-foot-tall, beardless, white-haired man who was highly accessible, laughed frequently, and was a lover of music. He had the distinguished appearance of a "fine old English gentleman." His fatherly demeanor had earned him the sobriquet "Old Pap," or as some called him "Old Dad Price." Davis nonetheless had him pegged. The former Missouri governor was an overrated prima donna who now found himself on the national stage and who was believing the press hype. It would take time for reality to catch up to the perception.[15]

General Sterling "Old Pap" Price detested Jefferson Davis; the feeling was mutual. (Library of Congress)

Precisely why the Missourian was in town was somewhat vague. The press claimed that the visit was official, and it was suspected that he would have an audience with the president. The *Dispatch* warned its readers, however, that any anticipated promotion might not be forthcoming—the West Point clique would prevent it. At his departure, however, there seems to have been a quid pro quo. "The Missouri difficulty," wrote the *Dispatch*, had received a "satisfactory arrangement." Despite the president's policy of reserving major general commissions only for West Pointers, coupled with the fact that he personally disliked the Missourian, the promotion was politically inevitable. The Missourians by that time were already being rapidly tendered into Confederate service. Besides, Davis could hardly make Hindman a major general but not Price. The Missourian therefore would be nominated once the transfer of his state troops was complete. On March 6, 1862, the Senate easily confirmed him. The Confederate rank of major general, according to the *Whig*, attracted attention to "the hero-statesman of Missouri."[16]

In June 1862, Price was with his division in Van Dorn's Army of the West, now at Tupelo, Mississippi. The Missourians had strongly resisted crossing the Mississippi River, and there was some fear of mutiny, but they went on Price's personal promise that they would be returned. Now the general wanted to make good on that promise. He was told by the army commander, Braxton Bragg, that he could return, but the troops had to remain. In the midst of the Peninsula Campaign, Old Pap therefore took it upon himself to take a leave of absence and, along with his aide, Colonel Snead, proceed to Richmond to make his case. His messiah-like entrance into the capital on June 19 was striking. Crowds cheered him, and the Virginia state legislature gave a reception and banquet. Unfortunately, there were accompanying political overtones. A group of anti-administration congressmen quietly floated a hair-brained idea of deposing Davis and placing Price, or even Tombs or the inept Pillow, as president or "generalissimo," commanding all the troops in the Confederacy. Both Missouri senators, Clark and William M. Cooke, were a part of the scheme, but there is no indication that Price was a participant. Congressman Boyce, who believed that Davis would be the death of the Confederacy, floated the absurd idea of having a convention of the states to make Price president. Some believed that Davis was jealous of the Missourian's popularity. The rumblings provided a further angst in his relationship with Price, whom he considered the "vainest man he had ever met."[17]

The meeting with the chief executive went about as well as could be expected under the circumstances. He was asked to submit his ideas in writing. The general proposed making the trans-Mississippi into a separate department, not merely a district answerable to a superior, while he would return with his Missourians to Arkansas. After several days, Price was again summoned. Davis, in the presence of Randolph and

Snead, regretted that the Missouri division had crossed the Mississippi, an order that had come from Sidney Johnston, not the administration. Perhaps so, but Davis knew about the transfer and did not stop it. As for the trans-Mississippi, it would be made into a separate department with Magruder as commander.

He then got down to the crux of the matter: he had decided not to let Price return with his Missouri troops. The general respectfully answered: "Well, Mr. President, if you will not let me serve *you*, I will nonetheless serve my *country*. You cannot prevent me from doing that. I will send in my resignation and go back to Missouri and raise another army there without your assistance, and fight again under the flag of Missouri, and win new victories for the South in spite of the Government." An incensed Davis showed controlled rage at the general's defiance. Slowly, but contemptuously, he replied: "Your resignation will be promptly accepted, General; and if you go back to Missouri, and win victories for the South, or do it any service at all, no one will be more *pleased* than myself, or"—he paused and then continued with emphasis—"more *surprised*." "Then I will surprise you, sir," Price replied, as he clinched his fist and slammed it on the desk, rattling a set of inkstands. Furiously he stormed out and returned to his hotel. Snead made an angry stump speech to an assembled crowd, then ripped the Confederate insignia from his uniform. Price also made remarks described as "turbulent."[18]

The next day cooler heads prevailed. Davis did not need more trouble in the trans-Mississippi. Already Rector was making veiled political threats of a separatist movement. Some 22 percent of the members of the House came from west of the Mississippi River, a power bloc that Davis did not wish to further agitate. Price's resignation was returned, and he was told that General Bragg would be instructed to transfer him and his Missourians back across the river as soon as it could be safely done. While Magruder would command the department, Price would serve as second-in-command, while Hindman would oversee the District of Arkansas, which included Missouri and Louisiana north of the Red River, and Major General P. O. Hébert would oversee the District of Texas (Texas and western Louisiana). Magruder would give priority to reclaiming Missouri. It would be enough to placate the pompous Price. When Price returned to Tupelo, Bragg appointed him to command the Army of the West (two divisions of 11,000 troops) to replace Van Dorn, who was now commanding the Vicksburg garrison.

Yet Price's transfer never came. Clark, in the Senate, expressed outrage. Price's troops "were promised that they would return to Missouri," he declared on the House floor. Now that the Conscript Act had been passed, these same troops were in the Confederate service and would be retained in Mississippi at a time when "they could undoubtedly do more good at home."[19]

Congressman Thomas A. Harris, representing Missouri-2, was also making waves. On June 10, the former army veteran and soldier of fortune–turned–lawyer called on the secretary of war with a list of familiar complaints. He believed that Missourians should retain the prerogative of remaining in the state army yet have equality with Confederate soldiers. Furthermore, all trans-Mississippi soldiers should be kept at home, and he fumed that Price's Missouri division (now east of the Mississippi) had not been returned. He constantly harped for Price's promotion and asked bluntly if the sacrifices of Missourians was acknowledged by Richmond.[20]

Senator Oldham meanwhile expressed outrage, beyond his merely philosophical objections, about the Conscript Act. He believed that the Texas frontier should be secured before its state troops were conscripted into the Confederate army. According to the *Dispatch*, the Lone Star State had a military population of 100,000, and by the spring of 1862 it had fielded forty-four regiments. Beyond that, Texas was a major food supplier. The grain crop that spring was the largest in the state's history. But it was beef that made Texas particularly vital. Lucius B. Northrop, heading the Commissary Department, had agents buying cattle—thousands of head. The steers were crossed at the mouth of the Red River in Louisiana and then ferried across the Mississippi River at Yazoo City, Mississippi. But Texas had a unique problem: Comanches. Fifteen years of fierce attacks meant that many Texans "won't go away from home, because they cannot—and leave their homes exposed to a ruthless enemy," argued Oldham. A motion to exempt a regiment of Texas Rangers for frontier duty failed after a lengthy debate, with Wigfall, Semmes, and Phelan all taking the floor. Discontent fermented in the trans-Mississippi delegation.[21]

Problems with Van Dorn also persisted. In mid-1862, Mississippi Senator James Phelan was with Bragg's army while at Tupelo. His private investigation raised grave concerns, which he promptly reported to his friend Davis. "Van Dorn is not only unpopular with his division [army], but [he] is the butt of their jeering and ridicule." He related a jingle that he heard the soldier's sing:

> Who lost the battle of Elkhorn [Pea Ridge] / Van Dorn–Van Dorn
> Who do we wish had never been born / Van Dorn–Van Dorn

The men desired Price at army command. "I do not hesitate to assert that there does not exist, in this army, one particle of enthusiasm towards any other General—unless it may be to a lesser degree—General Breckinridge."[22]

In early August, a shipment of Louisiana state-owned arms had almost made it across the Mississippi River when Van Dorn dispatched his cavalry and "forcibly seized" all the muskets and the battery. The troopers also stole the artillery saddles and broke open cases and helped themselves to the blankets. Sparrow and the entire Louisiana delegation erupted in anger—not only at what they saw as blatant theft but also because Van Dorn curtly responded to Governor Moore that he did not owe him any explanation. The general later thought better of it and released the battery and half the muskets. It was not enough; Sparrow remained incensed. "We have plenty of men but no arms," he barked, and some of the small arms were needed to keep the blacks in tow. In some parishes the ratio of blacks to whites was 10:1, and in two parishes it was 15–20:1. He was joined by Bob Johnson and Charles Mitchell, who were perpetually carping about the neglect of the trans-Mississippi. Gorgas fired back that the "reckless charges" of the Arkansas senators were unfounded. Some 5,000 arms earmarked for that sector had been confiscated as the shipment crossed the Mississippi River when the Federals captured the steamer *Fair Play*. An additional 2,000 muskets had successfully crossed, 1,000 were in route, and 6,400 more were then being repaired at both Macon and Chattanooga. It was also his intent to send one-fourth of the arms captured at Second Manassas. In short, everything that could be done was being done.[23]

8

Give Our Banners to the Breeze

Following the Battle of Shiloh, Confederate casualties were estimated at 7,000 killed and wounded and 361 missing. When Beauregard's after-action report subsequently appeared in the *Whig*, Richmonders were appalled to see that the number had soared to 10,699. The capital press nonetheless remained supportive, even adulating, of Beauregard, and there were those, including Sallie Putnam, who wrote admirably of him. But John Jones foretold another story: "I repeat, he is a doomed man."[1]

An April 9 Beauregard dispatch to Cooper had been intercepted and reprinted in the *New York Herald*. The Louisiana general estimated that his army at Corinth faced a combined Union strength of 85,000, while he could muster only 35,000. Van Dorn's small army from Arkansas was expected to juncture in a few days with an additional 15,000. He urgently requested reinforcements from the coast, even if it meant temporarily abandoning Charleston and Savannah. "If defeated here we lose the Mississippi Valley and probably our cause," he warned. The *Whig* dismissed the story as mere Yankee disinformation, but uncomfortable officials at the War Department knew that the document was genuine.[2]

Combined Union forces under Henry Halleck continued to press toward Corinth at a glacial pace. Time and again a major battle was anticipated, but the Federals appeared reluctant to engage. As late as April 23, the *Whig* admitted that it was "impossible to anticipate events at Corinth with anything like correctness. It is still believed that a great and decisive battle is pending at that place." Union artillerists began rolling siege guns into position, but on May 29 Cary Harriette "heard that Beauregard's army is doing well." Five days later, on June 3,

Ruffin updated his diary. Although he had heard nothing additional from Corinth, he nonetheless believed that "silence and delay there are good for our prospects."[3]

Much to Davis's chagrin, Beauregard was becoming the darling of the capital press. The *Dispatch* concluded that "he seems to bear a charmed life" and that "everything he undertakes seems to prosper"; the Creole was branded as "[t]he most successful General of the war." A Richmond civilian, weary of the retreating Joe Johnston, wrote his sister on May 26: "I wish we had olde Beauregard. I would have ten times more confidence than I have in the others—except Price and [Stonewall] Jackson."[4]

Despite press and public rising popular approval, in administration circles the general's stock remained decidedly low. According to Thomas Bragg: "He [Beauregard] has a great reputation with the public . . . but those who know him will doubt his capacity; the President, I think, does not esteem a high reputation of him." Davis, in fact, detested him. Senator Phelan, who was with the army at Tupelo, advised the president: "Beauregard is not popular and, so far as I can judge, he has entirely lost his early prestige." The word was also floating that Grant's army could have been destroyed on the first day at Shiloh but for Beauregard's cessation order. When the Louisiana general's after-action report arrived, Sidney Johnston's name was mentioned only four times, seemingly a dismissal of the slain general's role in the battle. The president was furious, and Preston Johnston, now living in the Confederate White House, could not swallow his anger. He denounced Beauregard as "that newspaper idol," adding "Beauregard is a vain creature and a little Frenchman. He is moreover a newspaper hero and a humbug."[5]

Beauregard's growing antagonism with the administration was widely known on the capital streets. A false rumor floated that both Beauregard and Bragg had "notified the authorities that they will obey no orders from Jeff Davis." The Creole, writing on May 19, notified the administration that ever since the Battle of Shiloh he had received no instructions relative to policy or strategy. He then explained in detail the obvious: the importance of Corinth as a rail junction. The town must be held—even at the risk of a defeat—*unless* the odds became overwhelming. Was he hinting at a possible withdrawal? It was left for War Department officials to interpret. Interestingly, the communiqué was sent by letter rather than dispatch, meaning that Cooper did not receive it for a week. It was Lee who would reply, and he quickly read between the lines. He approved of Beauregard's potential line of retreat along the Mobile & Ohio Railroad should it come to that, but he expressed disappointment that the town might have to be abandoned.[6]

Notification of the evacuation of Corinth, which occurred on the night of May 30, did not arrive in Richmond until June 3, and the press belatedly reported it on June 6. The army had quietly slipped away. "The enemy was firing at our banks of dirt, and killing rebels in their imagination, two days, it is believed after our army was far away," noted a correspondent. Precisely where the army had gone was unknown, at least to the public. Rumors in the Northern press claimed that Beauregard had taken his army to Virginia to join Joe Johnston. One account claimed that the army had fallen back only ten miles in a planned counterattack. Others reported that the troops had withdrawn twenty to thirty miles to Booneville and Baldwyn, while still others claimed fifty miles south to Tupelo. What remained undisputed was the praise heaped upon Beauregard: the *Enquirer*: "admirably executed," the *Dispatch*: "in every respect successful," and the *Whig*: "executed with great skill." Precisely why the army had withdrawn from such a vital position was unknown, but the press offered cover for the general: the retreat was "unquestionably for a good reason." Independent of editorials, Ruffin recognized that the withdrawal would involve the loss of Memphis.[7]

Privately, Phelan kept Davis apprised. "You can scarcely magnify the deplorable condition of the army at Corinth—both morally and physically—at a time of the retreat from that place," he confided. "Deaths numerous, desertions by no means, rare; whilst a general spirit of despondency seemed to pervade the entire march."[8]

To be sure, Beauregard faced an army twice the size of his own, and his options were unappealing. Davis, who simmered because he knew little beyond what he read in the papers, was not in a mood to be sympathetic. He vented his frustration to Varina, then in North Carolina, writing that "there are those who can only walk a log when it is near to the ground, and I fear he [Beauregard] has been placed too high for his mental strength, as he does not exhibit the ability manifested on smaller fields." Cabinet members also expressed their disdain. Mallory contemptuously wrote that the general "retreated without notice to the Prest. or War Dept. & up to this time no reason for his retreat is known." Unwilling to wait any longer, Cooper fired off a curt dispatch on June 12, reminding the general that the explanation for his withdrawal had not yet arrived. Beauregard responded the next day that he was busy and that he would get to it in time.[9]

Finding Beauregard's subsequent report unacceptable, Davis dispatched Preston Johnston to Tupelo, where the army eventually settled, armed with a list of pointed questions. Hardly unbiased, the colonel's loathing was further enflamed by "Uncle Will," Colonel William Preston, his mother's brother, who wrote him letters from Tupelo that were in turn shared with the president. "We miss your father. The double bees [Beauregard and Bragg] do not rise to the exigency," the colonel informed his nephew. Beauregard received the envoy cooly, inquiring directly "to what end his mission to him tended." If the president was not satisfied with his decision, he hostilely contended, then he would request a court of inquiry. In the end, Johnston's final report was mostly innocuous and even supported the general's reasons for retreating. It mattered not. Davis was already working on a scheme to transfer the general to Charleston, under the pretense of accommodating his health.[10]

Davis, on June 14, notified Bragg to report to Jackson, Mississippi, to replace Lovell in command of Department No. 1. A quick reply came from Beauregard, saying that the general could not be spared; Bragg would be temporarily commanding the army in his absence. Beauregard had decided to take a sick leave for an indefinite time, adding, "I must have a short rest." It was the first time that the administration had heard of his intentions. Unquestionably the general was frail, but for Davis, who at times suffered daily from his own health issues, the thought of the general leaving his post was tantamount to desertion.[11]

Gorgas had an appointment with the president on June 18, at which time Davis openly expressed his discontentment with Beauregard's movements. The next night, as Davis wrote Varina, he could not resist his sardonic side. "Beauregard left his command to seek rest[] and restore his health. The sedentary life at Corinth must have been hard to bear[,] as he reports himself exhausted and his army undergoing reorganization." On June 21, he again wrote that a desperate attempt must be made to win back what Beauregard had abandoned. The subject of the withdrawal came up in a "most interesting" cabinet meeting that same day. Mallary believed that Beauregard was simply collapsing under the weight of command and that, finding Bragg about to leave him, he "ran away from an army he could not manage." Davis ordered Beauregard's immediate removal for deserting his post and placed Bragg in command. "Beauregard has never voluntarily fought a battle—and never will," concluded Mallory. "Bragg is left in command and he may do better."[12]

It took a week for the story to break in the press, but whisperings soon became grist for the gossip mill. Jones heard (incorrectly) that Beauregard and a cadre of officers were planning to escape to France with some commandeered gold bullion but were thwarted by an alert officer. For public consumption, the administration announced that the general was removed from command due to health concerns. Jones continued: "There are charges against Beauregard. It is said that the Yankee army might have been annihilated at Shiloh, if Beauregard had fought a little longer." Reaction in the capital dailies was surprisingly muted, and only brief mention was made of the change. According to the *Dispatch*, the general was "positively in Richmond" to become second-in-command to Lee and had brought reinforcements from the West. Other articles, some Northern, speculated that the Army of the Mississippi had been dispersed to Charleston, Richmond, and Mobile. The June 28 *Dispatch* related the current street talk. Beauregard had been relieved of command, adding that "it has been known for some time that Beauregard and Jeff Davis are on antagonistic terms." In the House, Texas Congressman Frank Sexton made a motion that the secretary of war, later amended to the president, be requested to provide all Beauregard's documents related to the Corinth evacuation; the motion passed.[13]

Throughout 1861, Braxton Bragg had received good press. His record in the Mexican–American War had been highlighted, and the general's strict discipline policy had been applauded. He reportedly had a good sense of humor, which surely would have caused a groan from those who actually knew him. His conduct at Shiloh was even heralded in a poem that appeared in the *Enquirer*:

> "From height to height, from left to right, as cool as a glacial snow;
> He hurled that wide, fierce lava tide unbroken on the foe."

Politicians also embraced the new army commander. Congressman Pugh, one of Bragg's former soldiers, heard comments of high praise in his abilities being talked in the capital. Congressman Jabez L. Curry, representing Alabama-4, had visited the army in May, and he commended the general on the high state of discipline.[14]

Slowly, however, opposition began to build in the capital. William Preston, knowing well that his nephew had the ear of the president, warned of Bragg's excessive discipline, noting that "the men are indignant, and I fear trouble." Gorgas, based upon precisely what will never be known, came to his own conclusion: "Between Bragg & Buell there is little to [choose] on the score of morality. Both are like the common run of humanity." By mid-June, Curry had also turned on Bragg. With Congress in recess, he returned home and visited the army at Tupelo. He characterized the retreat from Corinth as more of a rout than a withdrawal. A force of 20,000 Federals could have captured the army, or at least put it to flight. Nearly 60 percent of the army was sick. All of that occurred on Beauregard's watch, but he soon got around to Bragg. "There is great dissatisfaction in the army," and the Tennessee troops were "well-nigh mutinous," because the general had stopped the practice of letting the men vote for their officers and was not allowing them to reorganize their companies "in spite of law and justice." Then there was the issue of the 17th Alabama, in which Curry's half-brother and brother-in-law served. Three strangers had arbitrarily been appointed as field officers, two of them being brothers-in-law to Navy Secretary Mallory. He concluded that "Price and Stonewall Jackson are universal favorites [for army command] because they fight and push forward."[15]

Cooper forwarded a copy of the letter to Bragg, adding that "charges of this sort have become so frequent[] as to greatly concern the President[] and the Department." The general answered that the congressman was angry because he had been refused a staff position. "I have no use for fawning sycophants on my staff or in my command," he informed Davis. In terms of appointing Mallory's two brothers-in-law, he said that he had no idea of the relationship when the appointments were made. Colonel Thomas H. Watts, commanding the regiment, had been called to Richmond as attorney general, the lieutenant colonel had resigned after Shiloh, the major deserted, and the two senior captains were on the disability list.[16]

Another incident that came to light was the case of Lieutenant Colonel Robert P. Blount of the 5th Alabama Battalion. His unit had seen limited action at Shiloh, and after the battle Bragg dispersed the companies to other Alabama regiments. Beauregard subsequently assigned

Blount as provost at Columbus, Mississippi. "Lieut. Col. B. has quietly submitted to the high-handed treatment of Gen. Bragg, simply for the good of our common cause," an anonymous author submitted to the *Whig*. The incident, in an of itself not serious, marked the beginning of a shift in press treatment. On July 31, Bragg forwarded to the president a Montgomery news clipping titled "The Army at Tupelo" that contained "false and malicious" remarks. Upon investigation, Davis became convinced that the source of the article was Yancey and that the intent was an attack upon the administration. Davis responded to the general that he had "the misfortune of being regarded as my personal friend."[17]

Even before Bragg ascended to command, an unfortunate incident occurred that had potentially serious ramifications. Phelan had warned Davis back in June that there were allegations that Bragg had several soldiers shot without benefit of trial for trifling offenses—"I do not doubt the charge." During the retreat from Corinth, the general issued strict orders not to discharge weapons needlessly. Despite numerous warnings the practice continued. On one occasion an Arkansas soldier shot at a chicken in a farmyard and accidentally killed a young black boy. Bragg, wishing to make an example, ordered the soldier's execution without benefit of a military trial. The order was ultimately revoked, but not before an anonymous report appeared in the *Mobile Advertiser & Register* under the pen name "Justice," later reprinted in the *Whig*. An accusation was made that Bragg had ordered five executions without due process. The case was taken up in Congress.[18]

In the Senate, James L. Orr of South Carolina offered a resolution proposing that the matter of the reported executions be investigated by the Military Affairs Committee; the motion passed. Four days later, on September 12, the committee reported that only one case was in question—that of the Arkansas soldier. Although it was not mentioned that the order of execution was ultimately stayed, enough exculpatory information was forthcoming that Senator Sparrow moved that the incident no longer be investigated; the motion passed. Orr was not satisfied. He moved that a select committee of three be appointed to continue investigating, with authority to question witnesses and examine documents. He had "implicit confidence" in his source, and he labeled Bragg a "tyrant." A rancorous two-day debate ensued. Burnette believed that the officers in the army would hardly sit quietly if indeed Bragg was a

Though not a westerner, James L. Orr became a staunch anti-Bragg opponent. (Library of Congress)

"tyrant and a murderer." Indeed, he wondered why the "the gentleman's informants" did not bring charges against the general. The matter should be left to military investigation, he argued, not the Senate. Orr quickly responded that he would never trust a military tribunal. His informants, whom he implied were officers, were "in the army of this tyrant and in his power." The sixteen guns of the execution squad would have made more noise that the single shot that killed the black child.

Clay likewise opposed the notion; indeed, he was very sorry that the issue had come to this. If such an unproven accusation got back to the troops, it "might incite insubordination and mutiny." Phelan of Mississippi angrily vented: "The name assassin and General Bragg should never be linked together and driven into the public ear." He also had done some personal investigating, and he was convinced that the army commander would be vindicated. Yancey, although sympathetic to Orr, believed that a Senate committee was not the appropriate course. Clark of Missouri, always the contrarian, admitted that he knew nothing of the matter, but he favored the motion, believing that the facts should come to light. Robert M. T. Hunter (Virginia) questioned whether the Senate even had the right to remove a general officer. Wigfall believed that the matter should be referred to the military. He asserted that even a lieutenant had the right to shoot a soldier who was deserting and creating disorder. The appropriate course was for the president to initiate a court of inquiry. If the pertinent facts turned out to be true, and the president failed to act, the House should take up impeachment proceedings. The Senate then went into executive session, where roving reporters were not allowed. When the senators shortly emerged, the incident had been dropped. The attempt to disparage Bragg, although unsuccessful, had nonetheless caused damage. The core of the opposition, thought Thomas Bragg, comprised Clark, Yancey, and Orr—"all 'soreheads.'" The narrative, at least at this point, was controlled by Phelan, Clay, Wigfall, and Burnette. Phelan, the general's strongest advocate, advised Bragg not to worry about Orr's verbal assaults—"Time will set all that even."[19]

Later that day, September 12, Senators Semmes and Sparrow of Louisiana called upon the president. They presented him a petition requesting that Beauregard be restored to army command rather than transferred to Charleston. It had been signed by fifty-one western senators and representatives and five South Carolinians. All of the Louisiana and Missouri delegates signed, and almost all those from Tennessee, Kentucky, Arkansas, and Alabama. Noticeably *not* signing was the entire Mississippi delegation and all but one of the Georgia delegation. The balance of the eastern delegates opted out. The petition claimed that the request had been undertaken without the knowledge or consent of the Louisiana general. It was a lie. Beauregard had in fact been in open communication with his brother-in-law, Louisiana Congressman Charles Villere, in a naïve attempt to get his old job back. He had even written to Cooper, stating his strategy plan once he returned. Additionally, the general encouraged Villere to stir up the western congressional delegates.[20]

Jones and Kean were not the only ones hearing rumors. Withers, in

Cooper's office, had heard that Leonidis Polk was in Richmond on September 13. He was wrong; the bishop was engaged in active military campaigning in Kentucky at the time. "It is believed now," Withers nonetheless wrote, "that Genl. Joe Johnston is to go to Tennessee to take command of Bragg's army." Johnston had not yet recovered from his Seven Pines wound, but that had not stopped his name from being batted about—not for the Army of Northern Virginia but the West.[21]

Davis closely read the document in front of Semmes and Sparrow, making verbal comments and corrections to the assertions as he read. He concluded by articulating the name of each of the signatories—all fifty-six. He believed that they clearly did not have all the facts, and he proceeded to give the background of how Bragg assumed command. Beauregard, sick though he was, should have remained in Tupelo, "even if he had to be carried out on a litter." Restoring the general to command was simply out of the question. Bragg was now in the initial stage of a complicated campaign, and he would not remove him "if the whole world united in the petition." The meeting was over.[22]

Meanwhile, in the House, Texas Congressman Frank Sexton continued to privately express his frustration at Foote's continued antics. "Foote spoke until the House adjourned. He tries everybody. He wants now to fetter the Military Committee with some foolish instructions." Again, on August 21, the Tennessee congressman "availed himself of the occasion to abuse Gen. Huger most violently & improperly on account of the circumstances, the places & manner of its being done." The following day he "consumed nearly the whole day in useless discussion of the Conscript Act," although his arguments were elegantly challenged by E. S. Dargan of Alabama. In a closed session at the end of the month, he continued his abusive talk "most dreadfully" against Mallory.[23]

Preston Johnston was coming to the conclusion that the core of the administration's woes lay in a cadre of malcontented congressmen from Missouri, Kentucky, and Tennessee. Although not naming specifics, it was clear that Clark from Missouri, Foote from Tennessee, and James Moore, George Ewing, and James Thomas from Kentucky were all on his list. The chief instigator, he believed, was Foote, whom he labeled as "a nuisance and an obstructionist to public business." He did not put it beyond a clique of "factionalists" to attempt an assassination against Davis or a political coup.[24]

The first that Richmond citizens heard of trouble brewing in East

Tennessee was in the *Whig* of June 23. The next day an ominous headline appeared: "Critical State of Affairs in East Tennessee." An enemy column, estimated to be 16,000 strong, had entered Powell's Valley, southeast of Cumberland Gap, in an apparent attempt to take the position in reverse. Many of the bluecoats, or so it was reported, were mountain volunteers eager to extract revenge against their Southern-leaning neighbors. War Department insiders had actually been monitoring the situation for a week and a half. Army intelligence estimated the column at 10,000 infantry and twelve guns. Major General Edmund Kirby Smith, well-known in the capital for leading a brigade (not his own) forward at an opportune moment at the Battle of Manassas, now commanded the department. Smith marched from Knoxville with 5,000 reinforcements, but he needed help—and quickly. Then came the troubling question: If he was forced to abandon the entire department, should he withdraw toward Georgia or Virginia? Cooper answered Georgia, but officials were alarmed. In a June 14 dispatch to the adjutant general, Smith wrote that, unless reinforcements arrived soon, he had no choice but to withdraw his 10,000–12,000 effectives to Chattanooga, which was then being threatened from the west by the Federal division at Huntsville, Alabama. Additionally, Don Carlos Buell's 25,000-man army, marching eastward from Corinth, was already at Tuscumbia, Alabama, and crossing the Tennessee River. Davis assured a rattled Congressman Swan that everything that could be done was being done.[25]

Smith, laid up at his headquarters with typhoid fever, bombarded Richmond with dire appeals for reinforcements. A dual threat was simply beyond his capacity; he was stretched even to handle the Cumberland Gap encroachment. He either had to relinquish Knoxville or Chattanooga, both of which were vital. Clearly no troops could come from Virginia, and officials in Charleston and Savannah were already screaming that they were being abandoned. Cooper pleaded with Bragg for help, but the general insisted that the reinforcements should come from North Georgia. War Department officials, scrambling for troops, rushed two recently organized Georgia regiments, an unarmed Alabama regiment (Randolph promised to expedite the needed arms), and a cavalry regiment to Chattanooga. By late June, Bragg, under continued War Department pressure, boarded McCown's understrength 3,000-man division on the boxcars. By that time, the spearhead of the Union advance had arrived at Battle Creek, a day-and-a-half march from Chattanooga.[26]

What ultimately impeded the Union advance was not the panicked response of administration officials but the twin lightning bolts of John Hunt Morgan and Nathan Bedford Forrest. Morgan rode almost completely untouched through Kentucky, taking 1,000 prisoners, destroying bridges, and generally disrupting rail traffic along the Louisville & Nashville Railroad. Forrest meanwhile captured Murfreesboro along with 1,200 prisoners. "Our army is doing well in the West," Judith McGuire jubilantly wrote in late July. Newspaper articles on the cavalier's exploits appeared daily in Richmond for a week. The raids, coupled with the arrival of reinforcements, checked the Federal advance.[27]

Richmond was aware that the Federals at Corinth had divided their forces, with Buell now bearing down on Chattanooga. This left Grant at Corinth and vicinity with a reported 15,000, with a like number in West Tennessee at Memphis, Boliver, and Jackson. Bragg had several options. He could attack Grant at Corinth, which he preferred to do. For once, by his own intelligence reports, he held the numerical superiority, and the Union forces were widely scattered. He could also shift his entire army eastward, midway between Grant and Buell, and then northward, but he could get crushed between them. He could move farther east to Chattanooga, thereby leaving Mississippi vulnerable, or he could, as did the Yankees, split his force; he chose the latter. Price's 16,000-man Army of the West would temporarily remain at Tupelo, as would Van Dorn's Division at Vicksburg. The balance of Bragg's 35,000-man army boarded the cars for a circuitous, 776-mile trek to Chattanooga via Mobile and Atlanta. After detaching several regiments to bolster the Mobile garrison, his army had been whittled down to 30,000. He hoped to juncture with Kirby Smith and strike at the rear of the Federal army in Middle Tennessee. This was essentially the information in possession of the War Department on July 23.[28]

Even before plans had been formalized, War Department gossip told of a major movement in the offing. A *Dispatch* article of June 14 mentioned that offensive preparations were underway in the Army of the Mississippi and that Bragg had told the troops that he should soon "give our banners to the breeze." A news blackout suddenly followed, and Bragg's army seemingly disappeared. Federal news reports predicted that either Memphis or Nashville would be threatened. A reprinted *New York Herald* article claimed that Bragg was at Vicksburg on July 30, while two days later the *Chicago Tribune* placed him at Tupelo with 60,000–70,000 troops. A *Mobile Advertiser & Register* article claimed that he threatened Memphis with an army of 80,000. While the general population in Richmond was kept in the dark, Grant knew precisely Bragg's location.[29]

The next reported sighting of Bragg came during the first week of August as he passed through LaGrange, Georgia. The *Whig* of August 23 bannered: "Our Cause Brightening in the West." Bragg was quoted as declaring that "things is workin" and that matters were more favorable "than could have been expected." Beyond the enticing hints, no specifics were forthcoming. After huge territorial losses in the West, capital citizens began to take heart.[30]

Although the papers (at least those in Richmond) were mum on Bragg's whereabouts, the War Department learned of his arrival in Chattanooga on July 31. The troops were still trailing in, and with resupply and a hurried reorganization (Polk and Hardee would each command a "wing,") it would be at least two weeks before an offensive could be undertaken. George Morgan's Union division remained at Cumberland Gap and Buell's army at Bridgeport, Alabama, and at Battle Creek.[31]

There were those who knew more than they were telling out. By August 18, the Kentucky congressional delegation had gotten wind of the plans to march into their home state by two columns, one under Smith in East Tennessee and the other under Bragg. A letter was drafted to the president, signed by both senators and eight of twelve representatives, addressing certain political realities. The current state government was obviously hostile. Votes in a recent election had reportedly been suppressed, and opposition candidates were threatened with imprisonment. It was of the highest importance that all of the Kentucky officers be immediately detached to unite with the two columns. A month earlier Burnette had wildly assured Davis that 40,000 Kentuckians would flock to the banner; the actual number would end up being under 3,000. Bragg was about to discover what Sidney Johnston had learned ten months earlier: Kentucky was a myth. Tennessee politicians also had their hands out. On the eve of Bragg's offensive, Governor Harris requested the return of three Tennessee regiments in the Army of Northern Virginia, a request that the War Department politely, yet promptly, denied.[32]

Despite the silence of the press, there were too many well-connected clerks, aides, and politicians who learned that Bragg had taken his army to Chattanooga. Withers, by September 8, had heard that the Federals were withdrawing from North Alabama and that "Bragg is after them."

By September 22, the *Whig* announced that Huntsville was again in Confederate possession. Large preparations were also underway for Bragg. Gorgas was requested for large shipments of small arms ammunition and 4,000 muskets to replace damaged ones. The delays, though necessary, proved bothersome. "Why does Bragg not attack? Will he never attack[?]" Preston Johnston wrote on August 15. As late as September 26, Ruffin wondered: "What can Gen. Bragg be waiting for?"[33]

The war in Virginia had always dominated the Richmond press. Thus, as Bragg and Smith commenced their operations in Kentucky, it was Lee's brilliant victory at Second Manassas on August 29–30 that swept the news cycle. With McClellan's still massive and lethal Army of the Potomac at Harrison's Landing under the protection of the Federal navy, Lee audaciously left a small garrison at Richmond and moved against another newly formed Federal army under General John Pope on the plains of Manassas. The result was a stunning Southern victory. While Pope's army limped back to the suburbs of Washington—to a large degree because McClellan had dallied in reinforcing him—Lee now sent Davis a shocking proposal. On the heels of the massive casualties sustained in both the Peninsula Campaign and at Second Manassas, he desired to march into Maryland. Capital citizens awoke on Tuesday morning, September 9, to read in the *Dispatch* that Confederate forces "now tread the soil of Maryland!"[34]

On the same day as the victory at Second Manassas, Smith scored a decisive win in a town in eastern Kentucky, about seventy miles from Cumberland Gap, with an unlikely name: Richmond. An 8,000-man Federal division had been routed with the loss of 3,000 prisoners. To Jones it was not a coincidence. "This is not chance—it is God[] to whom all glory is due." During the Peninsula Campaign, Jones had ignored the war in the West, but he now became mesmerized with the turn of events. "And Cincinnati is trembling to its center, the abolition city, half foreign and half American is listening for the Thunder of our avenging guns," he wrote on September 11. Three days later he observed: "Our army has entered the city of Lexington [Kentucky], and the population hail our brave soldiers as deliverers."[35]

Wildly exaggerated reports arrived in Richmond claiming the capture of Louisville and Cincinnati and the evacuation of Nashville. "I hope so," wrote Jones, adding: "I think we shall get Nashville soon."

Smith claimed that he could recruit 20,000 Kentuckians if he only had the arms. The elation spread to Congress. In the Senate, Haynes of Tennessee proposed building fortifications along the Cumberland and Tennessee Rivers, and a similar proposal in the House came from Foote and Thomas Jefferson Foster of Alabama-1, which unrealistically included the construction of a dozen gunboats to patrol the rivers. The jubilation continued on September 23, when it was reported that Bragg had captured the 4,000-man garrison at Munfordville, Kentucky.[36]

"War is the realm of uncertainty," the military theorist Carl von Clausewitz once wrote. It was such uncertainty that now came into play. Stonewall Jackson's great victory at Harpers Ferry, with the capture of 12,000 prisoners, ninety guns, and 15,000 arms—or so it was reported—was well known. Around this time, garbled reports trickled in of a great battle at Sharpsburg, Maryland, along Antietam Creek, in which Lee had been driven back. On September 21, Jones lamented: "We have one bad day of gloom. It is said that our army has retreated back into Virginia." Four days later, the *Dispatch* dismissed as "Yankee lies" the talk of a Confederate defeat. News that Lee was indeed falling back nonetheless continued to arrive, and there were accounts of a "great slaughter" at Sharpsburg. As late as September 30, the *Dispatch* proclaimed: "The victory, though not as decisive as that of Manassas, was certainly a Confederate victory." By that time, however, Davis knew otherwise. As Lee's veterans trudged back into Virginia, nearly 11,000 sick and wounded flooded the hospitals of Richmond. Everywhere there was suffering.[37]

Though the news in the East appeared uncertain, the turn of events in the West appeared bright. A Southern account and captured Northern letters "give very favorable accounts in Ten. & Ky. . . . Our forces occupy (or have no organized foe in) all of the territory of Ky. except the S. W. corner between the Tennessee & Ohio rivers—and all the towns except Louisville, & a few others in Ohio," Ruffin intoned. He expected to hear news of the capture of Louisville any day. As for Lincoln's recently issued Emancipation, "I think this proclamation will serve our cause good."[38]

The newspapers began posting dispatches on the bulletin board outside their doors on Tuesday, October 14. The gist was that a two-day battle had been fought at Perryville, Kentucky, on October 8 and 9, resulting in the capture of 25,000 bluecoats! The Richmond dailies ran detailed articles the next day from the *Knoxville Register* and the latest Northern news. The Battle of Perryville on October 8 resulted in 1,500 Federal casualties and 5,500 captured. The next day, twelve miles distant, there had been another fierce engagement, with the capture of another 4,000 Yankees and forty guns. One Southern dispatch placed Bragg's casualties at 5,000 and claimed "a complete victory." The *Central Presbyterian*, a Richmond weekly newspaper with mostly denominational news, indicated that the Confederate attack on October 8 had fallen on two divisions of Alexander McCook's corps. A reprinted article from the *New York Herald* admitted a defeat, placing Union casualties at 1,500–2,000, including two generals killed. Bragg's report, wrote Ruffin, was "most anxiously looked for."[39]

Yet in the ensuing days the buzz on the street and in the War Department seemed less than reassuring. Northern accounts, wrote Ruffin, "which (if credited) . . . declare a defeat of our army." Preston Johnston, hearing of the news of Perryville, wrote his wife on October 11: "We have had a bad day." Kean noted on October 19: "Bragg is retreating in Kentucky. No official news of the Battle of Perryville yet." Jones did not know what to believe. Though the unofficial news hailed a great victory, he admitted that "[w]estern accounts are generally exaggerated." Gorgas also expressed skepticism. The reports of a victory he dismissed as "doubtful," observing that "no one is satisfied with its [newspaper accounts] authenticity."[40]

The *Dispatch* nonetheless remained buoyant: "If Gen. Bragg has been as signally victorious as we hope and believe he has, it will have been, probably, the most important event of the war. It will throw the whole State of Kentucky into the arms of the Confederacy, and will free Tennessee, and eventually Mississippi. It will give new life and vigor to our cause everywhere." Even though the number of prisoners had been reduced from 25,000 to 10,000, Jones took heart: "We shall have our positive news."[41]

Meddlesome politicians now stepped forward. Following his defeat at Baton Rouge, John Breckinridge's Division, increased to 5,000 by exchanged prisoners, had arrived in Knoxville to reinforce Bragg. On October 1, a majority of the constantly agitated Tennessee delegation, including Senators Henry and Haynes and seven representatives, Foote among them, as well as Willis Machen and Bruce of Kentucky and Thomas Hanley of Alabama, requested that Breckinridge's Division be redirected to Murfreesboro in preparation for a move on Nashville. The way that Jones heard the story, the delegation verbally requested that the transfer be made with or without Bragg's approval. The president considered the request most extraordinary—as indeed it was—and promptly denied it. In time, however, the division, which never made it to Kentucky, was redirected to Middle Tennessee.[42]

The *Whig* of October 20 told the all-too bitter truth: Bragg was not advancing to Louisville; he was instead abandoning the state and retreating toward Cumberland Gap. Relating to the numerous dispatches of the previous two days, all declaring victory, the paper could only state: "We can scarcely conceive how such reports get into circulation." The truth, the paper continued, would be received with profound disappointment. More had been expected of Bragg than simply making pronouncements to "the people beyond the Ohio." The editor had long withheld his criticism despite Bragg's "long delay at Tupelo, his hesitancy at Chattanooga, [and] his tardy advance into Kentucky" that had shaken public confidence. The campaign in Kentucky, the editor declared, "turned out simply to be a fizzle." After Smith's victory at Richmond and reported victory at Frankfort, after Bragg declared victory at Perryville, and after Morgan's exploits, the campaign in the end had resulted in "just nothing at all." The *Enquirer* also added its voice, declaring the campaign a failure. The exploits of Smith and Morgan, though laudable, served no other purpose than to warn Buell that he was in trouble. The circumstances required more than a drill instructor and disciplinarian, and "public sentiment is now in favor of placing some general of larger brain and more active talents in command."[43]

Bragg's after-action report was printed in the *Dispatch* of October 22. He claimed 2,500 casualties at Perryville compared to 4,000 Union killed and wounded and 400 captured. The disappointment was not merely in the deflated Yankee casualties. Bragg had failed in Southern expectations, and his explanation proved insufficient to quell public sentiment. "Thus Kentucky is given up for the moment," Jones disgustedly wrote. Writing from his office on the fourth floor of the War Department, Colonel Jeremy Gilmer, heading the Engineer Bureau, divulged to his wife that the campaign in Kentucky "[i]s pronounced here a magnificent failure—big show and no result." Even though he had mostly dismissed "our lying telegraphic reports," Ruffin still expressed disappointment. He believed Bragg to be a good disciplinarian, but "he is too cautious, & too slow to command in chief [an] invasion—& his slow movements have lost nearly all that he was so near in gaining."[44]

Kentuckians used Preston Johnston as their sounding board. Brigadier General Preston related: "All in Kentucky was loose, incoherent[,] and pointless." Congressman George B. Hodge also wrote the president's aide that Kentuckians had been outraged by Bragg's accusation of their state's lethargy. William B. Manchen, representing Kentucky-1, joined the anti-Bragg maligners. In like tone, Preston Johnston told his wife: "I think Bragg in Kentucky is a signal failure." Senator Henry, writing from Knoxville, advised the president that the army was highly dissatisfied with Bragg—"not his rigid discipline, but on account of his retreat."[45]

The press—the "dogs of detraction" Bragg called them—continued their assaults. The *Dispatch* concluded that Bragg simply lacked the qualities of a great commander. John Daniel at the *Examiner* was brutal in his assessment: "As commander-in-chief[,] he is worse than inexperienced, for he has grown old and hardened." He concluded that the general had "an iron heart, and [an] iron hand, and a wooden head." Bagby also attacked the general, coming close to impugning his courage and prewar reputation, although he subsequently backed off his insinuation. Governor-in-exile Hawes had a letter printed in the *Enquirer* defending (unconvincingly) Kentucky's lack of response, and he then excoriated Bragg's tactical decisions. Even the Richmond correspondent of the *London Times* characterized the campaign as an "unquestionable fiasco."[46]

Congressional indignation continued to fester, with the Tennessee and Kentucky delegations leading the van. Henry of Tennessee informed Wigfall that he had never heard so much dissatisfaction coming from Bragg's army. Senators who had expressed support back in September, such as Burnette of Kentucky, now faltered. Five Tennessee congressmen signed a letter to immediately replace the general, while Dargan proposed the names of Joe Johnston or James Longstreet. Nonetheless, Phelan, widely known for his "frigid demeaner," Pugh, and Francis S. Lyon, representing Alabama-5, remained loyal apologists.[47]

With the Army of the Mississippi safely back in Knoxville, Bragg on October 24 was summoned to the capital. The street talk was that he would be superseded, probably by Joe Johnston, but some speculated Beauregard. Jones discounted the last, suspecting that "Beauregard is too popular, I fear, to meet with favor here." For the next week Bragg met with the president in lengthy closed-door sessions. On October 27,

Congressman George B. Hodge, like most of the Kentucky congressional delegation, expressed outrage at Bragg's characterization of their state's lethargy for the Southern cause. (Library of Congress)

the general was able to break away long enough to meet with his brother Thomas, who found him "well & in good spirits." Braxton seemed confident that his explanation of events had been entirely acceptable to Davis. The next day, word began to spread that the general would be retained. Jones discounted Bragg's supposed forty-mile supply train as a "Western *tale*, I fear." In Bagby's column of November 1, the journalist reported: "The president has been invisible since last Saturday

[October 25]. Up to yesterday [October 31] he was closed all the time with Bragg, who returns to his command with the supporting smiles of the Executive."[48]

Bragg may have kept his job, but it was more out of default than confidence. Davis openly conceded that the "results in Ky. have been to me a bitter disappointment." He likewise conceded that another general might "excite more enthusiasm." The question came down to a viable candidate. Joe Johnston was still recovering from his Seven Pines wound, Lee was needed in Virginia, and Beauregard was simply unacceptable to Davis. Besides, the retreat from Kentucky had not been as bad as Beauregard's from Corinth, Bragg was a good administrator who knew the army, and any replacement would have his own shortcomings. Davis did mull the thought that Bragg could be of "good use *here* in Richmond," perhaps as general in chief.[49]

Davis now summoned Kirby Smith, Polk, and Hardee to the capital, although the latter begged off. Randolph was noticeably kept out of the meetings. All three (Hardee in a letter to Preston Johnston) sabotaged their superior, and Smith and Polk openly requested that Johnston supersede Bragg. In their after-action reports, both Polk and Hardee blamed Bragg for being completely fooled by Buell's maneuverings and that at Perryville they had been unable to convince Bragg that Buell's entire army was on the field. An early snow covered the streets of Richmond and temperatures hovered around 38 degrees during the second week in November. Bagby observed that Smith was in town, and he wondered if "something is in the wind." A week later he noticed that Polk was in the capital—"for what purpose we can only conjecture. He [Polk] says, I understand that Kentucky and Missouri could have been reclaimed." Several officers from the Army of the Mississippi were also in the capital, and they all spoke of the army commander "without mercy." The president appealed to the patriotism of all three generals to support his decision to retain Bragg and to do their share to bring harmony. If his pleading was insufficient, he made all of them lieutenant generals. It was nothing more than a pathetic bribe. There were uncorroborated reports of Polk talking with congressmen before he departed. Smith thereafter kept quiet, but Polk and Hardee embarked upon a backstabbing campaign. "Unfortunately for Bragg, he has given his enemies just grounds for attacking him," Hardee wrote Preston Johnston. Davis should have directly addressed the issue, but he naively clung to his belief that his generals could put aside personal animosities for the sake of the cause.[50]

Whether or not Southern political and military expectations of capturing Louisville and Cincinnati and crossing to the north bank of the Ohio River had been a realistic goal or a pipe dream was not the issue. Reports were contradictory, and no one had a crystal ball. Two things were known. Following the failed invasions of Maryland and Kentucky, hopes for a quick end of the war faded, and Bragg—unlike Lee—had developed serious opposition in Richmond.

When Buell's army withdrew from North Alabama and Middle Tennessee into Kentucky, two depleted Federal armies remained in the rear: Grant's Army of the Tennessee in West Tennessee, and William S. Rosecrans's (Pope's old) Army of the Mississippi at Corinth and vicinity, totaling according to Confederate best estimates 42,500. Confronting these forces was Price's Army of the West, minus McCown's Division, which had reinforced Smith. Buttressed with some newly recruited Mississippi and Alabama regiments (men who hurriedly volunteered to avoid the onus of being drafted), Price had two divisions of 13,800 infantry and artillery and 3,000 cavalry. Bragg had left Price with instructions to keep Rosecrans's estimated 23,000 troops from joining Buell in Kentucky. There was little that Price could do beyond keeping the Federals pinned down with harassing sorties. As for Davis and the War Department, they were essentially kept out of the loop, and no one, absorbed as they were with events at Antietam, was asking questions. Bragg had notified Richmond that Van Dorn's force (at Vicksburg and Port Hudson, Louisiana) and Price each had 16,000, although Van Dorn's returns showed him with barely 10,000, 2,400 of whom were at Port Hudson.[51]

Van Dorn had essentially been reduced to a district command. Beyond the Vicksburg garrison, largely from the former New Orleans garrison, he was desperately attempting to piece together a field division using John S. Bowen's brigade of Shiloh veterans, which Bragg had left behind, a scattering of newly organized Mississippi regiments, former Island No. 10 and Fort Donelson prisoner exchangees, and 725 conscripts—in all slightly over 8,000 troops. Price, under extreme pressure from Bragg, felt that he could not wait for Van Dorn's troops to get organized and equipped. Rosecrans's army had moved toward Nashville (or so it was believed), and Price had to do the same.[52]

Following Price's Richmond brouhaha with Davis, he was content to keep a low profile. Nonetheless, Van Dorn was sending dispatches—lots of them. By mid-September it had become apparent that he and Price were not in consort. This was partly of the president's own making, since he continued to naively believe that ego-driven generals would cheerfully put aside their own agendas and cooperate for the greater good. When Van Dorn requested unified command, both Davis and Randolph were hesitant to become involved. Neither had sufficient information on what Bragg intended in Mississippi. Davis urged cooperation to avoid disaster.[53]

The next news came from the *Whig* of September 29. A terse Northern item claimed that Price's army had been nearly surrounded at Iuka, Mississippi, twenty-two miles east of Corinth, but managed to escape. It was news to the War Department. There was no additional intelligence until October 7, when the *Enquirer* ran a Southern account of the affair. An engagement had occurred at Iuka on September 19 as Price attempted to keep Rosecrans's army from joining Buell. The Missourian had scored a victory, inflicting 700–1,200 casualties at a loss of only 300 of his own. The casualty figure was subsequently raised to 482, but official reports (not released to the press) placed the true numbers at 979, including 485 sick and wounded who had been left behind. Reading between the lines, "Old Woodpecker," as Grant called Price, had had a close call—dangerously close. Randolph continued to push for cooperation, but Davis could wait no longer. Given Price's close call at Iuka, the president did what he was loath to do: get in the middle of his generals' squabbling. Van Dorn, as senior general, was given unified command.[54]

Bragg, in Kentucky, was notified of the bickering among the generals. He penned a peevish reply to Davis in early October. Van Dorn, he railed, had never been cooperative. He never submitted reports or returns unless specifically ordered to do so. He evaluated the Mississippian as "gallant to a fault, but he is self-willed, rather weak minded & totally deficient in organization and system. He never knows the state of his command, and wields it only in fragments." Bragg remained angry because he was under the impression (wrongly) that he was fighting Buell's, Rosecrans's and Grant's combined armies due to Van Dorn's and Price's lack of energy. By that time, however, Davis knew that his intelligence was incorrect.[55]

On Sunday night, October 5, a dispatch arrived in Cooper's office—a glorious victory at Corinth on October 3. Van Dorn had driven the enemy from every position. Even though the fighting had not yet ceased, "we may confide in the opinion & dispatch of Gen. Van Dorn[] that we have secured a victory," Ruffin jubilantly wrote. Although no additional information had arrived by October 8, Ruffin had gotten his hands on a disturbing telegram: Van Dorn had been driven. "The worse is that Van Dorn, the commander, is said to be unfit for such a trust. On that ground only I feel discouraged." The next day, four days before the War Department received official notification, capital citizens awakened to shocking news. A batch of New York newspapers had arrived at the office of the *Dispatch* on Monday, October 6. Northern accounts claimed that a two-day battle had been fought at Corinth on October 3–4, with the Federals winning an undeniable victory. The Confederates had sustained "great slaughter," leaving many dead and wounded on the field, with 700–1,000 prisoners. Van Dorn was in full retreat. "This news is the more painful that we had been led to anticipate at [a] complete victory [at] Corinth," declared the *Dispatch*. Indeed, Van Dorn's dispatch harkened back to that of Beauregard's "complete victory" telegram at Shiloh. A reprinted Mobile article of October 10 told of unparalleled slaughter. William Cabell's brigade had been reduced to 450 men. The Southerners momentarily gained the town but were driven back. A fresh Union division, marching from Boliver, Tennessee, had harassed the retreat. A depressed Davis wrote his brother Joseph: "A feeling of gloom seems to prevail here from the news of our late disaster at Corinth[,] the full extent of which is still not known." Jones confided in his diary: "This is bad for Van Dorn and Price."[56]

Such unwelcome news coming on the heels of the Kentucky retreat, capital citizens were mortified. "Bad news! The papers bring an account of the defeat of our army at Corinth (Mississippi)," wrote a consternated Judith McGuire. "This bringing up [of] reinforcements, which the Yankees do in such numbers, is ruinous to us. Ah! If we could only fight them on an equal footing, we could expunge them from the face of the earth; but we have to put forth every energy to get rid of them, while they come like frogs, the flies, the locusts, and the rest of the vermin which infested the land of Egypt, to destroy our peace." Ruffin expressed his utter contempt. "[A]s I feared latterly, instead of the victory at Corinth, which Gen. Van Dorn too hastily announced for a then unfinished battle, our army has suffered a defeat—& the reverse I fear will be very disastrous to our military operations in Tenn. & Ky."[57]

Prior to the battle, Davis had sent Major General John Pemberton, then at Charleston, to command at Vicksburg as Van Dorn continued conducting field operations. Pemberton had issues while in Charleston—some tactical (including the foolish idea of dismantling Fort Sumter), some engineering, and some personality traits; he could be stern and brusque. His greatest sin, however, was his Pennsylvania birth and being assigned to the most rabid secessionist city in the South. South Carolina politicians—notably Congressman William Porcher Miles and Governor Francis Pickens—not only opposed him but also made it their mission to nag Richmond until they got him transferred. Pemberton had been summoned to the capital back in August 1862. He came and left in obscurity. Having stuck Pemberton at Vicksburg (where Major General Martin L. Smith was already stationed), Davis was free to place Beauregard at Charleston. Now that Van Dorn had so spectacularly failed, Davis had no choice but to supersede him with Pemberton. As it stood, Van Dorn and Price both ranked him, so the administration had the Pennsylvanian promoted to lieutenant general, which the Senate approved with all speed.[58]

As for Van Dorn, he wallowed in victimhood: "The attempt at Corinth had failed, and in consequence I am condemned and have been superseded in my command. In my zeal for my country I may have ventured too far with inadequate means." Yet he piously concluded in his after-action report, which was never released to the press, that the dead at Corinth "do not rebuke me, for there is no sting in my conscience." No one was nodding approval. His zeal was not for his country but was a reflection of a little man's ego, and the widows of the dead now cursed him. His final casualty count tallied to 4,858, including over 2,100 captured. Along with Price's near miss at Iuka, the Confederates were down nearly 6,000 troops. Congressman Thomas Foster of Alabama, writing from Huntsville, observed that the denunciations against Van Dorn were "loud and universal." Yet Davis sustained him. Although superseded by Pemberton, he was placed at corps command, leaving Lovell without a command.[59]

Presidential support notwithstanding, the capital press screamed denunciations. The *Examiner* characterized the Battle of Corinth as a "serious reversal." "N'Importe"—in reality Albert J. Street—wrote for the *Mobile Advertiser & Register*, but his articles were carried in the *Whig*. His commentary on Van Dorn proved merciless. The general "blinded himself to the use of force," and he fell into a "murderous trap." Both Price and Lovell opposed the attack, but "with a determined madness, equal to that of Charles X," Van Dorn ordered the assault. Street admitted that no one knew anything about the new commander, Pemberton, but anyone would be an improvement over Van Dorn.[60]

The issue of Van Dorn's drinking and womanizing also came to light. Some Mississippi civilians claimed that they had "indisputable evidence" of his being a "seducer, drunkard, and libertine." It was not the first time that Davis heard of his drinking. Phelan had warned that some distinguished citizens had called upon the general only to find him too drunk to attend to business. As with his friend George Crittenden, Davis turned a blind eye. Van Dorn was aware of the accusations. Relating to the reported seduction of a young flirtatious Vicksburg lady (who happened to be married), the general flatly denied the accusation, although he sheepishly admitted that some indiscretions might have led to slanderous talk. "I am unfortunately not a good Christian—*but I am not* a seducer, nor a drunkard," he insisted to Randolph. He had never had intercourse with any woman other than his wife—a shaky claim given that three of his illegitimate children all bore his last name. The diminutive general requested to come to the capital to personally offer his explanations, perhaps believing that he would have better luck talking his way out of his predicament than writing his way out.[61]

According to Phelan, Van Dorn remained universally despised and was regarded as "the source of all our woes." There was much talk of his "whoring and drunkenness"; whether true or not he did not know, but the people believed it to be so. Lacking all respect for him, the troops would never fight again under his leadership. Northern Mississippi was filled with stragglers who had deserted under his command.[62]

Van Dorn got to tell his side of the story in a subsequent court of inquiry. Several eyewitnesses who were with the general both before and after the Battle of Corinth offered testimony that he was definitely not inebriated. The accusations that potentially had more sticking power were those leveled by Brigadier General John Bowen, which dealt with tactics, strategy, and later even drunkenness. The primary question became: Should the Battle of Corinth have ever been fought? To be sure, Van Dorn and Price had been placed in a difficult, although not impossible, situation. The court of inquiry, which was highly stacked in Van Dorn's favor, ultimately exonerated him, but reputational damage had nonetheless been done. Thomas Bragg spent an evening with the president, and he observed that Davis was quite depressed with the turn of events. He openly expressed that "we have been outgeneraled" and that Van Dorn had allowed himself to be "drawn into a trap, & getting his forces very much cut up." All of the facts were still not known, but it was a "mournful result, risked without an object." Van Dorn had become more trouble than he was worth.[63]

9

A Storm in Congress

The failure of the fall campaigns in both the East and the West dashed Southern hopes, perhaps overly delusional hopes, of a quick resolution to the war. Correspondent Peter Alexander began to write about a war of attrition and exactly what that would mean. Already, during the first ten months of 1862, Confederate armies had sustained, according to his best estimates, 25,000 dead and mortally wounded. There were probably more—perhaps many more—who had died of disease, plus another 25,000 who had been left maimed and physically incapacitated. The total dead or disabled before the end of the year would doubtless bring the total to 100,000. The reporter offered a grim prediction: the Confederacy should be prepared to sustain annual losses at that level each year the war continued. He left it to the reader to deduct the obvious question: Could the numerically inferior South long survive under such horrific losses?[1]

Joseph E. Johnston was no stranger to Richmond. The Virginian was known as the co-victor, along with Beauregard, of First Manassas, and a popular perception developed that "Old Joe" was a master strategist. As he led troops through the streets of Richmond at the beginning of the Peninsula Campaign, crowds "cheered themselves hoarse." Perhaps it was his appearance; his goatee gave him the look of a French officer. He could be affable, but he also had the ability to "keep people at a distance when he chooses." Johnston stood erect, making him appear taller than his five feet six inches, and he possessed a "striking air." He was shy, to the point of blushing during public appearances. The general was sensitive about his baldness and wore a hat whenever possible, even at the dinner table. By the fall of 1861, the Johnston–Davis relationship had devolved into acrimony, and matters worsened as the war progressed. The estrangement was stoked by Lydia Johnston, the general's wife, who saw herself as an old Virginia aristocrat who was above the western Davises, and despite overtures on the part of the president and first lady, she harbored suspicions against them. The general believed that the president had intentionally denied him his proper seniority rank, and he was forever bitter and resentful. As for the president, Davis saw Johnston as selfish, insubordinate, and forever carping. Neither trusted the other. Neither could entertain the thought of being wrong. Both were thin-skinned. Johnston's increasing association with the congressional anti-administration clique exacerbated the friction. At a function in which Yancey, Foote, and Wigfall were all present, Yancey stood and made a toast: "Gentleman, let us drink to the health of the only man who can save the Confederacy—General Joseph E. Johnston." Cheers of "Hear, hear!" followed. The story made the rounds in the capital.[2]

It was not politics but a Yankee bullet and shell fragment that ultimately resulted in Johnston being assigned to the West. During the Peninsula Campaign, at the Battle of Seven Pines, he was severely wounded in the shoulder and chest and knocked unconsciousness. The chest wound, which resulted in adhesions between the lungs and the chest wall, would require six months to heal; even then the general was frail. Davis graciously extended an invitation for him to recuperate in the Confederate White House; it was declined. The general instead chose to stay at the home of Senator Wigfall, who by that time was clearly in the anti-Davis camp. It was a slap in the face to the president. In the meanwhile, Robert E. Lee, whom Johnston saw not as a comrade in a shared cause but as a competitor, took command of the Army of Northern Virginia. Already resentful that Davis had given Lee a higher seniority ranking, Johnston became increasingly jealous of Lee's successes (on the Peninsula and at Second Manassas) and of his rival's harmonious relations with Davis. He wanted his old command back; it was never going to happen.[3]

Now that Sidney Johnston was dead, Old Joe was the second-highest-ranking field officer in the Confederacy. On November 1862, he reported to the War Department for duty. Precisely where to place him was problematic, if not somewhat embarrassing. To leave him idling in the capital and potentially stirring up trouble was politically unacceptable in addition to being, in the eyes of most, a waste of talent. Davis thus devised a plan that would, simultaneously, offer Johnston a field command commensurate with his rank, remove him from the capital and his political allies, and take care of a western problem, namely, the lack of voluntary cooperation between Bragg, Kirby Smith, and Pemberton. Even while Johnston recuperated, the president informally suggested to him the role of supreme western command, essentially combining Tennessee and Mississippi. An early snow began falling in the capital when, on November 12, Johnston reported for duty at the War Department. Randolph told him that he would be assigned to his new command "in a few days." The next day Johnston again went to Randolph. Believing that he could negotiate the parameters, the general told the secretary that he wished to expand his authority to include Holmes's Trans-Mississippi Department. It simply made more sense, he argued, that any reinforcements to Pemberton should come from Holmes, not Bragg. Grant should be defeated first before taking care of Rosecrans, who by that time had replaced Buell as commander of the Army of the Cumberland. Johnston was in essence proposing *two* theater commands—one for Pemberton and Holmes, the other for Bragg and Smith. Randolph was in full agreement, but Davis had already rejected the notion. Two subsequent closed-door meetings occurred among Johnston, Davis, Cooper, and G. W. Smith, the temporary secretary of war. Whatever was said, and the tone in which it was said, the end result was that the president proved intractable.[4]

The announcement was hailed by the press. The *Examiner* believed that the one redeeming factor of an otherwise bleak outlook in the West was the assignment of Johnston. Apparently concluding that Johnston would replace Bragg—which was not the case—the paper added that if the Virginian had been in command in Kentucky, then "Louisville would have been ours [and] the shipyards of Cincinnati would have been destroyed. . . . The appointment of Bragg was a terrible mistake." In an article carried in the *Whig*, the *Charleston Mercury* declared that Johnston was a "real strategist" who possessed "the confidence of the country."[5]

But haunting problems remained. Eight months earlier, on April 14, 1862, Davis, Randolph, Johnston, and Lee (then serving as presidential adviser) met to discuss strategy for the Peninsula Campaign. The marathon meeting became heated and ultimately devolved into a tug-of-war between Johnston's strategy of retreating toward the capital versus Lee's strategy of holding the line. Davis ultimately sided with Lee. Johnston seemingly accepted the decision, but he left the meeting with the full intention of doing what he had originally proposed. That begged the question: If Johnston ignored orders in the very shadow of the capital, would he follow the administration's policy any better at his headquarters in Chattanooga, some 545 miles distant?[6]

For his part, Johnston suspicioned that he was being set up as a scapegoat should matters in the West further deteriorate. Additionally, as long as all department heads reported directly to Richmond and the president, why was it even necessary to have a theater commander? Wigfall related to Clay that he did not believe that Davis genuinely desired a unified western command. He instead wished to simultaneously direct army operations as well as oversee civilian affairs, something that even Napoleon did not attempt. Notwithstanding his serious reservations about the whole concept of shifting troops between Mississippi and Tennessee, Johnston departed Richmond on November 29. Senator and Mrs. Wigfall accompanied the Johnstons for the first sixty miles of the journey. "Gen. Joe Johnston and staff have left Richmond for the West, where he will take command," reported Richard Yarington, the Richmond correspondent of the *Columbus Sun*. "This is a desirable change, and it is hoped will produce a great revolution in affairs in that section."[7]

Ruffin did not have the slightest idea where Bragg's army was camped, there having been a news blackout for over two weeks. "[I]f it were possible," he wrote, "[I] might well suppose that the army was no longer existing." While the capital public remained in the dark, the War Department had known for over two weeks that Bragg intended moving into Middle Tennessee. Indeed, the general openly discussed the move when he consulted with Davis in late October. Breckinridge's Division, which got as far as Knoxville, had been redirected to Murfreesboro and, along with Forrest's cavalry, had taken up a position at Murfreesboro.[8]

By November 22, Bragg's two corps, renamed the Army of Tennessee, along with two of Kirby Smith's divisions, had arrived at Tullahoma. The ranks were rapidly filling up, and with the addition of Smith's 11,000 troops, the army now numbered 40,000 infantry and artillery and 5,000 cavalry. Rosecrans's army, estimated at 60,000, remained huddled around the environs of Nashville. While the War Department made a serious effort to keep Bragg's movements out of the press, reprinted Northern dispatches openly told that Frank Cheatham's Tennessee division had arrived at Tullahoma. On December 2, the *Examiner* was the first to report that Bragg had concentrated his army around Murfreesboro and Tullahoma. "At the latter place it is supposed the battle between the two armies will soon take place," suspected Ruffin.[9]

As Bragg disappeared from the headlines, the exploits of John Hunt Morgan filled the news vacuum. Richmonders knew the cavalier only through his swashbuckling reputation. Few, perhaps beyond some in the Kentucky delegation, were aware that the thirty-seven-year-old widower fought bouts of depression with gambling, drinking, and womanizing. He even had quiet trysts while his invalid was wife wasting away. This was war, however, and private indiscretions could be overlooked for battlefield victories, especially in the West. His ride around the Federal army in Kentucky was compared in the *Dispatch* to Jeb Stuart's June 1862 ride around the Army of the Potomac. On December 7, 1862, the Kentuckian attacked an isolated Federal brigade at Hartsville, Tennessee, inflicting 300 casualties and taking 1,800 prisoners, with Morgan sustaining only 139 killed and wounded. The colonel was hailed in the Richmond press, and Johnston requested his immediate promotion to brigadier general: "He is indispensable." Equally as aggressive, Nathan Bedford Forrest in December raided throughout West Tennessee, capturing 1,500 prisoners and killing and wounding (by his estimates) 1,000, and creating havoc in the Union supply chain.[10]

Western raids paled compared to the massive battle fought at Fredericksburg, Virginia, on December 13. Lee was attacked by the huge Army of the Potomac, now led by Major General Ambrose Burnside. The bluecoats were repulsed in repeated nearly suicidal frontal assaults. The exuberant capital press wildly exaggerated Federals losses—5,000 dead, 25,000 wounded, and 3,000 captured—but the truth was sufficiently stunning: 13,000 Union casualties, with the Confederates losing a third of that number. While Davis remained the symbol of Confederate nationalism, it was clearly Lee who had won the hearts and minds of the South.[11]

Ever since the fall of Fort Donelson, politicians had pleaded with Davis to come to the West. In early December, despite continued health problems, he made plans to go. The idea was to leave on December 10 and return by New Year's Day. The trip was made in utmost secrecy; the president was accompanied only by a servant and two aides, although War Department insiders quickly got wind of it. Even though the capital press was kept in the dark, western papers openly reported the tour. Thus, Richmonders awoke on January 12 to read in both the *Dispatch* and *Whig* that Davis had arrived in Knoxville the previous night. He made a speech and appeared to be in "fine health and spirits." The *Whig* ventured that he was on an inspection tour to raise morale and to get an opinion of Bragg's capacity to command. Kean wrote pointedly: "Private information from many sources represents the tone and temper of the people of the Mississippi Valley are very unsound. *They are submitting*. Whether he [Davis] can reassure them is doubtful."[12]

The *Dispatch* reprinted a *Chattanooga Rebel* item that detailed the leg of the president's journey from Chattanooga to Murfreesboro. The trestle at Bridgeport, Alabama, was down, so the presidential railcar was loaded aboard a barge and floated across the Tennessee River. He was greeted on the west bank by a thirteen-gun salute of the New Orleans Washington Artillery (Fifth Company). On Saturday, December 13, he reviewed Breckinridge's Division. Johnston related to Wigfall that he saw "no evidence of the want of confidence & dissatisfaction [with Bragg] of which we heard so much in Richmond." No public mention was made of a large troop detachment until Davis's December 15 dispatch to James Seddon, notifying him that Carter Stevenson's 8,000-man division was being sent from Tennessee to Mississippi. Pemberton clearly needed reinforcements, but Johnston continued to argue that they should come from Holmes rather than Bragg, which would "take several weeks."[13]

During December 19–22, a severe cold snap hit the capital. Truant boys were seen playing on the local ice ponds, but temperatures moderated as Christmas approached. Harry McCarthy, the "Arkansas Comedian," happened to be in town at the Broad Street Theater. The twenty-eight-year-old English-born singer, composer, and comedian, who had emigrated from England in 1849, was well-known throughout the South, especially for his most famous composition, "The Bonnie Blue Flag." He was a crowd-pleaser, and Richmond was sorely in need of diversion. Despite the war, the blockade, and inflationary prices, Christmas Day in the capital passed pleasantly. The traditional eggnog still flowed, the wealthy sat down to a roasted turkey dinner, and there were numerous small parties. Reportedly a few fights occurred among those who over-imbibed. The children played with pop-crackers, which seemed to be in abundance. The more sedate attended church services. To John Withers, it appeared as though there was no war. "This is a lovely Christmas day," he wrote, "and thousands in this city[] are enjoying it to the full." Still, the *Enquirer* could not help but feel that it was a bittersweet occasion. "Victory has adorned the arms of the Confederacy [at Fredericksburg], but death shadows are gliding against every threshold." Nonetheless, it was a day of peace and time "to throw aside the tears of sorrow and be happy."[14]

The diversion did not last long. On December 27, a Johnston dispatch got the attention of civilian authorities. "General Bragg reports that the enemy are advancing on him [at Murfreesboro] in heavy force, and [he] asks for all available assistance. He [Bragg] is rapidly concentrating." The next day a telegram indicated that the Federals were within ten miles and closing fast. Cooper implored Kirby Smith for help. The general dispatched the 39th North Carolina, which was all that he could spare; Bragg was on his own. Someone at the *Dispatch* was beginning to pick up on the news. On the morning of December 29, a brief statement indicated a potential battle near Murfreesboro "early next week." The morning of December 31, a two-day-old dispatch reported that Rosecrans's army was advancing in force and was within three miles. A general engagement was shortly expected; unsettling hours ticked away. "All eyes now turned towards the Department of the West," voiced the *Whig*.[15]

Triumphant news arrived from Murfreesboro on a warm New Year's Day 1863. Bragg's dispatch of the previous day declared that the enemy's center and right had been driven from the field, with the capture of 4,000 prisoners, 31 guns, and 200 wagons. Loss on both sides was great, but that of the enemy was far greater. Elation on the city streets proved overwhelming. The news "put us almost 'beside' ourselves with joy, and caused even enemies to pause and shake hands in the street," related Jones. True, it was a western dispatch, which could be notoriously inaccurate, but this one came directly from Bragg, seemingly adding some validity. Nonetheless, Jones awaited additional telegrams "with anxiety." To Ruffin, the news portended "good hopes."[16]

No additional dispatches arrived the next morning, but by afternoon Jones could hardly restrain his joy as he transcribed: "We are in great exaltation again." Bragg's cavalry commander, General Joseph Wheeler—"Fightin' Joe" to his men—had ridden completely around Rosecrans's army. There were indications that the Federals had withdrawn from the field. "I think we will get Nashville now," he confidently concluded. "The Year Opens Brightly!" hailed the *Enquirer*. Additional arriving dispatches nonetheless revealed that the Federals had not quit the field but had only slightly pulled back. The *Whig* was still prepared to declare Murfreesboro the greatest victory in the West to date—Shiloh not excepted. The *Dispatch* was more tempered in its remarks but admitted that the battle stood "high in the scale" of great battles. "You are glad to see our great victory near Nashville. It seems to be complete," Preston Johnston wrote his wife.[17]

Sometime during the day on January 5, a dispatch arrived from Bragg. He had been unable to dislodge the Federals, and hearing that they had received reinforcements, he was compelled to withdraw from the battlefield on the night of January 3. The enemy had not followed. Although the news was not at that time public knowledge, Jones knew its contents. "During the day an absurd rumor was invented, to the effect that Bragg had been beaten. We are anxious to learn the precise particulars of the battle," he wrote.[18]

Bragg's telegram appeared in the *Dispatch* of January 7, but by that time the *New York Herald*'s version of events had also arrived. Rosecrans claimed that the "rebels are whipped decidedly" and that Federal forces had advanced nine miles beyond Murfreesboro. Ruffin was left shaking his head. "The confident expect[at]ions of continued success of Gen. Bragg have been woefully disappointed," he sighed. Even though the accounts were "meager & obscure," it was beginning to appear as though Bragg had met with a reversal. "[T]his victory seems to be like those of the first days at Fort Donelson, at Shiloh & Perryville, a bloody & truly glorious success leading to disappointment, reverse, & disastrous defeat or loss."[19]

Jones was at a loss for words. He simply could not reconcile Bragg's initial dispatches claiming that he had gained the whole field to the latest telegram declaring a retreat. For the next three days, nothing new arrived from Tennessee (at least nothing reliable). Although the public still knew little or nothing about the detachment of Stevenson's Division to Mississippi, there was quiet talk in the War Department that perhaps too large of a detachment had been made. "If that blunder should prove disastrous, [then] the authorities here will have a hornet's nest about their ears," Jones surmised. Preston Johnston had heard from his Uncle "Will," who related in disgust: "We lost a fourth of the army & achieved nothing but a retreat." The colonel came to the conclusion that Bragg would "have to go under. He is not equal to his position." The president was nonetheless "loath to yield a general to the popular clamor or sacrifice one for failure. He always hopes for better luck next time. But Bragg is incompetent."[20]

Sporadic details continued to trickle in, mostly of the Union rout of the first day's battle. It was January 12 before a reliable Southern source told of the fierce fighting on January 2. The Federals managed to gain a foothold on the south bank of Stones River. Breckinridge's Division unsuccessfully attempted to dislodge them, but it was bloodily repulsed. "We drove them across the river[] but encountered so vast a body so securely posted that we retired to our position again. Our loss, for numbers engaged, was very heavy," related a participant. The army had withdrawn behind the Duck River. The slaughter had been horrific; Bragg later admitted his loss exceeded 10,000, although the figure was never released to the public. Captain B. C. Yancey, son of the Alabama senator, had his horse shot from under him while leading his battalion of sharpshooters, but, wrote the senator, "God in his merciful Providence preserved his life throughout that terrible battle."[21]

Despite his disappointment, Davis again sustained Bragg. At the transfer of Stevenson's Division to Mississippi, the president had instructed the army commander: "Fight if you can and fall back beyond the Tennessee River." The general could argue that he had followed his orders. Also, on the first day's battle, he had scored a great victory. It was not his fault that Rosecrans had been heavily reinforced. Preston Johnston wrote Rosa that "Bragg's retreat is not a defeat. The President seems contented with the results," although he could not resist adding a personal note, "but has not Bragg a way of dashing down the cup of hope from our lips that is shocking." Joe Johnston confided to Wigfall that "we ought to have won at Murfreesboro." A friend of Judith McGuire's remarked that "the Bragg victories never seem to do us much good."[22]

Given the expectation of a victory, the press now exploded in anger. "General Bragg has certainly retreated . . . from his victory at Murfreesboro, as he did last fall at Perryville," howled the *Examiner*. The *Dispatch* concluded that Bragg became "alarmed at his own success and ran away from it." Bagby had just enough time to complete his monthly editorial in the *Southern Literary Messenger*; he did not hold back. When the victory of December 31 was first announced, "Our joy knew no bounds." Then the whole story came out; Breckinridge's Division had been shattered on January 2 and the army had been forced to retreat. "One thing is for certain. The campaign in Tennessee has failed. . . . Bragg has been given two fair trials. He has failed in both of them." The general was nonetheless retained due to his "friend in Richmond [Davis]." The accounts deeply pierced the general, and he related to his friend Senator Clay that he feared that the criticism had reduced his "usefulness."[23]

Supportive articles appeared from two Bragg staff officers—John Forsyth, editor of the *Mobile Advertiser & Register* who was temporarily serving as an aide; and Josiah S. Stoddard, who wrote anonymously under the initials "J. S. J."—but Richmond had made up its collective mind. Kean told his diary on February 15: "It is quite manifest that there are deep quarrels in that army and that Bragg is cordially hated by a large number of officers."[24]

Politicians were in a surly mood. Wigfall pressed Seddon to remove Bragg. Ten Tennesseans, including five Confederate congressmen and John Bell, a presidential candidate in 1860 and undisputed leader of the Whigs in the state, petitioned Davis to remove Bragg from command. Congressman Dargan of Alabama-9 advised the president that the loss of confidence in Bragg was "universal." Representative Foster pleaded that Bragg be ordered to return to Mississippi or that Van Dorn be immediately reinforced; otherwise North Alabama and northern Mississippi "will be overrun this winter & spring." Congressman Wiley Harris, representing Mississippi-6, urged the government to abandon the coast for the defense of the Mississippi Valley. There were no limits to the demands and urgent requests.[25]

Kirby Smith meanwhile had been summoned to the capital. It was soon announced that he had been relieved of command of the Department of East Tennessee and replaced by Brigadier General Daniel Donelson. Senator Robert Johnson of Arkansas proposed a joint resolution, expressing the thanks of Congress for his great victory at Richmond, Kentucky; it passed unanimously. But where was he now going? No one knew for sure, but many speculated the Army of Tennessee. Even Bragg knew of the talk and suspected that he might be relieved. But Davis had other plans for Kirby Smith.[26]

Representative James Pugh of Alabama strongly supported General Bragg in the House. (Alabama Department of Archives and History)

Eventually, almost predictably, questions began to be raised in Congress about Bragg's leadership. When Bragg ally James Pugh made a resolution in the House (HR-4) to express thanks to the general for his conduct in the late battle, there were those who hesitated. Henry Read of Kentucky, still perturbed at the loss of his state, voted against it, but a supportive letter from General Johnston, read by Henry Foote, turned the tide. The vote passed 78 to 2. "I voted in the affirmative with many misgivings," admitted Franklin Sexton. "Did it solely because J. E. J. sent in orders [General Orders] that his [Bragg's] conduct was good &

his generalship able." John Wright, representing Tennessee-10, was a staunch Bragg ally. He declared the resolution as "one of the highest compliments that had been paid to any general." Abstaining was Kentuckian George Hodge, who now proposed a reconsideration. While he did not question Bragg's patriotism, "before God" he would not vote to support the resolution. Surprisingly, the only other negative vote was James Lyons of Virginia. He explained his vote by saying that he did not disapprove of the resolution as it stood, but he felt that the impression existed that it was linked to the failed campaign in Kentucky. John Crockett (Kentucky-4) showed an independent streak and openly voiced support of Bragg.

The next afternoon, February 27, Foote, who had been uncharacteristically cooperative the day before, showed his colors. He had long since established himself as the most predictable irritant in the House. The fact that he had only briefly spoken the previous day was now apparently more than he could bear. In his support of HR-4, he did not mean to imply that he supported Bragg; he did not. He had long considered him an inferior general and had said as much, and he "had not word one to take back." He had supported the resolution only because of the Johnston document. Robert Breckinridge (Kentucky-11) rose to state that, if the vote were taken today, that he, James Christman, and Willis Machen would all change their votes. Hodge asked if he could change his abstention vote to "nay," but there was objection. Pugh nonetheless wrote the general that the vast majority in the House expressed "overwhelming" support. "You have got a strong friend in the President—let the disorganizers howl. There is no danger of shaking him," Pugh reassured the general.[27]

The issue in the Senate was more problematic. Clay, Phelan, and Semmes all expressed support, but there were others who had turned on the general. Burnette of Kentucky demanded that no action be taken until Bragg's after-action report had been submitted and debated. From all the information Pugh could gather, he believed—and related to Bragg—that "the two Kentucky senators [Simms and Burnette], old Clark of Missouri, Orr of S. C. & Wigfall of Texas will vote against you in the Senate. All the other Senators are for you strongly." But such was not the case. Yancey of Alabama, Oldham of Texas, Henry of Tennessee, and Robert Johnson and Charles Mitchell of Arkansas all stood in opposition. Jillson P. Johnson, a Breckinridge aide, was convinced that Clay was *against* the general. Pugh admitted to Bragg: "This city has been the focal point of all the malignity against you—false representations have been made [by Polk's envoys] to members of Congress, and a dissolute press has teemed with communications originating with these croakers and malcontents."[28]

Attempting to mitigate the political damage, Bragg sent his own lobbyists to Richmond. Forty-five-year-old Captain John B. Sale, an Aberdeen, Mississippi, attorney and son of a preacher, and Captain Felix Robertson, a Texan who quit West Point only three weeks before graduation to cast his lot with the Confederacy, arrived quietly in the capital on March 2. They had come to explain Bragg's Murfreesboro after-action report to congressmen, but it would take several days for clerks to make sufficient handwritten copies to be distributed. In the meantime, Sale roamed the halls of Congress and held private conversations. It was clear that a number of senators were disturbed by reports of dissatisfaction within the Army of Tennessee. The captain nonetheless wrote the general that he had no doubt that supporters would ultimately win out over the "croakers and malcontents." Bragg subsequently made an addendum to his original report, which did not arrive until congress had recessed. The original resolution was therefore never considered; Bragg would not get his thanks.[29]

The addendum, published in the press, proved highly prejudicial against Breckinridge, essentially placing the blame of the failed January 2 assault on his shoulders. It was not well received. "It makes him [Breckinridge] a laggard on Wednesday, reveling in a circle of false rumors, and incompetent on Friday, in pushing his men beyond the point that he was instructed to take, and which he had secured. In a word the report turns the little end of the telescope upon him [Breckinridge] in a very damaging way," Preston Johnston wrote. William Gale, Polk's aide and son-in-law, happened to be in the capital when the issue came to a head. The report "raised a storm in Congress. . . . [Senator] Henry says however that General Bragg will not be removed. Others . . . speak with equal confidence at his being retired at an early day and say that it is the object of his being ordered to Richmond at this time. . . . I venture to predict his certain removal. His [report] has done the work." Breckinridge requested a court of inquiry and quietly sent a letter to Preston Johnston to see that it was granted. The colonel went to Cooper and sought his help. For practical reasons the inquiry was never held, but Cooper cooperated by releasing Breckinridge's report for press publication.[30]

The rumblings in the West had long been known in Richmond. Kean knew of the talk: "Bragg is said to have lost confidence of his command completely," he wrote. He later added: "It is quite manifest that there are deep quarrels in that army, and that Bragg is cordially hated by a large number of his officers." Polk, writing directly to the president, freely criticized the army commander. The disaffection in the Army of Tennessee, "which [the president's] visit was intended to heal, is likely to revive under the depressing influence of Bragg's retreat and his continuance in command," the *Examiner* editorialized. It was Bragg's next step, however, that took the administration by surprise. He asked his generals (corps, division, and brigade) if he had lost the confidence of the army. Apparently expecting them to rally in his favor, the generals in Hardee's Corps instead took the opportunity to say that a change was necessary. When the news got back to Davis he was taken aback: "Why General Bragg should have selected that tribunal and have invited its judgements upon him is to me unexplained," he wrote Johnston, who was instructed to proceed immediately to Tullahoma and find out exactly what was happening.[31]

Polk's Corps never took a formal vote, but the general informally discussed the issue with his generals and assured the president that they were in accord with the "officers of the other corps." Polk then proceeded to do what he did best: stab his superior in the back. "My opinion is that he had better be transferred," he wrote. Recalling Davis's words that "I can make good use of him here [in Richmond]," he suggested a position akin to inspector general. The suggestion was actually a good one despite its conniving author. The bishop desired to have Johnston placed at army command. The *Whig* ran a *Chattanooga Rebel* article that mentioned "a rumor in army circles" that Bragg was being transferred to another unnamed department.[32]

Johnston proceeded to Chattanooga, doubtless wondering about a curious sentence in Davis's communiqué: "[Y]ou have a right to direct its [Army of Tennessee's] operations and to do whatever else belongs to the general commanding." It was not difficult to read between the lines and understand that the president was suggesting that Johnston could replace Bragg as its commander should he so desire. The Virginian did not take the bait. He arrived at Tullahoma on either January 28 or 29. By that time, it was being reported openly in the press that Johnston had arrived to assume command of the Army of Tennessee. "We trust the report may be true," concluded the *Examiner*.[33]

In reports to Davis on February 3 and 12, Johnston enthusiastically supported Bragg's leadership and boasted of the condition of the army. Bragg was aware of the fractious feelings, but "[he] thinks it is passing away." Governor Harris believed that the want of confidence was primarily due to the Kentucky Campaign and that it was declining. The complaints of certain generals notwithstanding, the army remained "full of confidence." Both Polk and Hardee related to Johnston that they had requested the president to place him at army command. Such a move would have the obvious appearance of conniving to get the appointment, which seemed perfectly reasonable to the conniving corps commanders, but it did not make sense to Johnston, who made it clear that such an appointment would be "inconsistent with my personal honor." Writing to Davis on February 23, Bragg wrote: "Assailed, myself, for the blunders of others, and by them and their friends, my mind is made up to bear no sins in the future but my own." Davis may not have appreciated the import of those words, but Bragg had declared war on his enemies.[34]

Johnston's resistance to assuming army command presented a problem for the administration, which clearly desired him to make the move to thereby avoid the political ramifications. Davis did not agree with Johnston's "honor" argument, but even so he wrote theater commander that the short list for a Bragg replacement was indeed short. Secretary of War Seddon was more direct. But for Johnston's "scruples," the fact seemed obvious that "you should at once take command of the largest army (that of General Bragg), most likely to be engaged in the field." If Bragg was recalled to Richmond, Johnston's embarrassment would be even greater. The secretary was perhaps hinting that he was not beyond forcing the issue. If the administration was not exactly pure in its arguments, then neither was Johnston in his replies. He desired an army—just not in the West; he indirectly (through Wigfall) proposed a swap with Lee. At the very least—it would raise the issue of what would become of theater command—would it simply dissolve? Additionally, if Seddon believed that Johnston should take command of the army "most likely to be engaged," then he would be going to Vicksburg, not Tullahoma.[35]

Johnston's carping became a sore point with the War Department. "General Johnston has written another of his brief unsatisfactory, almost captious letters, protesting against Bragg's removal. . . . He never treats the Government with confidence, hardly with respect," wrote Kean. On April 16 he added: "He treats the [War] Department as an enemy with whom he holds no communication which he can avoid and against which, he only complains and finds fault. He is a *very little man*, has achieved nothing, full of himself, [and] above all things, eaten up with morbid jealousy of Lee and his superiors in position, rank, or position, rank, or glory. I apprehend the gravest disasters from his command in the western department."[36]

Wigfall, whose friendship with Johnston was less personal than political expediency, was irked with the general. His support of Bragg had seriously complicated matters. Seddon had finally gotten the president to the point of removing Bragg when he received Johnston's complimentary report. This allowed Davis "to shuffle off the whole responsibility for continuing him in command. In protecting Bragg[,] you have at the same time protected the President."[37]

Strangely, the Richmond public was kept in the dark about the potential command change that spring, although it was openly reported in other Southern papers. The *Charleston Courier* reported that "a gentleman just from Richmond" (a congressman?) noted that Bragg's Murfreesboro after-action report had caused such ire among senators and congressmen "that neither the President nor General Bragg can withstand it, and that if General Bragg is not relieved of his command, it may lead to an unfortunate contest between the President and both houses of Congress. It is already rumored that General Bragg has been called to Richmond." There were whispers that he would be reassigned to Mobile. The *Appeal*, which was frequently quoted in the capital dailies, also mentioned that a change would be forthcoming, and yet the Richmond press remained noticeably silent. The single mention came from a Northern article, which reported (wrongly) that Price would be replacing Bragg.[38]

Davis, under continued political pressure, concluded that Bragg had to be deposed. Johnston, then in Mobile, was ordered to report to Tullahoma and assume command of the Army of Tennessee. Upon his arrival, Bragg would report to Richmond. When Johnston subsequently arrived, however, Mrs. Bragg was deathly ill. For humanitarian purposes, Johnston stayed the order. By the time she recuperated, Johnston's old Seven Pines wound had flared. As a result, Bragg remained at this post and no change occurred. At the very least, the president could have transferred Polk, the chief troublemaker, yet no decision was made. As a result, trouble continued to fester.[39]

10

The Vicksburg Obsession

In late 1862, the *Whig* reprinted an article by an enterprising correspondent of the *Knoxville Register*. In 1860, some 400,000 tons of freight were shipped by steamboat from St. Louis to Memphis and other cities south. More than a million tons passed Cairo, Illinois, all headed for the lower Mississippi Valley. Annually, some 1,500 to 2,000 steamboats plied the Mississippi River. True, the North could always ship midwestern wheat and corn via rail, but the added freight cost would surpass $12 million per year. "The people of the Northwest cannot for an indefinite period be induced to make war upon the South," deduced the reporter. Put simply, the economics of shutting down the main artery of the nation would ultimately prove debilitating. Whether or not such a strategy was indeed viable was not the issue; the South believed it to be so.[1]

Conversely, the possible loss of Vicksburg sent chills down the collective spines of Southerners. War Department clerk John Jones encountered the burly, salt-and-pepper–bearded postmaster general, John H. Reagan, on the streets of the capital one day. His concerns about Vicksburg had brought him to the point of despondency. If the Federals controlled the Mississippi River, "the Confederacy would be 'cut-in-two.'" He implied that he would be willing to give up Richmond to thereby save his adoptive state of Texas. It was a ridiculous notion but revealed the passion surrounding Vicksburg as a political and strategic symbol. Even Davis referred to the potential loss of the Mississippi River as the "dismembering of the Confederacy." Vicksburg would increasingly become an obsession of the administration.[2]

A heavy snow still blanketed the streets of the capital on Sunday, November 9, 1862, although temperatures later in the day climbed to 38 degrees. A dispatch arrived from Mississippi; Grant's army near the Tennessee–Mississippi border was in motion. The department commander there, General John Pemberton, had little choice but to withdraw his army from Holly Springs, Mississippi, to the south bank of the Tallahatchie River north of Abbeville. The Richmond public took little notice save for a Northern article claiming that Grant was advancing down the Mississippi Central Railroad to take Jackson and Vicksburg from the rear.[3]

Federal operations then suddenly stalled; for what reason no one knew. On November 27, Pemberton wired that Grant, with 60,000 troops, was once again advancing along a wide front, with another Federal column, 12,000 strong, marching south through the Delta along the east bank of the Mississippi River, that threatened to get in his rear. A third expedition was gathering in Memphis to move directly on Vicksburg, which was garrisoned by only 4,500 troops. Mississippi was clearly being overrun. The War Department first asked, then directed, Holmes to send 10,000 infantry to the east bank of the river, an order that was ignored.[4]

Mississippi Congressmen John McRae, Wiley Harris, and Ethlebert Barksdale sent the president a frenzied letter stating that, if Pemberton did not receive immediate reinforcements, Jackson and Vicksburg would be overrun within two weeks. "Can nothing be done to arrest this catastrophe[?]" A week later, on December 8, Harris again addressed Davis, wildly advising the government to abandon the entire Eastern Seaboard to concentrate all troops in Mississippi. The loss of the Mississippi Valley, he believed, would be "fatal to the cause." And if Mississippi and Alabama were to be overrun, "the people would submit to U.S. control."[5]

By December 5, Pemberton had withdrawn another fifty-five miles to the south bank of the Yalabusha River, with headquarters at Grenada. Although Richmond papers gave only passing notice to the loss of most of northern Mississippi, officials in the War Department were scrambling. A brigade of East Tennessee conscripts was boarded on the boxcars, but they would not arrive at Jackson until midmonth. Stevenson's Division was also on the way from the Army of Tennessee, but it would barely arrive before the end of the month. A brigade, sent from Mobile to Meridian, Mississippi, trailed far behind. Johnston, who by that time had assumed theater command, also ordered 8,000–10,000 infantry from Holmes in Arkansas, but again the order was ignored.[6]

A letter arrived on the president's desk from his old friend James Phelan. The senator from Mississippi told of the "unhappy condition of affairs in this State." Since the retreat from the Tallahatchie, army moral had plummeted. Furthermore, Pemberton had "not impressed himself with either the people or the army." Indeed, few even knew that he was the new department commander; the men in the ranks still referred to "Van Dorn's Army." In what was becoming a common—if not desperate—refrain, the senator urgently requested that the president come West to take personal command.[7]

Just as matters appeared their bleakest, a December 30 dispatch clicked over the wires bringing jubilation. Earl Van Dorn, in a Pemberton-approved raid, had led a division of cavalry in Grant's rear; on December 20 they had destroyed the Union forward depot at Holly Springs, Mississippi. The destruction was total, according to the *Dispatch*: 1,950 prisoners, 1.8 million rounds of ammunition, 5,000 rifles, 2,000 revolvers, 100,000 suits of clothing, 5,000 barrels of flour, 1,000 bales of cotton, $1.6 million of medical stores, and $600,000 of sutler's goods. Coupled with Forrest's West Tennessee raid, Grant's overland supply chain had been effectively shut down.[8]

Troublesome intelligence nonetheless arrived on December 27 of a large-scale expedition under William T. Sherman, streaming south from Memphis with as many as eighty transports. "Preparation for an Attack Upon Vicksburg," warned the *Enquirer*. Whether or not the president was still in Vicksburg on his western tour was unknown. With nothing more than newspaper accounts to rely on, War Department officials could only anxiously wait. "We have a dispatch from Vicksburg at last," Jones wrote on December 29. A series of attacks by 25,000 Federals was repulsed at Chickasaw Bayou, the Federals losing 400, the Southerners thirty. A second attempt was made on December 30 with similar results—300 Federals killed and wounded and 400 captured, to the Confederates fifty killed and wounded. Johnston's predictions notwithstanding, some of the Tennessee reinforcements made a timely arrival on the battlefield. Coming on the heels of Bragg's initial triumphant telegrams from Murfreesboro, matters in the West appeared uncharacteristically bright.[9]

The conventional wisdom was that the Federals had given up on the Yazoo River approach to Vicksburg. The deduction proved correct, but the enemy quickly turned to another avenue. A January 24 dispatch arrived warning that Sherman's corps, estimated at 21,000, was only five miles above Vicksburg and that Grant's army, of equal or greater size, was also concentrating. Spies had counted a massive collection of 107 steamers, including fourteen or fifteen gunboats. The Federals were feverishly working on a canal on De Soto Peninsula opposite Vicksburg. The purpose was for the Mississippi River to fill the ditch and allow transports to emerge south of the city, thereby circumventing the heavy batteries. "I fear the Yankees will succeed in this [canal] scheme," intoned Ruffin. An ominous Johnston dispatch arrived two days later: "Enemy, in full force, again opposite city, with indications of forcing his way below." Some feared that a Federal battery would deploy on the west bank between Vicksburg and Port Hudson, disrupting river traffic. Others predicted that a major crossing was in the offing at Warrenton.[10]

The Confederates had long been aware of Grant's canal. Indeed, Northern articles detailed the progress of the project. Reassuring Southern accounts proclaimed that the project, unlike the successful canal dug at Island No. 10, would be a failure. On February 1, the ram *Queen of the West* completed a successful run past the batteries and made for the mouth of the Red River, where it created havoc. "This shows that iron-clads [cotton-clad] steamers can safely pass by our batteries[] to reinforce the [Baton Rouge] fleet below," observed a concerned Ruffin. If the canal was completed, he realized that the strategic purpose of Vicksburg would be neutralized. Jones noted on March 4 that the Yankee papers claimed that the Federal fleet had successfully passed through the canal. "This is not true—yet," he cautiously wrote. On February 9, Pemberton wired Cooper of the "great probability of his [Grant's canal] getting through." He was wrong; the project subsequently failed. That was not the only good news. *Queen of the West* and the ironclad *Indianola*, both of which had slipped past the batteries, had to be scuttled to prevent capture by the Southerners. Richmond papers jubilantly announced their demise.[11]

The snow that had blanketed northern Virginia during the first week in April had, by February 15, been replaced by a seasonal rain, with temperatures climbing to the mid-sixties and vegetation showing signs of new life. Jones fretted over the president's declining health; he could no longer come to the office, but he continued working in the Executive Mansion. And then there was the West. "It seems that we lose all the battles of any magnitude in the West," he wrote. The two dispatches arriving on April 17 did little to allay his fears. Pemberton notified Cooper that a convoy of ironclads and transports had passed the Vicksburg batteries during the early-morning hours of April 16. One of the transports had been disabled, but updated reports confirmed that seven heavily armed ironclads, a ram, and two transports were a mile below New Carthage, Louisiana. There was more bad news on April 23: a gunboat and six more transports had made a mostly successful run, with perhaps two of the latter being disabled. The gunboats appeared to pass the batteries with "comparative impunity," observed Kean. Grant now began concentrating on the west bank of the Mississippi River, the apparent target being Grand Gulf, Mississippi, several miles downriver from Vicksburg. Virginia-centric Richmond took little notice.[12]

"We have had bad news from the West," Jones noted on April 25. A raid the previous day had penetrated deep into Mississippi, striking the Southern Railroad at Newton Station, between Meridian and Jackson. Telegraph wires were cut, tracks ripped up, and two trains torched. The initial report placed the number at 300 raiders, but the number was subsequently raised to 1,600. A small detachment had turned back, laden with stolen loot—watches, jewelry, spoons, and the like. The main column headed for Enterprise, south of Meridian, but "the impression prevails that but few of them will ever return," Jones noted. The incident received only scant mention in the capital press.[13]

On April 28, the Federal fleet opened a fierce bombardment on the Grand Gulf fortifications, and according to Pemberton, there was every indication that the attack would be renewed the next day. He was again wrong. Grant's expedition continued south and established a beachhead at Bruinsburg, south of the Big Black River. On the night of April 30, the Pennsylvanian sent an urgent dispatch to Davis: "The enemy has landed this side Miss. River." Grant did not advance north, toward Warrenton, but continued south of the Big Black River. The target appeared to be Jackson. Pemberton needed reinforcements—immediately. Seddon assured him that they were on the way, but most were one to two weeks out. Kean could only shake his head: "Western matters are in a sad way."[14]

In late April, Richmond once again fixated on Lee. On April 29, General Joseph Hooker's massive Army of the Potomac crossed the Rappahannock above and below Fredericksburg. During the first days of May a massive battle raged around the crossroads of Chancellorsville. By May 4, a Union cavalry raid under George Stoneman approached the suburbs of the capital, creating panic among civilians. Even Major General Arnold Elzey, commanding the city defenses, thought that the capital's luck had run out. Mary Chesnut, who happened to be in Richmond visiting her husband, was in the Executive Mansion as officers came and went in a scene of excitement. Varina whispered to Mary that the Federals were only three miles away but cautioned her to remain quiet, as the president was ill. In what would become Lee's masterpiece, however, his army emerged victorious and the capital was once again safe. Victory nonetheless came at a heavy price: Stonewall Jackson fell mortally wounded. All business was suspended as the general's body was taken in a slow procession to the capital building, where his casket was placed in state in the House chamber. A line of 20,000 mourners paid their respects. In Virginia, once again, the enemy had been checked. In the West, once again, there was looming disappointment.[15]

During the first week of May, even as the capital convulsed with anxiety over the unknown outcome at Chancellorsville, two Mississippians, Congressman James Harrison and former Governor James Whitfield, arrived in Richmond for a conference with the president and secretary of war. They represented a citizen's committee from Columbus, Mississippi, and the Tombigbee Valley to plead their case to improve security in northeastern Mississippi. Davis listened sympathetically but admitted that what he could do depended on "the fluctuating tide of war." His only advice was to raise more state militia. Meanwhile, Davis remained aware of the continued lack of confidence in Pemberton's leadership. Fleet T. Cooper and A. N. Kimball, editors of the Jackson *Mississippian*, informed the president that "three-fourths of the people in [the] army and out doubt him. Send us a man we can all trust—Beauregard, [A. P.] Hill, or [James] Longstreet—and confidence will be restored." The chief executive replied that there was simply insufficient time to chose a new commander.[16]

More troubling reports continued to arrive from the West. Johnston needed reinforcements, and a hurried decision had to be made. In early May, three brigades from Beauregard's department—one from Savannah and two from Charleston—were ordered to take the trains for Mississippi. South Carolina and Georgia officials howled, and there were predictions of gloom. It was nonetheless a correct decision, but as in the case of Fort Donelson over a year and a half earlier, would it be too little, too late? The van would not arrive for nearly three weeks. Seddon reassured Johnston that 10,000 troops had been ordered; the actual number was 6,900. Meanwhile, Johnston, along with two brigades (2,789 troops) from the Army of Tennessee, were ordered to Jackson.[17]

The question of transferring troops from Virginia to the West was not a new one, and Davis, expressing "intense anxiety" over the fate of Vicksburg, now revisited the issue. Three brigades of George Pickett's division (about 6,700 troops) were at that time in the vicinity of Richmond. On May 9, Seddon telegraphed Lee asking if he would approve the transfer of these brigades to Mississippi. Lee, who had his own problems, responded promptly and uncharacteristically bluntly. The distance was too great, and the issue of the Mississippi Valley would be decided before they arrived. Even if the division made it in time, he questioned whether or not the troops would be deployed effectively—a not-so-veiled reference to Pemberton. Besides, flushed with the stunning victory at Chancellorsville, Lee was once again eyeing a second Northern invasion. Thus, as Johnston was asking Davis for a decision between Mississippi or Tennessee, Lee saw the dynamic as "between Virginia and the Mississippi." The president heeded the warning; the division would not be sent.[18]

Lee discussed the issue of Vicksburg with his "War Horse," Lieutenant General James Longstreet. The South Carolinian suggested that, if reinforcements were to be sent West, then they should go to Bragg's army to defeat Rosecrans. Desiring independent command, he volunteered his corps to be sent. Lee, however, was averse from allowing a portion of his army "so far beyond his reach." Eventually Longstreet wrote his friend Wigfall, clearly expressing not only his views but also probably those of Lee. "Grant seems to be a fighting man and seems to be determined to fight. Pemberton seems not to be a fighting man." If troops were sent West, they should be sent to Bragg for a second Kentucky invasion. "That being the case we can spare nothing from this army to re-enforce the West." He implored the senator to use his influence to send all available troops to the Army of Northern Virginia. If Lee could march into Pennsylvania with 150,000 men, then the South could "either destroy the Yankees or bring them to terms."[19]

Lee was proposing a go-for-broke campaign that would break the current cycle of attrition and, if not result in total victory, at least bring President Lincoln to the bargaining table. Davis did have options; he could swap geography for time and send one of Bragg's corps to

Virginia for Lee's proposed invasion. It was a radical thought, and there is no indication that it was ever proposed. Even so, it would have been dismissed out of hand. The move would surely be detected, and Rosecrans would match it. If troops could not be sent East to West or West to East, if the trans-Mississippi was off the table, and if the Atlantic Coast had already been stripped, then what other options were available? It was time for a meeting; the date was set for May 15.[20]

Lee quietly arrived in the capital on May 14 (the newspapers did not mention his visit) on the afternoon train of the Richmond, Fredericksburg & Potomac Railroad. The next morning, appearing gaunt and pale (Davis and Seddon were hardly better), the general arrived at the War Department for what would be a marathon session. The day before, news had arrived in the capital of the fall of Jackson, Mississippi. An unnerved Seddon was determined that something had to be done to immediately reinforce Pemberton. Barely a week earlier, Governor Pettus had pleaded that the "[h]our of trial is on us. We look to you [Davis] for assistance. Let it be speedily." The editors of the Jackson *Mississippian* advised that some Mississippians thought Pemberton incompetent; all thought him distrustful. Commenting on the loss of the Mississippi capital, the *Whig* questioned "if Pemberton was not competent for the duties assigned him, why was he sent there, and why was he so long retained[?]" In a reprinted article from a correspondent of the *Columbus Sun*, it was noted that the people of Jackson were "greatly incensed at General Pemberton[] and openly accuse him of bad faith."[21]

During the grueling War Department session, the only one arguing against Lee's proposed Northern invasion was John Reagan. Obsessed with securing Vicksburg, he argued that 25,000–30,000 troops from the Army of Northern Virginia should be sent to Mississippi. To Lee's argument that threatening Washington and Baltimore might result in a Union withdrawal from Vicksburg, the postmaster general remained unconvinced. With Lee dominating the meeting, it became clear that Reagan's views were not favored by anyone else, and so he "gave it up." Writing years later, he recalled: "I will not now repeat the expression I made when this conclusion was reached." Even so, the issue was not over. The next day Reagan requested that Davis reconsider the issue. Redebating issues was something that Davis rarely, if ever, countenanced, but on this occasion he agreed to do so. In the ensuing days, however, enough impromptu cabinet gatherings had been held that it was clear that further debate would be pointless.[22]

Postmaster General John H. Reagan opposed Lee's Pennsylvania invasion in favor of troops from the Army of Northern Virginia going to Vicksburg. (Library of Congress)

Beyond the cabinet, not all approved of the current course of action. South Carolina Congressman Robert Rhett, an openly avowed member of the anti-administration clique, adamantly declared that it was the "plainest dictate of the most ordinary prudence, after defeating the armies of the Unites States in the East [Chancellorsville], immediately to have crushed them out in the West, and then, if necessary, to return them to the East." As for the Pennsylvania invasion, he denounced it as an "absurdity," and he could not—would not—believe that the idea had actually come from Lee.[23]

With Virginia no longer available as a manpower source, Davis frantically looked elsewhere. On May 22, he pleaded with Bragg to send still more troops from the Army of Tennessee. Already two brigades had been ordered to Mississippi, and Philip Roddey's cavalry brigade had been redirected to North Alabama. Ordinarily Bragg would have strongly objected to yet another drawdown, but the army commander saw an opportunity. Having been in a serious row with Breckinridge over the failed January 2 assault at Murfreesboro, he notified Richmond that he would immediately dispatch Breckinridge and three of his four brigades (5,269 troops) plus William Hicks "Red" Jackson's cavalry division (3,269 troopers), the same unit Johnston had previously removed from Pemberton. Between May 10 and May 23, there had been draws of over 11,000 troops from the Army of Tennessee. Weeks earlier Johnston had loudly protested such transfers; he now kept quiet.[24]

Kean did not share the public's adoration of Johnston. Following the occupation of Jackson, he confided in his journal: "His 'strategy' seems of the mind Yankee correspondents ascribe to all their commanders—retreat and sacrifice is always 'strategical.' I have little confidence in the General who came near losing Richmond and who thinks so much of himself." Gorgas nonetheless remained hopeful. He doubted that Grant had 30,000 troops so far from his base; the number he surmised was closer to 12,000. "I trust Gen Johnston will yet send them back staggering, & that Vicksburgh will be maintained."[25]

A Johnston dispatch of May 18, received in Richmond the next day, related that Pemberton had fought a nine-hour battle between Jackson and Vicksburg and fallen back behind the Big Black River. "Pemberton was *forced back*. This is all we know yet," Jones nervously wrote. Seddon privately described the engagement as a "grave disaster." Vicksburg became the talk of Richmond. "I feel depressed tonight," Judith McGuire admitted. "Any news from the South [West] is bad. General Pemberton has been repulsed between Jackson and Vicksburg." Ruffin trembled at the ramifications. "[I]f Johnston should be compelled to lose Vicksburg, & retreat—or, worse, be defeated in battle, if would be one of the heaviest blows that could fall upon the Confederate States." The next day, Gorgas noted that "Grant appears to have out generaled us, & is now said to have invested Vicksburgh." Since there were reports that the city had two months supplies, he continued to believe that "this effort of Grant's may prove his ruin." Additional Southern dispatches claimed the loss of 3,000 casualties and thirty guns at Champion Hill, but Northern accounts placed the number at a staggering 4,000 prisoners and twenty-nine guns at Champion Hill and 2,000 prisoners and seventeen guns at the Big Black River Bridge. Kean heard that

"Stevenson's division broke and officers of different grade were heard to say that they were betrayed." Gorgas wrote despondently and quietly expressed that the garrison might not have sufficient ammunition supplies to sustain a lengthy siege.[26]

No news arrived on May 24, although there were "plenty of Sunday rumors as usual." Hoping against hope, Kean speculated that perhaps the city's investment had been exaggerated—"a sugar speculation story." Monday morning, May 25, brought renewed hope. "Vicksburg—the Enemy Repulsed," heralded the *Dispatch*. Three assaults had been beaten back with thousands of Union casualties. "If indeed the enemy's assaults have been made repeatedly, & so successfully repulsed, there is little ground to fear the capture of Vicksburg soon," concluded Ruffin. Judith McGuire prayed that God might yet save that "heroic little city."[27]

The siege dragged on wearily throughout June and early July, with Northern articles claiming that the fall of Vicksburg was certain if not imminent. Some accounts said that the city had surrendered, although such claims were dismissed. Capital newspapers remained sanguine. "Our hopes rise as the resistance is prolonged," voiced the *Whig*. Ruffin likewise took heart. "Vicksburg is still ours," he wrote on June 3. "[U]p to June 1st Vicksburg is still ours. Even if there had been a total absence of late reports, in the existing condition of things, no news is, for us, equivalent to good news." Jones saw the issue as more muddled. "They [dispatches] say, up to third [June] instant, yesterday, everything is encouraging; but the Memphis papers say Grant's losses have not been so large as was supposed. Then it is reported that Grant has retired to Grand Gulf. Yet it is expected the town [Vicksburg] will be stormed in twenty-four hours!" Nineteen-year-old Emma Tyler, daughter of the Richmond commission merchant John Tyler, was simply glad that "Dear, brave old Vicksburg still holds out. . . . I wish some deadly pestilence would come and sweep Grant's army from the earth in one single night."[28]

The question on everyone's mind related to Johnston and his army: When would he make his move to rescue Vicksburg? Richmond was growing nervous. "If Vicksburg is lost without a desperate battle to save it by Johnston, he will be ruined too, and justly," thought Kean. "The stake is worthy of a desperate throw. Such venture is inconsistent with Johnston's character as I understand it, and I greatly fear he will not make it." The *Whig* questioned "why he [Johnston] delays so long in going to the rescue." It also ventured a warning: "He cannot but know that if he allows Vicksburg to surrender without an attempt to give succor, he is a ruined man." Jones likewise fretted. "Where Johnston is we have no knowledge; but in one of his recent letters he intimated that the fall of Vicksburg was a matter of time."[29]

The document Jones had seen was a June 5 dispatch from Johnston. "Our resources seem so small, and those of the enemy so great, that the relief of Vicksburg is beginning to appear impossible to me," it read. Grant had 60,000–80,000 troops, with more arriving. Unless significant additional resources arrived, "the surrender of the place will be a mere matter of time." It was not what the administration wanted to hear, and the predictable bickering between Richmond and Johnston resumed. According to the War Department, Johnston should have 34,000 troops, but he claimed 24,100 "effectives." The latter term was a calculating device frequently used by Johnston to downplay his true present-for-duty strength, which on the day on which he wrote his response was actually 28,438. Within a week, June 7, his present-for-duty strength, a report that Seddon had on his desk, totaled 35,400, exclusive of Pemberton's 30,000.[30]

It was becoming increasingly evident that Johnston might not make any effort to relieve the city. Kean's opinion of the general continued to plummet. "He seems more anxious to make a point than to gain a battle, to put the Government in the wrong [than] to defend a state. It is very clear to me that the *Mississippi will be lost*." The *Dispatch* questioned why in seven weeks no action had been taken. If Vicksburg fell without any serious attempt to save it, then "his [Johnston's] military fame will be gone *forever*."[31]

Johnston's June 15 telegram—"I consider saving Vicksburg hopeless"—sent administration officials into a tailspin. Seddon immediately fired back: "Your telegram grieves and alarms me. Vicksburg must not be lost without a desperate struggle. The interest and honor of the Confederacy forbid it. I rely on you still to avert the loss." Johnston answered that the War Department clearly did not understand what he faced, but Johnston clearly did not understand what the administration faced. The secretary reminded the general that the "eyes of the Confederacy" were watching. Wigfall nonetheless feared that Johnston was being set up to take the blame if disaster occurred.[32]

On June 17, Lieutenant Colonel Arthur J. L. Fremantle, an officer in the British army, arrived in the capital, the final leg of his Southern tour. For the next two days he met with several government officials, including Cooper, Benjamin, and Preston Johnston, during which time the subject of Vicksburg came up. It was clear that there was anger in the capital about Johnston's inactivity—and despair that he might not rescue the beleaguered city. With surprising candor, perhaps to the point of indiscretion, they expressed that the fate of the city was sealed. The talk, noted the British officer, came from "the highest quarters."[33]

Richmond, its collective mind never far from Lee's army, began to once again focus on the East. During the first week of July, the capital papers were flooded with accounts of a major battle at Gettysburg, Pennsylvania. The overwhelming majority of the articles were from Northern papers, most of which claimed a major victory—indeed, that Lee's army had been dealt a mortal blow. "We pause for the truth," Judith McGuire wrote on July 6. Two days later she noted that the accounts from Gettysburg remained "very confused." Gorgas expressed "great uneasiness and anxiety" about the outcome.[34]

At 1 p.m. on Tuesday, July 7, a stunning dispatch arrived at the Richmond telegraph office. It was not an official telegram but rather a press telegraphic signed "Woodson," referring to Will O. Woodson, a correspondent of the Confederate Press Association. Dated July 5, the message announced the surrender of Vicksburg as reported by an unnamed officer arriving in Jackson. Shown the message, William S. Morris, president of the Southern Telegraph Company, doubted its authenticity. Rather than release it to the press, he promptly took it to the War Department. Having heard nothing from Johnston, Seddon immediately telegraphed him and requested verification. At 8:30 p.m. the general answered: "Vicksburg capitulated on the 4th instant." Seddon forwarded the message to the president, declaring his "deepest regret at being compelled to inflict the pain of such disastrous intelligence, tho only confirmatory of our fear." Five days later Port Hudson capitulated; the Confederacy was divided.[35]

The *Examiner* released the news on the morning of July 8. The headline proved so startling that many in the capital dismissed it as a mere rumor gotten up by a shrewd sugar speculator. Yet Sallie Putnam noticed that government officials were maintaining a sullen silence. Eventually the "paralyzing" truth was realized. "The sad tidings from Vicksburg have been confirmed by subsequent accounts," Jones lamented. Writing the same day, Judith McGuire noted in her diary: "Vicksburg has fallen!

So say the rumors; and we are afraid not to believe." Ruffin nonetheless felt that the dispatch left "much room for doubt," and he continued to cling to hope. Gorgas expressed shock: "The announcement is so unexpected, after the assurance given heretofore, that it appears incredible."[36]

The news caused stunned despair in Richmond—Davis: "disastrous"; Henri Garidel: "caused a great sensation in Richmond"; Seddon: "shock of despondency and despair"; Jones: "has cast a gloom over everything"; Gorgas: "It is indeed a terrible blow to our cause. It apparently sets us back indefinitely"; Christopher Tompkins: "People are decidedly blue as to the homefront—Port Hudson has followed Vicksburg—of course Natchez will go next"; Sara Pryor: "should we, too, be starved into submission" Seddon: "the fatal turning point of the war."[37]

The *Sentinel* editorialized that the enemy would doubtless be "vastly encouraged" by the fall of the citadel. Having only partial news on the outcome of Gettysburg, the *Whig* declared that the "heavy blow" represented by the Vicksburg loss would be "more than counterbalanced by our glorious victory in Pennsylvania." By July 11, however, the truth of Lee's defeat had become apparent. Although the Northern papers notoriously lied, believed Ruffin, there was little doubt that the third day's battle had been a "disastrous defeat" for Lee and that his army had retreated "in disorder and demoralized." During the second week in July, even the weather appeared to announce the ominous news of the twin disasters. Without a cloud in the sky, a haze permeated the atmosphere in Richmond that caused the sun to omit a bright-red glow, imparting a menacing appearance.[38]

Precisely how many troops had surrendered at Vicksburg was unknown. Southern accounts had previously placed Pemberton's strength at 17,000. The number of prisoners, according to Ruffin, was somewhere between 15,000 and 27,000. An article by "One of the Garrison" placed the number at 23,000, along with a staggering ninety guns. With the subsequent fall of Port Hudson, Jones fumed that Pemberton's 50,000-man army "has been completely destroyed."[39]

Most of the indignation was aimed not at Johnston but at one person in particular: Pemberton. The *Examiner* berated the administration in its efforts to protect Pemberton by making a "brave old soldier [Johnston]" the scapegoat. The president's office was barraged with telegrams and letters from politicians, officers, and citizens. Davis was warned that the reorganizing Vicksburg parolees were in "almost a mutinous condition, denouncing in the most furious language, General Pemberton. . . . This feeling of the People against Genl. Pemberton, tends to encourage the Deserters, which are quite numerous in the Eastern [Mississippi] counties." L. N. Walthall wrote bluntly: "Nine in Ten think him unfit to command an army[] and are very unwilling to serve under him again. Indeed many go so far as to say they *will not* do so." Congressman Barksdale did not mince words: "The *enthusiasm* of the masses is *dead*." If the question of reunification was put to a vote of the people, it would pass. Phelan candidly wrote to Davis that he "cannot realize the unhappy, disaffected, dangerous sentiment which pervades the whole people[] upon this subject [Pemberton]." The Vicksburg troops would be "gone to the winds, if Genl. Pemberton is retained." The criticism also bled over to the president. The senator did not mince words, stating flatly that it was commonly believed that Davis "disregard[ed] as ignorance or resent as dictation[] any effort to change your convictions." Even Lieutenant General Hardee and the president's own brother, Joseph Davis, warned that Pemberton could not be reassigned to his former position. Davis nonetheless continued to support the Pennsylvanian. During his western tour, he made a statement at Brandon, Mississippi, that ultimately wound up in the *Whig*: "My confidence in Gen. Pemberton has not abated in the least—he is one of our most gallant and skillful Generals in the service."[40]

Those outside the administration and War Department largely supported Johnston. The *Whig* admitted that there were those who declared that "Johnston is a coward. Kept idle an army larger than that which he won Manassas, while Vicksburg was starved. Johnston is a dunce and a coward." The paper nonetheless took a too-early-to-tell position, and Ruffin would rise in his defense. "Why Gen. Johnston had not attempted to relieve the garrison, by an attack, is unknown. But it must have been his utter inability even to hazard the attempt. . . . I still believe that Gen. Johnston did all that his means enabled him to do." The general's allies in the Congress, led by Wigfall, held steadfast.[41]

The *Examiner* went on a bitter attack against the administration. "The apologists of the President have attempted to cast the blame on General Johnston[] and to blacken the hard-won reputation of the ablest strategist of the Confederacy," he editorialized. "The people, clinging fondly and proudly to their old battle-scarred favorite, pointing to Richmond, angrily proclaim: '*Not General Johnston, but Mr. Davis is to blame*.'" The public, he went on to say, "cannot be hoodwinked, deluded[,] or persuaded to cast one iota of blame upon him [Johnston]." He then became more pointed: "The people do not share his [Davis's] chronic hallucination that he is a great military genius[] and [that he] can direct the campaigns in distant states with unerring skill." Constituents would rather that he content himself with "correcting [administrative] evils near his own door."[42]

The sole condemning voice came from the pro-administration *Sentinel*, which belched forth a canister of condemnation:

> The people are asking, and the whole world will ask, where was General Johnston and what part did he perform in the grand tragedy. In answer it will be said that with an army larger than [that which] won the first battle of Manassas, he made not a motion, he struck not a blow, for the relief of Vicksburg. For nearly seven weeks he sat down in sound of the conflict and he fired not a gun. He heard the confident declarations with which the besieged animated their courage— "'Never mind! *Johnston* is coming!'" But JOHNSTON never came. He did not so much as harass the enemy. . . . [H]e has done no more than sit by and see Vicksburg fall[] and send us the news.[43]

By July 10, Grant's advancing army was again on the outskirts of Jackson. Johnston, though heavily outnumbered, vowed to fight, but those in the War Department never doubted that he would have to withdraw. By July 16 there was no news and, wrote Jones, "no news is generally bad news." Congressman Barksdale, then in Jackson, wired Davis that the "result may be easily conjectured." The city was evacuated.[44]

Davis fumed. Meeting with Gorgas on July 16, his bitterness became apparent. The colonel remarked that Vicksburg apparently fell from want of provisions. "Yes, from want of provisions inside and a general outside who wouldn't fight." Johnston defended himself by writing that, once in Jackson, he had been relieved of theater command and could no longer order troops from Tennessee. Davis replied days later with a fifteen-page denial that smacked of a legal brief. Indeed, some in the War Department, as well as Wigfall, suspected that Davis's friend Judah Benjamin, a lawyer, played a role in its writing. "The President is furious with Johnston," Kean remarked. Mary Chesnut, though living in South Carolina, kept abreast of capital matters through her husband on the presidential staff. "The President detests Joe Johnston for all the trouble he has given him," she wrote, "and General Joe returns the compliment with compound interest. His hatred of Jeff Davis amounts to a religion. With him it colors all things." Wigfall, on July 21, informed

Senator Clay that Davis was denouncing Johnston "in the most violent manner . . . & attributing the fall of Vicksburg to him and him alone."[45]

Despite its practicality, the entire theater command concept—perhaps designed out of a genuine attempt to create unified command in the West or, as Johnston suspected, perhaps because Davis simply did not know what else to do with him—was doomed from the outset. As long as the president saw his own role less as a politician and more as a quasi-supreme secretary of war, Johnston would have responsibility but no authority. As long as Johnston saw his own role only from a parochial military view, ignoring serious political consequences, he could only offer militarily correct, but politically unacceptable, solutions. He either did not grasp the concept of a super-command or, more likely, resisted the concept to prove the president wrong. The relational rupture was no longer repairable. Wigfall reported: "I did not see Davis but heard that he was blind as an adder with rage & ready to bite himself."[46]

Although there was talk in the Senate among some of Davis's staunchest supporters of removing Johnston, Wigfall kept the western delegation in line. Even Semmes and Burnette, who were typically tepid about opposing the administration, promised to stand by the general. Wigfall continued to believe that it was Davis's "pig-headedness & perverseness" that had brought disaster to Mississippi. When Pemberton wrote a letter to the president stating that he had fought the Battle of Champion Hill at the positive order of Johnston, Wigfall denounced it as "a piece of unmitigated meanness."[47]

Pemberton subsequently submitted his after-action report. Wigfall went to the War Department and demanded to see a copy of it. Seddon, who now seemed to be turning on Johnston, refused. Wigfall promptly replied that all correspondence regarding Johnston had been kept and that it would show the "stupidity of Davis." In the event that there was blame attached to the theater commander, he would release all documents to the press. Additionally, he was prepared to take the issue to the floor of the Senate. According to Wigfall, Seddon's high horse suddenly became a "gentle & diminutive pony."[48]

In terms of the vilified Pemberton, Davis could do little else but yield to the popular clamor, which in every way went against his grain. He still supported the general, whom he saw as a victim, and felt that he had made the right decision by taking his army within the Vicksburg defenses. Nonetheless, Davis assigned Hardee to replace him, temporarily leaving the Pennsylvanian without a command.[49]

What to do about Johnston was more problematic. When Hardee was reassigned to Mississippi, Preston Johnston urged the president to have the Georgian replace Johnston. The issue, according to Kean, was openly discussed in a cabinet meeting, but there was a split on the issue. As much as Davis detested Johnston—and he did—the president ultimately chose to retain the Virginian rather than risk the political backlash. "Johnston has very influential supporters and more real popularity in the country than the President has. It [removal] would be a first[-] class disaster," admitted Kean, who was no Johnston supporter. Nevertheless, Davis did detach Tennessee and North Georgia from Johnston's operational control.[50]

The Vicksburg disaster was interwoven with political ramifications. Congress was not in session during the summer, but western congressmen, even on hiatus, voiced their fears and anger. Representative Dargan, writing from Mobile, informed Seddon that the loss of Vicksburg and Lee's retreat had "nearly ruined us" and that unless Britain and France came into the conflict the outcome would be predictable. For that reason, he argued, slavery might have to be abolished to gain independence, something that he would be willing to entertain. It was not the first time he had floated his emancipation for independence theory. "Mr. D[argan] has an unhappy disposition," Jones slyly wrote. An alarmed Phelan wrote Davis that "the *enthusiasm* of the masses[] *is dead*" and that Mississippi was ripe for "blood" and for "fluent demagogues to organize a reconstruction party." An incensed Foote referred to Pemberton as the president's "bosom friend." He—along with Dargan, Barksdale, and Reuben Davis—all advised the president that Pemberton had to go.[51]

Georgia Senator Herschel Johnson was looking to make a deal. England would be of no help, but Louis Napoleon III might move toward recognition, since he would never be able to maintain a foothold in Mexico without Confederate help. Davis had to tread lightly, however; a persistent rumor said that the trans-Mississippi states might be looking for their own separate deal, with France as their protectorate.[52]

Yancey went on another Davis tirade, writing that it was the "prejudice and bitterness" of the president that had lost Vicksburg, and he predicted that "this will be the verdict of history." Several chafed letters had recently passed between the two, each accusing the other of

Senator William L. Yancey of Alabama made peace with Jefferson Davis as he was dying at the age of forty-eight. Courtesy of the Southern Historical Collection. (Benjamin C. Yancey Papers #2594, Southern Historical Collection, Wilson Library, University of North Carolina at Chapel Hill)

bias. Since mid-June, the Alabamian had been in declining health from fever and inflammation of the bladder, which resulted in excruciating pain. Facing death, Yancey, who often referred to the president as "a military dictator," extended an olive branch to his nemesis, an offer graciously accepted by the president. The senator died on July 27 at the age of forty-eight. He was buried in Oakwood Cemetery in Montgomery. Yancey had been second only to Wigfall in his influence in the western delegation. The *Examiner* praised him, then used the occasion to go on another rant against the president. The *Dispatch* called Yancey "the most brilliant man in the Senate." He was indeed a Goliath in the chamber, but one wonders if Davis inwardly was glad that there was one less giant to slay.[53]

Mississippi Senator Albert Brown also found his name in the papers—the Northern papers. A letter appeared in the *Cincinnati Commercial* stating that, upon the surrender of Vicksburg, Brown went to Snyder's Bluff and took the Oath of Allegiance. His wife was with him, and she bitterly complained that his service in the Confederate Congress "had ruined her." Further, she said, there would be no need to fear that he would be disloyal in the future. The *Dispatch* dismissed the story as Yankee disinformation. Brown would continue to serve in the Senate until the end of the war.[54]

Clay was having his own issues. Although he had at times been critical of the administration's policies, he had been a longtime friend of the president and was seen as a Davis man. Being one of eight senators who had drawn a two-year term at the start of the war, he was now up for reelection. Writing to a friend, the Alabamian noted that "there is a strong feeling of dissatisfaction with those in office that is very natural & not entirely unfounded [and] that threatens to throw us all out—especially those regarded as the President's especial friends." He was defeated by Richard W. Walker of the politically powerful Walker family in the November election. Clay and Congressman Jabez Curry, who had been defeated in the August congressional election (he failed to carry even his hometown), both had their names placed on the ballot for Yancey's unexpired term. The Alabama legislature appointed Robert Jeminson.[55]

Indeed, in the fall 1863 elections disaffected constituents, reconstructionists, moderates, and anti-administrationists, put several of Davis's western congressional allies on the defensive. Dargan warned that the trend "is to seek peace[] upon any terms *whatever*." Georgia Congressman David W. Lewis, generally friendly to the administration and an avowed nationalist, lost his seat. Arkansas Congressman Grandison Royston, another nationalist, was defeated by Augustus H. Garland, a bitter Davis opponent who was now disillusioned over the loss of Vicksburg. Phelan, a longtime Davis ally (who had been burned in effigy in Mississippi) lost his seat to the Holly Springs attorney John W. C. Watson, "an old[-]line Whig." Nevertheless, Georgia Senator Herschel Johnson retained his seat by easily defeating his virulent anti-administration

Senator James D. Phelan, Sr., of Mississippi was a staunch administrative ally; it ultimately cost him his seat in Congress. (James D. Lynch, *The Bench and Bar of Mississippi* [New York: E. J. Hale and Son, 1881]).

opponent Robert Toombs, described by Preston Johnston as "a seditious, turbulent, able, shrewd, drunken, pestilential demagogue."[56]

A letter arrived on Seddon's desk in August. It was from a Mississippian named Mr. Reanes, who was once a millionaire but now lived in a shed. He had been a zealot for the cause and even now claimed that he would be willing to give his life for it. But harsh reality told him that

According to the Northern press, Senator Albert G. Brown of Mississippi was reported to have taken the Oath of Allegiance. The reports proved "ridiculously preposterous." (Library of Congress)

independence was no longer possible—"numbers must prevail." His advice to Richmond: get the best terms and rejoin the Union. Jones read the letter and wondered if in the first revolution there was such suffering and despondency among certain classes of the people.[57]

Vicksburg had been a national trauma. Both militarily and politically its loss had resulted in deep scars—not just in the West but also in Richmond. Sides were being drawn, fingers pointed, and accusations made. The breach between the pro-administration and anti-administration forces widened. There was little nuance recognized as politicians, the

Clement C. Clay's close association with Jefferson Davis cost him his seat in the Senate. (Library of Congress)

press, and civilians increasingly clung to their entrenched positions. Perhaps beneath all the recriminations and blame Richmond realized that the war was being lost in the West. Kean peered into a crystal ball and concluded: "This is a mortal blow."[58]

11

Look Beyond the Mississippi!

From the outset, Davis and Randolph had a collaborative but formal relationship. Although their wives were friendly, the husbands had no such personal interaction. Randolph was given responsibility but not authority, and his "clerk" status increasingly annoyed the Virginian. It was not unusual for the micromanaging president to issue orders and plan campaigns without consulting his secretary, and he unilaterally submitted the names of all general officers. Following the Kentucky Campaign, when Bragg and his corps commanders were summoned to Richmond, Randolph was pointedly excluded from the conferences. As for Davis, he became perturbed at Randolph's evolving "independent character"—or at least that is how Kean (Randolph's relative) saw it.[1]

The strategic situation in the trans-Mississippi was radically altered with the retreat of Bragg in Kentucky and the defeat of Van Dorn at Corinth. It was no longer feasible for Holmes to advance into Missouri, since the enemy had possession of the upper Mississippi Valley and could cut his line of communication. A joint movement by the armies of Bragg, Pemberton, and Holmes could perhaps be undertaken while the rivers were low. This would present the best opportunity to move into Kentucky and Missouri and to retake the cities of Nashville, Memphis, and Helena, Arkansas. At the very least, two of the three armies would have to cooperate. This was the Davis strategy as set forth in the fall of 1862.[2]

Randolph followed up the president's letter by writing to Holmes. The trans-Mississippi commander should immediately cooperate with Pemberton to reclaim the Mississippi Valley. Once accomplished, Bragg could move into Kentucky. The first move on the strategic chessboard should begin with Holmes, who should immediately occupy Helena before crossing the Mississippi River into Tennessee. So far, so good. It was a sentence in Randolph's October 27 follow-up letter to Holmes that created a firestorm. The secretary granted the department commander authority to leave Arkansas, cross the Mississippi River, and, by virtue of his rank, "conduct the combined operations on the east bank." Jones was taken aback. "Perhaps Mr. Randolph has resolved to be really Secretary. This is the first thing I have ever known him to do without previously obtaining the President's sanction—and it must be confessed it was a matter of some gravity and importance. Of course it will be countermanded."[3]

The letter had indeed not been cleared by Davis, who took offense. He never intended for Holmes to cross the Mississippi River, which would "have disastrous effect[] and was never contemplated by me." He simply intended him to share intelligence and occupy Helena, not to take command in Pemberton's department. Randolph promptly rescinded the order and sent Holmes a copy of the president's letter. It was not enough. The secretary received another rebuke, stating that all orders related to troop movements must pass the president's desk before being issued. Randolph had clearly been put in his place. On November 15, he did what he had been planning to do for some time: resign ("in a huff," according to Preston Johnston). Although taken aback, Davis promptly accepted it.[4]

Kean was beside himself. "Thus[,] the President actually evicted him of his office, exercising it himself without General Randolph's knowledge of the fact till such acts were done." The press expressed outrage, the *Examiner* declaring that "if cabinet ministers are to continue as mere automatons, it matters little by what names those machines are called." Nevertheless, Jones believed that Randolph had gotten out of his lane. W. C. Corsan, a touring Englishman who happened to be in the capital at the time, noted how little comment was heard on the street about the secretary's dismissal. "I suppose the President knows best what he is doing," said some, while others commented with a shrug: "We have too much to do and to think about just now."[5]

Finding a successor took top priority. Alfred T. Bledsoe, assistant secretary of war, suggested Polk, who had executive experience and who would have good work habits. Davis wisely dismissed the idea. Bledsoe opposed a name that was floating about, that of the Richmond political insider James Seddon. In fragile health, Seddon would be a failure in the demanding role, and he was "neither by nature nor habit" a "worker." The president nonetheless chose him, despite the fact, or perhaps because, he lacked military experience. The former lawyer was a thinker, not an executioner; in short, he would not be a threat. Foote, in characteristic style, dismissed him as a "foul and incompetent secretary. Seddon left his estate, twenty miles outside the city, and moved into the Spotswood [Hotel]." His skullcap and long graying hair soon became a fixture in Richmond as he walked to work each morning. It did not take long for him to stagger under the load.[6]

The secretary quickly recognized the West as the weak cog in the Confederate war machine. Perhaps under the influence of Wigfall (they could "be on terms" with Seddon, the senator from Texas advised Clay), he became a strong supporter of Joe Johnston. When it came to ordering more troops east of the Mississippi River, however, Wigfall was a political outlier. Other trans-Mississippi congressmen strongly disagreed with the transfer of additional troops; indeed, they desired Missourians, Arkansans, and Texans already in the Heartland to be promptly returned. Wigfall nonetheless held firm. Writing to the secretary, he related: "When Oldham [the Texas senator] and Bob Johnson [the Arkansas senator] were badgering me for not joining them in insisting that all the troops from the other [east] side of the river [Mississippi] should be returned," he promptly told them that if it were up to him "every soldier from Arkansas and Texas" would be sent across the river, political misgivings notwithstanding.[7]

Davis encouraged, but did not peremptorily order, Holmes to reinforce Vicksburg. Initially it appeared as though the department commander intended to comply. John G. Walker's Texas division was ordered from Little Rock to the Mississippi River, but Holmes later reneged. Hindman was at that time engaged in active campaigning in northwestern Arkansas, and sending in Walker would leave the Arkansas Valley totally unprotected. It would be best for the president to "leave the matter at my discretion."[8]

In early January 1863, the Richmond papers announced a victory. Hindman, with 14,000 troops, had marched out from Van Buren and encountered the enemy, 25,000 strong, at a place called Cane Hill, Arkansas. Senator Clark had been in Arkansas at the time and returned to announce the news: 1,000 enemy troops killed and wounded, 300 captured, with Southern losses totaling only 350. The senator's son, Colonel John B. Clark, Jr., had been struck from his horse, but he was

James A. Seddon, who was frequently seen around the capital in his skull cap, fit the president's concept of a secretary of war—a clerk, not a decision maker. (Library of Congress)

not killed. It was all joyous news. It was also—all of it—a lie. The Battle of Prairie Grove, fought on December 7, had been an unmitigated disaster for Hindman. He sustained about 1,400 casualties among his 11,000-man corps and suffered hundreds of desertions during his retreat, many of them mountain conscripts who never wanted to be in the ranks in the first place. Holmes confided to Davis that only 6,000 troops arrived in Little Rock, with 3,000 sick abandoned at Fort Smith and a like number deserting. The only hint to the Richmond public of the true state of affairs came from a reprinted Northern article in the *Whig*. Hindman, whose papers had been captured, admitted to a loss of 4,000.[9]

There was more bad news. Arkansas Post, at the mouth of the

Arkansas River, fell to a joint Union army–navy expedition on January 11, along with its garrison of 5,000 Texas and Arkansas troops. The *Dispatch* initially dismissed the story as a "fabrication," and Davis, having received no official verification, did not know what to believe. He wrote Holmes of the Northern accounts appearing in the papers and expressed hope that such was not the case. By February 5, however, the surrender was confirmed. The *Examiner* wanted to know why a division had been placed in such an exposed position. It was the *Whig*, however, that unleashed a torrent: "With the experience of Fort Donelson before him [i.e., Holmes], he sends an inferior force to that Post . . . as if he intended to invite the enemy to capture them." Holmes was denounced as an "old fogy" and an "imbecile, a man without decision of character."[10]

Joe Johnston saw the movement of troops as tantamount to pawns on a chessboard; Davis had to deal with the political realities. The Missouri congressional delegation had always been a collective gadfly, but lately Arkansas politicians had become increasingly irascible. Governor Harris Flanigan, who had previously threatened to secede from the seceding states, was on a tear. He strongly protested the removal of any additional Arkansas troops from the state. Admitting the provincial thinking of many, he reminded Davis that "soldiers do not enter the service to maintain the Southern Confederacy alone but also to protect their property and defend their homes and families." Holmes also warned the administration that the state was being overrun by tories and deserters.[11]

Vociferous complaints were made against both Holmes and Hindman. Arkansas Congressman Grandison Royston railed against martial law and price-fixing, which earned Holmes a gentle rebuke from the president. The Arkansas delegation urged the appointment of General Kirby Smith to supersede Holmes in command in addition to the transfer of Hindman and the return of Price and his Arkansas regiments serving east of the Mississippi River. Even Holmes complained of the unpopularity of Hindman, which was bleeding over to him. As for Holmes, Congressman Augustus Garland considered him "deficient in the extreme. . . . He is too slow and does too little," and he was "regarded as but an instrument in Genl Hindman's hands." He begged for the removal of both officers. Holmes insisted that the reinstitution of martial law had been absolutely necessary. Arkansas and the Indian Territory had been overrun with disloyal persons, deserters, and draft dodgers, many of whom preyed upon the citizens.[12]

On January 29, the Arkansas congressional delegation called on the

Representative Augustus Garland was not beyond firing off angry letters to Jefferson Davis. (Courtesy of the Butler Center of Arkansas Studies, Central Arkansas Library System, Little Rock)

president at his office, with some cabinet members present. Several requests were made, namely, that martial law be maintained in the state, that Hindman be recalled, and that Holmes be superseded by Kirby Smith. In an unusually cooperative gesture, Davis granted all of the requests. In a February 2 letter, signed by the entire delegation, all appeared to be in agreement.[13]

Davis was thus taken aback when he received a sharp (bordering on insulting) letter from Garland, endorsed by Congressmen Thomas B. Hanly and Royston. The delegation, the president was told, had strongly *opposed* the reinstatement of martial law in their state and that it had been reauthorized against their desire. Garland believed that the delegation had "been sadly trifled with here [Richmond] by the administration" and that "the call of the Senators and Representatives was useless and ridiculous." Four days later Garland fired off another letter. He had actually received numerous letters from constituents "complaining bitterly of the state of affairs" and had forwarded only a few to the president. He considered Davis's lack of a response to be "disrespectful." The president promptly answered to avoid the "inference that my silence on the subject would be a tacit assent to the accuracy of your recital." He had, in fact, gone out of his way to be accommodating to the delegation. His only denial was in the return of Arkansas regiments. Further, he disagreed with the assumption that regiments should serve only within the bounds of their respective states. In terms of being "disrespectful," the president reminded him that there were simply not enough hours in the day to meet with all 120 congressional members, various officers, and department heads and that he had never intentionally failed to meet with any member of Congress if his schedule permitted.[14]

Kean was aware of the unsettling Arkansas political crisis. "The Arkansas delegation, except [Senator] Johnson, insist on a change of commanders out there. Garland wrote the President a very strong letter on the subject a few days ago, declaring the want of confidence in Generals Hindman and Holmes," Kean wrote on February 15, 1863. The next month he noted: "There are indications that Arkansas is in a state of great irritation and disloyalty. Their delegation in Congress show many indications of dissatisfaction with the Government and complain of neglect of the Trans-Mississippi."[15]

In short, Davis was under extreme political pressure to address the fragile state of the trans-Mississippi. While Johnston had to deal with Rosecrans and Grant, the president had an equally odious task: addressing the demands of raucous western politicians. If Davis ordered more troops east of the Mississippi River, would they munity rather than cross? If Arkansas did in fact secede from the Confederacy, would it ignite a domino effect, thereby causing Missouri, Louisiana, Texas, and the Indian Territory to establish their own Confederacy? If Arkansas was essentially abandoned, could the Federals outflank Vicksburg and Port Hudson by advancing to the Red River via Louisiana? Under the circumstances, Davis did not dare transfer additional troops. The security of Arkansas, and the department's ability to transfer troops to Vicksburg, were a decision that had to come from Holmes in Little Rock, not the president in Richmond. That is how Davis saw it, anyway, and that is why he was reticent to issue peremptory orders; it was the correct decision.[16]

There was also the issue of numbers. Johnston was under the impression that Holmes led a department of 50,000 troops against only sparse opposition. Perhaps, as when Beauregard came to the West, he got the figure from Cooper. If such was the case, it must have represented an "aggregate present," which was useless. By the end of 1862, Holmes counted in Arkansas only Hindman's "corps," reduced to 6,000, and John G. Walker's 5,000-man division. Even as late as March 1863, Seddon insisted that Holmes had whittled his army down from 40,000–50,000 to 15,000–18,000. Jones admitted that the figures came from a pamphlet published by the contentious and insubordinate Albert Pike. Seddon apparently accepted the faulty number without question. In short, sending 10,000 infantry from Arkansas to reinforce Pemberton, as Johnston requested, would have resulted in the de facto abandonment of the state.[17]

The political fallout continued long after events had passed. Seddon's desk was swamped with letters telling of the disastrous state of affairs. Foote, quoting from Pike's pamphlet, denounced Hindman in the House. Congressman Malcolm D. Graham of Texas spewed similar words of condemnation. Johnson continued his fight in the Senate to have all of the skeleton Arkansas regiments serving east of the Mississippi returned home, a demand that the War Department "bitterly opposed." Ruffin heard the mistaken rumor that Holmes had died; he declared his death "a public benefit—& (as I said of Pres[iden]t [William Henry] Harrison, after my voting for him), his dying is the only service he has ever rendered to the public welfare."[18]

Daniel, at the *Examiner*, continued his ruthless criticism of Holmes: "Look beyond the Mississippi! What a humiliating spectacle meets the eye. Missouri utterly abandoned to her persecutors. . . . A large portion of Arkansas overrun, simply because Mr. Davis's protégé No. 2—General Holmes—is kept in command, despite the prayers of the State and the irrepressible complaints of the army. If General Holmes be not [in] his dotage, the English language possesses no synonym to indicate his stupidity and inertia."[19]

Edmund Kirby Smith, a favorite of both Davis and Lee, had been summoned to Richmond. He arrived on Thursday, January 12, 1863, and checked into the Spotswood. Two days later, the native Floridian was assigned to the command of Louisiana and Texas, but the appointment was soon expanded to include the entire trans-Mississippi. Smith took with him his staff, which included Major Hugh L. Clay, his adjutant and longtime friend and the brother of Senator Clay. Holmes was quite relieved to be superseded and to be rid of what he termed his "elephant." He was reassigned to the District of Arkansas, which included Missouri. Hindman, to Senator Johnson's delight, was ordered to report to court duty (sitting on a judge panel) east of the Mississippi River.[20]

Having dispensed with the Holmes–Hindman headache, the Price dilemma once again reared its head. In late 1862, Missouri Governor Claiborne Jackson died of natural causes while in Little Rock, which could not have been a disappointment to Davis. The mantle thus passed to Thomas Reynolds, who had already been warned by the Missouri congressional delegation to stop meddling in their business. Nonetheless, he arrived in Richmond in early January 1863, determined to get Price back to the trans-Mississippi. When he learned of the bad blood between Davis and the general, he quickly backed off. Price's name had been associated with a hair-brained congressional scheme to depose the president and later to the so-called Northwest Confederacy scheme, another absurd plot between Missouri and the Northwest states to form their own Confederacy with Price at their head. Price had not personally been involved in either instance, but his name was out there.[21]

Under the circumstances, Jackson assumed the role of negotiator rather than advocate. When Price arrived in the capital in late January, the governor attempted to convince him to return to Arkansas without the Missouri brigade, which would be returned as soon as possible. The general was hesitant, not only mistrusting the government but also wanting the Missouri brigade to become the nucleus of a new Missouri army. But this was the offer on the table, and Reynolds made it clear that he would not revive the State Guard. Under the circumstances, Price—who distrusted Reynolds's friendship with Davis—took the deal. Seddon happily rubber-stamped the agreement.[22]

Once in Arkansas, Holmes (still in command at that time) offered Price a division at Jacksonport. "Deacon" J. W. Tucker, editor of *The Argus* and of late the *Southern Crisis*, then in Jackson, Mississippi, was furious. Normally that would be inconsequential, but Tucker's inflammatory articles and letters to the editor were picked up in several papers, including the *Whig*. He thus had an influence well beyond his own circulation. Price "might as well for the time being be stationed in Australia," he bemoaned. It was all due to that "old imbecile" Holmes. Price "chafes like a caged eagle" to lead an offensive into Missouri, but he was prevented. Tucker claimed that a former U.S. senator had related to him that Holmes had "not the capacity, unaided, to take a carriage and horses and make his way out of Arkansas."[23]

When the War Department assigned Kirby Smith to the trans-Mississippi, it was with the clear intention of shifting strategy. The department had always been and would continue to exist in a supporting role, but the pending crisis at Vicksburg now took priority. Ideally, he would "throw troops across the river," but at the least he should create a diversion, strike at Union bases, or harass shipping. Smith assured his cooperation. He arrived in Little Rock in early March 1863 and found matters generally stabilizing following the Prairie Grove debacle. Nonetheless, there were only two field divisions in the state, each with 5,000 troops. Price predictably pushed for a Missouri invasion as a diversion to draw enemy troops away from Vicksburg. Holmes, fearful that the Arkansas Valley would be left undefended, opposed the move. Smith agreed with Holmes and retained Walker's Division in Arkansas, rather than dispatch it to Louisiana, where Taylor was being heavily pressed. Reynolds was nonetheless pleased with the turn of events. Using Preston Johnston as his conduit to the president, Reynolds wrote: "Do not feel much anxiety about us over here. There have been great blunders & great deficiencies, but croakers have exaggerated them. Kirby Smith is emphatically the right man at the right place."[24]

In mid-April, Smith received word that Nathaniel P. Banks's 18,000-man Union army at Baton Rouge was advancing west toward Berwick Bay. Taylor, who had fewer than 4,000 troops, could do little to check the advance. Rather than assisting Pemberton, Smith now pleaded with Cooper to get reinforcements from Port Hudson! It was wishful thinking; Pemberton was in no position to offer assistance. With Banks closing on Alexandria and the Union navy steaming up the Red River, Smith declared Fort DeRussy untenable and moved his forces to Shreveport. In mid-May, Banks marched down the Red River and advanced on Port Hudson.[25]

Unfortunately, communications were poor and rumors filled the vacuum. A press report in June related that Smith, with 10,000 troops, had captured Grant's supply base at Milliken's Bend, Louisiana, and that it would not take long for the Vicksburg siege to be raised. Other stories claimed that the general was instead at Port Hudson with 18,000 troops and had scored a major victory. A "tolerably authentic report" indicated that Price, with an army of 17,000, had captured Helena. An entire black regiment, along with its white officers, had been executed. None of the stories panned out. An assault by a Texas brigade had been repulsed at Milliken's. Smith had in fact not been at Port Hudson; the garrison had repulsed a May 27 attack on their own. Taylor had reportedly captured the Union railhead at Brashear City (Morgan City), west of New Orleans, along with its garrison, which included, according to press accounts, 1,800 prisoners (actually 1,300), 7,000 arms (2,500), and 16 (11) guns. As for the July 4 attack on Helena, Davis, as late as July 15, had heard only rumors. Eventually he received Holmes's dispatch announcing his defeat with a loss 1,636, not the 500 reported in the press. He never desired the attack, he claimed, but Senator Johnson told him "that you [Davis] had expressed surprise that it had not been done." He especially blamed the defeat on Price, whom he considered "utterly and entirely worthless in the field."[26]

Smith's temporary transfer of Walker's Division and James C. Tappen's Brigade to northern Louisiana raised the ire of Senator Johnson, who repeated the now-familiar refrain that Arkansas was being abandoned. Gorgas fired back that his department had kept up a steady flow of material. Between February and May 1863, ordnance shipments to the trans-Mississippi included 28,235 muskets (5,000 of which were captured in transit), 9,651 rifles, 304 carbines, 823 shotguns, and 130 Colt revolvers. An additional 6,000 arms went to Texas through the blockade. Other ordnance included 39 field guns, four 20-pounder Parrott rifles, 2,225,000 rounds of small arms ammunition, 1,138,000 percussion caps, 14,705 rounds of field artillery ammunition, 1,238 rounds of siege artillery ammunition, in addition to a large assortment of knapsacks, canteens, and haversacks. About two-thirds of the material and nearly all of the artillery went to Arkansas.[27]

Davis's patience with the relentless anti-administration senator was nearing an end. "Your letter [of June 18] found me in the depth of gloom in which the disasters on the Mississippi have shrouded our cause," he wrote. Under the circumstances "it pained me to observe how far your confidence was shaken and your criticism severe on men who I think deserve to be trusted." The president lectured the Arkansan that "we must all cling together, judge charitably of each other, and strive to bear and forebear." He dismissed the talk of a trans-Mississippi separatist movement as "mad" and "suicidal."[28]

In the end, Smith's attempts failed to check Grant and relieve the Vicksburg garrison. The enemy may have Vicksburg, rationalized the *Enquirer*, but it not have the Mississippi River. Jones was nonetheless under no delusion. On July 19, he sadly noted: "Texas, Louisiana, and Arkansas are now isolated, and no protection can be given them, by the government here." In a report to the War Department, Taylor noted that Vicksburg *might* have been relieved from the trans-Mississippi but that "the whole situation was treated with levity." Seddon agreed that the greater blame for the city's loss came from Smith, not Johnston![29]

Davis apprised Smith of the fall of Vicksburg and Port Hudson, which presented "not merely a military but also a political problem." Rumors persisted of a separatist movement by the trans-Mississippi states. "Unreasonable men think that they have been neglected," the president continued, "and timid men may hope that they can make better terms for themselves if their cause is not combined with that of the Confederacy." It was hoped that Smith could squash the separatist whispers, which were especially active in Arkansas, and keep them from spreading.[30]

Faced with geographic isolation, Smith called a meeting of political dignitaries in Marshall, Texas, on August 15. Among the attendees were Governor F. R. Lubbock and Senator Oldham of Texas, Governor Moore of Louisiana, Reynolds of Missouri, and Senators Johnson and Charles Mitchell of Arkansas. It was a necessary conference, but not one without risks. Smith was popular in the trans-Mississippi, but Reynolds wrote Richmond that he feared matters could always take a "dangerous political direction." He also made mention of "*political* generals," a not-so-veiled reference to Price. The subsequent meeting took on an organizational tone, with committees assigned to discuss a series of issues ranging from Smith's civil authority to recruitment, communications with Mexico and the French, and logistics. It was the beginning of a de facto fiefdom run by Kirby Smith.[31]

In late July 1863, Holmes, stricken with a severe headache and clearly shaken by his disastrous repulse at Helena, took sick leave. Price, who was placed in command of the division, soon faced trouble. The loss of Vicksburg meant that the Federals sent reinforcements to occupied Helena. A 10,500-man column under General Frederick Steele advanced on Little Rock. Civilians in Richmond (and, for that matter, the administration) were kept abreast only by sparse news accounts. A Northern article, reprinted in the *Enquirer* of August 19, noted that Price "is said to be in a dangerous situation." By early September, again via the Yankee press, Price was reported to be in full retreat, a story dismissed by the *Enquirer*. With only 7,700 troops to check the advance, Old Pap abandoned the city on September 10. The *Enquirer* reported the news five days later. Holmes resumed command on September 25 and promptly lambasted Price for having abandoned the state capital without a fight. Price made his case to Senator Johnson, and Holmes (at least according to the Missourian) retracted his "slanderous" statements.[32]

Governor Flannigan meanwhile fired off yet another letter to Richmond stating that Kirby Smith clearly intended to write off Arkansas in favor of Louisiana. Smith had not said that in so many words, but the implication was there. Davis denied the assertion, but he wrote to Smith stating that much discontent could be avoided by not revealing his hand to the complaining governor. In a reference to the separatist movement, the president noted that "timid men" might conclude that they could make a better deal than with the Confederacy. Adding to the president's headaches, Senator Henry was now urging that McCown be restored to command and assigned to the trans-Mississippi, adding yet one more washed-out general to what was fast becoming a dumping ground. The McCown request was fortunately rejected.[33]

On September 24, the Richmond papers hailed a stunning Southern victory three weeks earlier at Sabine Pass, Texas, which saved Houston from occupation. According to the reports, a single Irish artillery company, the name of which, the "Jeff Davis Guards," must have brought a smile to the president, had fought back an expedition of four gunboats and twenty transports with 10,000 (actually 5,000) troops. So easy was the victory that Taylor suspicioned that it must have been a feint.[34]

Smith's end-of-month letter to Davis, conveyed by Senator Johnson, offered a bleak outlook. The despondency of civilians and the desertions among the ranks indicated both "despair" and "abandonment." The enemy force at Little Rock was estimated at 25,000, against which Holmes had only 7,000 troops, and those were in an appalling condition. As for Louisiana, Taylor's 10,000 faced a Federal force at Berwick Bay comprising of Bank's army reinforced by two of Sherman's corps. It was further reported that Sherman intended to march with the balance of his army against either Shreveport or Camden. These combined forces would total 80,000, against which Taylor could muster perhaps 15,000. It was possible that by winter the occupation of Arkansas, Louisiana, and the coast of Texas would be a fait accompli. If all of this were not enough, Holmes and Price were again at loggerheads. One of them had to go—Smith recommended Holmes, to be replaced by Buckner.[35]

News was slowly arriving in Richmond of the bloody guerrilla raids led by William Quantrell. Word was that he "collected some thousands of desperate men[] and *killed* several regiments of the enemy." They also burned several Union towns and captured Booneville. "These are the men against whom Kansas Abolitionists have sworn vengeance—no quarter is to be granted them. I suspect they are granting no quarter!" noted Jones. No mention was ever made in the press of the Lawrence, Kansas, raid and the massacre of scores of men. The purpose of all of Quantrell's raids was simple: revenge-killing and plunder.[36]

12

The Hollow Winds of Autumn

Matters remained quiet in Tennessee throughout April and May 1863—at least on the battlefield. Polk's and Hardee's Kentucky Campaign after-action reports were made public, and Bragg—predictably—did not come off well. The old feuds were reignited. Writing directly to the president, Bragg expressed his ire that "confidential conferences of the generals" had been released for public consumption. "No harmony can ever prevail in any army where these buncombe reports are made for the public, instead of a simple narrative of facts for the War Office." The *Enquirer* meanwhile lifted a story from the Union-controlled Nashville papers that "upon perfectly reliable authority" General Breckinridge, on April 19, killed Bragg in Tullahoma in a "personal matter." Breckinridge, of course, did not actually kill Bragg; he only wished him dead. A nonetheless accurate report, ripe with gossip, made public the death of Major General Earl Van Dorn—shot by a jealous husband. Van Dorn, well known about Richmond as "a horrible rake," received little sympathy.[1]

The June 27 *Whig* repeated an editorial from the *Appeal* that the enemy had made no progress in Middle Tennessee since last winter and boldly predicted "nor is he likely to make any." The armchair generals once again got it wrong. In late June, Rosecrans easily punched through Bragg's advance line and occupied Hoover Gap and Liberty Gap. Events now occurred in rapid succession. On June 27, Richmond became aware that Bragg had fallen back to Tullahoma, and by July 2 his army was at the Elk River. As matters developed, confusing and totally false press accounts then indicated that Rosecrans had fallen back and that the Southerners had reoccupied Tullahoma. Nonetheless, on

July 4, as Pemberton surrendered Vicksburg 450 miles distant, Bragg notified Cooper that the army had retreated to the Tennessee River, a move that was completed by July 8. Jones fretted that Bragg was "in no condition to face Rosecrans." In less than two weeks, all of Middle Tennessee had been lost, and by the third week of August most of the Army of Tennessee was deployed around Chattanooga. Bragg reported his casualties as "trifling," but a subsequent ordnance tally listed the loss of 6,000 arms and 200,000–300,000 rounds of small arms—all with barely a shot having been fired! A dispirited Kean believed that the entire West was now open to the enemy.[2]

The reaction in the capital proved remarkably mute. The South was still reeling from the twin disasters at Gettysburg and Vicksburg, and such events in Tennessee went largely overlooked in the shock of the moment. A *Chattanooga Rebel* editorial, reprinted in the *Whig*, declared that the retreat had been inevitable. Bragg held a sixteen-mile overextended line with too few troops. Despite the territorial loss, it was doubtful if Rosecrans would attempt any further movement. As to the reaction in Richmond, the *Whig* admitted: "To this hour, we venture to affirm that the majority of our citizens are quite in the dark as to the great change that has occurred in Tennessee." Perhaps there would have been a greater reaction had the city "not been absorbed in anxiety about the battle of Gettysburg[] and had been better acquainted with [Tennessee] geography." Truth be known, the Tennessee events evoked "scarcely a comment" on the streets.[3]

What drew the capital's attention were the exploits of Nathan Bedford Forrest and John Hunt Morgan. That summer the Federals, led by Abel Streight, launched a raid against Rome, Georgia. In a masterpiece of deception and boldness, Forrest captured the entire 1,600-man brigade, earning him the thanks of Congress. Unfortunately, a subsequent dispute between the general and one of his lieutenants led to Forrest being seriously, though not fatally, shot. Morgan meanwhile led a 2,500-man brigade in an Indiana raid, creating havoc in the Union rear. Kean labeled it "one of the most remarkable smaller events of the war," and Ruffin thought it "unprecedented for its boldness." With the brigade so deep into enemy territory, however, Jones fretted that "they may be lost." He was right; the cocky cavalier got his command captured.[4]

Davis, only July 26, received a dispatch from Polk in which he floated a strategically difficult and logistically challenging idea. If Grant's and Banks's now uncommitted armies merged, the Mobile garrison and Johnston's small army would inevitably be overrun. The bishop therefore proposed a concentration of Bragg's, Johnston's, and Buckner's forces (70,000–80,000) to go on the offensive against Rosecrans's 60,000, then seize Memphis and neutralize Federal operations in the trans-Mississippi. Mobile and Alabama would necessarily have to be risked. Such a concentration would cause Mississippi and Alabama congressmen to howl, but something obviously had to be done. Under the circumstances, Cooper asked Bragg whether he would he go on the offensive if such a concentration were to occur. Bragg initially seemed agreeable, but in subsequent consultation with Johnston, who opposed the strategy, he backed down. A concentration of his and Johnston's armies would total only 50,000. Rosecrans was believed to have 60,000, and Burnside's returning army from Mississippi would doubtless add 30,000. The figures on file in the War Department, however, gave Bragg a present-for-duty strength of 40,000, Johnston 26,000, and Buckner 15,000 for a total of 81,000. Seddon wanted Davis to order an offensive, but the president refused to force the issue.[5]

By August 22, word had reached the War Department, through both intelligence and news reports, that Burnside's army was preparing to march into East Tennessee. Johnston, upon Seddon's request, boarded six brigades of 9,000 troops on the cars to reinforce Bragg. "This signifies battle," noted Jones. As August concluded, Richmond citizens were well aware that the Federals were bearing down on Knoxville. "Fears are expressed by correspondents from that region [East Tennessee], and I fear too well founded, that our forces will be defeated, & Chattanooga, Knoxville, & all East Tennessee occupied by the enemy. Indeed[,] Knoxville is said to be in imminent danger—& its capture is already rumored," related a shaken Ruffin. Despite jittery nerves, by the first week in September all was quiet in Knoxville; Bragg reported that Burnside was sixty miles distant.[6]

By early September, it had been eight months since the president had visited the West. Preston Johnston suggested that perhaps it was time for a return visit. The president initially considered going, yet with other matters pressing, the trip was delayed three weeks. By that time, western matters had measurably altered.[7]

Rosecrans's army was moving fast. Bragg's August 22 dispatch to Cooper stated the Army of the Cumberland was on "this side of the mountains" and that Chattanooga had been shelled by advanced enemy cavalry units on August 21. The papers reported that little damage had been done and that the city remained in Confederate possession. Enemy cavalry feints had been made twenty miles above Harrison, Tennessee, northeast of Chattanooga, but Northern articles placed Rosecrans's main army at Stevenson, Alabama, thirty-two miles from Chattanooga.[8]

Despite Northern press accounts, from all information received at the War Department, Rosecrans and Burnside were moving to juncture. Buckner's forces in the Knoxville area were withdrawn to Chattanooga, resulting in Federal troops taking possession of Knoxville. With attention focused on Bragg's right, civilian authorities were shocked to learn on September 5 that the bluecoats had instead crossed the Tennessee River *below* Chattanooga and were advancing on Rome, Georgia. "Your success must depend upon fighting the enemy in detail," Davis urgently advised. If he could not attack the column moving against Rome, then he should "detach a sufficient force to crush the small army [Burnside]," ignoring the fact that the "small army" could always withdraw. In the meantime, Johnston sent two additional brigades (2,500 troops) to Atlanta, and the Georgia militia was activated.[9]

With two-thirds of Rosecrans's army well over forty miles southwest of Chattanooga and crossing the Lookout Mountain range, Bragg had little choice but to abandon the city. The Federals took possession on September 9. Senator Haynes notified the president of the news, stating: "I have no other intelligence of this, and [I] hope it is exaggerated." Gorgas was left shaking his head: "Bragg has shown his usual readiness for retreating, and has retreated us out of the whole of East Tenn., Rosecrans being in possession of Chattanooga, & Burnside of Knoxville, without the pulling of a trigger." The *Enquirer* expressed outrage. "As long as General Bragg commands in that Department, the public will not expect other than defeat. He has lost Tennessee, and this is enough for one man. Cannot another be tried?" The editor quickly answered his own question: "General Longstreet, Lee's right arm, the Massena of Northern Virginia, quiet, unpretending, unobtrusive, would revive confidence, drive Rosecrans back, and soon redeem Kentucky. . . . Try 'old Pete.'" Senator Henry also lobbied for Longstreet. The loss of East Tennessee was worse than the loss of "fifty Charlestons." "I think Bragg exhausts himself in organizing his army[] and that Buckner has not developed that dogged resolution that wins victories," he bluntly wrote Seddon.[10]

The idea of sending large-scale reinforcements from the Army of Northern Virginia was nothing new. It had been considered when

Vicksburg was in dire straits but was shelved at the time in favor of Lee's invasion of the North. Now that his army was safely back in Virginia, Lee wished to again assume the offensive; Davis had other ideas. The general was summoned to the capital for two weeks of consultations, much of it spent on horseback as Lee and the president inspected the Richmond defenses. Davis initially appeared to acquiesce to Lee's renewed offensive, but the strategic and political pressures proved so intense that he decided instead to reinforce the West. Indeed, he desired Lee to go and command a concentrated western army. The general politely begged off, and Davis reluctantly agreed. It was ultimately decided that two reinforced divisions of Longstreet's Corps would be sent, with Pickett's Division, decimated in the disastrous charge at Gettysburg, remaining to guard the capital.[11]

At this point a strange lapse of communication occurred. The *Dispatch* reported the capture of Knoxville on September 3, yet Longstreet remained in the dark and continued formulating plans to go through East Tennessee. Not until September 8 did Davis inform Lee that Knoxville was in Union possession. Longstreet's 15,000 troops thus had to traverse a circuitous 950-mile route through the Carolinas to Savannah, then to Atlanta, and finally north to Chattanooga. What would have required two to four days thus turned into seven to eleven days. The first train departed Richmond at 8 p.m. on September 8, followed by 1,700 troops the next evening and 1,800 in the morning the day after that. Despite the news blackout, Richmonders clearly saw troops flooding into the city: "It is said for Tennessee," wrote Jones. Seddon disclaimed any knowledge of the capital rumor that Lee was going to the West. "That may be true," thought Jones, but a corps of his army was "already marching thitherward." On September 13, Ruffin received a letter from a Petersburg friend telling him of the troop trains passing through that town. The president was heard to exclaim to a circle of friends at the capital that he was determined to "snatch Tennessee from the clutches of the Abolitionists, if it took the united armies of the South to accomplish it."[12]

In a dispatch dated September 6, Bragg informed the War Department that Rosecrans had crossed the Tennessee River and was advancing on Rome. There was no communication beyond Loudon, Tennessee, and Burnside's position was unknown. Luck now smiled on the Southerners. It became clear that Burnside was content not to venture far beyond Knoxville. With Confederate reinforcements rapidly arriving,

Bragg was in position to strike Rosecrans's widely scattered corps. He focused on the enemy's center corps, but bungling generals (Daniel H. Hill, Hindman, and Buckner) foiled the trap at McLemore's Cove on September 10. A second opportunity occurred on September 13, when Polk was ordered to annihilate Rosecrans's left wing, but he refused to attack. These incidents received scant notice in the capital press at the time; Jones and Kean never mentioned them. The rare articles that appeared were mostly from Northern papers claiming that Bragg was continuing to retreat. The general's dispatch of September 18 nonetheless made it appear that a battle was looming.

The president was pulled out of Sunday worship on September 20 and for three hours huddled with Seddon and Cooper. A report indicated that the enemy occupied Bristol, Tennessee, on the Virginia & Tennessee Railroad. About 1,300 cavalry stormed into town, burned some buildings, and tore up rails. Four major railroad bridges, including the one at Bristol, remained out of commission from the enemy raid of the previous December, and the Federals apparently intended them to stay that way.[13]

The East Tennessee news paled to the jaw-dropping dispatch that arrived from Bragg the next day. A major two-day battle had been fought on September 19 and 20 along the banks of Chickamauga Creek in northwestern Georgia. The enemy had been driven from the field with a loss of 2,500 prisoners and twenty guns. There was cautious optimism. Seddon did not think that it was possible for Longstreet's Corps to have yet arrived. "We await the sequel—with fear and trembling, after the sad experience [misrepresentation] of Western victories," Jones admitted. As late as September 23, the *Dispatch* was still expressing skepticism. Although there appeared to have been a great victory, "there is a feeling of uncertainty in this community, who will but remember Murfreesborough, and know the glorious promise of one day was turned to sorrow by the dispatch of the next." Even the pro-administration *Sentinel* was tentative in its joyful expression: "We trust that fortune is not to tantalize us at Chickamauga, as at Shiloh and Corinth[] and Murfreesborough."[14]

But Chickamauga was not Murfreesboro. At 11 a.m. on September 21, Governor Harris telegraphed: "Our victory is complete!" Jones believed that the effect would be "electrical." Bragg's September 24 dispatch claimed 7,000 prisoners, 2,000 of whom were wounded, 25 stands of colors, 36 pieces of artillery, and 15,000 small arms. "The hollow winds of autumn are almost upon him [Rosecrans]," observed the *Sentinel*. The *New York Tribune*, declaring Chickamauga one of the greatest battles of the war, acknowledged the defeat. Rosecrans had fallen back to Chattanooga. and as of 9 p.m. on September 25 the Army of Tennessee was reportedly near there. Casualties on both sides were horrific: 10,000–15,000 for the Confederates and 25,000–30,000 for the Federals, later adjusted to a still-overinflated 20,000 and 5,000 prisoners. By the end of the month Bragg conceded that his losses would exceed a breathtaking 18,000 casualties.[15]

Congratulatory letters were sent to Bragg from his congressional supporters. Senator Semmes wrote of the general's "twofold victory—one over the enemy & the other over detractors and calumny." Pugh likewise hailed the victory, accomplished "under the pressure of hostile editors and correspondents, croakers, worthless officers, and trashy soldiers." Swan visited the army twice post-Chickamauga and submitted a letter to the *Enquirer* in response to its editorial that the general had no support in the army. On the contrary, wrote the representative: He had mingled with officers and soldiers alike, and to a person they expressed unequivocal confidence in Bragg.[16]

Critics soon began to consider Chickamauga an unacceptable half-victory. Rosecrans's defeated army had been allowed to escape to the defenses of Chattanooga, while Bragg occupied the heights stretching six miles from Lookout Mountain to Missionary Ridge outside town. Harris related that a victory had not been won and that a severe battle would be fought the next day. Gorgas expressed concern: "As however we do not hear that Rosecrans has abandoned Chattanooga the fruits of so great a victory are not yet reaped, and the people are still in a state of anxious suspense, fearing that all this bloodshed may have been in vain, and that Tennessee may not be recovered." The Federals would obviously send reinforcements and at some point "may become too strong to dislodge." "Sallust," the pen name of the anti-Bragg correspondent of the *Dispatch*, wrote what many were thinking: "Possibly an energetic pursuit Monday [September 21] would have compelled them to recross the river." As it became increasingly clear that there was no prospect of dislodging Rosecrans, Gorgas wrote in exasperation: "[T]he blood of 5[,]000 poor fellows has been shed in vain." An anonymous soldier correspondent wrote a letter to the *Whig* in which he declared the campaign "a failure" and the battle, "though a victory," was "not a success." The paper lamented: "Grave mistakes have been committed—rare opportunities lost—and the fruits of a splendid victory entirely thrown away."[17]

The raw manpower and industrial complex of the United States now became apparent. Grant replaced Rosecrans as commander, and reports arrived on Seddon's desk, also reported in the press, of heavy Union reinforcements on the way to Chattanooga—16,000 from Sherman's now idle army at Vicksburg, two corps under Joseph Hooker from the Army of the Potomac, and Burnsides's Army of the Ohio finally marching from East Tennessee. On the afternoon of September 30, the president summoned Cooper and Seddon to discuss the turn of events. Having won the battle, Bragg could soon be on the defensive.[18]

Bragg did in fact go on the offensive—just not against the Yankees. Writing directly to the president, he unleashed on Hill for the bungled McLemore's Cove affair. He denounced the corps commander as "despondent, dull, slow," and "always in a state of apprehension." He also considered him a constant croaker "who does not hesitate at all times and in all places to declare our cause lost." Bragg also continued his attack on Polk, who at Chickamauga had failed for hours to launch an assault ordered for sunrise on September 20. The bishop in turn blamed Hill. As for Bragg, he was perfectly content to blame them both. He considered Polk "luxurious in his habits," as someone who "rises late, moves slowly, and always conceived his plans the best—He has proved an injury to us on every field where I have been associated with him."[19]

Hill requested a court of inquiry, which Cooper promptly denied. There were no charges pending; he had simply been relieved of command. The president's acquiescence made Hill suspicious that Davis desired to make him a scapegoat to protect Polk and also because he desired a corps command for Pemberton, who had suddenly shown up in camp. Representative Dargan got wind of the Pemberton's presence and wrote Seddon that if the failed general received a new command "our cause is ruined beyond reputation." As for Polk, he was placed under arrest and ordered to Atlanta, Davis's plea to "overlook the offense" notwithstanding. The bishop did not take it laying down. Firing off a letter to Davis, he denounced Bragg as an incompetent who had allowed Rosecrans's defeated army to slip the noose.[20]

The trouble was not over. Hindman was suspended temporarily from command, and Forrest submitted his resignation. Davis intervened by transferring Forrest to Mississippi and West Tennessee. As for Hindman, the *Whig* dismissed him as "no loss to any army." Davis, anxious about the growing tensions, sent his aide Colonel James Chesnut to investigate. The colonel had barely arrived when he dispatched Davis on October 5: "Your immediate presence in this army is urgently demanded." Realizing the gravity of the situation, Davis made immediate plans to travel to the West. Meanwhile, Longstreet—who clearly coveted Bragg's job—sent Seddon a damning letter about the army commander. "I scarcely hope anything from the President's visit," Kean admitted. "He temporizes too much, takes took long to make up his mind, [and] is as much wanting in vigor as his enemies say he is in amenability to public opinion."[21]

Davis's western visit was widely reported in the capital, but the reason behind the tour could only be speculated. Was he going to mingle with the troops, questioned the *Dispatch*, or resolve an internal cabal? Rumors filled the news vacuum. An Army of Tennessee correspondent claimed that the news had "leaked out" that Bragg related to the president that if he wished to relieve him "it would take an immense burden from his shoulders." But if Bragg was relieved, who would take his place? The *Enquirer* pressed for Joe Johnston, but the *Dispatch* believed that it would "likely be by either Lee or Longstreet." "Sallust" of the *Dispatch* surprisingly reported that the president had sustained Bragg and that Hill had been ordered to Richmond and replaced by Breckinridge. One army correspondent reported a "camp rumor" that Davis had offered Pemberton a corps command but that he had turned it down. An agitated Senator Henry fired off a letter to Seddon that the Tennessee troops would mutiny if Pemberton was given a corps.[22]

As Davis continued his tour by traveling to Mississippi, Kean took stock of what occurred. "No fruits of his visit to the army at Chattanooga have yet transpired," he wrote on October 18. "I confess I do not look for any. He is not a man of quick and vigorous resolves and none others are likely to yield fruit worth the plucking. . . . It is one month tomorrow since the battle of Chickamauga and the fruits are almost *nil*." As the word of Bragg's retention slowly became public, Senator Orr, the general's longtime critic, expressed his disdain: "The President's attachment for Genl. Bragg could be likened to nothing else than the blind & gloating love of a mother for a deformed & misshapen offspring."[23]

Although the president was still absent, Seddon got wind of a troubling officer's cabal in the Army of Tennessee. Davis acknowledged that there had been a "conversation," but he dismissively added that it was "of little importance." It was the *Enquirer* that got the scoop. Somehow the news leaked out that anti-Bragg generals had "memorialized" their opposition in a signed document. Breckinridge and Longstreet did not add their signatures, being "restrained by considerations of personal delicacy," but in fact Longstreet did. The paper sounded an alarming warning: "A separation must take place; either General Bragg must cease to command the army, or, we fear, the army will soon refuse to be commanded by Gen. Bragg." Jones saw trouble brewing. Davis sustained Bragg "in spite of the tremendous prejudice against him in and out of the army." Unless the general made some spectacular move by the end of November, when Congress would again be in session, there would be more "clamor against the government than ever." Already the political pressure was beginning to mount, with Henry remarking that Bragg remained, in his words, "on very bad terms with his officers." The president, concluded Kean, nonetheless "seems fatally bent on retaining him."[24]

The *Enquirer* ran yet another article about the troubling meeting that took place between Davis and certain generals. According to "a friend" who was an eyewitness, the corps commanders met with the president and Bragg at army headquarters. Longstreet was asked to give his frank opinion of the late campaign. According to the insider, the general did not mince words. From the hour he arrived on the scene, he saw that Bragg "was not the man to command an army." His disposition of troops was "horrible" and his tactics "wretched." If the president did not remove him, then he wished to be sent back to Virginia. Other generals said the same and likewise asked to be relived. D. H. Hill called Bragg a "personal coward," words that deeply grieved the president. Whether or not the reporting was accurate (the accounts differed), it was clear that bitter internal quarreling was occurring at the highest levels in the Army of Tennessee. Jones read the handwriting on the wall: "It was necessary perhaps to have a scapegoat," he wrote in reference to Hill. "Bragg will *probably* be sustained by the President—but then what will become of *P*[olk], who is so inimical [harmful] to Bragg." It was too late, however. In what one historian would later term Davis's "fateful—and terrible—decision," Bragg retained his command.[25]

The same cold northwest wind and rain that caused homes in Richmond to light their first log fires on October 24 also swept through Chattanooga, creating misery among the ranks. According to a soldier who submitted an account to the *Whig*, the hillsides around the army were rapidly being stripped for fuel. A citizen who was able to slip past the

Yankee lines related that only three hundred civilians remained in town. A considerable number of Confederate deserters had come into the city, and they were promptly put to digging trenches alongside the blacks.[26]

By early November, the *Whig* was predicting—"Just intimations," mind you—that Grant would soon be making his move. The assault could come from the Army of the Cumberland making a frontal assault, or that army might feint and the actual move would be in Bragg's southern rear. In a reprinted editorial from the *Charleston Courier*, future maneuvers appeared vague. Some in the army were predicting a Federal flank attack by way of Bridgeport or Shellmound, others that the Yankees were content to do nothing until spring. If Grant did anything, the paper predicted, "it will be to take possession of Lookout Mountain."[27]

On November 12, Seddon received a lengthy letter from the Georgia politician Howell Cobb, writing from Atlanta. He had just returned from the Army of Tennessee and happily reported that there was a renewed spirit in the army since the president's trip. Nonetheless, there needed to be improved relations (as Jones worded it) between "Bragg and _____, his _____," an apparent reference to Polk, his second-in-command. He also thought that "Generals *B* [Buckner] and *C* [Cheatham] might be relieved without detriment," if they could not improve their relations with the army commander. Colonel Isaac St. John, who headed the Nitre and Mining Bureau, nonetheless shared a letter that he had received from Captain John Clarke, one of Longstreet's engineer officers, who believed that the "same state of hopeless distrust" continued in the army. Davis's answer to the growing army intrigue was to swap Hardee (then in Mississippi) and Polk. His letter to Polk dismissing all charges was released to the *Whig* for publication. Hindman's suspension was likewise voided.[28]

Union reinforcements were known to be rapidly arriving. From atop Lookout Mountain, a Southern correspondent could see "a long, dark column of troops . . . moving steadily up Lookout Valley." In embarrassingly short order, Grant reopened a supply line via Brown's Ferry, effectively lifting the siege, which even at its height had never been totally effective. A subsequent attack by Longstreet failed to close the so-called Cracker Line, causing Davis to express his "bitter disappointment." "It is much regretted that the rains have interfered with your projected operations upon your left flank," the president began his letter of October 29. "It is reported here [Richmond] that the enemy are crossing at Bridgeport." If nothing substantive could be accomplished on his left, could Bragg detach Longstreet's two divisions to drive Burnside from Knoxville? Communications could then be reestablished with the capital and Longstreet would be closer to Lee, who was growing nervous about increased enemy strength.[29]

The suggestion may also have had political overtones. Senator Henry had been pressing for an East Tennessee offensive. Failing to grasp the complexities of logistics and strategy, he had suggested that Lieutenant General Richard "Dick" Ewell's corps from Lee's army could be detached to drive Burnside from Knoxville. Once successful, Ewell could then proceed down the Tennessee River and unite with Johnston's army in Mississippi for operations in Rosecrans's rear. The defense of Virginia, he argued, should be made in Tennessee. Even if the capital was invested in the meantime, Lee could hold out for six months. By that time the combined western army could relieve Richmond and the war could be closed out in a "blaze of glory." It was an impracticable if not absurd idea, but Lee—in a vintage Lee reply—answered that the strategy, though intriguing, would currently prove unfeasible. Davis continued to hope that the same thing (or at least the East Tennessee portion of it) could be accomplished by Longstreet.[30]

In early November, Bragg saw an opening: perhaps a quick strike at Burnside would force Grant to detach troops from Chattanooga. It was risky. Detaching Longstreet's two divisions (12,500 troops), plus Wheeler's cavalry (5,000), during a Union buildup in his front was controversial. Once the campaign was underway, the troops could not be quickly recalled. Bragg nonetheless thought that he could hold Lookout Mountain and Missionary Ridge without Longstreet, and it would be the perfect way to be rid of the irksome corps commander.[31]

With Congress currently not in session, Senator Haynes—whose Knoxville home was now being used as a Federal headquarters and whose Jonesboro, Tennessee, summer house had been converted into a hospital—was now living in Wytheville, Virginia. In mid-November, he journeyed to the Army of Tennessee to get a firsthand view of affairs and keep the president abreast. He watched the enemy movements from atop Lookout Mountain, and it appeared to him that the bluecoats were no more near a battle than they were two weeks earlier. He then commented on the Bragg situation. "I have mixed freely with the army & have held free conversations with the officers," he wrote. "To say that there is no dissatisfaction in the army would not to be to tell the truth, but there is not as much as I expected to meet." The reorganization of the divisions, undertaken to separate the anti-Bragg element, had had a detrimental effect, including some desertions.[32]

Foote arrived back in Richmond on November 24, having been in the vicinity of Bragg's army. He claimed that Grant had 90,000 troops and Bragg 20,000–30,000, and he implied that disaster was unavoidable. The next day, November 25, a dispatch arrived from Bragg—and it did not bear good news. Federal forces had gained ground on Lookout Mountain, and a Confederate division had "suffered severely." Whether or not the mountain had been taken was not certain. In the War Department, the general belief existed that the Confederates would retreat. "To us it seems as if Bragg has been in a fog ever since the battle on the 20th of September," thought Jones. He winced at the thought of a potential disaster—and what it would mean for the administration. Davis had retained Bragg "when the whole country (as the press says) demanded his removal." "Sallust" submitted his article before the battle had concluded, but he declared that Lookout Mountain would probably be abandoned, "it being of little importance since the loss of Lookout Valley." Subsequent Northern articles vowed that the mountain had been taken "at the point of the bayonet" and that hundreds of Rebel prisoners had been taken.[33]

On November 26, a Thursday, Bragg's dispatch of the previous night arrived on Cooper's desk. It told of the unthinkable: "After several unsuccessful assaults on our lines today, the enemy carried the left center about 4 o'clock. The whole left soon gave way in considerable disorder." There were no specifics pertaining to losses, but that did not stop the *Whig* from releasing the news: "For the first time, in a great battle, Confederate troops have been put to flight by the enemy." The paper admitted the "painful spectacle of a whole wing of a Confederate army . . . breaking into a disorderly flight." Bragg's Friday dispatch related that a stand could not be made at Chickamauga Station and that the army continued to fall back. Seddon admitted how he knew nothing more than what he read in the papers.[34]

On the last day of the month, Bragg's dispatch of November 29 for the first time mentioned the word "disaster." Underscoring the magnitude of events, the general offered his resignation. It had been rumored that the cabinet had earlier broken in its support for the general, the majority being for removal. Davis now had no choice but to accept his resignation; Hardee was given temporary command. By that time, independent news sources were filling in the details. The *Whig* reported the loss of 5,000 prisoners and conceded that the Battle of Missionary Ridge had resulted in "little short of a rout." Soon Northern articles began to appear. George Thomas's dispatch to Halleck claimed 6,000 prisoners and forty guns, with Union losses totaling only 300 killed and 2,500 wounded. Subsequent Yankee reports claimed that Bragg's line atop the ridge was broken simultaneously at six points and the Rebels had been "utterly routed," although some continued to believe that such reports were exaggerated. There were no reliable updates by December 1, but private reports read by Ruffin claimed that Bragg had apparently lost eighteen guns and had been "compelled to retire," though the Union "suffered much the heavier loss of men." Senator Henry placed the losses at 1,000 prisoners and thirty guns, but Kean knew better: The army was not defeated; it disgracefully "ran away." By December 1, Jones had heard that Bragg's army had retired to Dalton, Georgia—"His army must be nearly broken up." The army in time would be rebuilt, surmised Gorgas, "but its morale is I fear badly shaken."[35]

Fury erupted in the capital over the shameful rout, and the rage was directed squarely at Davis. In the words of the *Whig:* "We find no fault with General Bragg. Doubtless he did the best he could. It is no fault of his that he has held a command for which he is incompetent." Several days later the paper added: "An army of asses led by a lion is better than an army of lions led by an ass." Daniel's *Enquirer* screamed its indignation: "We have no doubt that General Bragg has done the best he could, and for all the ill that has befallen him and us, Mr. Davis alone is responsible. . . . Let us hope that Mr. Davis is not weak enough to trifle longer with the interest of his country, and that he will immediately appoint some other man to command. . . . It would be difficult to find another, save perhaps Pemberton and Holmes, who would not inspire more confidence than General Bragg." On December 10 the paper questioned who was the "military genius" who ordered Longstreet to Knoxville at a time when Grant was being heavily reinforced.[36]

The House was called to order on December 6, the session opening with prayer by the Rev. Dr. Jeremiah B. Jeter of the Grace Street Baptist Church. Never one to miss an opportunity to voice his displeasure at the administration, Foote was quick to take the floor. Swan, he claimed, attempted to shift the blame of Davis by pointing to Johnston, who repeatedly wrote letters supporting Bragg. Foote understood that in the past there was a certain "delicacy in superseding a brother officer," but under the present circumstances "why is Johnston not now appointed? Why is not Beauregard? Why is that army left so long without a permanent commander?" He continued his rant. Bragg should have been replaced after Kentucky. He had been in the Army of Tennessee and mixed with officers and soldiers alike. He found "nothing but a feeling of distrust with Bragg." He had "made a martyr of Polk—he had calumniated the gallant Breckinridge." Furthermore, he was "on bad terms even with Hardee. This was well known." He charged the president with "gross misconduct in retaining his favorites in office."[37]

Davis added fuel to the fire by adopting Bragg's excuse for failure by censuring a portion of the army for its dismal conduct. In his address to Congress, the president stated that at Missionary Ridge "some of our troops inexplicably abandoned positions of great strength" and engaged in a "disorderly retreat." Both in the House and in a letter to the editor, Foote furiously denounced the president's remarks as "cruel" and "unpardonable," adding that there was not a dishonorable regiment in the Army of Tennessee. "[T]he President is himself the cause of that deplorable occurrence [i.e., the rout]." The public had long demanded that either Johnston or Beauregard be given command, but Davis stubbornly resisted. Swan had shown Foote a letter from Bragg stating that he would never be able to command effectively until he was rid of at least twelve brigadiers and a "full regiment of field officers." Then Foote told what the administration had attempted to keep quiet: "Sir, Gen. Bragg was so odious to this army[] that rumors, which I believe to be well-founded, assert that the whole body of the officers of rank who belonged to it[] besought the President to displace him." Doubtless Foote spoke what had been widely whispered.[38]

When Bragg's removal was announced, the *Dispatch* declared that he "ought to have been removed long since." The *Whig* was more brutal in its assessment. It stated that the rumor of Bragg's removal "was received with as much, or more, satisfaction by the public yesterday, than would the official news of a victory over the Yankees." Mary Chesnut happened to be visiting her husband in Richmond when she heard the news. "He has a winning way of earning everyone's detestation. Heaven! How they hate him."[39]

Congress convened on Monday, December 7—"They were in a very

Senator Robert "Bob" Johnson of Arkansas was part of the constantly carping trans-Mississippi political bloc. (Courtesy of the Arkansas State Archives)

bad humor," wrote Kean. The trouble, as usual, emanated from the western delegation. Senator Johnson introduced a bill on December 10 that would limit cabinet terms so that nominations would come every two years. "This is a direct attack upon Mr. Davis, so intended and regarded," wrote Kean. "If it passes, as Mr. Wigfall told me yesterday it probably will, it will be a radical change in the system of government." Kean was appalled, understanding that the heads of departments would "constantly be beholden to individual senators." The motion had been undertaken due to recent military losses, notably Chattanooga. The *Examiner* applauded the idea, but the *Dispatch* denounced it, claiming that it would be a violation of the separation of powers. Rumor had it that Davis would resign if the motion passed. Although the president ultimately won the congressional skirmish, Kean admitted that the president had lost most of his friends.[40]

Further stirring trouble was the resolution of Augustus R. Wright (Georgia-10) proposing that the president open peace negotiations with the United States. The proposal failed; sensing the backlash, he withdrew from Congress. Georgia Representative Warren Aiken was told by a member of the Kentucky delegation that "Wright would have been expelled from Congress if he had not left Richmond so suddenly." Aiken was glad he "left and prevented another topic for exciting newspaper articles."[41]

Back on November 18, the *Whig* had reported that Longstreet was across the Tennessee River at Loudon and that Wheeler's cavalry was within nine miles of Knoxville. The Confederates were closing on the enemy's works by November 22, and there were early reports that Burnside had abandoned the city along with 1,500 prisoners. "But as its capture has been falsely reported some half dozen times, I wait for positive proof," declared Ruffin.[42]

A siege was undertaken, but when Bragg's army was routed at Missionary Ridge, it spelled trouble. "Great fears for Gen. Longstreet's safety are felt," reported the *Whig* of December 2. "Three thousand of the enemy are advancing towards Knoxville from Cleveland [Tennessee]." By December 4, word had arrived at the War Department that Longstreet had been repulsed at Knoxville. The next day the talk was "prevalent on the streets" that the siege had been raised and Longstreet was withdrawing toward Virginia. The news remained mixed, however, and according to the *Dispatch* "nothing really definite or reliable" was known. Kean heard the whispers: with Bragg's army in retreat, Longstreet was "in a critical situation." Confirmation arrived on December 7: Longstreet was "flying from superior numbers." Ruffin expressed contempt: "It has been reported, for 10 or 12 times, that Longstreet had defeated Burnside, & taken Knoxville—& yesterday it was more confidently asserted than ever. Today [December 5] it has come out that the object, if not the army of Longstreet, has been defeated, & that he is retreating to Virginia."[43]

It was not until December 13 that Longstreet gave details. He had heard "rumors"—later confirmed by a captured document—that Grant was heavily reinforcing Burnside. A go-for-broke assault had been made on Fort Sanders, but it was bloodily repulsed with the loss of 700 (later increased to 813). Bragg instructed Longstreet to unite with the Army of Tennessee or, if unable, to return to Virginia. With the rail link between Bragg and Longstreet broken, the decision was eventually made to retire to Virginia.[44]

Richmond went through the façade of yet another joyous Christmas—the third one at war. The *Whig* believed that "people generally will be joyous and gleeful today, as they have ever been at Christmas." Yet there was too much suffering, and too many empty chairs at dinner tables never to be filled again, to fully believe the paper's admonition. It rained all day in Richmond on New Year's Day 1863. John Daniel sat down at his desk to pen his editorial to close out the year. As he reflected upon the disastrous losses at Gettysburg, at Vicksburg with the capture of an entire field army, and now Missionary Ridge, he concluded that it had been "the gloomiest year of our struggle."[45]

13

Crossing the Rubicon

Precisely what would become of Braxton Bragg following his resignation became fodder for capital chatterboxes. Assistant Adjutant General Samuel W. Melton told Kean in his stammering way that Bragg should become inspector general: "He would make us all howl but I'd be willing to howl if I could hear some other people howl too. We'd be a perfect menagerie." Gorgas heard that Bragg was willing to serve as Johnston's chief of staff, while the *Whig* reported that he would be replacing Seddon as secretary of war. Others claimed that Bragg and Johnston would swap armies, still others that he would supersede Kirby Smith in the trans-Mississippi.[1]

In a dispatch to Bragg on January 27, 1864, the president instructed the deposed general: "Come to Richmond, if your health permits. I wish to confer with you." It was bitter cold when the general arrived in mid-February, with the temperature rising to only 20 degrees by noon, freezing pipes in the Spotswood Hotel. Although the press took no note of his arrival, North Carolina congressmen—William Dortch in the Senate and Burgess Gaither in the House—welcomed their native son with resolutions offering an honorary chair in both chambers to observe the proceedings during his stay (a rather perfunctory gesture, as the Congress would adjourn in two days). Gorgas had the general to supper on February 16, along with Alabama Congressman Francis Lyon—"Bragg was talkative," noted the colonel. The *Enquirer* did not know precisely what Davis was up to but implored him in an editorial "not to dappen the enthusiasm of the people[] and dishearten them this early in the Spring by the appointment of Gen. Bragg to any important command, where he has no superior officer."[2]

On February 23 the president issued the poorly worded General Orders No. 23, which appeared to make Bragg general in chief of all Confederate armies. It was quickly clarified that he would serve as the president's military adviser. It was a risky move that created "quite a buzz" in Richmond. The *Examiner* erupted in anger, calling the decision "a bucket of water on a newly kindled gate." The paper sarcastically admitted that some would not go so far as it did, believing that Bragg might "make a tolerable brigadier." The *Whig*, likewise, went on a tirade, calling Bragg an "utterly 'played out' officer" who was "floating about." He would be used "as a mere tool to force the public into acquiescence with the President's partial opinion of his abilities." Seddon, who did not need assistance a year ago, would now end up "playing second fiddle to Gen. Bragg." Wigfall likewise carped that Bragg's appointment was "discourteous" to Seddon. The paper also noted the peculiar timing of the appointment—right as Congress adjourned. Davis, according to Jones, shrugged off the criticism. Indeed, the president privately reveled in "triumphing thus over the popular sentiment, which just at this time is much adverse to Gen. Bragg. The President is naturally a little oppugnant."[3]

To be sure, there were supporters. The *Dispatch* claimed that the other papers in town had created a "tempest in a teapot." Lee, Cooper, and Seddon had all been consulted in advance of the appointment and had given their support. Even the *Enquirer*, which only two days earlier had disapproved any assignment of the general, now hypocritically fell into line. The paper found the assignment to be "very proper" and the general "eminently fit." It reminded the public that the appointment would be "under the President" and that he would not outrank Lee or Johnston. Bragg would not be a commander in chief with executive authority but would merely take work off Seddon and Cooper. Skeptics predicted trouble.[4]

When Congress reconvened in May, the issue of Bragg's appointment came before the Senate. Orr, a longtime critic, expressed opposition to approving the general's salary. The argument soon became personal. The South Carolinian declared that the general was not "fit for any other position than that of a commandant of a camp of instruction" and that his appointment was discourteous to Seddon. Sparrow rose to say that the legislation before the body should not be influenced by personal feeling; the only issue to be resolved was that of pay. Orr replied that he was not a military man and that he had met Bragg only once, but even in that brief encounter he could tell "that he had neither the head nor the heart to lead our armies to victory." Henry described the general as a man of "valor and wisdom." When asked by Orr if Bragg had not quarreled with all of his general officers, the Tennessee senator candidly admitted that he had but that it had been "unavoidable." "He [Bragg] ought to have shot some of them," shouted Benjamin Hill of Georgia. Henry insisted that it was the generals in question who had lost the fruits of Chickamauga by disobeying orders. Semmes likewise defended Bragg's war record. Wigfall pointedly argued that the want of confidence was in Davis for having retained him. Jones heard the rumor that Bragg might withdraw his name and resign. If he did, thought the clerk, it would humiliate the president, "for the attacks on Bragg are meant principally for Mr. Davis. But I doubt the story." The bill, though initially tabled, subsequently passed.[5]

Newspapers pondered who would be Bragg's successor. *Whig* commentary acknowledged that, while both Beauregard and Johnston had the ability to command the Army of Tennessee, there was an "immovable impediment" in their path: Robert E. Lee, who was "the only General of known ability." Davis was actually in communication with Lee on the subject. On December 6, he wired the Virginian asking if he was any more open to the suggestion (i.e., temporarily going to the West) than he had been two weeks earlier. Lee saw no benefit and even believed that, given the intra-army bickering, he would "not receive cordial cooperation." Commanding the Army of Northern Virginia in Lee's absence would be the senior corps commander, Dick Ewell; Lee expressed opposition. Davis subsequently summoned the army commander to Richmond, which led to the general's fear that he would be ordered to go against his wishes. But Lee would not be sent to the West. He initially advocated for Beauregard, but sensing the president's opposition he recommended Johnston.[6]

Davis now faced the odious dilemma of choosing between the lesser of two evils, a difficult task; he despised Johnston only slightly less than Beauregard. The Louisiana general privately feared that he would send him "at the eleventh hour and without adequate resources." "Sallust," the prolific Army of Tennessee correspondent for the *Dispatch*, predicted that "Gen. Beauregard will be sent to us." By December 2, clerk Jones at the War Department had heard unofficially that Beauregard had been selected, although it "may be changed." As for Johnston, Wigfall sensed a trap. If the Virginian was tapped, the president would make every effort to ensure his defeat. Indeed, it would be better, the Texas senator sardonically continued, if Pemberton assumed army command. Though Pemberton was totally incompetent, the administration would do everything possible to support him.[7]

In a cabinet meeting on December 14 or 15, the issue of Bragg's successor was debated at length. Some preferred Hardee, who had been appointed temporary commander, but he quickly removed his name from consideration. Seddon, although disappointed in Johnston's Vicksburg performance, proposed his name, and he was hesitatingly supported by one or two others. A majority nonetheless opposed Johnston, chief among them Benjamin, who detested him. Indeed, initially there was no name that received a majority. Slowly Benjamin came around to Johnston as being the only viable option. Davis reluctantly, perhaps painfully, agreed, although Seddon remarked that the president showed "doubt and misgiving to the end." The general was notified of his appointment in a curt dispatch on December 16. Possibly thinking that he would be sidelined to Mississippi for the balance of the war, Johnston immediately thanked Wigfall, but the senator admitted that Lee had more to do with his appointment than he did. Varina let it be known that Johnston was not the president's first choice. Even Mary Chesnut understood that the president must have harbored deep reservations.[8]

Since Bragg had preferred charges against Breckinridge for his conduct at Missionary Ridge, the western army was in need of another corps commander. Davis had previously promised Bragg that he would promote John Bell "Sam" Hood when a vacancy became available. As a division commander, the Texan had lost an arm at Gettysburg and, more recently as a provisional corps commander, a leg at Chickamauga. He recovered at the Spotswood during the winter of 1863–1864, where he became the toast of Richmond. He had his photograph taken on crutches, probably at the studio of Julian Vannerson at Main and Fourteenth. While he won the hearts of Richmonders, he noticeably failed to win that of Sally "Buck" Preston, who saw him as a "rude soldier" who "can't talk of literature and high art." She was taken aback by his "rough Texas wooing." At one point he grabbed her by the waist and kissed her neck, causing her to recoil—and him to express profuse apologies. Hood was highly ambitious and not beyond becoming an "awkward flatterer," especially with Davis. Mary Chesnut shocked the thirty-two-year-old general when she bluntly told him that, if he stayed in the capital much longer, he would "grow to be a courtier. You came a rough Texan!" Davis nominated Hood for lieutenant general, and the Senate confirmed him on February 4. Not all were pleased. Senator Herschel Johnson questioned if he was physically up to the task. Virginia Congressman Alexander Boteler grumbled that Jeb Stuart of the Army of Northern Virginia should have been tapped. Lee, who noticeably passed up Hood twice for corps command the previous spring, was silent. Sam Hood would soon be on his way to Dalton.[9]

Davis's letter of December 23 awaited Johnston at his arrival in Dalton. The president impressed upon him the "imperative demand" for an offensive to regain Tennessee. This could be done because the reports (Hardee's exaggerated assertions) in his possession indicated that the losses at Missionary Ridge were "not great," the artillery had been "reorganized and equipped," the transportation was "not unfavorable," and "stragglers were rapidly coming in." He was in hopes that the general would soon be able to commence active operations. Senator Henry, who had two sons in the Army of Tennessee, wrote to Johnston expressing his hope that Tennessee would soon be redeemed. By doing so, he claimed, the army could add to the ranks 30,000 Tennesseans and 20,000 Kentuckians. It was, of course, a pipe dream, but there were believers.[10]

Preston Johnston was ordered to immediately catch the next train to Dalton. He was not even permitted to go home, tell his wife goodbye, and get a fresh shirt. He arrived the day after Christmas, one day before Johnston's arrival. "[M]uch is expected of him [Johnston] I see by *the public*, and no great things by *the Army*," the colonel observed. He was frankly taken aback by the "feeling towards Bragg," finding it much stronger than he had expected—"almost every officer and man I have spoken to hopes he will return." It was not in the cards.[11]

General Johnston's correspondence indicated that he was far from initiating a winter offensive. His intelligence indicated that he was outnumbered nearly two-to-one (43,000 to 80,000). In addition, field transportation was inadequate, and the 120 wagons promised from Polk in Mississippi had not yet arrived. Indeed, there was sufficient transportation for only eight days' subsistence. Rations were poor, the artillery horses remained in wretched condition, and the cavalry was "not very efficient." Additionally, the secretary of war had informed him that he could not expect reinforcements. Under the circumstances, he could only beat the Federals as they advanced and then push forward. It would be a refrain often repeated in the coming weeks.[12]

While the administration bantered with Johnston over strategic proposals and counterproposals, Davis received a petition, signed by thirty-two ranking officers in the Army of Tennessee, stating that the draft age should be lowered to fifteen and raised to sixty. It also recommended that slaves be conscripted for menial support roles such as teamsters, laborers, and cooks. Davis denied the proposal based on the proposed new draft ages; the use of slaves for menial army tasks had by this time become established policy. Johnston claimed that 10,000 men could be placed in the ranks of his army if blacks were conscripted. Even Thomas Hindman's anonymous December 1863 proposal to temporarily arm the slaves when needed was nothing new, although it could not find a single congressional sponsor.[13]

Georgia's Senator Johnson then presented the president a communication from Major General William H. T. Walker, a division commander in the Army of Tennessee, that spelled potential trouble. Walker was a bitter opponent of Major General Patrick Cleburne, the very officer who had just received the thanks of Congress for checking the Federal pursuit after Missionary Ridge. Cleburne had presented a memorandum proposing the arming of slaves with the promise of emancipation. To the Irishman the question was simple: Did the South want independence or slavery? It could not have both. The proposal, signed by a few general and field officers, was presented to several of the army's ranking generals; it received a mostly hostile reaction. Johnston, who quietly opposed the idea, attempted to suppress the memorandum, but a seething Walker went over the general's head and sent it to Davis. Walker characterized the idea as sedition and denounced Cleburne as a leader of the "abolitionist party." Bragg agreed, claiming that the signers were "abolitionist men" who "should be watched."[14]

Cleburne also discussed his proposal with newly elected Tennessee Congressman Arthur S. Coylar while in Atlanta. "I admire General Cleburne's boldness and the fearless manner in which he comes up to a question which he must know may overwhelm him in ruin," wrote Coylar, "but I cannot agree with him in the necessity for such a move." Cleburne nonetheless related that he "considered slavery at an end." The Cleburne memorandum was discussed in the cabinet, but only Reagan supported it. Davis instructed Johnston to suppress not only the document but also the controversy. A correspondent in the Army of Tennessee informed Bragg a few weeks later: "The Free Negro scheme seems to be down with chill and fever," although not on a scale suggested by "the originator of the '*Scheme*.'"[15]

Little substantive news arrived from Dalton throughout February apart from the "Latest from the North" column in the *Dispatch*. Even that feature was contradictory, one dispatch claiming that Johnston was withdrawing forty miles to Kingston, Georgia, and the other that he was advancing on Chattanooga. The Richmond inner circle—Davis, Lee, Bragg, and Seddon—were meanwhile formulating offensive plans for the Army of Tennessee. The only person left out of the discussion was Johnston. One of the more absurd ideas, which originated from Longstreet, was to mount his corps, then wintering in East Tennessee, on mules and send it on a raid into Kentucky. Davis rightfully rejected the proposal. Longstreet continued to press for a Kentucky raid, while Lee's army marched into East Tennessee and the Army of Tennessee held Virginia. By the first week in March, Davis and Bragg were conjuring another idea. The Army of Tennessee would sidestep Chattanooga and unite with Longstreet around Madisonville, forty miles from Knoxville. The combined forces would then invade Middle Tennessee via Sparta and McMinnville. Again, Johnston was kept in the dark short of terse messages from Bragg to hold his army in readiness. It was imperative that Johnston struck first—"prompt and vigorous action" before the Federals advanced.[16]

On March 4, Bragg related Richmond's strategy. Johnston was to advance east of Chattanooga and cross the Tennessee River at Kingston, where he would juncture with Longstreet's Corps. If the Federals did not offer battle, then the consolidated Southern forces would march on Nashville via Sparta. This would force the bluecoats to abandon Chattanooga. Once Nashville had been captured, Johnston would proceed into Kentucky with his own 44,000 and Longstreet's 16,000, reinforced by 5,000 from Polk and 10,000 from Beauregard, amounting to 75,000. Johnston immediately, and not surprisingly, rejected the strategy. There were a litany of objections, not the least of which was that he was heavily outnumbered. Additionally, the juncture point with Longstreet was too close to the enemy, opening the possibility that Southern forces could be caught in a pincer move between Chattanooga and Knoxville. A far more practicable approach was to advance into Middle Tennessee via North Alabama. He needed the reinforcements *before* the campaign commenced, there was still insufficient transportation, and in any event Grant "will be ready to act before we can be."[17]

Revealing that he also could write to Wigfall, Hood sent the Texas senator a pointed letter. "I think he [Johnston] should have said to Bragg: 'I am delighted to have the chance to regain Tenn & Ky and am ready to move as you propose, but would prefer the other route.' So Bragg [could have] replied that as he had failed to accept the plan to move forward, nothing could be done, and no troops furnished." He made clear that he "urged all this before I left Richmond and I told Genl J. that I did not care where or what route we took, provided our troops were concentrated." His evaluation of Wigfall's pet: "He is too petulant to administer an army well, and I regard Lee as far his superior. There is more fight in Lee than J."[18]

Throughout March and April, Hood also sent a series of letters to Davis, Bragg, and Seddon expressing what the administration longed to hear. This meant undercutting Johnston, which the ambitious Hood unhesitatingly undertook. Hood wrote Seddon on March 10: "We have a sufficient number of troops, if thrown together, to defeat his entire army." He later added: "We should march to the front as soon as possible, so as not to allow the enemy to concentrate upon us." The president did not reprimand the new corps commander for his obvious breach of protocol, for he had obviously been instructed to keep Davis informed. Indeed, Bragg continued to receive numerous letters from his former allies in the army stating essentially the same as Hood. On April 3, the Texan wrote to Bragg stating, among other things: "Should we fail to move forward and act only on the defensive—and troops should have to go from this Army to Va.—you know I am fond of large engagements and hope you will not forget me." Again, on April 13, he wrote Bragg: "I . . . am sorry to inform you that I have done all in my power to induce General Johnston to accept the proposition you made to move forward. He will not consent."[19]

It was a rainy April 12, a Tuesday, when Colonel Benjamin Ewell, still suffering from varicose veins and diarrhea, stepped off the train at Richmond and took residence at the Linwood House. The West Point graduate, educator, civil engineer, and older brother to Lieutenant General Dick Ewell, was on a mission from Johnston. Sensing that the administration was growing impatient, Johnston had sent the staff officer to present his side of the story. It also helped that the colonel was on friendly terms with Bragg. Perhaps the general would be able to "pour oil on troubled waters."[20]

Ewell happened to arrive on the anniversary of the firing on Fort Sumter, thus announcing the beginning of the fourth year of the war. Despite two million Federals having been hurled at the Confederacy, boasted the *Whig*, the South held firm. To be sure, there had been setbacks: "New Orleans fell because its defenses were not completed, and Vicksburg [likewise fell] because it was entrusted to incompetent hands." Yet the question was not why the South kept fighting but rather how much longer the North would persist in its "mad attempt" to militarily dominate the Confederacy. Far from sounding a defeatist note, the paper believed that a successful campaign by Lee would make the fourth year the last year of the war.[21]

Nonetheless, as the cherry blossoms began blooming in Richmond and the papers boasted of how the world marveled at Southern resilience, the press could not refrain from reporting the undeniable reality. Grant, flush from his western victories at Fort Donelson, Vicksburg, and Missionary Ridge, had now arrived in Virginia to take overall command of Federal operations. Two Yankee corps (XI and XII), reportedly 15,000 troops, had come from the West to reinforce the Army of the Potomac. With other reinforcements likely to arrive, Grant would begin his spring campaign 100,000 strong. Other reinforcements were traveling from the West—the IX Corps. Its destination was Annapolis, Maryland, where Burnside was organizing a massive expedition to where—Wilmington? Charleston? the Virginia Peninsula?[22]

The next day, April 13, Ewell went to see Bragg. He wished to give assurances that Johnston was not opposed to an offensive—just not the one suggested by Richmond. He then proceeded to list the army commander's needs—1,000 wagons, 1,000 artillery horses, and reinforcements—and that he desired Longstreet's Corps. As for the offensive, it should be south of the Tennessee River, where a defeat would be less disastrous. Bragg assured the colonel that the route of the offensive would be entirely left to the discretion of the army commander. As for Longstreet, Ewell was surprised to learn that the corps had been ordered to Virginia. With all available reinforcements needed for Virginia and the North Carolina coast, Bragg suspected that "little could be done." Nonetheless, he desired to have his old army reinforced. He therefore posed a hypothetical to the colonel: If 15,000 troops could be sent to Dalton from Polk in Alabama and Beauregard on the coast, would Johnston unequivocally take the offensive? He must have an answer by the next day, when Ewell had an appointment with the president. The staff officer immediately telegraphed Johnston for an answer.

The next day, Ewell met with the president; he had received no response from Johnston. The scene was reminiscent of St. John Liddell's January 1862 visit from another Johnston—viz. Albert Sidney—but the request this time was not for more arms but more men. Unlike the Liddell visit, Davis was at least affable, although he was no more cooperative. Ewell took it upon himself to say that, if reinforcements were received, Johnston would emphatically launch an offensive. Davis believed that it was too late for an offensive. Union reinforcements had already arrived from the West in Virginia—the very thing that Johnston's offensive was supposed to have prevented. Nonetheless, he should still attempt it. The president assured the colonel that there was no intent to "force a plan of campaign." As for reinforcements, he said that none could come from Polk and that all reinforcements from Beauregard had to go to Lee. Besides, Davis by now suspicioned that Johnston had no other intention than to await the Federal advance and that any troops sent him would only be squandered. Indeed, when Ewell did receive Johnston's reply later that day, the general equivocated. If given reinforcements, he answered, an offensive would depend on the enemy's strength in Tennessee. Even so, he would need another four to six weeks for preparation. There is evidence that Bragg saw the telegram; if so, he unquestionably shared it with Davis. The president nonetheless promised to give the issue of reinforcements some thought.

While waiting for a reply, Ewell took the opportunity to visit his brother Richard at Orange Court House. He remained there several days and even had a brief meeting with Lee, who repeated that no reinforcements were available. While in Richmond, the colonel got his hands on an old *Enquirer*, in which Johnston was criticized for his conduct in the Vicksburg Campaign. Irked by the article, he went to the editor, Nathaniel Tyler, and inquired who submitted it. He was taken aback when told that it was turned in by a member of the cabinet. On April 19, Ewell again returned to the War Department. Bragg related that the "pressure at Richmond" made substantial reinforcements impossible but that additional troops would be sent "when circumstances warranted." Meanwhile, a brigade would be ordered to Dalton from Mobile, and five large regiments from the coast would be exchanged with five depleted ones at Dalton. The accessions would send an additional 4,000 troops to Dalton. A disappointed Ewell departed the next day.[23]

Johnston saw Richmond's response as one more rejection. He took pen in hand and wrote Wigfall: "The U.S. have the means of collecting two great armies—here & in Virginia. Our government thinks that they can raise but one, that of course in Virginia." Intelligence reports were nonetheless arriving in Richmond that 30,000–40,000 Union reinforcements had flooded into Virginia from the West. The administration was convinced that the Federals were not planning a coordinated two-front advance but rather a single massive offensive—and that would come in Virginia.[24]

On Monday, April 21, the sun finally broke through in Richmond. Brigadier General William Pendleton, artillery chief of the Army of Northern Virginia, arrived in the capital, fresh from his inspection tour at Dalton. He had been sent to investigate the differences between Hardee's report on the condition of the artillery as compared to Johnston's claims. Before departing North Georgia, the brigadier had a lengthy discussion with the army commander. Johnston repeated his view that he was heavily outnumbered. Wheeler, who happened to be in the room most of the day, concurred. His scouts estimated Union army strength at 75,000 infantry, exclusive of 15,000 black troops and 5,000 unassigned Tennesseans. The enemy cavalry comprised 15,000 troopers, making a total army strength of 95,000. To oppose this force, Johnston had 37,311 infantry and artillery and 2,085 effective cavalry. The army commander repeated his argument that a defeat north of the Tennessee River would be "ruinous," and Wheeler agreed that it would be "probably fatal." Every effort should be made to immediately reinforce his army. At that time, he would push against the enemy first at Ringgold and then Cleveland, Tennessee. This would force the enemy into a battle. Simultaneously, Polk's cavalry should raid into the enemy's rear in Middle Tennessee. Pendleton concurred with the strategy.[25]

Unfortunately, Bragg, who had always been suspicious of Johnston, was not so easily convinced. The Union army, according to his estimate, was 70,000 strong, only 60,000 of whom "could be brought against us." W. W. Loring's reinforced division of 7,000 troops from Polk's army should be sufficient for Johnston to initiate his offensive. Forrest could meanwhile raid into Middle Tennessee. "This can all be done," he insisted, "without the elaborate preparation now deemed necessary for an advance." Because Bragg's numbers fit the administration's narrative of events, it was accepted.[26]

Johnston was not the only one sounding an alarm. Senator Walker returned from a trip in North Alabama and reported to the assistant clerk of the House of Representatives, who forwarded the message to Davis that heavy reinforcements had been passing through Nashville for three weeks, all headed for Chattanooga. In addition to the XV Corps at Bridgeport, 7,000 troops from Vicksburg had been marching through North Alabama—all going toward Chattanooga. "Either the Yankees mean to make two simultaneous campaigns—one in Virginia and one in Georgia—or they are intending one grand campaign in the latter state," wrote Walker. "I believe the latter is their intention[] and that their real movement will be against Atlanta, not Richmond." On April 23, Johnston reported to Bragg that the XXIII Corps was not in Kentucky but had traveled from Knoxville to Cleveland. The message was clear: massive forces were gathering against Dalton in Georgia.[27]

The reinforcements promised by Richmond were nonetheless slow in arriving. The proposal to swap two large South Carolina regiments for two smaller ones had to be scrapped. The three oversized regiments from Savannah, to be exchanged with smaller ones, trailed far to the rear; none had arrived by the end of April. William T. Martin's cavalry division, reportedly 3,300 strong, was ordered from East Tennessee to Dalton but upon arrival counted only 2,000. George Cantey's 2,000-man Alabama brigade, ordered from Mobile, was at Rome by the end of April. As for Loring's Division, Polk resisted every call, and Davis refused to order him. By the end of the month, however, Johnston's army, counting returning hospital patients and stragglers, had swelled to 54,500.[28]

On April 30 at 1 p.m., Varina took her husband a lunch basket as he worked in his office. In her absence, the Davises' four-year-old child, Joseph—his father's favorite—ventured out on the rear balcony and slipped over the railing, plummeting twenty-feet to his death on the brick portico below. Even much later that day, Mary Chesnut could hear the hysterical screaming of Varina. The president was devastated. The next day, a Sunday, the child was buried in Hollywood Cemetery, with hundreds of children covering the grave with flowers. "We attended this afternoon the funeral of one of the Presidents little boys (Joe), who was killed yesterday evening by a fall from the back piazza," Gorgas sadly entered in his diary. "No one saw the little boy fall, & he probably had been lying some little time when he was found. His legs were both broken & his head fractured. It is a very sad thing to see a fine healthy child, gamboling about yesterday, & to-day carried along in his little coffin. The President is very much attached to his little children, & very caressing toward them, and this is a heavy sorrow to him." The next day, Monday, Davis was back at his desk.[29]

"The long[-]threatened effort to take Richmond has begun." Thus read Lee's May 4 dispatch to Davis. Grant had crossed the Rapidan River and moved into the Wilderness, where Lee quickly engaged him. Brutal but inconclusive fighting raged throughout May 5 and 6, resulting in horrific casualties. More fighting occurred around Spotsylvania Court House between May 5 and 26. Meanwhile, Benjamin Butler's 39,000-man expedition threatened from the southeast as it pushed up the Peninsula, and 10,000 cavalry under Philip Sheridan endangered the northern suburbs of the capital. "It is too late now for the evacuation of Richmond, and a *desperate* defense will be made," Jones wrote on May 13.[30]

The capital papers were consumed with the operations in Virginia. What news arrived from the West appeared in terse items on page two. By May 7, it was reported that the Union army, now under Sherman, "had advanced but little." Officials at the War Department, however, knew that the enemy—in an obvious coordinated plan with Grant—was in motion. Cooper notified Polk to immediately dispatch Loring's Division "and any other available force at your command" to Rome in Georgia. Interpreting the order literally, the bishop redirected both of his infantry divisions and Red Jackson's cavalry division (some 10,000 infantry and 4,000 cavalry) to Rome. Bragg, who had not been notified, was miffed about the removal of the cavalry, which he said was never intended; Polk ignored him. By May 7, the bluecoats had closed to within five miles of Dalton.[31]

Johnston, on May 11, notified Richmond that the enemy was making a demonstration on Resaca and that Polk's troops had been directed to that place. For some unknown reason, it took six days for the telegram to arrive. The general's dispatch of the next day, May 12, must therefore have raised eyebrows: "I am convinced that the Federal army, having failed in its attempts on this place [Dalton], is now, covered by Rocky Face Ridge, in motion for Calhoun or some point on the Oostanaula." The *Dispatch* on the morning of May 13 carried a very brief article that mentioned "the affair at Resaca" and that the enemy was "moving in force on Resaca." Johnston's dispatch of the same day confirmed that the army had indeed withdrawn to Resaca. Since that town was thirteen miles south of Dalton, civilian authorities were left wondering what "affair" had taken place. It was later confirmed that several enemy assaults had been repulsed on May 14. The only mention of Snake Creek Gap came through an intercepted Sherman dispatch. Nonetheless, the entire mountain sector of North Georgia had been surrendered; the administration had been left to figure out the details.[32]

A dispatch arrived later on May 16 that portended trouble. The enemy had laid a pontoon below Calhoun and, under cover of two divisions, crossed to the south bank of the Oostanaula River. Johnston, as he predicted four days earlier, had been forced to withdraw to Calhoun. Davis read the dispatch "with disappointment." The president's return dispatch dated May 18 did not arrive at Johnston's headquarters until May 20, and the general responded the next day. The reply was not placed on the president's desk until May 23, however, a time lag of five days. The general related that he was looking for opportunities to attack but that Sherman entrenched at every halt, making an assault "too hazardous." Kean noted: "We have no specific intelligence of the fighting which has occurred or the movements made except that Johnston fell back first to Resaca and then to Colburne [Calhoun] to meet him, and that he [Sherman]was repulsed with loss in an attack on Rome. The campaign is not, so far as we know, yet developed."[33]

Johnston's dispatch of May 21 was written "near Allatoona." He admitted having fallen back thirty-two miles within six days, warning that attempting an assault on such superior numbers was simply "too hazardous." The administration was actually receiving more details from reading the morning papers. On May 20, a *Dispatch* report placed the Federal army at "well over 100,000," with casualties to date being 2,500 Confederates and 12,000–15,000 Federals—an absurd number. On May 23—bearing the dateline "Atlanta, May 21"—a correspondent revealed that the enemy had crossed the Etowah River, eight miles above the railroad bridge, on May 20, with the column marching on Marietta, Georgia. Union Major General James B. McPherson meanwhile had crossed twelve miles below Etowah Station to flank Johnston's left. The

Southerners were already across the river, burning the railroad bridge as they withdrew.[34]

Sherman now began to shift his line west, some twenty miles from the railroad, near a town called Dallas. Three sizable engagements were fought at the end of May: New Hope Church on the twenty-fifth, Pickett's Mill on the twenty-seventh, and Dallas on the twenty-eighth. Johnston reported that the Federals were repulsed at the former "with considerable loss" and the latter "with slaughter." Only New Hope Church was widely reported in the Richmond press. A western civilian told that Hooker's corps was repulsed "with great slaughter," while the Southern loss was "comparatively light." The Union casualty loss was placed at 1,500 killed and wounded. An exploding shell came close to striking both Johnston and Hood. At Pickett's Mill, Patrick Cleburne's division so thoroughly repulsed the Federals that many threw up their hands and surrendered. The engagement on May 28 resulted in the repulse of Confederate Major General William Bate's division. A scant news item placed the Southern loss at 72 killed, 350 wounded, and 56 missing.[35]

Government officials were beginning to get jittery. The president faced, in his words, "steadily increasing pressure" to relieve Johnston of command. An alarmed Gorgas feared that Johnston would "reach Macon in a few days at the rate he is retreating. I trust the country will sooner or later find out what sort of a General he is." As for Kean himself: "I don't think he will suit the emergency." Kean encountered a greatly perturbed Seddon. He was frustratingly told "that General Johnston's theory of war seemed to be never to fight unless strong enough certainly to overwhelm your enemy[] and under all circumstances merely to contrive to elude him. This is a very just criticism upon all of General Johnston's campaigns."[36]

The *Dispatch* nonetheless continued to trumpet support. "[W]e see no reason for the uneasiness which so many persons hereabouts express[] but which the Georgians do not appear to feel. Gen. Johnston has fallen back, not because he has been beaten, but apparently upon a well[-]considered and well matured plan." The paper again remarked: "The public, as is the habit of those who know nothing of military matters, have judged Gen. Johnston too hastily. . . . When the country shall have found him hesitating, uncertain, and unbalanced, then it will be time enough to take the alarm. We see nothing of this." The *Enquirer* assured its readers that Johnston's "retrograde movements have not in the least dispirited his army, and the most implicit confidence is felt in his strategy." Gorgas remained unconvinced. The papers "assert that he [Johnston] is a 'master of the situation,' a meaningless phrase copied from Yankee papers."[37]

In Virginia, Lee had also been retreating. By early June he had been pushed back to Cold Harbor, only ten miles northeast of the capital. But Grant had been unable—even with the sheer force of numbers—to take Richmond, and his army in the process had sustained murderous casualties. The Union drive in the Shenandoah Valley had been checked, and Butler's attempt to take the capital from the Peninsula had been bottled up at Bermuda Hundred. Though fixated on the Virginia front, and exhausted by long hours of discussions and tedious cabinet meetings, Davis was forced to also turn his attention to the West.[38]

Bragg wired Davis in early June that "[t]he condition of affairs in Georgia is daily becoming more serious." He was aware of six Federal corps already assembled in North Georgia, with a seventh on the way. Should all these forces concentrate, "we may well apprehend disaster." It was precisely what Johnston had been warning Richmond since last winter. Johnston's June 1 dispatch, which the War Department uncharacteristically released to the press, indicated that Sherman was now shifting back toward the railroad. Heavy rains had slowed the enemy pace to a mile per day. The new line ran roughly parallel to the Chattahoochee River, about fifteen miles south. The Confederate left, held by Polk's Corps, rested on Lost Mountain, while Hood held the center and Hardee the right. In the fighting of June 14, Polk was killed by a Federal artillery round. Davis lamented the death of his old schoolmate by stating that his loss was only surpassed by Sidney Johnston and Stonewall Jackson, revealing how out of touch he was about the bishop's wartime contribution. Nevertheless, Jones noted that the Louisianian's death was "lamented by a great many."[39]

On June 27, a dispatch from Johnston clicked over the wires. He had been attacked in his new defensive position along the Kennesaw Line. Details were scant, but the Federals had been repulsed with heavy losses. It would be more than a week before the Richmond public learned additional details. Some 2,000 Federals had reportedly been buried in front of Cheatham's Division and another 1,500 bodies on Cleburne's line. Several thousand Enfield rifles had been collected, plus a large number of Henry repeating rifles.[40]

That summer, in the midst of the Virginia and Tennessee Campaigns, internal strife began brewing within the administration. Seddon's relationship with the president, in part due to Bragg's "endless meddling," caused a rift. Davis began to indiscreetly tell out that he desired a change at the War Office; the stories got back to the secretary. Seddon and Cooper also clashed, the adjutant general complaining that he was "not simply a bureau [officer] as some view me." A mini–civil war had long transpired between the president and his vice president. Davis snipped at Gorgas over a minor issue, and he quarreled with former congressional friends, such as Senator Sparrow, chair of the powerful Military Affairs Committee. As the Confederacy's territorial losses continued to mount, the president's Richmond support circle correspondingly dwindled.[41]

The tension between Johnston and the administration continued to mount. Bragg informed Davis that there was simply no other way to reinforce Johnston, "and he has been so informed several times." One of the general's aides, Lieutenant Richard Manning, began privately writing of "the enemy at Richmond." While visiting in Columbia, South Carolina, he "talked Joe Johnstonism run mad," wrote Mary Chesnut. "He coupled Lee and Davis and abused them with equal virulence." As for his part, Seddon believed that Johnston's continued reticence about his plans indicated that he had no plans at all.[42]

The president had never believed that Sherman's army disproportionately outnumbered the Army of Tennessee. There was also the issue of casualties. Through early July, Johnston had reported his casualty losses at 10,000 killed and wounded and 4,700 sick. But this did not include 7,000 prisoners, the number that was on file in the Adjutant General's Office; nor did it account for cavalry losses. Johnston admitted that the incessant rains were depleting his ranks at the rate of 300 per day. Davis thus believed his total losses to be not less than a staggering 25,000. Johnston's estimate of Union casualties was three times his own, some 30,000 killed and wounded. But would this not give Johnston near parity of strength? The only reinforcements received by Sherman was the XVII Corps, which Johnston estimated to be 5,000–7,000 but the War Department placed at 20,000.[43]

Despite the resounding victory at Kennesaw Mountain, Sherman once again outflanked Johnston, causing him to withdraw another six miles. The *Dispatch* suppressed the news for two days but eventually reported that the Army of Tennessee was now within a mile of the Chattahoochee

River. Davis was left "more apprehensive for the future." With Atlanta facing immediate danger, an impending command shakeup appeared all but certain. There were Georgians who urged Johnston's replacement. Wigfall, on his way to Texas, paid a visit to the general on June 28. He related that there were reliable reports in the capital that the general would be replaced, the pretext being he had lost confidence among Georgians. Johnston told the senator that he planned to fight Sherman not as he crossed the south bank of the Chattahoochee River but rather as he crossed to the south bank of Peachtree Creek, a tributary of the Chattahoochee northwest of Atlanta. If defeated at Peachtree Creek, Sherman would then have to fight with his back against the Chattahoochee. As it was, Johnston was comfortable fighting with *his* back against the Chattahoochee, stating that he had six bridges behind him.[44]

Alabama Senator Richard W. Walker, of the politically powerful Walker family of Huntsville, also traveled to Georgia and found absolutely no loss of support for the general. On the contrary, he wrote the assistant secretary of war, "I doubt whether any army ever existed which felt a more entire or implicit confidence in its leader." The power brokers, however, were not in the ranks of the Army of Tennessee, or in Georgia, but instead in Richmond. "Johnston has I fear fallen behind the Chattahoochee just as I surmised long ago," Gorgas remarked on July 7. "Will he fight at last? I do not expect it, & yet I do not see how he *can* give up Atlanta without a fight—a general action."[45]

Nathan Bedford Forrest was fast becoming the toast of Richmond. His stunning June 10 victory in northern Mississippi at Brice's Crossroads, in which his reported 3,000 troopers routed Samuel D. Sturgis's 10,000 infantry and cavalry (the Federals claimed 8,000), had netted 2,000 prisoners, 17 guns, 250 wagons, and 3,000 arms—his "proud trophies" as Forrest called them. A resolution of thanks was passed in the House. There was also a resolution presented by John Murray of Tennessee-4 declaring Forrest among the most brilliant military leaders of the day, but the Military Affairs Committee offered an amendment echoing the same wording as the praise resolutions offered to Lee, Stonewall Jackson, and Beauregard, ostensibly so that Forrest would not receive "more praise than others." Foote customarily cried foul and insisted that Murray's resolution should remain unchanged, but Swan and Miles quieted him.[46]

Senator Louis T. Wigfall of Texas, arguably the most influential member of the Senate, was also one of the most boorish. (Library of Congress)

There was also an Atlanta news article, carried in both the *Whig* and *Dispatch*, written by an anonymous officer who had known Forrest over fifteen years, that told of the man. He claimed that Forrest was normally mild-mannered, loved to "laugh much," possessed a "nervous manner," could never "stand still," loved children, and longed for the close of the war. The subject of Forrest's "ungovernable temper" then came up. The general "loves a fight as other men do a game of cards." At Brice's Crossroads, it was reported that he personally killed eight Yankees.[47]

The subject of exactly what to do with Forrest and his cavalry following their victory at Brice's Crossroads now became the subject of much debate. Johnston had long claimed that the only solution in stopping

Sherman's massive Federal army was for Forrest to cut his rail communications. Indeed, between June 3 and July 10, Johnston addressed the subject with Davis twice and Bragg five times, openly suggesting that Mississippi should be abandoned to support the operations in Georgia—and further conceding that he had no other cards to play.[48]

Johnston's political and newspaper allies ("the Cartel," as Bragg called them) began mounting a concerted effort to pressure the Confederate White House. The *Examiner* led the charge, followed by the *Whig*. The latter declared that that there were two railroads from Stevenson, Alabama, to Nashville, "both of which are open to Forrest if he should choose to operate in Middle Tennessee," or he could strike the track south of Chattanooga. Such an operation could "possibly starve his [Sherman's] army." The sole government ally, the *Sentinel*, pushed back by stating that Forrest, by remaining in Mississippi, *was* aiding Johnston, who otherwise would be "overwhelmed by superior numbers." As for cutting Sherman's rail line, Johnston's own cavalry could have done it "had they been ordered to do so."[49]

Demanding and unrelenting politicians were harder to ignore. When Governor Joseph Brown's request for a Forrest raid was rejected, the Georgian was quick to respond. "The whole country expects this, though points of less importance should, for a time, be overrun," he barked at Davis. He added that he did not see how Forrest's operation in Mississippi and Morgan's raid in Kentucky directly interfered with Sherman's advance. Governor Thomas Hill Watts in Alabama also fired off a sharp letter. Asking to be forgiven for the bluntness of his communication, he then proceeded to be blunt: "I fear you have permitted yourself to be unjustly influenced against Gen'l Johnston and his movements [i.e., retreats]," which he characterized as "necessary and proper." He then got to the point: a Forrest raid on Sherman's rail line was the only remaining option. The governor concluded with a dire warning: "If Johnston's army should not succeed, the public opinion of this section of the Confederacy will attribute failure, not to Johnston, but to the neglect to give him that aid, which is now in your power."[50]

It was at this point that Senator Hill became a player in the ongoing Johnston drama. Hill was a personal friend of Davis and an outspoken defender of the Davis administration. He was hardly reticent in taking on the president's opponents. Back in early 1863, Hill and Yancey had gotten into a heated debate over the issue of the Confederate Supreme

Court. Words were exchanged, and before it was over the Georgian hurled a glass inkstand at Yancey, striking him in the cheek and causing profuse bleeding. When the defiant Alabamian attempted to respond, Hill threw a heavy glass tumbler at him, although it failed to connect. Colleagues kept the neighboring senators apart, quelling the embarrassing episode.[51]

Johnston had convinced Wigfall, in Atlanta on his way to the trans-Mississippi, and Governor Brown that his only chance of defeating Sherman was in a Forrest raid. Convinced that they would not be heard, which indeed they would not have been, Wigfall and Brown believed what they needed was a Davis ally to relay the message. They called upon Hill to go to Richmond and address the president. The senator agreed—but not before he spoke with Johnston personally. The meeting occurred at army headquarters in Marietta on July 1. In Hill's retelling of events to both Davis and Seddon on July 12, he explained that Johnston believed that cutting the enemy's rail lines "could be easily done." The army commander was under the impression that Morgan had 5,000 cavalry at Abingdon, Virginia, but if he was not available then Stephen D. Lee had 15,000 cavalry in Mississippi and Alabama and would agree to release a third of them to Forrest.

Hill questioned the general about the possibility of Federal counterraids. What if Sherman attacked the Atlanta & West Point Railroad, the main Selma–Atlanta artery? If so, Johnston said, he would get his supplies via Selma–Columbus, thirty-five miles south of the West Point line. The senator suggested that if one rail could be cut, then the other could as well. Johnston did not think that it would come to that, since Sherman had only 12,000 ineffective cavalry. Hill queried: If the opposing forces were about proportionally equal to what they had been back to Dalton, to which the general agreed, then why not send Wheeler on the raid? Johnston insisted that Wheeler was indispensable to screen the army and protect its flanks. The senator expressed his concern that Sherman would continue his flanking maneuvers until Johnston was forced back into the Atlanta defenses. "Well, before the enemy shall get the position you mention, of course we shall have a bloody fight," Johnston replied.[52]

Senator Walker, writing the assistant secretary of war, was also convinced that a raid by Forrest was Johnston's only hope of success. Indeed, he wrote, there was "universal surprise" that, immediately after Forrest's success at Brice's Crossroads, his cavalry was not sent to

Senator Benjamin H. Hill of Georgia, a staunch Davis ally, traveled to Richmond to plead Joe Johnston's case; he ended up turning on the general. (Library of Congress)

Sherman's rear. With 10,000 men or less, Walker argued, Forrest could totally reverse Sherman's progress. He was aware that a "formidable expedition" was about to leave Memphis to raid Mississippi and central Alabama but insisted that attacking Sherman's communications would more than counterbalance any damage done in the Federal raid. Senator Henry likewise advocated for the Forrest raid.[53]

Hill arrived in Richmond on July 10. He immediately proceeded to the Confederate White House, where he received an audience with Davis and Seddon. The senator explained Johnston's position and then joined in the call for the Forrest raid. But there was intelligence that Hill did not have in his possession: Morgan had been defeated in his

Northern raid, his command limping back to Abingdon with only 1,800 men. As for Forrest, S. D. Lee's department was then being overrun. A 16,000-man column under A. J. Smith had departed Memphis, while a 20,000-man Federal army was reportedly marching from New Orleans to Mobile. "My opinion is that it is Mobile via bay or up Mississippi River," S. D. Lee wrote the president. To meet this threat, Lee had only 7,500 cavalry and 1,500 dismounted cavalry and the Mobile garrison of 4,000 troops. From that number Johnston now wished to draw 5,000.[54]

Davis then asked Hill how long Johnston could hold Sherman north of the Chattahoochee River. According to the general's estimate, he answered fifty-four to sixty days, which would place the date in early September. The president then related to the astonished senator that Johnston was already across the river! Bragg, in Georgia on a factfinding mission, wired a dispatch on July 13: "[I]ndications seem to favor an entire evacuation of this place [Atlanta]." Yet another telegram that day concluded: "I find but little encouraging." Kean, who knew of the Davis–Hill conference, noted that Johnston was supposed to make several stands between Marietta and the Chattahoochee, "[b]ut he went it at one leap." The anti-Johnston *Sentinel* noted on July 7 that it had known for a day or two of the general's plans to cross the Chattahoochee. The stunned Georgia senator immediately got to the dispatch office and telegraphed Johnston: "You must do the work with your present force. For God's sake do it." Before leaving Richmond, Hill, on July 14, wrote a memorandum of his conversation with Johnston. That evening, he sat down and wrote a love letter to his wife back in Georgia; he made no mention of the war.[55]

The political pressure appeared to have an effect. Bragg ordered S. D. Lee to put Forrest in motion, and—responding to Polk and Hardee—he wrote that "assistance now on way to you from S. D. Lee and Forrest." The troops were recalled, however, when Lee advised that a "formidable expedition" under A. J. Smith from Memphis was advancing against him "to repair the disaster of Sturgis" (referring to Samuel D. Sturgis's June 10 rout by Forrest at Brice's Crossroads). The operation resulted in the Battle of Tupelo on July 14–15. Lee was defeated, Forrest's Corps mauled, and Forrest seriously wounded. Even if Forrest had been detached, he was some 225 miles west of the Western & Atlantic Railroad, meaning that it would be the end of July before he reached the intended target. He would then have to negotiate the Federal division at

Rome, a Yankee cavalry division guarding the rail line, and a string of smaller garrisons. In addition, the people of Mississippi and Alabama were badly dispirited enough already, and the president did not wish to appear to abandon both states.[56]

Davis sent Johnston a snippy message in which he was told that he should know precisely how much cavalry S. D. Lee possessed, since only six months earlier he had commanded that department. There had never been more than 10,000 troopers, not the 15,000 spoken of. Why then send 4,000 cavalry from over two hundred miles distant when Wheeler could perform the same mission? Johnston replied that he got his numbers from Polk and that dispatching Wheeler was simply out of the question, since he was constantly engaged in protecting the army's flanks. When Wheeler, with 4,000 troopers, finally did strike north in August, his efforts to disrupt communications proved ineffectual. There was brief damage done between Chattanooga and Knoxville and Chattanooga and Nashville, where the railroads were less protected, but still not the major destruction necessary to stall Sherman's progress.[57]

Patience was growing thin in the capital. Writing on July 20, Missouri Congressman Thomas Snead observed: "At Richmond everybody is determined and hopeful. No one doubts the ability of Lee to defend that city. His army is invincible." Snead believed that "[o]ur greatest danger is in Georgia—in fact, our only danger." Johnston would simply not fight unless assured of a victory: "The only fear is that the government will compel him to fight or ask him to be relieved. I cannot believe that this fear is well founded."[58]

Newspaper accounts claimed that, if the enemy could not be checked along the Chattahoochee River, then Johnston could not possibly do so south of the river. Yet here it was mid-July, and the Federals *were* south of the river. The *Whig* was becoming irritated: "Gen. Johnston is either unable to make up his mind to fight or unwilling to risk a general engagement. . . . The Atlanta papers seem to be satisfied that Gen. Johnston will give up that important city without a struggle." The *Sentinel*, which had long shared the administration's loathing for Johnston, editorialized: "He is standing still, with folded arms, as during the siege of Vicksburg, Yorktown, and Dalton. He will never risk a battle until every possible advantage exists on his side." Gorgas, writing on

July 13, noted: "Everybody has at last come to the conclusion that Johnston has retreated far enough." Seddon wanted Johnston gone, but Davis hesitated.[59]

Even while Hill was in Richmond, Davis toyed with the idea of replacing Johnston. The president had written Robert E. Lee that it appeared as though Atlanta would be lost. He asked his view of Hood as a possible successor. In two dispatches on July 12, Lee warned against replacing Johnston in the midst of a such a dangerous and pivotal campaign. He nonetheless offered Hood his restrained approval, although he seemed to prefer Hardee. On July 14, the president sent Bragg, then in Georgia, a coded message: "I can only say that if C. [Hardee] is thus indicated adopt advice and execute proposed." The next day Bragg replied: "I am decidedly opposed, as it would perpetuate the past and present policy which he [Hardee] has advised and now sustains. Any change will be attended with some objections. This one could produce no good."[60]

"A very gloomy view of affairs in Georgia prevails in the cabinet," Kean wrote after Hill's presentation. "The subject now in hand with the President is the removal of Johnston. . . . [I]t is apparent from the tone of cabinet officers and others intimate with the President, by representing that the responsibility of the failure of the campaign in Georgia is on the President for not sending Forrest against Sherman's communications." The problem, Kean thought, would be his successor. The only solution was to send Beauregard, "but the President thinks as ill of him as of Johnston."[61]

On July 15, Bragg sent a letter to Davis, to be delivered by Lieutenant Colonel H. W. Walter. In conversation with Johnston, Bragg said that he learned nothing more than was already known. Three enemy corps—25,000 troops—were across the Chattahoochee some nine to fifteen miles upriver from the railroad. Since the retreat from Dalton, the army had lost a breathtaking 20,000 men and was now down to 52,000. "Where can we supply such a waste of men?" Gorgas wondered. Sherman's strength was estimated at 60,000 infantry and 10,000 cavalry. Bragg related that, according to Hood, numerous opportunities had been lost. Hardee had generally favored retreat, although he was frequently noncommittal. In the event of a command change, Bragg recommended Hood, although he admitted that he was not a "genius" or a "great general."[62]

Events transpired quickly on July 15. Seddon took the morning train to Petersburg to consult with Lee on the subject. He returned on the afternoon train and immediately related to Davis that the general opposed replacing Johnston on the grounds that "if he could not command the army we had no one who could." Nevertheless, if Johnston was removed, then Lee supported Hardee for his replacement. That same day, Davis received a dispatch from Bragg stating: "I cannot learn that he [Johnston] has any more plan for the future than he has had in the past"; in short, there would be no offensive. Even then Davis showed reluctance and, according to Seddon, was prepared to retain the general. He sent a dispatch to Johnston that forced the issue: "I wish to hear from you as to present situation[] and your plan of operations so specifically as will enable me to anticipate events." Johnston did not have to read between the lines to understand that this dispatch amounted to a presidential ultimatum.[63]

Under the circumstances, Johnston's response, received the same day, was nothing less than astonishing. "As the enemy have double our number," he began, "we must be on the defensive. My plan of operations must, therefore, depend upon that of the enemy. We are trying to put Atlanta in condition to be held for a day or two by the Georgia militia, [so] that army movements may be freer and wider." Davis could not—would not—wait any longer. He considered the response as "conclusive that Atlanta was also to be given up without a battle." Johnston's tenure was now down to hours.[64]

In the cabinet meeting of July 16, Benjamin continued to harp on his "favorite theme"—his hatred of Johnston. "We'll never have a fight of his army as long as Johnston keeps the head of it," he insisted. Still later he added: "Johnston is determined not to fight; it is of no use to reinforce him, [for] he is not going to fight." Benjamin also referred to Johnston's "nervous dread of *losing a battle*." Seddon was embarrassed that he had backed his name in the first place. Davis later related to James Lyons, a Virginia attorney, that the removal could not be helped, as Seddon was furious and "would not listen to nothing." That also went for Senator Hill, who had been invited to sit in on the meeting and who by now had clearly turned on the general. The cabinet voted unanimously: Johnston had to go. Consumed with his hatred of Beauregard, and aware of the political ramifications of removing Johnston, Davis demurred. "Gentlemen," he remarked, "it is very easy to remove the Genl.[,] but when he is removed his place must be filled and where will you find a man to fill it." He had earlier related to a Hood staff officer who was visiting the capital that he could not appoint Hardee. The Georgian was "always importuning the War Department for a general in chief to be sent there—over him." Davis made a default decision: he chose Hood. Kean somehow got wind of the meeting, for he wrote in his journal that evening: "The trouble about Johnston may have come to a head."[65]

The next day Cooper notified Johnston that he had been relieved of command, "as you have failed to arrest the advance of the enemy to the vicinity of Atlanta, far into the interior of Georgia, and express no confidence that you can defeat or repel him." He could not have been surprised, but he responded in a not-so-veiled comment about Hood: "Confident language by a military commander is not usually regarded as evidence of competency." Seddon informed Hood that he was now in command, concluding: "God be with you." Sometime during July 18, Jones heard the talk being whispered that Hood had been placed in command. Three days later, July 20, the Richmond public was "surprised this morning" to read the news in the *Dispatch*. Johnston's skill was well known, lamented the *Whig*, "but his habit of retreating has been so often indulged in" that that a change of command was inevitable. The *Examiner* denounced the removal as deplorable if not unexpected.[66]

The *Dispatch* approved of Hood's appointment. It argued that Hardee had not been slighted; he had already turned down the position out of a "sincere distrust of his own abilities." Nor did Bragg have anything to do with the appointment. "He is Johnston's friend, although it is known that he wished Johnston to fight and not retreat." Admittedly, Hood "may not do as well as the military editor at the foot of Capital Square [the *Whig*]," the *Dispatch* sardonically noted, but he would do the best he could. In the end, "the President was reduced to the alternative of retaining Johnston and losing Atlanta; or losing Johnston and the possibility of saving Atlanta." The *Whig*—no fan of Johnston—nonetheless questioned the selection of Hood. Hardee was "certainly his equal." Additionally, on the threshold of a major battle, Davis chose "a young, inexperienced, and not very remarkable officer," yet Hood might "prove to be a lucky hit; we certainly hope that he will." Even the *Sentinel* broke ranks and questioned the selection. There was no need to appoint Hood "when a full General of the first order of ability is playing the part of a division commander in the army defending Petersburg"—an obvious reference to Beauregard.[67]

Civilians, politicians, and bureaucrats expressed grave concern. Removing Johnston with a battle imminent "I fear is one of President

[Davis's] great military blunders & wrongs. He and his favorite Gen. Bragg are both hostile to Johnston—& this is the fruit of their feud," Ruffin concluded. Writing from Jackson, Mississippi, Congressman Barksdale warned the Confederate White House that Johnston's removal had evoked "much comment." Many believed that he was "a victim of mere personal malice," while others wondered why the government "so long tolerated" his retreats. Wigfall advised Hood to reject the appointment. Hood's selection, thought Gorgas, "of course means fighting, and a battle must soon be the result. Gen. J will doubtless have a strong party who will condemn his removal."[68]

Johnston's removal remained hotly debated, but Davis held firm. "You are no doubt right in your conclusion that Gen'l Johnston was not removed soon enough," Davis replied to Senator Johnson. Had he known that the general would have abandoned the vital mountain region of North Georgia, "he would have been sooner relieved."[69]

Hood, knowing well what was expected of him, quickly made his move. On July 21, the War Department received his dispatches of the previous day. Portions of both A. P. Stewart's Corps (Polk's former command) and of Hardee's Corps attacked the enemy along Peachtree Creek, driving the bluecoats back to their trenches, although the works were not gained. The *Dispatch* placed the number of Yankee prisoners at 430, although there were no estimates of Southern casualties. "It would seem that Gen. Hood has made a successful debut as a fighting general," Jones concluded. Davis's gamble on Hood appeared to be paying off. It was clear to the *Whig* that the president had finally gotten serious about defending Atlanta "at every hazard and to the last extremity" rather than retaining Johnston and his "particular line of military strategy [retreating]," in which he was "without a rival."[70]

Two days later, July 25, another optimistic dispatch arrived. Hardee's Corps had made a night march and, on the afternoon of the July 22, had attacked Sherman's extreme left, driving the enemy troops from their works with the loss of 2,000 prisoners and twenty-two guns (later reduced to thirteen). "Glorious News from Georgia," hailed the *Whig*. Hood was the man of the hour, the *Enquirer* proclaiming him as "not only a 'fighting man' but a general of unusual ability." Bragg wrote of the morale effect on Southern troops and how casualties were small in comparison to the enemy. Yet a third "sharp engagement" was fought on July 28, which ended "with no decided advantage to either side," according to Hood. Hood's attacks, hailed the capital press corps, had "forced the enemy to cease extending his flanks."[71]

What the Richmond public (or, for that matter, the War Department) was not receiving was the truth about the hideous Confederate casualties. Davis was getting nervous and, after encouraging Hood's aggressiveness, now advised him to avoid assaulting intrenchments if possible. Seddon was also beginning to ask questions, and he ordered an agent to Georgia to prepare a list of casualties. Having recommended Hood for command, Bragg felt compelled to cover for him. He assured Richmond that the casualties in the first two battles were "about" 3,000, although the *Dispatch* placed the number at 5,000, with 1,500 for the engagement on July 28 alone. Yet civilian officials had access to the Northern accounts that were being reprinted in the Richmond dailies, and although much of it could be dismissed as wild exaggerations and Yankee lies, some articles must have given pause. The *New York Herald* published General George Thomas's official report. He stated that in the Battle of Peachtree Creek on July 20 the XX Corps buried 563 Rebels, the Southerners were permitted to bury an estimated 250 more, and a division of the IV Corps buried an additional 300—a staggering total of 1,113 killed. In the Battle of Atlanta on July 22, Thomas placed his losses at 3,500. At least 2,142 Rebels were buried and 3,200 captured. In the Battle of Ezra Church on July 28, the XV Corps buried 642 Southerners. All three battles were trumpeted as Union victories. Who was telling the truth—Bragg or Thomas?[72]

Thursday, July 30, was sweltering in Richmond, with a "burning sun" by 9 a.m. William D. Gale, son-in-law to the recently deceased Leonidas Polk, was in town and had an appointment with the president at the Executive Mansion. Davis was "gracious and charming" as he extended his hand and motioned for Gale to have a seat. The president fondly reflected on his West Point days with Polk. Davis then seemed to "writhe in his chair in torture" as he reflected on Johnston's retreats. Had he known that Johnston would have given up the mountain highlands of North Georgia, he would have ordered Polk's Corps into Tennessee to operate in Sherman's rear. Yet he insisted that, contrary to popular thought, he was "not unfriendly" with the general. It was hardly believable.[73]

Following the battles around Atlanta, command upheaval once again reared its head. Hardee had never accepted Hood's appointment. Even though he had declined the position back at Dalton, he felt wounded that he, as senior officer, had not been given first preference. He considered serving under a junior as "humiliating," and he lacked confidence in Hood—a feeling that was reciprocated. In early August, Hardee requested to be transferred from "an unpleasant situation," a request that he believed was due him as "an old soldier." Davis initially refused and implored Hardee to put patriotism over personal sentiment, but "Old Reliable" would not hear it. The issue eventually leaked out to the Richmond press. Davis relented, but it would take time to find a replacement.[74]

More bad news arrived on August 5 when it was confirmed that Admiral David Farragut's fleet had passed the forts of Mobile Bay, destroyed the Confederate fleet, and, despite the loss of one *Monitor*-class ironclad to a mine, was now in position to ascend the narrow, six-mile-long Spanish River to Mobile. The *Dispatch* gave assurance, however, that the river was heavily fortified and that the city was not in imminent danger. Reports soon emerged, however, of a 2,000-man expeditionary force marching toward the city from Pensacola. The editors pointed to Charleston and declared that Mobile would never be taken as long as its defenders were defiantly determined that "she shall not be surrendered!"[75]

Jones meanwhile began hearing "an ugly rumor" as he walked the streets on September 3. Hood had suffered a disaster and Atlanta had fallen. Since there was no confirmation in the War Department, the talk must have originated with telegraph operators. Later that night, Hood's dispatch confirmed the news that Atlanta had fallen and the Army of Tennessee was twenty-five miles south of the city. The only specifics known were that the bluecoats had made a lodgment along the Flint River at Jonesboro and cut the Macon & Western Railroad, the lifeline to Atlanta. Hood had dispatched two of his three corps (S. D. Lee's and Hardee's) to intercept. The subsequent Southern assault utterly failed.[76]

The details of the Jonesboro affair eventually came to light in Southern accounts and republished Northern articles. Jonesboro had actually been a two-day battle. After the repulse on August 31, Hood recalled S. D. Lee's Corps to Atlanta. The next day, September 1, the Federals attacked Hardee's understrength corps, already thinly stretched for two miles. It was partially overrun by a Federal attack and only by hard fighting and a bit of luck managed to escape during the night. Hood ungraciously reported that "our effort was not a vigorous one" and as evidence noted that Lee and Hardee sustained only 1,476 wounded and a small number of killed on the attack of August 31. (The Federals claimed that they buried 400.) Sherman's after-action report, taken from the *Philadelphia Inquirer*, told a different story. He reported that the Rebels during the operation left 500 dead on the field, with 3,000 prisoners taken, and he estimated their wounded at 2,500—for a total of 6,000![77]

The loss of Atlanta had not only been a military disaster; it also portended political ramifications. A *New York Herald* article, reprinted in the *Whig* of September 9, told the story: "The entire North is ablaze with joyful excitement over the downfall of Atlanta and the consequent disaster to the South." Destroyed in the evacuation were eighty-one carloads of ammunition. Jones, who considered the loss a "stunning blow," believed that there would now "be a new clamor against the President[] for not removing Johnston and for *not* putting Beauregard in his place." Kean saw the loss as "a triumph for Johnston and his friends. The 'authorities' look rather black today. General [Robert E.] Lee is over here for consultation." The *Examiner* was soon denouncing Hood as "notoriously incapable of commanding anything larger than a division," and it demanded the restoration of either Johnston or Beauregard.[78]

For weeks, some in the capital believed—probably to the point of delusion—that if the Southerners could only maintain Atlanta then it would prevent Lincoln's reelection and result in a negotiated peace. The capture of the city would now "have the effect of consolidating all parties in the North in favor of a continued prosecution of the war," analyzed the *Dispatch*. A disgusted Daniel at the *Examiner* believed that the city's capture came "in the very nick of time when such a victory alone could save the party of Lincoln from irretrievable ruin." It would unquestionably "render incalculable assistance to the party of Lincoln and obscures the prospects of peace, late[ly] so bright."[79]

Judith McGuire expressed her disdain at the fickleness of a public that once denounced Davis for not removing Johnston yet now blamed him for Hood's aggressiveness. "For weeks the President was abused without measure because he [Johnston] was not removed, and now the same people are using the same terms towards him [Davis] because the course they absolutely required at his hands disappointed them." Six weeks earlier there were those who "curled the lip in scorn at General Johnston's sloth and want of energy, and praised Hood's course from the beginning of the war, now shrug their unmilitary shoulders, who straps have never graced a battlefield, and pronounce the change 'unfortunate and uncalled for.' General Hood, they say, was an 'admirable Brigadier' but his 'promotion was most unfortunate' while General Johnston's 'Fabian Policy' is now pronounced the very thing for the 'situation' the course of which would have saved Atlanta, and have made all right." The unforgiving rage against Hood nonetheless continued to carry the scuttlebutt about town. The rumor floated that he would soon be superseded by Beauregard. "[N]ot at all probable," thought Gorgas. "It would however be popular. The general judgment is that Hood has not the capacity for such a command. The President is strongly prejudiced against Beauregard." Such irascible conversations nonetheless continued.[80]

The vice president heard from the blustery Tombs. Hood was "getting rid of Bragg's worthless pets as fast as he can, but Davis supports a great number of them." His evaluation of the army commander was far from encouraging: "Hood I think the very best of the generals of his school; but like all of the rest of them he knows no more of business than a ten[-]year[-]old boy, and [he] don't know who does know anything about it."[81]

While Robert E. Lee was holding the line against Grant's hordes in Virginia, the war was clearly being lost in the West. The struggle for Atlanta had been a national trauma. Precisely how badly the Army of Tennessee had been shattered, and the current temperature of western morale, remained uncertain. It was time for Davis to make a visit to Georgia.

14

Trouble in Kirby-Smithdom

The Missouri congressional delegation was in a state of chaos. Back in April 1863, Representative Charles M. Cooke (Missouri-1), former judge, Sterling Price aide, and virulent anti-Davis critic, died of consumption at the age of thirty-nine after a long illness. Five months later, on September 3, Senator Robert L. Y. Peyton, engaged to Price's daughter, died while in Alabama. There were different stories about his demise—some claiming inflammation of the bowels and others that he contracted pneumonia while serving in Vicksburg. Congress was not in session, so Governor Reynolds had time to reflect on his replacement. Senators Johnson and Mitchell advised him to appoint "your big man"—meaning Price—but the governor was not interested in placing another anti-administration Missourian in Congress. Price claimed that he was not a debater and that he was not interested in the position, although there were those on his staff who pressed for his nomination. Reynolds instead appointed Waldo P. Johnson, a former U.S. senator and friend of the president. Senator Clark, who drew a two-year term, was hoping to be appointed to fill out Peyton's unexpired term, but Reynolds had had enough of his drunken sexual escapades. Clark did not help his case by referring to Davis as a "slow coach," by denouncing Benjamin as "a cut-prick Jew," and by unceremoniously climbing through a window in the War Department to see Randolph. Reynolds succeeded him with Colonel L. M. Lewis, who at the time was a prisoner of war. This led to a Missouri divide between the anti-Davis faction, led by Price (who supported Clark for Peyton's seat), and the pro-Davis faction, led by Reynolds.[1]

The next congressional race would be in May 1864, and already candidates were throwing their hats in the ring. Reynolds apprised Davis of the prospects: the able Nimrod L. Norton, who was running on the "sobriety and morality platform," Peter S. Wilkes, a "sensible man," Robert A. Hatcher, a "man of ability" who had served in the Army of Tennessee, and Thomas Snead, a Price man who would oppose the administration. Those running to keep their seats included Casper Bell, who remained unpopular because of his support of the obnoxious Foote, Aaron Conrow, "an avowed administration man," Thomas Freeman, Thomas Harris, whose "personal habits" (alcoholism) were well known, and George Vest, whose "habits and neglect of office seekers at Richmond may defeat him." But Vest was not defeated; nor was the troublesome Clark yet out of the picture. Although a Senate seat was no longer available, he ran for a seat in the House. If he lost, Reynolds warned the president to offer him a military appointment far from Missouri, "as he is an agitator." But Clark, with the strong support of Price, won. He openly touted his victory as a "popular rebuke" of Reynolds for not having supported him in the Senate.[2]

Then there was the case of Major Edwin Price, son of the famed general, who after his prisoner exchange resigned his commission and publicly renounced the Confederacy. General Price offered a feeble explanation for his son's conduct to Vest, who in turn related it to Reynolds. The explanation only fueled Reynold's suspicions that the general himself was merely an opportunist whose devotion to the South was at best tepid. The governor continued to strongly suspect that the general had a hand in the so-called Northwest Conspiracy and that perhaps he was now hatching some other plot with his traitorous son. He did not relate his concerns to either Davis or Kirby Smith, fearing that they would transfer the general and create a "fuss." Despite disingenuously assuring Price that he remained his "*warm personal friend*," Reynolds kept his eye on Old Pap.[3]

The political deaths continued to mount. On September 20, Arkansas Senator Charles B. Mitchel passed away while in Little Rock. He was forty-nine-years old. "By the death of Senator Mitchel, you have sustained the loss of a very true and faithful friend," Senator Bob Johnson wrote the president. "It makes a gap in the role of your earnest supporters, not easily filled from this State." He was right. The state legislature appointed Augustus Garland, one of the administration's political enemies, to fill Mitchel's unexpired term.[4]

Ever since late January 1864, Richmond had been aware that the Federals were building up their forces at New Orleans. According to his spies in the city, Smith placed Nathaniel Banks's strength at 21,000. Although a move against Mobile was possible, Smith thought otherwise. Intelligence related that Banks resisted being drawn east into Grant's orbit. This left only one possibility: "The only true line of operations by which the enemy can penetrate the department is the valley of the Red River," wrote the department commander. As soon as the river gauge rose, he predicted a joint army–navy expedition toward Shreveport. Smith thus began concentrating forces from Texas and Arkansas toward Louisiana. A reprinted Houston article in the *Enquirer* openly stated that Texas, not Mobile, was the intended target. What Richmond officials did not know was that Smith and Richard Taylor were now bickering, the latter desiring to make a preemptive strike before the bluecoats reached the interior. Taylor insubordinately hinted that he might even disregard his superior's orders. Smith's plans also delayed Price's grandiose projection for a Missouri offensive. None of this infighting, at least for now, got back to the War Department or found its way into the capital press.[5]

The first that Richmond knew of a Louisiana victory came on April 12 when an intercepted Union dispatch was sent to the chief surgeon in Baton Rouge. The captured message was forwarded to the capital via Mobile: "We met the enemy near Shreveport. Union forces repulsed with great loss. How many [Federal patients] can you accommodate in hospitals at Baton Rouge? Steamer Essex, or Benton destroyed by torpedoes in Red River, and a transport captured by the Confederates." The next day, April 13, Kirby Smith's dispatch of the previous day clicked across the wire: "Providence has given us a signal and glorious victory." With 16,000 troops he had defeated Banks's expeditionary force of 35,000 in battles at Mansfield and Pleasant Hill. Confederate killed and wounded were given as 2,000, but the Federals had lost 3,000 prisoners, 21 guns, and 200 wagons. An updated report later listed Union casualties as 5,000 killed and wounded and 4,000 captured. President Davis related to Representative Thomas Hanley of Arkansas that for the first time in the war he "saw a bright day dawning" for the trans-Mississippi.[6]

Insiders such as Gorgas soon began hearing the talk, but it would be nearly a month before the papers caught up with the news. A courier arrived in Richmond from Louisiana and related the details. Smith intentionally fell back toward Shreveport hoping to draw Banks into the interior and the Union fleet toward the shallows. The defeated Federals were in full retreat. The general now had the option of reclaiming either New Orleans or Arkansas and Missouri. The Federal fleet, trapped by a lowering river gauge, escaped by the construction of an ingenious dam. "If *our* boats had been so caught, we should simply have blown them up," admitted Gorgas.[7]

Even though Banks's army remained a threat in Louisiana, Smith received word that the northern portion of the Federal "pincer"—a 12,000-man army under Frederick Steele marching from Little Rock and another column proceeding from Fort Smith—still threatened Shreveport. To combat this advance, Price in Arkansas had only 6,000 cavalry and 1,500 infantry. Taylor implored Smith to continue after Banks, believing that the certain destruction of his army could have been achieved. Taylor further argued that once Steele learned of Bank's defeat he would withdraw. In the final battle at Pleasant Hill, the Confederates had been defeated, however, revealing that a Confederate pursuit would be far from a mop-up operation. Believing that Banks had been severely crippled and no longer presented a threat, and asserting that Arkansas could be "saved politically," Smith redirected three divisions from Taylor to reinforce Price. It would be the beginning of a bitter dispute that would reach all the way to Richmond, one in which Davis sided with Taylor.[8]

Steele's column made it to Camden, Arkansas, when the Confederates struck. According to reprinted Northern accounts, two of his supply columns were ambushed, one on April 18, the other on April 25, with Union losses totaling 1,401 casualties, six guns, and 420 wagons. What the accounts did not reveal, even the Northern papers, was that matters had spun out of control. Many of the captives were black troops, who were then massacred by the Southerners and their Indian allies, the latter taking scalps. There was no gentleman's war in the trans-Mississippi—only merciless killing.[9]

On May 11, the *Whig* semi-announced a Price victory. Steele, with 9,000 troops, had been captured at Camden. The report awaited confirmation, but the paper remained hopeful that Price would make a "clean thing of it." Three days later, Robert E. Lee issued his General Orders

No. 41 declaring, among other things, that Steele's army had indeed been captured. The only problem was that it was not true. On a dark and rainy night, Steele escaped the noose and beat a hasty retreat back to Little Rock. In the press, Price was nonetheless hailed as "the deliverer of Arkansas and Missouri." In the War Department, Kean gloated at the near destruction of Banks and Steele, the former limping back to New Orleans with only 5,000 men, the latter arriving in Little Rock "with a remnant."[10]

The truth was far less dramatic. Although both Federal forces had been defeated, both had been allowed to escape. Taylor pointed the finger at Smith, and Smith at Price. By late April, Taylor had unleashed a tirade of criticism of the department commander, in part claiming that he was merely seeking personal glory. Smith had abandoned the "certain destruction of an army of 30,000 men" to "chase after a force [Steele's] of 10,000 in full retreat with over 100 miles the start."[11]

Taylor's case was not helped by the Richmond press corps. The *Whig* editorialized that the enemy had been thoroughly expelled from western Louisiana as well as Arkansas, "thus leaving Missouri open to another advance of our troops." An *Appeal* article, reprinted in the *Dispatch*, assured readers that there were "no other Federal troops in southwestern Louisiana" and that Magruder had "little or nothing" to contend with in Texas. The *Whig* declared that Banks's army had been so badly crippled that it would remain out of service for the balance of the summer. The capital dailies saw a cup overflowing, but Taylor could see only a cup half-empty.[12]

Taylor had powerful friends in the Louisiana congressional delegation, starting with Duncan F. Kenner, a millionaire sugar plantation owner, thoroughbred horse breeder, and chairman of the powerful Confederate Ways and Means Committee; as fate would have it, his sister-in-law was married to Taylor. Kenner had worked under the tutelage of John Slidell—in short, he was arguably the most powerful politician in the state. In March 1864, Kenner visited Smith in Louisiana and pleaded Taylor's case for reinforcements. He was shocked when told that Taylor did not desire additional troops. A stunned Kenner exclaimed that it could not be so, but Smith showed him a letter, calling attention to a particular passage. Kenner, of course, immediately wrote to Taylor, who in turn fired off a letter to Smith that his words had been misconstrued.[13]

Although the increasingly bitter dispute between Smith and Taylor

The Trans-Mississippi. Map by Mary Lee Eggert.

never became press fodder, it was not free of Richmond chatter; even Mary Chesnut heard the talk. Taylor made his case to Kenner, while E. Warren Moise, a powerful Louisiana magistrate, appealed to Congressman Charles F. Conrad. Thomas Snead, now representing Missouri-1, believed that the talk was common knowledge. He was sorry to hear it, as Taylor had "powerful friends at Richmond" and Smith had "powerful enemies there." Congressman Garland, now back in Arkansas, lamented the "unfortunate difficulty" between Smith and Taylor but assured Seddon that it was a capital story that received little notice in Arkansas.[14]

Smith, who finally removed Taylor from command, wrote directly to the president, a risky move given Davis's family connection to the Louisiana general. He initially attributed Taylor's complaint to his "sickness and irritation," although subsequent letters crossed the line of insubordination and could not be excused. Taylor had written that he had thrown himself "between you [Smith] and popular indignation" but that he intended to tell him the truth "however objectionable to you." Smith had heard that a campaign was afoot in Richmond to have him relieved of command. "I know that facts will be misrepresented and distorted by certain parties in Louisiana who are waging a bitter war against me." The department commander was also not beyond undertaking his own letter-writing campaign, and soon Governor Reynolds was firing off missives of support to Waldo Johnson of Missouri and Mitchell of Arkansas. When Congressman Robert Hilton of Florida subsequently defended Smith, however, the general criticized him for not having all the facts.[15]

Then there was the ongoing dispute between Smith and Price. When Congress adjourned in mid-June 1864, most congressmen remained in town and hung around the War Department to get the latest news. Unfortunately, the wires were down in all directions, meaning that couriers had to relay dispatches, slowing down the flow of information. In the Missouri delegation, Vest and Conrow remained in Richmond, but the other five representatives traveled to Mobile and Mississippi, and one, Robert Hatcher, went to Johnston's army in Georgia. Writing from Mobile, Representative Snead addressed Price about an embarrassing incident. Following the recent campaign, Congress had extended a formal thanks to both Taylor and Smith for their roles in the operation, but Price received no such acknowledgement. Snead suspected that Smith was behind the snub. "I know the principal cause of the failure to embrace you in that vote was the opposition of General Taylor's [Louisiana] friends." Snead nonetheless suspicioned that "General Smith has not reported you faithfully at Richmond, where one of his staff, Major [Guy M.] Bryan, was during the last ten to fifteen days of this session." There seemed to be an open secret in the capital that Smith, through his proxy Bryan, was quietly undercutting Price.[16]

With the trans-Mississippi now, in the words of the *Dispatch*, "in a most promising condition," the time seemed ripe for an offensive. From Smith's perspective, Federal naval power meant that an attack on New Orleans was impracticable. He therefore turned his attention to a Missouri offensive. Who would lead the expedition was the issue. Still angry with Price for allowing Steele's army to escape, he strongly opposed the Missourian. Although admitting to Davis that Price's "name and popularity" would be an asset, he was "neither capable of organizing[] nor operating an army [and] should not be left in command of the district [or] of an army in the field." He preferred Taylor, but with the Louisiana general mired in vitriolic attacks, Smith, after consideration of several others, had no choice but to unenthusiastically assign Price. Buckner, who recently reported for duty, would command in Arkansas in his absence.[17]

Before the offensive began, however, the War Department insisted that Smith send troops across the Mississippi River to reinforce Johnston in Georgia. While Smith pledged his support, he warned of serious consequences. If Banks renewed a large-scale offensive in Louisiana, "I will be powerless to oppose his advance." Smith's planned Missouri offensive, minus infantry support, would necessarily be reduced to a cavalry raid, and in the meantime the Arkansas Valley would be left defenseless. Davis's sharp response made it clear that he was not in a sympathetic mood. To start, he was not aware of any planned offensive. That aside, he wondered how the plans for a Missouri drive, "for which you say had been perfected," could have been reliant "on infantry which was below the Lower Red River." He pointedly wrote that "you must expect frequent diversity of views unless fuller information is given." He then proceeded to lecture Smith on his failure to send troops east of the Mississippi River.[18]

Taylor, recently promoted to lieutenant general (the first non–West Pointer to receive that rank), proceeded to march two understrength divisions—together not more than 4,000 infantry—toward the Mississippi River for crossing. Enemy spies quickly got wind of the movement, however, and by mid-August the Union navy's constant patrolling made a transfer impossible. But there were other problems. As the column neared the river, several hundred desertions occurred. Three companies of Texans walked off and headed home; they were arrested and brought back. Taylor, fearful that he might lose half his troops, suspended operations. Gorgas heard that Taylor's troops "will not serve on this side of the river if they can help it. If we get no troops from Trans-Miss the plan of operations for the relief of Hood will be seriously interfered with." Jones also read the dispatches and sadly wrote that there would be no more troops crossing the Mississippi, "or they will be sure to desert." The ringleaders of the mutiny—a captain and ten others—were arrested, tried, and shot, but the operation proved an utter failure. The faintly delusional plan of crossing troops east of the Mississippi River was forever settled. The only one who ultimately crossed (in a canoe) to the east bank of the Mississippi was Taylor, who assumed command of the Department of Alabama, Mississippi, and East Louisiana.[19]

Price outmaneuvered Steele's forces in Little Rock and began his Missouri offensive on September 19. Richmond citizens were kept remarkably current on events through the usual source: reprinted Northern articles. Price began the campaign by some accounts with 12,000–15,000 troopers, while other sources placed the number at 20,000–25,000. The Northern papers insisted that, as the Confederate column pushed through Missouri, all males aged 16–50 were forcibly conscripted—even those with Federal sympathies. Given that Smith's September 30 return to the War Department was so "unintelligibly prepared," it is doubtful that Seddon had any more information than what he read in the papers.[20]

Price's original plan was to advance in three columns to Fredericktown, Missouri, and then push on to St. Louis. Standing in the way, however, was the Union garrison of Fort Davidson at Pilot Knob, about sixty-five miles south of St. Louis and sixty miles west of the Mississippi River. Not wishing to leave the garrison in his rear, Price assaulted on September 27. He was bloodily repulsed, with the Northern papers claiming seventy-five Federal casualties and 1,500 Confederates. That night the garrison slipped away. Official Richmond had no other information.[21]

"If General Price continues his march upon St. Louis with the rapidity which has already characterized his movements the city will fall into his hands." Thus read the *Dispatch* of October 5. But Price had a change of plans. Having been bloodied at Pilot Knob, and hearing of Union reinforcements arriving at St. Louis, he abandoned his original plan. He only feinted toward the city, capturing a hundred militia at Franklin, on the outskirts of St. Louis. He then veered toward Jefferson City, where according to the *New York Herald* he closed to within ten miles by October 8. Meanwhile, William "Bloody Bill" Anderson, a sadistic Confederate guerrilla, murdered every Federal he could get his hands on, including twenty-four unarmed soldiers at Centralia and, in an ambush later that day, over a hundred more. Richmond citizens read of his murders but not of his savage tortures, scalpings, beheadings, and corporeal mutilations.[22]

Unwilling to tackle a well-guarded Jefferson City, Price continued west. The campaign came to a head during the Battle of Westport, south of Kansas City, on October 23. Richmond received only Northern accounts, which were dismissed as useless, but even so there appeared to have been a significant Union victory. One account claimed that Price's Missourians had vowed not to retreat back into Arkansas, meaning that they intended to continue an insurgency in their home state. There was also reported infighting. Confederate Brigadier General John S. Marmaduke had been captured and was talking to Northern reporters. He openly declared that he had never favored Price's raid, "on the ground that nothing could be accomplished that would affect the final result of the war." Governor Reynolds and Price were also said to be squabbling. Indeed, Reynolds complained to Representative Vest that the campaign had been nothing more than a "weak and disgraceful plundering raid." It mattered not. Neither Jones nor Kean, who were preoccupied with more pressing military matters, bothered to even mention the trans-Mississippi events. In early January 1865, a report came to Richmond that Price had died. He was not dead; only irrelevant.[23]

In December 1864, the *Whig* launched a blistering attack against Smith titled "The Military Administration of the Trans-Mississippi Department." The paper observed that A. J. Smith's corps had shifted east of the Mississippi River and had reinforced George Thomas's army at Nashville. Additionally, the XIX Corps had arrived in Washington, D.C., just in time to save the city from the attack of Jubal Early. These draws were made from the trans-Mississippi because the Federals "knew they had but little to fear from the languid and indecisive operations of the Lieutenant General commanding." The Union transfers to the east side of the Mississippi River were due "almost entirely[] to the hesitancy and lassitude of Lieutenant General Kirby Smith." The paper further blamed the department commander's "extraordinary tenderness" on Banks's defeated army, which would have resulted in the recapture of New Orleans. He instead sent his infantry against Steele in Arkansas, eighty miles from Shreveport, although the enemy was already retreating before Price's cavalry. The *Whig* asserted that if Beauregard had been in command Bank's army would never have escaped. The next month another savage article appeared, which clearly revealed that the editor's source was almost certainly one of Taylor's staff officers.[24]

Smith wrote directly to the president addressing the fact that he had "been attacked in the columns of the Richmond Whig." He continued: "I know that efforts have been made through other journals east of the Mississippi to prejudice the public mind and destroy confidence in the purity of my motives and in my ability to command." He then offered to be relieved of command. Two days later, March 9, 1865, he received the president's December 24 letter that had the effect of piling on. The president regretted that the transfer of Union troops east of the Mississippi River "was not promptly met by the forwarding of reinforcements from you." Again, the department commander offered to be relieved.[25]

With the Confederacy collapsing, and the president himself attempting to flee to the trans-Mississippi, Smith, Price, and Reynolds, among others, crossed the Rio Grande into Mexico. In the end, the Confederates west of the Mississippi River failed to affect the more significant war in the Heartland, in large part due to a roster of inept leaders. Senator Oldham would later conclude that the trans-Mississippi became a place where washed-out generals could be sent "in a kind of honorable exile." There would be those who would argue, then and now, that the region was not worth the effort that Richmond put into it. From a political point of view, however, it must be remembered that the theater accounted for a third of the Senate and over 20 percent of the House of Representatives, including Louis Wigfall, arguably the Senate's most powerful voice. They were not going to be ignored and served as a bloc that kept up unrelenting political pressure on the Confederate White House.[26]

15

Your Faces Will Be Turned Homeward

By the early fall of 1864, war-weariness was fast reaching a breaking point. Atlanta was gone, as was virtually all of the Upper Heartland. So desperate had times become that the *Enquirer* advocated for Congress to purchase 250,000 slaves, train them in camps of instruction, and then place them in the ranks. It was virtually the same proposal that ten months earlier had caused such a backlash in the Army of Tennessee and had probably cost Pat Cleburne a corps command. It was time for the chief executive to make yet another western tour.[1]

Accompanied by two aides, Davis quietly boarded the afternoon train of the Richmond & Petersburg Railroad on a "bright and pleasant" Tuesday, September 20. Richmonders learned of the departure only through reprinted news accounts from other cities. The purpose of the trek was to get a personal appraisal of the Army of Tennessee and its leadership, to discuss strategic plans, and to raise damaged civilian morale. Davis had received a disturbing letter from Major General Samuel French written on behalf of "several officers" and relating a "feeling of depression" in the army. The president determined to, as Seddon wrote, "see and judge for himself."[2]

Sherman had proposed a "peace conference" to Georgia officials—Governor Brown, Alexander Stephens, and Senator Johnson. The purpose, according to the *Dispatch*, was to "detach the State of Georgia, if possible, from the Confederacy." The paper was certain that the meeting would not take place, but it also expressed concern. "We make these remarks because separate State action has been agitated of late in more quarters than one," thereby giving encouragement to the "peace delusion" advocates. The paper queried if Georgia would now abandon Virginia "after having dragged her into this war?" Georgia leadership, however, felt that their state had been neglected in favor of the Old Dominion. A Georgian warned the president of a rumor that the state had already sent an agent to negotiate with Washington. He also had heard of a general in the Army of Tennessee who entertained "reconstruction opinions," and he was certain that there were others. The political fragmentation that had characterized the western congressional delegation had metastasized to the Heartland; Davis was worried.[3]

The presidential party pulled into Macon on September 23, where Davis made a prepared speech. In the course of his remarks, he could not resist an ungraceful jab at Johnston. "I even heard that I had sent Bragg with pontoons to cross into Cuba," then added: "But we must be charitable." The remark prompted an angry letter from "A Georgian," who noted that the sardonic comment, which deviated from "your usual dignified course," could only have been made out of fatigue or "perhaps a little too much wine." He pleaded that Hood, "a supercilious braggart," be replaced by Beauregard.[4]

The only account read by Richmond citizens of Davis's visit to the Army of Tennessee came from a reprinted article from the *Columbus Enquirer*. The president arrived at Palmetto, Georgia, at 3:30 p.m. on a rainy Sunday, September 25. On Monday he reviewed the army and that night Delivered a twenty-minute speech to a large gathering of soldiers who were left "spell-bound." He turned to the Tennesseans of Cheatham's Division and, in a rather astonishing security breach, said: "Be of good cheer, for within a short while your faces will be turned homeward, and your feet pressing Tennessee soil," words greeted with a thunderous cheer. Hood was also called for a speech. He rose from his chair, admitted that he was not an orator, and said: "Within a few days more I expect to give the order 'Forward' and I believe that you are, like myself, willing to go forward, even if we live on parched corn and beef." Governor Harris then made a speech and Senator Sparrow addressed the Louisiana brigade. The *Enquirer* cited a Northern source claiming that Davis received a "cold reception" from the troops. When he asked his generals why, they related that the army was dissatisfied with Johnston's removal.[5]

Hood was ultimately retained, but command changes were in the offing. Robert E. Lee, perhaps at the president's bequest but more likely on his own volition, asked Beauregard if he would be willing to go to Georgia and command the Army of Tennessee. Anxious to regain his independent command and get out from under Lee's shadow (he was essentially a full general serving as a corps commander under the Virginian), the Creole agreed. While the president was on his tour, the news leaked out in Charleston, and was repeated in the *Whig*, that Beauregard would indeed supersede Hood. In the *Enquirer* of October 4, it was again reported that "the general impression here [Griffin, Georgia]" was that the Louisiana general would replace Hood. When the subsequent Davis–Beauregard meeting occurred in Augusta, the general was doubtless taken aback and disappointed to hear that he was instead being offered the new Military Division of the West. His jurisdiction would include the Department of Alabama, Mississippi, and East Louisiana, now under Richard Taylor, and Hood's Department of Tennessee and Georgia, but his role would be advisory only except when present with either army. The decision was essentially political; it silenced Hood's critics by giving Beauregard nominal control, placated the public clamor, and removed the troublesome Creole, who had been clashing with the Richmond hierarchy—Lee, Bragg, and Seddon. In desperation, Beauregard accepted. Jones's comment that the general had been tapped "in response to the universal calls of the people" left much unsaid.[6]

Hardee had long desired to be away from Hood; the feeling was mutual. In conversation with the Georgian, Davis transferred him to Charleston. After three and a half years in the West, Old Reliable would now be on the coast. Although the *Enquirer* would report the rumor that Richard Taylor would be his successor, it would end up being Cheatham. Hardee's transfer was widely publicized in the Richmond press; Cheatham's promotion was never mentioned.[7]

There were press claims that recruits were flocking to Hood's army, that two of Sherman's divisions had been sent to recruit in Kentucky, and that Blair's Union corps had been disbanded, their service commitments having expired. Hood related to Bragg, whether it was true or not, that "Sherman is weaker now than he will be in the future, and I as strong as I can expect to be." As officials pored over the September returns, however, there was grave concern. Government officials could readily see that the army's 33,479 present-for-duty infantry and artillery on September 20 were down more than 21,000 since June 10. Johnston, according to Hood, had lost 25,000 men in seventy days as compared to his loss of 8,000 in fifty-four days. Operating with Hood's army would be Red Jackson's 5,000-man cavalry division (Wheeler was then in North Alabama), making a total of approximately 38,000 to oppose Sherman, who Hood estimated could field "about sixty-five thousand (65,000) effectives[] and two divisions of cavalry." The Texan pleaded for reinforcements from the trans-Mississippi and even requested that Lee give him his old division from the Army of Northern Virginia. Davis intended to do neither, writing: "No other sources remain."[8]

Hood's plans toward the end of September were known only to Davis, Bragg, and Seddon. His letter of September 21 indicated that he would march north, cross the Chattahoochee River, skirt Marietta, and then strike the Western & Atlantic Railroad, described by the press as the "esophagus of the Yankee army." Some surmised that Hood's next move would be to Blue Mountain, Alabama, to operate in Sherman's rear, forcing him to give up Atlanta and pursue. Forrest was meanwhile wreaking havoc, capturing Athens, Alabama, with its garrison of 1,300 troops, along with 500 horses, 50 wagons and ambulances, and two trains of quartermaster and commissary supplies, all of this with a loss of five killed and twenty-five wounded. He then raided into Middle Tennessee, destroying five bridges on the railroad from Decatur, Alabama, to Pulaski, Tennessee.[9]

Hood frankly conceded that he was uncertain about the enemy's next move but guessed that Sherman would march back to Alabama and move on Columbus (Georgia) or Montgomery so as to open communication with Mobile. Such a maneuver would threaten the industrial complexes at Selma and Columbus. Under the circumstances, Hood would strike Sherman's flank and rear. The Northern press, however, openly reported that the intended Federal target was Savannah. The city was a 250-mile trek from Atlanta, requiring twenty to twenty-five days. The soldiers could carry ten days' rations in their knapsacks and the wagons could haul another ten days' worth. Sherman, according to the report, had stockpiled sixty days' rations in Atlanta. The *Enquirer* conceded that such a move would destroy the railroads "but otherwise do no harm." The country to the north would then be open to the Ohio River.[10]

Not waiting for Sherman to make his move, Hood, with Davis's permission, determined to seize the initiative. He planned to move north and disrupt Northern rail communications between the Chattahoochee and Etowah Rivers, hoping to draw Sherman after him and away from the interior. If Hood proved unable to fight an open battle, he would withdraw west toward Gadsden, Alabama. If Sherman instead moved east toward Augusta and ultimately the Atlantic Coast (as the Northern papers had been claiming), then Hood would attempt to get ahead of him—a dicey proposition, indeed. He would be drawing his supplies from Selma via the West Point & Montgomery Railroad. Kean read the telegram and recognized the danger, but he also saw potential. He called the strategy "a very bold purpose—nothing less than to turn Atlanta on the west, crossing the Chattahoochee and falling on Sherman's communications. This is extremely hazardous. It is an imitation of Sherman's own maneuver, and exposes Hood as Sherman exposed himself. If it is successful, it will be a very great success as it will compel him to evacuate Atlanta and come out and fight on Hood's own ground."[11]

On October 6, a Hood dispatch clicked across the wire; he had successfully crossed the Chattahoochee River and was in Sherman's rear. A. P. Stewart's Corps had struck Big Shanty and Ackworth, capturing 350 prisoners, ripped up ten miles of track, and was now moving on Allatoona Pass. "We shall soon have stirring news," wrote an encouraged Jones. But the news, received on October 9, proved far from encouraging. French's Division was repulsed at Allatoona—no further details. Subsequent Yankee reports claimed a grisly affair with 200 Rebel dead and 1,000 wounded and captured and 700 Union casualties, but Jones withheld judgment until Southern accounts arrived.[12]

Wild rumors swirled, including the recapture of Atlanta; Jones frankly did not know what to believe. For the next week, only Beauregard's dispatch of October 9 arrived, stating that Sherman had left a corps in Atlanta and was pursuing Hood with five corps—some 40,000 troops. Despite the dearth of official information, the clerk remained optimistic: "No doubt we have gained advantages there." He was right; on October 17 it was learned that Dalton had been captured with its garrison of 1,000, later revealed to be mostly black troops. The *Dispatch* of October 19 claimed that Atlanta had been cut off from all supplies for ten to fifteen days. With the notable exception of the Allatoona debacle, Hood's North Georgia foray appeared to be working.[13]

"The whereabouts of General Hood is as uncertain to the Confederates as it is to Sherman." Thus read the *Dispatch* editorial of October 26. There appeared to be evidence, however, that Hood had shifted his maneuvers to North Alabama. The paper saw bright days ahead. Even if Sherman could defend his rail line to Chattanooga, Hood could move through Wills Valley and strike at Bridgeport. His line being perpendicular to Sherman's, Hood had only one point of vulnerability—his terminus at Blue Mountain (Anniston), Alabama—but "our army covers that." Forrest meanwhile had been operating along the Tennessee River below Florence. The *Southern Confederacy*, now being published in Macon, pronounced Hood a "genius" and claimed that his men cheered him as he passed. The Northern papers were telling a different tale, the *Chicago Tribune* declaring: "Hood cannot hope to escape annihilation; but what follies will not desperation sometimes generate."[14]

War Department officials actually knew precisely where Hood was headed: Gadsden, Alabama. Hood arrived there on October 20, and the army trailed in over the next two days. From there, according to Beauregard's dispatch of October 22, it would march to Guntersville, Alabama, where the army would cross the Tennessee River. On the last day of the month, however, Richmond officials were surprised to read that the army had been drawn much farther west, bypassing Decatur and proceeding to Bainbridge, Alabama. Again, a crossing proved impossible and the troops thus continued their march to Tuscaloosa, across the river from Florence. The Richmond public knew none of this until November 5, when it was revealed through the Northern press.[15]

Unfortunately, Beauregard conceded that he had lost sight of Sherman's army. The Northern papers typically filled in the details, but even they appeared muddled on the subject. Eventually it became clear that Sherman had not taken the bait and that he was forging his own path to the south toward Macon. An irritated Davis wrote Hood that he should have beaten the Federals in detail before advancing to Tennessee. It was ultimately divined that Sherman's target was Savannah. "Possibly this may be mere rumor, but [we] think the public [is] entitled to know exactly what is bruited about," reported the *Dispatch*.[16]

It would be seventeen more days, November 5, before the next communication arrived. Beauregard advised that Hood would proceed to Middle Tennessee, leaving Sherman on his flank and rear. "It is a desperate conception, and will probably be a brilliant success—or a sad disaster," concluded Jones. By that time, it was known that Sherman was content to leave Hood to a hodgepodge Federal army assembling in Nashville under George Thomas while he began his own March to the Sea. "[Sherman's] army is, beyond all question, to secure a position on the seaboard," the *Whig* concluded.[17]

As desperate fighting continued in the West, embarrassing fistfights erupted between western congressmen. The genesis of the disruptions was once again Henry Foote, who was now advocating a negotiated peace with the North. While Davis was touring in the West, Foote openly told out that if Richmond was ever lost he would advocate appointing a dictator, at which time he was warned that such loose talk could get him shot. As Arkansas Representative Thomas Hanley made a presentation in a committee, Foote disrespectfully laughed. This led to words that eventually ended in a tussle before they were pulled apart. Foote later got into an argument on the House floor with Edmund Dargan, who called the Tennessean a "damned rascal." He then rushed Foote with a Bowie knife but was restrained by colleagues. Foote, with typical dramatic flair, shouted: "I defy the steel of the assassin."[18]

In November 1864, Foote made derogatory remarks about John Mitchell, a correspondent for the *Examiner*, whom he described as having "crawled from one newspaper to another." Mitchell, a fiery Irishman, determined to take the issue to the next level and challenged the aggressively opinionated representative to a duel. He sent the written challenge via Congressman Swan—a poor choice since the East Tennessean himself detested Foote and had not spoken to him for a year. Not knowing how to find him, Swan was led by H. Rives Pollard, editor of the *Examiner*, who was totally unaware of his intentions. The duo arrived at the five-story Ballard House at the northeast corner of Fourteenth and Franklin Streets. Knocking on the room door, Mrs. Foote was heard to say, "Come in." Swan and Pollard entered and saw Foote dozing by the fireplace. As they walked into the room, Pollard said: "Governor"—referring to Foote's former Mississippi title—"you are acquainted with your colleague, Mr. Swan?" Foote snapped back, "That man is not a gentleman, and I can't see him." Swan, carrying a heavy umbrella, then struck him on the forehead, causing a bloody gash. One eyewitness, hearing women screaming, came out of his room to see Swan in the hallway with a raised chair in his hands. Foote ran to his bedroom, grabbed a revolver from his dresser, and cocked it. Swan recoiled as Pollard got between them. General Williams Wickham, rushing from his room, whisked Swan down the hallway.

Foote, not content to let the matter go, now determined to challenge Swan to a duel. A warrant was issued against both Foote and Swan, and on November 23 they were arraigned in mayor's court. Three hours of testimony were taken, with all the city's papers printing the juicy details. The mayor ultimately ordered a cash bond for both men and instructed them to stay away from each other. The proposed Swan–Foote duel likewise never occurred. In the midst of the context of massive death, suffering, and a crumbling Confederacy, the incident offered a momentary diversion.[19]

Meanwhile, Johnston's after-action report of the Atlanta Campaign arrived on the president's desk. Not surprising, the general mentioned his numerous calls for S. D. Lee's cavalry to raid in Sherman's rear, all to no avail. Various accusations had been made against him, he wrote, "some published in newspapers, in such a manner as to appear to have official authority, and others circulated orally in Georgia and Alabama and imputed to General Bragg." The primary accusation was the issue of his retreats and his purported refusal to defend Atlanta. He responded by saying that, having done precisely what Lee had done in Virginia, he supposed that he would not be censured. Davis initially withheld the report from Congress, stating its "potential for controversy." Wigfall loudly protested and demanded its release. Beverly Johnston, the general's brother, who happened to be in the capital and had a copy of the report, privately leaked it to selected congressmen. Eventually the president released it to the Senate, with the addendum that it not be made public.[20]

The only news from the Heartland came from the Northern press. There were those who believed that Hood, with the occupation of Florence, would go into winter quarters and gather supplies. Soon, however, his army—estimated at 40,000 troops—was on the move and had crossed the Tennessee line. The bluecoats, under John M. Schofield, evacuated Pulaski and fell back to Columbia, a town of 6,000 forty miles south of Nashville on the Decatur Railroad. A Northern correspondent formed the opinion that Hood was attempting to avoid a fight and intended to skirt past Nashville into Kentucky. Indeed, Gorgas heard that Hood was veering toward East Tennessee for an apparent march into Kentucky. Richmond citizens knew only what they read in the papers, and even those accounts came from Union sources. The New York papers claimed that Stephen D. Lee's Corps was at Florence and Cheatham's corps was advancing on Waynesboro, Tennessee, halfway between Florence and Columbia, Tennessee. Forrest's cavalry was in undisputed control of the region within a thirty-mile radius of Florence. George Thomas's two Union corps, the IV and the XXIII, were at Pulaski, sixty to seventy miles from Nashville.[21]

Richmonders awoke on Monday, December 5, to jubilant news:

"Hood's Advance on Nashville—Victory Over Schofield—The Enemy Driven Fifteen Miles." Thus read the *Dispatch*—its source being Yankee accounts. George Thomas, commanding at Nashville, claimed that hundreds were fleeing toward the capital; the Confederates were said to be confiscating all horses, mules, hogs, and cattle. There were some Northern papers that claimed the Battle of Franklin was a victory, but the *Dispatch* warned its readers not to be misled. These accounts were based on the fact that a thousand Confederate prisoners were taken early in the battle and removed to Nashville.[22]

The next day, the *Dispatch*'s header read: "General Hood's Victory—The Yankees Stick to Their Lies." Federal news accounts continued to claim a victory, adding that several Rebel generals, including Pat Cleburne, had been killed. Thomas's army was nonetheless huddled within the Nashville defenses. "It seems certain that the Yankee army sustained a severe defeat at Franklin," noted Ruffin, but he conceded that Hood had apparently "suffered heavy loss." As late as December 3, Jones wrote: "Our people . . . perceive a Confederate victory." Hood's December 3 telegraph did not arrive at the War Department until December 14. The account was terse: the Federals had been driven from their lines at Franklin, and they evacuated the town on the night of November 30. He told of the capture of a thousand prisoners and the loss of several generals, including Cleburne. The first Southern account of the battle did not arrive until December 14. Hood's losses were given as 3,500. A later account gave 2,000–4,000, with five generals killed, five wounded, and one captured.[23]

Richmond's only communication with the affairs in Tennessee remained the Northern press. Hood's army had advanced northward and deployed outside Nashville, where there was daily skirmishing. The weather remained bitter cold with heavy snow. The first hint of any trouble came on December 19. The *Sentinel* printed a Union dispatch dated 10:40 p.m., December 15. Hood had been driven three miles with the loss of 3,000 prisoners and seventeen guns. This news was flatly denied. The next day—still through Northern sources—affairs at Nashville sounded more ominous. A two-day battle on December 15–16 had been fought during which Hood was defeated with the loss of thirty guns and 2,000 prisoners. "This is a gloomy day here," wrote Gorgas. If Hood's army was indeed defeated, it could well be destroyed before it reached a place of security. He blamed Beauregard, whose "favorite plan" had always been to reach Kentucky. The next day, December 21, the numbers had risen to a stunning 5,000 prisoners and forty-nine guns! The *Dispatch* continued to express doubt. By December 22 and 23, however, the word "rout" was being openly used. The paper lamented: "If half they tell be true, Hood is in a bad fix indeed."[24]

By December 18, Georgia Congressman Warren Aiken had heard the rumors that Hood had been "terribly beaten, and I fear it is true. If so[,] that whole army is lost I fear." Five days later he wrote his wife: "From all I can learn I fear Hood's army is ruined—scattered, and will never be good for any thing again." Jones winced as he read the Northern news accounts. "We are still incredulous—although it may be true," he admitted. "If so, the President will suffer, and Johnston and Beauregard will escape censure—both being supplanted in command by a subordinate." News accounts continued to arrive of "an irretrievable disaster, which may involve the loss of Tennessee, Georgia, etc." December 22 dawned cold but sunny, "but all is dark in Congress," Jones admitted. "The Tennessee members say Hood's army is destroyed, that he will not get 1[,]000 men out of the State, for the Tennesseans, Kentuckians, etc. refuse to retire farther south, but struggle and scatter to their homes, where they will remain." On December 24, a *New York Times* article, claiming to be an official dispatch from General Thomas, reported 6,000 prisoners and fifty-four guns captured at Nashville, not counting 3,000 Rebel wounded left in Franklin. Total Union losses came in at 3,500.[25]

Davis continued to suffer from his persistent fevers. During the second week of December 1864, another of his recurrent illnesses returned—Joseph E. Johnston. Davis was thoroughly done with the general, but a clamorous public was unfortunately not. Johnston's brother Beverly, also in Richmond, had written him to hurry to the capital. He had heard from "several persons having good means of information" that the general's Atlanta report was about to be released to Congress, accompanied by the War Department's refutation. Johnston, who had been in virtual retirement since the Atlanta Campaign, quietly arrived in the capital, where he probably stayed with Beverly in the Spotswood. He visited with Gorgas on December 18—"he is looking very well," observed the colonel—and Johnston spoke freely of the terrible loss of generals at Franklin.

Johnston appeared in the hall of the Senate, where he was given a formal introduction and offered a "privileged seat" on the floor. A House invitation was subsequently offered and accepted. Then came the invitation from the Virginia state legislature. Despite the hoopla, Johnston was disappointed to find that only Wigfall was seriously taking up his cause. "It was painful, in Richmond, to observe the apathy in both branches of the Government & still more absolute subserviency of both legislatures to the executive branch," he wrote a friend. There was much talk in Richmond about the recent Nashville disaster, the fault of which "seemed to be attributed generally to the administration." Johnston had heard the talk of reinstating him in command of the Army of Tennessee (the *Whig* declared such in an editorial), but he was no longer interested. "No general can be useful who is not supported by his government—& moreover, I have endured as much insolence from our administration as ought to fall to the share of one man." There is no indication that Johnston met with Robert E. Lee while in town, but he privately advocated that Davis be deposed and Lee made dictator, an indication, given his checkered feelings about Lee, of just how deeply he hated the president. Johnston planned on returning to Columbia, South Carolina, by Christmas, but troop movements from the capital to Wilmington, North Carolina, prevented his departure until December 28.[26]

The *Dispatch* editorial on Christmas Eve was befitting of the grim outlook in the capital: "There is scarcely a fireside in the Confederacy which has not a vacant chair in the Christmas circle. The father, the husband, the brother, gone forever, or miserable captives in a Northern prison." Thus, rather than celebrating the occasion by intemperance, the citizens, like the people of Ninevah, should don sackcloth and ashes and invoke God to "spare his people." The next day, however, drunks were seen stumbling in the streets.[27]

In early 1865, Henry Foote was once again in the press. Back in September 1864, the Tennessee congressman began advocating for a Southern peace conference. He composed a lengthy memorandum titled "Of Peace and the Means of Obtaining It" that appeared in the *Whig* and other Southern papers. Foote condemned Lincoln and Northern Republicans for "this unpardonable war" but praised Northern Peace Democrats. Although feigning hope that the South would yet win independence, he clearly believed that the war was on its last legs. In truth, he was not only seeking an off-ramp for the Confederacy; he was also attempting to ingratiate himself to Northern peace advocates and distance himself from Southern Democrats. "Virginus" promptly submitted a rebuttal in the *Enquirer*.

Lincoln's subsequent reelection torpedoed Foote's plan, but the issue did not end there. He and his wife attempted to sneak across enemy lines to Washington. Captured by the Confederates, he returned to Richmond and attempted to feebly explain his actions before a furious House of Representatives. He was ultimately expelled by the House, and it was now Benjamin's turn to denounce the Tennessean as a coward and traitor. In February 1865, he resigned his position and traveled to Washington and subsequently to New York. The Northern press ridiculed him, claiming that he was "not a repentant rebel" and that his "late colleagues were glad to get rid of him." His personal appearance was even mocked. Lincoln refused to meet with him, and he was told that he could either leave the United States or be arrested. He thus traveled to England and later spent time in Europe. For the bellicose Henry S. Foote, the war was over.[28]

Everywhere despondency reigned. Congressman Aiken painfully heard that there were those in his home state of Georgia who rejoiced at the reported death of Jefferson Davis. Indeed, one Georgia regiment offered up three cheers. "The fate of the Confederacy will be settled in six months, one way or another, and I very much fear the *worst*," he wrote his wife on January 10. He had been in conversation with the president, who admitted that he did not have control of the generals in the field and that he did not send Hood to Tennessee. Under his diary entry for February 23, Gorgas reflected: "Did we dream six months ago that Hood's movement to Tenn. would bring us to this pass?"[29]

Sunday, April 2, 1865, dawned brightly. Dr. Moses Hoge, minister at the Second Presbyterian Church, was in the middle of his sermon when someone handed him a message. After reading it, he announced: "Brothern. Trying times are before us. General Lee has been defeated; but remember that God is with us in the storm as well as in the calm. We may never meet again. Go quietly to your homes." The president was worshipping at St. Paul's Episcopal, having sent Varina and the children away a week earlier. A note was handed to him. Secretary of War Breckinridge had forwarded Lee's message that his lines had been broken and that he had been forced to withdraw from Petersburg. "I advise that all preparations be made for leaving Richmond tonight." The government was hastily moved to Danville, Virginia, with Davis and the cabinet leaving at midnight. Chaos ruled the streets. Barrels of whiskey were broken into, and many soldiers, blacks, and "rough women" became basely drunk; mobs pillaged local stores. By night the whole riverfront was in flames. Ironically, Davis sought refuge in the West—the very place where the war for the Confederacy was lost.[30]

The South's epic struggle was soon over, and the inevitable postmortems began. In reflecting on the Confederacy's demise, Senator Oldham would later blame personalities, specifically Bragg, Holmes, Pemberton, and notably Davis. He believed that the crucial mistake of the war was not placing Johnston in direct command of the Army of Tennessee as well as giving him theater command. Davis's failure to order troops from the trans-Mississippi to Vicksburg "changed the fate of the war." Perhaps. But it could also be argued that placing Johnston in command rather than Beauregard had a similar effect.[31]

To be sure, personalities played a role in battlefield losses, but what is often underappreciated was the role of politics in the events that transpired. The failed policy of territorial defense, the insistence of defending the rivers to the bitter end, the refusal to peremptorily order trans-Mississippi troops to Pemberton, and equally splitting troop strength between Virginia and the West—all of these policy decisions were grounded in politics. Battles were not fought in a vacuum. The decisions of the administration resulted from demagogic congressmen, shifting political alliances, an often contentious capital press corps, and hundreds of petitioning citizens who, beneath the surface of their parochialism, were fearful and desperate. What played out hundreds of miles from Richmond—the "frontier" as many Virginians viewed it—cannot be understood in isolation from the seat of power.

NOTES

Abbreviations

BRCC — Ezra J. Warner and W. Buck Yearns, *Biographical Register of the Confederate Congress* (Baton Rouge: Louisiana State University Press, 1975)

DER — William K. Scarborough, ed., *The Diary of Edmund Ruffin*, 3 vols. (Baton Rouge: Louisiana State University Press, 1972–1989)

DU — Duke University, Rubenstein Rare Books and Manuscript Library, Durham, NC

JCCS — *Journal of the Congress of the Confederate States, 1861–1865* (Washington, DC: Government Printing Office, 1904)

JDC — Dunbar Rowland, ed., *Jefferson Davis, Constitutionalist. His Letters, Papers, and Speeches* 10 vols. Jackson: Mississippi Department of Archives and History, 1923

LSU — Louisiana State University, Louisiana and Lower Mississippi Valley Collection, Baton Rouge, LA

MU — Miami University Special Collections and Archives, Oxford, OH

NARG — National Archives Record Group, Washington, DC

OR — *The War of the Rebellion: A Compilation of the Official Records of the Union and Confederate Armies*, 128 vols. (Washington, DC: Government Printing Office, 1880–1901) [all citations are in series 1 unless otherwise stated]

ORN — *The Official Records of the Union and Confederate Navies in the War of the Rebellion,* 30 vols. (Washington, DC: Government Printing Office, 1894–1922)

PJD — Linda Laswell Crist et al., eds., *The Papers of Jefferson Davis*, 14 vols. (Baton Rouge: Louisiana State University Press, 1971–2015)

SHC	Southern Historical Collection, University of North Carolina, Chapel Hill, NC
SHSP	J. Williams Jones et al., eds., *Southern Historical Society Papers*, 52 vols. (1–49, Richmond: William Ellis Jones, 1876–1957); (50–52, Richmond: Virginia Historical Society, 1958–1959)
TSLA	Tennessee State Library and Archives, Nashville, TN
TU	Tulane University, Special Collections, New Orleans, LA
UGA	University of Georgia, Hargrett Rare Book and Manuscript Library, Athens, GA
VHS	Virginia Historical Society, Richmond, VA
WRHS	Western Reserve Historical Society, Cleveland, OH
WM	The College of William & Mary, Earl Gregg Swem Library Special Collections, Williamsburg, VA

Preface

1. Earl J. Hess, "Revitalizing Traditional Military History," in Andrew S. Bledsoe and Andrew F. Lang, eds., *Upon the Fields of Battle: Essays on Military History of American's Civil War* (Baton Rouge: Louisiana State University Press, 2018), 20–33.

2. Andrew S. Bledsoe and Andrew F. Lang, "Military History and the American Civil War," in *Upon the Fields of Battle: Essays on the Military History of America's Civil War* (Baton Rouge: Louisiana State University Press), 7.

3. William J. Cooper, *Jefferson Davis, American* (New York: Vintage, 2000), 368; Williamson Murray and Wayne Wei-siang Hsieh, *A Savage War: A Military History of the Civil War* (Princeton: Princeton University Press, 2016), 61–62; Steven E. Woodworth, *This Great Struggle: America's Civil War* (New York: Rowman & Littlefield, 2011), 40–41; Ernest B. Ferguson, *Ashes of Glory: Richmond at War* (New York: Vantage Books, 1996), 47–48; Emory M. Thomas, *The Confederate State of Richmond: A Biography of a Capital* (Baton Rouge: Louisiana State University Press, 1971), 21.

4. Ferguson, *Ashes of Glory*, 51, 53–54; Thomas, *Confederate State of Richmond*, 46.

5. Davis J. Eicher, *Dixie Betrayed: How the South Really Lost the Civil War* (New York: Little, Brown & Company, 2006), 86–87; William C. Davis, "Richmond Becomes the Confederate Capital," in William C. Davis and James I. Robertson, Jr., eds., *Virginia at War 1861* (Lexington: University Press of Kentucky, 2005), 116; Richard M. McMurry, *Two Great Rebel Armies: An Essay in Confederate Military History* (Chapel Hill: University of North Carolina Press, 1989), 24, 26; James M. McPherson, *Embattled Rebel: Jefferson Davis and the Confederate*

Civil War (New York: Penguin Books, 2015), 33–34; William C. Davis, *Jefferson Davis: The Man and His Hour* (New York: HarperCollins, 1991), 363. For a map of the Confederate congressional districts, see Thomas B. Alexander and Richard E. Beringer, *The Anatomy of the Confederate Congress: A Study of the Influence of Member Characteristics on Legislative Voting Behavior, 1861–1865*, 12. See Doris Kearns Goodwin, *Team of Rivals: The Political Genius of Abraham Lincoln* (New York: Simon & Schuster, 2005), xvi–xvii. Westerners in the Davis cabinet included Robert Toombs of Georgia, secretary of state; John H. Reagan of Texas, postmaster general; Judah P. Benjamin of Louisiana, attorney general; and Leroy P. Walker of Alabama, secretary of war.

6. Earl J. Hess, *The Civil War in the West: Victory and Defeat from the Appalachians to the Mississippi* (Chapel Hill: University of North Carolina Press, 2012), xi; C. Van Woodward, ed., *Mary Chesnut's Civil War* (New York: Princeton University Press, 1981), 148; Thomas W. Cutrer, *Theater of a Separate War: The Civil War West of the Mississippi River, 1861–1865* (Chapel Hill: University of North Carolina Press, 2017), 1. McMurry (*Two Great Rebel Armies*, 24) divides the Confederacy differently and concludes that the West (including Texas) totaled 65.7 percent of land size.

7. Greg D. Kimball, *American City, Southern Place: A Cultural History of Antebellum Richmond* (Athens: University of Georgia Press, 2000), 106–07.

8. William H. Russell, *My Diary North and South* (London: T. O. P. H. Burnham, 1861), 305; biggrdtuscities.com/1860, accessed July 24, 2023; Larry J. Daniel, *Soldiering in the Army of Tennessee: A Portrait of Life in a Confederate Army* (Chapel Hill: University of North Carolina Press, University of North Carolina Press, 1991), 13; Thomas B. Connelly, *Army of the Heartland: The Army of Tennessee, 1861–1862* (Baton Rouge: Louisiana State University Press, 1967), x.

9. Davis, *Jefferson Davis*, 338–39, 355; Ferguson, *Ashes of Glory*, 50–51; Thomas B. Connelly and Archer B. Jones, *The Politics of Command: Factions and Ideas in Confederate Strategy* (Baton Rouge: Louisiana State University Press, 1973), 50–51; Woodward, ed., *Mary Chesnut's Civil War*, 136; Allen Tate, *Jefferson Davis: His Rise and Fall* (Nashville: J. S. Sanders & Company, 1998), 101; Varina Davis, *Jefferson Davis: Ex-President of the Confederate States* (New York: Bedford Company, 1890), 2:202–03; Joan Cashin, *First Lady of the Confederacy: Varina Davis's Civil War* (Cambridge: The Belknap Press of Harvard University Press, 2006), 111.

10. Albert Castel, *Decision in the West: The Atlanta Campaign of 1864* (Lawrence: University Press of Kansas, 1992), 6.

11. Connelly and Jones, *Politics of Command*, 54–57, 86; George Rable, *The Confederate Republic: A Revolution Against Politics* (Chapel Hill: University of North Carolina Press, 1994), 211. Rable questioned whether organized coalitions or alignments ever developed. Thomas (*Confederate State of Richmond*, 46) believed

that "[t]he Richmond government wielded even more power perhaps than its counterpart in Washington."

12. McMurry, *Two Great Rebel Armies*, 148–49.

Chapter 1

1. Ferguson, *Ashes of Glory*, 52–53; John B. Jones, *A Rebel War Clerk's Diary of the Confederate States*, 2 vols. (Philadelphia: J. P. Lippincott, 1866), 1:46–47; *Dispatch*, May 31, June 17, 20, 21, July 12, 1861; *Examiner*, June 18, 1861; Judith McGuire, *Diary of a Southern Refugee During the War* (New York: E. J. Hale & Son, 1867), 88; laptrinhx.com/news/the-custom-house-richmond-s-first/federal building-oQpJoJv, accessed January 13, 2023; Eli N. Evans, *Judah P. Benjamin: The Jewish Confederate* (New York: The Free Press, 1988), 137.

2. *The City Intelligencer, or, Stranger's Guide* (Richmond: MacFarland & Ferguson, 1862); William B. McCash, *Thomas R. R. Cobb: The Making of a Southern Nationalist* (Macon: Mercer University Press, 1983), 250.

3. Davis quoted in Rable, *The Confederate Republic*, 85–86 (emphasis in original); Richard M. McMurry, *The Civil Wars of Joseph E. Johnston, Confederate States Army* (El Dorado Hills, CA: Savas Beatie, 2023), 61. All emphasis appearing in quotations is true to the original unless otherwise noted.

4. *Whig*, July 11, 1861.

5. *Dispatch*, May 23, 1861; Thomas C. Mackey, "Not a Pariah, but a Keystone: Kentucky and Secession," in Kent T. Dollar, Larry H. Whitaker, and W. Calvin Dickinson, eds., *Sister States, Enemy States: The Civil War in Kentucky and Tennessee* (Lexington: University Press of Kentucky, 2011), 32–33.

6. William C. Davis, *Jefferson Davis*, 19, 21, 191–94, 197, 201–05, 263; Murray and Hsieh, *A Savage War*, 83–84; John W. Simon, "Lincoln, Grant, and Kentucky in 1861," in Kent Masterson Brown, ed., *The Civil War in Kentucky: Battle for the Bluegrass State* (Mason City, IA: Savas Publishing Company, 2000), 4–5; Donald Stoker, *The Grand Design: Strategy and the U.S. Civil War* (New York: Oxford University Press, 2010), 48–49.

7. *Enquirer*, May 3, June 22, 1861; *Dispatch*, June 26, July 12, 1861.

8. James I. Robertson, Jr., "The Civil War's Most Valuable Diarist," lecture at the Virginia Museum of History and Culture," vimeo.com/165155545, retrieved December 12, 2022; Jones, *Rebel War Clerk's Diary*, 1:55; *Whig*, November 22, 1861; Steven E. Woodworth, *Jefferson Davis and His Generals: The Failure of Confederate Command in the West* (Lawrence: University of Kanas Press, 1990), 28; Glenn Robins, *The Bishop of the Old South: The Ministry and Civil War Legacy of Leonidas Polk* (Macon: Mercer University Press, 2006), 146–48; Russell Bonds, "Leonidas Polk: Southern Civil War General," *Civil War Times Illustrated* 45 (May

2006), 46; William G. Stevenson, *Thirteen Months in the Rebel Army by an Impressed New Yorker* (New York: A. S. Barns & Burr, 1862), 77–78.

9. Huston Horn, *Leonidas Polk: Warrior Bishop of the Confederacy* (Lawrence: University Press of Kansas, 2019), 39–40, 153, 159; William K. Polk, *Leonidas Polk: Bishop and General*, 2 vols. (New York: Longmans, Green, 1915), 1:355; William Preston Johnston, *Life of Gen. Albert Sidney Johnston, Embracing His Services in the Armies of the United States, the Republic of Texas, and the Confederate States* (New York: D. Appleton, 1879), 321.

10. William C. Davis, *Jefferson Davis*, 8–9, 390–91, 447, 448, 462, 692–93; Cooper, *Jefferson Davis*, 17, 20, 25, 266.

11. Woodworth, *Jefferson Davis*, 31, 32; Polk, *Leonidas Polk*, 1:166, 359, 372; Nathaniel C. Hughes and Roy P. Stonesipher, *The Life and Wars of Gideon J. Pillow* (Chapel Hill: University of North Carolina Press, 1993), 76, 157; Johnston, *Life of Gen. Albert Sidney Johnston*, 322.

12. *War of the Rebellion: A Compilation of the Official Records of the Union and Confederate Armies* (Washington, DC: U.S. Government Printing Office 1880–1901, Series I, Volume 4:362 [hereafter cited as *OR*, with all references to series 1 unless otherwise noted, followed by volume and part number]; *OR*, 52(2):115; Woodworth, *Jefferson Davis*, 33.

13. *Whig*, September 16, 1861; *Dispatch*, June 26, July 2, August 19, 1861; *Enquirer*, June 27, August 2, 24, 1861; Jones, *Rebel War Clerk's Diary*, 1:55.

14. Ferguson, *Ashes of Glory*, 43–44, 45, 71–72; Cobb as quoted in McCash, *Thomas R. R. Cobb*, 250.

15. *Whig*, August 5, 7, 19, 1861; *Enquirer*, July 30, August 21, 1861; *Dispatch*, July 30, August 3, 7, 1861; *OR*, 3:612, 617, 620; Hughes and Stonesipher, *Life and Wars of Pillow*, 176; Jones, *Rebel War Clerk's Diary*, 1:53–54.

16. *OR*, 3:667, 52(2):188, 4:363–64, 371; Jones, *Rebel War Clerk's Diary*, 1:48.

17. *OR*, 4:395–96.

18. Lynda L. Crist et al., eds. *The Papers of Jefferson Davis*, 14 vols. (Baton Rouge: Louisiana State University Press, 1971–2015), 7:289, 291 [hereafter cited as *PJD*].

19. *OR*, 4:395–96.

20. Crist et al., eds. *PJD*, 7:289, 291.

21. Horn, *Leonidas Polk*, 174–76, 182; *OR*, 3:666–67.

22. *Whig*, September 17, 1861; *Dispatch*, September 14, 1861; *Enquirer*, September 20, 1861; *OR*, 4:188–89; Dunbar Rowland, ed., *Jefferson Davis, Constitutionalist: His Letters, Papers, and Speeches*, 10 vols. (Jackson: Mississippi Department of Archives and History, 1923), 6:156–57 [hereafter cited as *JDC*]; E. Merton Coulter, *The Civil War and Readjustment in Kentucky* (Glouster, MA: P. Smith, 1966), 111; John A. Rawley, *Turning Points of the Civil War* (Lincoln: University of Nebraska Press, 1966), 38; Woodworth ("Davis, Polk, and the End of

Kentucky Neutrality," 14) concluded that Polk's "silence toward the president on so momentous an issue suggests that he had made up his mind what to do and did not want any direction from his commander-in-chief." In terms of Polk's premise for taking Columbus, Albert Castel believed that he was not necessarily wrong. "Even so, he committed an egregious blunder" by violating Kentucky's "legally specious but emotionally precious neutrality." See Albert Castel, *Victors in Blue: How Union Generals Fought the Confederates, Battled Each Other, and Won the Civil War* (Lawrence: University Press of Kansas, 2011), 33. Stoker (*The Grand Design*, 51) believed that Davis "put the military cart before the political horse, ignoring that 'political elements' are a part of war and that a conflict, effectively waged, is governed by political policies and necessities."

23. *Enquirer*, September 20, 30, 1861; *Dispatch*, September 12, 1861.

24. *OR*, Series 2, 2:1380–81; *Whig*, September 23, 1861; *Dispatch*, September 19, 1861; *Enquirer*, September 18, 24, 1861; William C. Davis, *Breckinridge: Statesman, Soldier, Symbol* (Baton Rouge: Louisiana State University Press, 1974), 288.

25. civilwar-history-fandom.com/wiki/Gustavus_Adolphus_Henry,_Sr., accessed December 15, 2022; *OR*, 4:192–93; Crist et al., eds., *PJD*, 7:330.

26. *OR*, 4:191; Horn, *Leonidas Polk*, 181; *Whig*, September 26, 1861, October 11, 1861.

27. William K. Scarborough, ed., *The Diary of Edmund Ruffin*, 3 vols. (Baton Rouge: Louisiana State University Press, 1972–1989) 2:137, 141 [hereafter cited as *DER*].

28. *Whig*, September 18, 1861; Horn, *Leonidas Polk*, 181; Evans, *Judah P. Benjamin*, 135, 137, 199–200, 203–04; William C. Davis, *Jefferson Davis*, 354–55; Woodworth, *Jefferson Davis*, 22–23.

29. *OR*, 3:304, 311; *Dispatch*, November 9, 1861; *Dispatch*, November 9, 15, 21, 21, 23, 1861; *Whig*, November 18, 20, 22, 23, 1861; *Enquirer*, November 19, 1861.

30. Scarborough, ed., *DER*, 2:143, 152, 156, 173.

31. Scarborough, ed., *DER*, 2:173, 183; Thomas Bragg Diary, December 7, 1861, SHC. For the particulars of the Russellville Convention and Kentucky's admission into the Confederacy, see Lowell H. Harrison, "The Government of Confederate Kentucky," in Kent Masterson Brown, ed., *The Civil War in Kentucky: Battle for the Bluegrass State* (Mason City, Iowa: Savas Publishing Company, 2000), 83–87; J. L. M. Curry, *Civil War History of the Government of the Confederate States, with Some Personal Reminiscences* (Richmond: Johnson Publishing Company, 1901), 104–05; Coulter, *Civil War*, 43; *OR*, Series IV, 1:755, *OR*, 52(2):240. Kentucky was admitted on December 10, 1861.

32. Ezra J. Warner and W. Buck Years, *Biographical Register of the Confederate Congress* (Baton Rouge: Louisiana State University Press, 1975), 31, 36, 37, 38, 39, 48, 65, 82, 121, 159, 177, 220 [hereafter cited as *BRCC*]; Woodward, ed.,

Mary Chesnut's Civil War, 310; *New York Tribune*, July 18, 1861; *New York Dispatch*, September 14, 1861; Sarah L. Wiggins, ed., *The Journals of Josiah Gorgas, 1857–1878* (Tuscaloosa: University of Alabama Press, 1995), 132–33.

33. Thomas Bragg Diary, January 16, 1862, SHC.

34. *Dispatch*, December 19, 28, 30, 1861; *Whig*, December 16, 28, 1861.

Chapter 2

1. Jones, *Rebel War Clerk's Diary*, 1:55; *Enquirer*, July 2, July 19, 1861; *Dispatch*, June 17, 20, 21 and 25, 1861.

2. Cutrer, *Theater of a Separate War*, 1; *Whig*, May 22, 1861; *Dispatch*, June 12, 19, 1861; *Enquirer*, June 22, 1861.

3. *OR*, 53:698–99; bioguide.gov/search/bio/C000003, retrieved December 3, 2022.

4. Thomas L. Snead, *The Fight for Missouri: From the Election of Lincoln to the Death of Lyon* New York: Charles Scribner's Sons, 1886), 30–31; Albert Castel, *General Sterling Price and the War in the West* (Baton Rouge: Louisiana State University Press, 1968), 30; *Sedalia Weekly Bazoo*, November 13, 1861; *Iron County Register*, April 7, 1887.

5. Castel, *General Sterling Price*, 30; Crist et al., eds., *PJD*, 7:294; *Enquirer*, May 28, 1861.

6. *Dispatch*, July 27, 1861; *Whig*, July 15, 1861; Castel, *General Sterling Price*, 14, 17–22, 31–32; Ezra J. Warner, *Generals in Gray: Lives of the Confederate Commanders* (Baton Rouge: Louisiana State University Press, 1959), 200.

7. Castel, *General Sterling Price*, 20–21; *Dispatch*, June 18, 1861; *OR*, 3:605.

8. Scarborough, ed., *DER*, 2:107.

9. Crist et al., eds., *PJD*, 7:188–89; William C. Davis, *Jefferson Davis*, 380–81; *Enquirer*, June 22, 1861; Castel, *General Sterling Price*, 32n11; *OR*, 3:605.

10. *OR*, 3:600–01; *Dispatch*, July 13, 1861.

11. William R. Geise, *The Confederate Military Forces in the Trans-Mississippi West, 1861–1865: A Study in Command* (El Dorado Hills, CA: Savas Beattie, 2022), 13–15, 17; *OR*, 3:687–88.

12. Scarborough, ed., *DER* 2:107–08; McGuire, *Diary of a Southern Refugee*, 51; *OR*, 3:104; *Enquirer*, August 21, 27, 29, 30, 1861; *Whig*, August 19, 26, 1861; *Dispatch*, August 17, 1861. The *Enquirer* of May 27, 1862, estimated that, of the 160,000 residents of St. Louis County, 60,000 were Germans.

13. Crist et al., eds., *PJD*, 7:290–91.

14. *Enquirer*, September 16, 26, 30, 1861; *Whig*, September 23, 30, October 8, 1861; *Dispatch*, September 30, October 3, 14, 1861.

15. *Whig*, August 16, October 12, 1861; *Enquirer*, October 10, 1861; *OR*, 3:717–18; Snead, *The Fight for Missouri*, 274; Jones, *Rebel War Clerk's Diary*, 1:86.

16. *OR*, 3:726, 733, 734, 742, 8:716, 746. McCulloch's strength at the time totaled 8,767 present for duty.

17. *Whig*, December 14, 1861; *Dispatch*, December 9, 1861. Only a handful of Iowans ever joined the Confederate army.

18. Cooper, *Jefferson Davis*, 386; *Enquirer*, November 12, 28, 1861; *Whig*, December 7, 1861.

19. Arthur J. Kirkpatrick, "Missouri Delegation in the Confederate Congress," *Civil War History* 5 (June 1959): 189–90, 193, 196–97; Warner and Yearns, eds., *BRCC*, 49–50, 193; W. D. Vandiver, "Reminiscences of General John B. Clark," *Missouri Historical Review* 20 (January 1926): 223–25, 232; Clayton C. Jewett, ed., *Rise and Fall of the Confederacy: The Memoir of Senator Williamson B. Oldham* (Columbia: University of Missouri Press, 1986), 76; bioguide.congress.gov/search/bio/C00041, accessed January 2, 2023.

20. See snaccooperative.org/aric/99166/w68d4rbj, accessed January 2, 2023; *OR*, 4:562–63; Jones, *Rebel War Clerk's Diary*, 1:46–47; William C. Davis, "General Samuel Cooper," in Gary W. Gallagher and Joseph T. Glatthaar, eds., *Leaders of the Lost Cause: New Perspectives on Confederate High Command* (Mechanicsburg, PA: Stackpole Books, 2004), 102, 105–06, 108–14, 116–17.

21. James L. Morrison, ed., *The Memoirs of Henry Heth* (Westport, CT: Greenwood Press, 1974), 159–60.

22. *Whig*, December 7, 11, 1861; *Dispatch*, December 11, 1861.

23. Scarborough, ed., *DER*, 2:181–82.

24. Rowland, ed., *JDC*, 5:179.

25. *OR*, 53:761–63.

26. *Whig*, December 6, 11, 12, 17, 1861.

27. *Enquirer*, December 14, 1861; *Whig*, December 17, 1861.

28. Morrison, *Memoirs of Henry Heth*, 160.

29. *Enquirer*, December 14, 1861; Jack D. Welsh, *Medical Histories of Confederate Generals* (Kent, OH: Kent State University Press, 1995), 147; Victor M. Rose, *The Life and Services of Gen. Ben McCulloch* 1958 reprint (Philadelphia: Pictorial Bureau of the Press, 1888), 195–96.

30. *Whig*, December 16, 1861, January 16, 18, 1862; Castel, *General Sterling Price*, 63; *OR*, 53:765, 3:743–46; *Whig*, October 5, 1861.

31. *OR*, 6:788, 797, 813.

32. *OR*, 7:717, 724–25, 728–29, 8:733–34, 53:767–68.

33. Thomas Bragg Diary, January 2, 1862, SHC.

Chapter 3

1. James W. Bellamy, "The Political Career of Landon Carter Haynes," Master's Thesis, University of Tennessee, 1952, 13, 15–25, 76–78; W. Todd Groce,

Mountain Rebels: East Tennessee Confederates and the Civil War, 1860–1870 (Knoxville: University of Tennessee Press, 1999), 30; Warner and Years, *BRCC*, 113–14, 234.

2. *OR*, 4:364–65.

3. *Dispatch*, October 17, 1861; *Whig*, October 18, 1861; Groce, *Mountain Rebels*, 2, 4, 10–12.

4. Warner and Yearns, *BRCC*, 234; Robert McKenzie, *Lincolnites and Rebels: A Divided Town in the American Civil War* (New York: Oxford University Press 2007), 46, 88, 107; *OR*, 4:366–67; *Dispatch*, June 28, 1861.

5. *Dispatch*, August 26, 1861; Thomas L. Connelly, *Autumn of Glory: The Army of Tennessee 1862–1865* (Baton Rouge: Louisiana State University Press, 1971), 41–42; C. David Dalton, "He Died on the Field of Glory: Felix Zollicoffer and the Confederate Defeat at Mill Springs," in Lawrence C. Hewitt and Thomas E. Schott, eds. *Confederate Generals in the Western Theater: Essays on America's Civil War*, 4 vols. (Knoxville: University of Tennessee Press, 2018), 4; Jack D. Welsh, *Medical Histories of Confederate Generals* (Kent, OH: Kent State University Press, 1995), 243–44; *OR*, 4:326; Jones, *Rebel War Clerk's Diary*, 1:72; Johnston, *The Life of Gen. Albert Sidney Johnston*, 394–95. Harris was reelected by West and Middle Tennessee votes, but he still lost East Tennessee by 62 percent. See Charles F. Bryan, Jr., "The Civil War in East Tennessee: A Social, Political and Economic Study," PhD diss., University of Tennessee, 1978.

6. Noel C. Fisher, *War at Every Door: Partisan Politics & Guerrilla Violence in East Tennessee, 1860–1869* (Chapel Hill: University of North Carolina Press, 1997), 45–46; *Whig*, July 15, 1861; *Enquirer*, July 16, 1861; *Dispatch*, August 20, 26, 1861; http://tennesseeencyclopedia.net/entries/albert-miller-lea, accessed January 12, 2023.

7. Fisher, *War at Every Door*, 50; *Enquirer*, August 3, September 7, 11, 1861; Larry J. Daniel, *Conquered: Why the Army of Tennessee Failed* (Chapel Hill: University of North Carolina Press, 2019), 9–10.

8. *OR*, 4:397, 402; *Enquirer*, September 24, 1861.

9. *Whig*, September 18, 1861; *Dispatch*, October 8, 1861.

10. *Dispatch*, August 13, 20, 26, 28, 1861; *Enquirer*, 9, 13, 28, 1861.

11. *Enquirer*, June 13, 1861; *OR*, 4:381–82, 389, 409.

12. *Dispatch*, June 7, August 23, September 5, October 9, 1861; Myers to Zollicoffer, August 31, 1861 and Benjamin to Myers, September 24, 1861, www.csa-railroads.com, website by David L. Bright.

13. *Enquirer*, September 25, November 12, 1861; *Dispatch*, November 13, December 4, 6, 24, 1861; *Whig*, November 11, 15, 21, 26, 1861; *OR*, 4:425, 239, 529–30, 511, 7:745, 764, 685.

14. *OR*, 4:529–30, 511–12, 540, 534, 559. Groce (*Mountain Rebels*, 38, 75–76) concluded that no more than 25,000 East Tennesseans fought for the South, representing only 13.4 percent of the military-age population.

15. Scarborough, ed., *DER*, 2:173, 222; Dispatch, August 20, December 10, 1861; *Whig*, June 30, 1861; James M. Pritchard, "Glory Denied: The Hard Fate of George B. Crittenden" in Lawrence B. Hewitt and Arthur W. Bergeron, eds. (Knoxville: University of Tennessee Press, 2010), 1–7; *OR*, 7:745, 764; Oliver Perry Temple, *East Tennessee in the Civil War* (Cincinnati: R. Clarke Company, 1899), 66–72, 399; McKenzie, *Lincolnites and Rebels*, 106–08, 135–37; Thomas Bragg Diary, November 28, 29, 1861, SHC.

16. Thomas Bragg Diary, November 29, 1861.

17. *Dispatch*, December 11, 1861.

18. Pritchard, "Glory Denied," 7; Woodworth, *Jefferson Davis*, 67; *Dispatch*, December 5, 1861.

19. *Dispatch*, December 20, 25, 30, 31, 1861, January 4, 1862.

20. *Whig*, December 24, 1861.

21. *Dispatch*, January 2, 1862; *Whig*, January 2, 1862; Cooper, *Jefferson Davis*, 400; William C. Davis, *Jefferson Davis*, 389, 391–92, 402; Eicher, *Dixie Betrayed*, 89–90; *Examiner*, January 2, 1862; *Whig*, January 2, 1862; Thomas Bragg Diary, January 1, 1862, SHC.

22. Harrison to wife, January 8, 1862, James T. Harrison Letters, SHC.

23. *Dispatch*, January 18, 21, 1862; Jones, *Rebel War Clerk's Diary*, 1:103, 104.

24. *OR*, 7:844–45, 102; Benjamin F. Cooling, *Fort Donelson's Legacy: War and Society in Kentucky and Tennessee, 1862–1863* (Knoxville: University of Tennessee Press, 1997), 35.

25. Thomas Bragg Diary, January 23, February 4, 1862, SHC.

26. *Dispatch*, January 24, 27, 28, 29, 30, February 7, 8, 10, 1862; *Enquirer*, January 24, 28, 1862; *Whig*, February 1, 8, 1862; John Withers Diary, January 24, 1862, Adjutant General's Department, NARG 109. Official casualties at the Battle of Mill Springs were 434 Confederate and 248 Union. Hess (*Civil War in the West*, 32–33) concluded that Mill Springs caused "shock among Southern sympathizers in the region" and left loyalists "jubilant at the prospect of a Union drive through Cumberland Gap."

27. *Charleston Mercury*, January 28, 1862 (article submitted January 25); Thomas Bragg Diary, January 31, 1862, SHC.

28. *OR*, 7:262.

29. Thomas Bragg Diary, January 24, 31, 1862, SHC.

30. *Whig*, February 8, 1862; *Dispatch*, January 27, 1862.

31. *Whig*, January 27, 1862; *Dispatch*, February 6, 1862; Woodworth, *Jefferson Davis*, 70.

32. *OR*, 7:848, 849; Warner and Yearns, *BRCC*, 8.

33. *OR*, 7:749, 750, 52(2):256–57; Bragg Diary, January 24, 1862, SHC; *Dispatch*, February 14, 1862, February 6, 1862; Kenneth A. Hafendorfer, *Mill Springs: Campaign and Battle of Mill Springs* (Louisville: KH Press, 2001), 538; Crist et al., eds., *PJD*, 7:29, 28.

34. *Charleston Mercury*, January 28, 1862; Thomas Bragg Diary, January 31, 1862, SHC; Cobb as quoted in Hafendorfer, *Mill Springs*, 533.

35. Jefferson Davis, *Rise and Fall of the Confederate Government*, 2 vols. (New York: D. Appleton, 1881), 2:21; *OR*, 7:862–63, series 4, 1:961. The case dragged on, but Crittenden's resignation was ultimately accepted. For details, see Woodworth, *Jefferson Davis*, 69.

Chapter 4

1. *Dispatch*, September 2, 1861; Johnston, *Life of Gen. Albert Sidney Johnston*, 291; Daniel, *Conquered*, 14.

2. Charles P. Roland, *Albert Sidney Johnston: Soldier of Three Republics* (Austin: University of Texas Press, 1964), 12, 59–61, 112, 151–53, 207; Johnston, *Life of Gen. Albert Sidney Johnston*, 718–19; William C. Davis (*Jefferson Davis*, 360) described Davis's relationship with Johnston as a "friendship approaching idolatry."

3. *OR*, 4:193, 405; Crist et al., eds., *PJD*, 7:329; Roland, *Albert Sidney Johnston*, 247–50.

4. *OR*, 4:193; *Enquirer*, September 21, 1861.

5. *Enquirer*, September 21, October 1, 1861; *Whig*, October 4, 14, 1861; *OR*, 4:465, 468–69, 528, 53:218; *Dispatch*, October 22, 1861; Jones, *Rebel War Clerk's Diary*, 1:87.

6. Jones, *Rebel War Clerk's Diary*, 1:86–87; *Dispatch*, October 17, 1861.

7. Jones, *Rebel War Clerk's Diary*, 1:88; *Dispatch*, September 24, 1861; *Enquirer*, November 26, 1861.

8. *OR*, 4:745–46, 813, 728. After the battle, Polk met aboard a Union boat under a flag of truce to discuss the release of a seriously wounded Federal colonel. A reporter who witnessed the meeting described the general as wearing a blue shirt with no shoulder insignia. Indeed, the only thing to indicate rank was a sash.

9. *Dispatch*, January 6, 7, 8, 9, 1862; *Whig*, January 8, 18, 1862; John F. Henry to Gustavus A. Henry, January 22, 1862, Gustavus A. Henry Letters, SHC.

10. *Dispatch*, January 4, 6, 1862; John M. Daniel, *The Richmond Examiner During the War* (New York: Arno, 1970), 21–22, 24.

11. *OR*, 7:824–25, 52(2):237, 7:779, 828–29.

12. *Examiner*, January 31, 1862; Bragg Diary, January 6, 1862, SHC.

13. Nathaniel C. Hughes, *Liddell's Record: St. John Liddell: Brigadier General CSA, Staff Officer and Brigade Commander in the Army of Tennessee* (Dayton: Morningside, 1983), 41–46.

14. Woodworth, *Jefferson Davis*, 70; Archer Jones, *Confederate Strategy from Shiloh to Vicksburg* (Baton Rouge: Louisiana State University Press, 1991), 25; Connelly and Jones, *Politics of Command*, 91.

15. Jones, *Rebel War Clerk's Diary*, 1:107.

16. Thomas Bragg Diary, January 17, 1862, SHC.

17. Thomas Bragg Diary, January 8, 10, 17, 1862, SHC.

18. *OR*, 7:844–45.

19. Thomas Bragg Diary, January 22, 1862; *Whig*, January 23, 1862; *Dispatch*, January 27, 30, 1862.

20. Steven E. Woodworth, *Davis & Lee at War* (Lawrence: University Press of Kansas, 1998), 74–76, 77–79, 84; William C. Davis, *Jefferson Davis*, 361; McMurry, *Two Great Rebel Armies*, 121–22; *Dispatch*, February 6, 7, 1862; Earl C. Woods, *The Diary of Edmund Enoul Livaudais* (New Orleans: Archdiocese of New Orleans, 1982), 19; *Mobile Advertiser & Register*, February 8, 1862.

21. William A. Link, *The Last Fire-eater: Roger A. Pryor and the Search for a Southern Identity* (Baton Rouge: Louisiana State University Press, 2023), 38, 40–41, 47; Warner and Yearns, *BRCC*, 197.

22. Alfred Roman, *The Military Operations of General Beauregard in the War Between the States, 1861–1865; Including a Brief Personal Sketch of His Service in the War with Mexico, 1846–48*, 2 vols. (New York: Harper & Row, 1883), I: 210–22; *Dispatch*, January 20, 1862. Beauregard was "too popular to be sacked," concluded Steven Woodworth, so Davis "cleverly got one of the general's friends to talk him into accepting the move." See Woodworth, *Davis & Lee at War*, 1998, 84. T. Harry Williams, *P. G. T. Beauregard: Napoleon in Gray*. 1995 reprint. (Baton Rouge: Louisiana State University Press, 2011), 114. Williams deduced that Pryor "may have been acting as a hatchet man for Davis."

23. *OR*, 7:813–14; Roman, *Military Operations of General Beauregard*, 1:213, 214; Jones, *Rebel War Clerk's Diary*, 1:107. Upon Beauregard's arrival at Bowling Green, he found that Johnston had 42,500 "effectives" in middle and western Kentucky to oppose an estimated 130,000 Federals. He expressed disgust at the "fanciful figures" that had been given to him.

24. Williams, *P. G. T. Beauregard*, 113–14; Jones, *Rebel War Clerk's Diary*, 1:106. Connelly (*Army of the Heartland*, 63) concluded that Beauregard perceived himself as the "savior of the entire Second Department" and saw himself as "the real leader behind the scenes." Woodworth (*Davis & Lee at War*, 91) suspected that "Moving the Louisianian away from Richmond was probably the best thing Davis could have done under the circumstances and with the information then available to him, though command in New Orleans might have been a more profitable assignment."

25. *OR*, 5:1053; Cobb to wife, January 15, 1862, as quoted in Evans, *Judah P. Benjamin*, 144–45.

26. *Dispatch*, February 6, 1862; Jones, *Rebel War Clerk's Diary*, 1:108, 109. For the details of the February 4 attack on Fort Henry, see Timothy B. Smith, *Grant Invades Tennessee: The 1862 Battles for Forts Henry and Donelson* (Lawrence: University Press of Kansas, 2016), 82–83.

27. Jones, *Rebel War Clerk's Diary*, 1:109; Scarborough, ed., *DER*, 2:230; Thomas Bragg Diary, February 7, 1862, SHC.

28. *OR*, 7:130–31.

29. *Dispatch*, February 8, 1862.

30. Jones, *Rebel War Clerk's Diary*, 1:110; *OR*, 7:862, 867, 869, 876, 6:823–24, 825. The Federals actually captured six field and seventeen heavy guns.

31. *Dispatch*, February 11, 1862; Thomas Bragg Diary, February 10, 1862, SHC.

32. *OR*, 9:110; J. Cutler Andrews, *The South Reports the Civil War* (Pittsburgh: University of Pittsburgh Press, 1985), 164–65; Jones, *Rebel War Clerk's Diary*, 1:109; *Whig*, February 10, 11, 13, 14, 17, 1862; *Dispatch*, February 10, 13, 14, 15, 17; *Enquirer*, February 14, 1862; *Examiner*, February 17, 1862; Bragg Diary, February 25, 1862, SHC.

33. Thomas Bragg Diary, February 11, 1862, SHC; Edward Younger, ed., *Inside the Confederate Government: The Diary of Robert Garlick Kill Kean* (New York: Oxford University Press, 1967), 110.

34. *Dispatch*, February 13, 1862; *Enquirer*, February 14, 1862; Jones, *Rebel War Clerk's Diary*, 110; Daniel, *Richmond Examiner During the War*, 40–41.

35. Thomas Bragg Diary, February 14, 1862, SHC.

36. Roman, *Beauregard*, 1:224; *OR*, 6:826, 827, 828; Thomas Bragg Diary, February 19, 1862, SHC. The "taking the helm" comment convinced Connelly (*Army of the Heartland*, 130) of Beauregard's desire to take command in Department No. 2.

37. John Withers Diary, February 16, 1862, NARG 109; Scarborough, ed., *DER*, 2:235–37; *Dispatch*, February 18, 1862.

38. *OR*, 52(2):275, 7:890, 892, 889. Some news, perhaps the Leroy Walker dispatch, arrived at the War Department at 11:30 p.m. on February 17, 1862, reporting that a disaster had occurred. Thomas Bragg Diary, February 18, 1862, SHC.

39. Cobb to wife, February 18, 1862, Howell Cobb Papers, UGA; *OR*, 6:828; Scarborough, ed., *DER*, 2:237, 238.

40. Thomas Bragg Diary, February 19, 20, 1862, SHC; *Dispatch*, February 20, 21, 1862; *Whig*, February 20, 1862; Reuben Davis, *Recollections of Mississippi and Mississippians* (Boston: Houghton, Mifflin and Company, 1889), 428. See also Salley Brock Putnam, *Richmond During the War: Four Years of Personal Observation* (New York: G. W. Carleton & Co., 1867), 106–07.

41. Thomas Bragg Diary, February 19, 20, 1862, SHC; *Dispatch*, February 21, 1862; Jones, *Rebel War Clerk's Diary*, 1:110–11; Crist et al., eds., *PJD*, 8:53.

42. Thomas Bragg Diary, February 21, 1862, SHC.

43. *Dispatch*, February 20, 21, 22, 1862; *Enquirer*, February 21, 1862; *Whig*, February 24, 1862; Scarborough, ed., *DER*, 2:240. Confederate losses tallied at 16,623 killed, wounded, and captured; about 2,000 escaped.

44. Wiggins, ed. *Journals of Josiah Gorgas*, 43.

45. Larry J. Daniel, "'The Assaults of the Demagogues in Congress': General Albert Sidney Johnston and the Politics of Command," *Civil War History* 37 (December 1991): 328–29; Woodworth, *Davis & Lee at War*, 98; *Enquirer*, Extra edition, February 22, 1862; Jones, *Rebel War Clerk's Diary*, 1:111; William C. Davis, *Jefferson Davis*, 389, 480; Davis, *Recollections of Mississippi*, 429–31; Rable, *The Confederate Republic*, 67; Thomas E. Schott, *Alexander H. Stephens of Georgia: A Biography* (Baton Rouge: Louisiana State University Press, 1988), 350.

46. McGuire, *Diary of a Southern Refugee*, 95–96; Younger, *Inside the Confederate Government*, 25; *DER*, 2:241.

47. *Dispatch*, February 25, March 4, 5, 1862; Scarborough, ed., *DER*, 2:243; *OR*, 7:437–38.

48. Davis, *Recollections of Mississippi*, 432–32.

49. Woodworth, *This Great Struggle*, 70–71; Howard Jones, *Union in Peril: The Crisis Over British Intervention in the Civil War* (Chapel Hill: University of North Carolina Press, 1970), 104–07.

50. Jones, *Rebel War Clerk's Diary*, 1:111; *Dispatch*, February 26, 1862.

51. Wiggins, ed., *Journals of Josiah Gorgas*, 47; Frank F. Vandiver, *Ploughshares into Swords: Josiah Gorgas and Confederate Ordnance* (College Station: Texas A&M University, 1980), 11, 26, 41, 42.

52. *Dispatch*, March 4, 1862; George Rable, *God's Almost Chosen People: A Religious History of the American Civil War* (Chapel Hill: University of North Carolina Press, 2010), 152–53.

Chapter 5

1. Thomas Bragg Diary, January 8, 1862, SHC; Johnston, *Life of Gen. Albert Sidney Johnston*, 511–13.

2. Crist et al., eds., *PJD*, 8:54, 57.

3. Tennessee Delegation to Davis, March 8, 1862, Gustavus A. Henry Papers, TSLA; Davis, *Rise and Fall*, 2:38. See also J. Williams Jones et al., eds., *Southern Historical Society Papers*, 52 vols. (1–49, Richmond: William Ellis Jones: 1876–1957) [vols. 50–52, Richmond: Virginia Historical Society, 1958–1959], "Proceedings of the Confederate Congress," 44:135 [hereafter cited as *SHSP*]. Precisely where the meeting occurred is not known. Representative Foote later wrote that he never once went into the Confederate White House. The three congressmen who did not sign were Merideth P. Gentry, William G. Swan, and John V. Wright.

4. Davis, *Recollections of Mississippi*, 317, 322–23. The Southern diarist Mary Chesnut wrote: "They [Tennesseans] say he [Johnston] is stupid. Can human folly go further than this Tennessee madness?" See Woodward, ed., *Mary Chesnut's Civil War*, 306.

5. Ben Wynne, *The Man Who Punched Jefferson Davis: The Political Life of Henry S. Foote, Southern Unionist* (Baton Rouge: Louisiana State University Press, 2018), 19, 37–39, 52, 90, 148, 156–57, 162–63, 175, 177, 214–15, 220, 228, 230; Joanne B. Freeman, *The Field of Blood: Violence in Congress and the Road to the Civil War* (New York: Picador Farrar, Straus and Giroux, 2018), 152–54, 156–58, 271; Davis, *Recollections of Mississippi*, 317; *Pulaski Citizen*, May 27, 1880. Mary Chesnut noted in her diary on February 24, 1862: "The irrepressible Foote, who once found our name [Chesnut] so amusing, now has turned his attention to annoying and impeding as much as lies in a Foote—Mr. Davis and his cabinet." Woodward, ed., *Mary Chesnut's Civil War*, 295–96. See also Foote's postwar books, *War of the Rebellion: or Scylla and Charybdis* (New York: Harper & Brother, 1866) and *Casket of Reminiscences* (Washington, DC: Chronicle Publishing Company, 1874), in which he continues his feud with Davis.

6. Warner and Yearns, *BRCC*, 21; McCash, *Thomas R. R. Cobb*, 235, 283, 284, 286, 290, 293, 325.

7. William C. Davis, *Jefferson Davis*, 445; Thomas H. Taylor, ed., "Boyce-Hammond Correspondence," *Journal of Southern History* 31 (May 1937): 349; Ruth Anna Nuermberger, *The Clays of Alabama: A Planter-Lawyer-Politician Family* (Lexington: University Press of Kentucky, 1958), 192.

8. Alvy T. King, *Louis T. Wigfall: Southern Fire-eater* (Baton Rouge: Louisiana State University Press, 1970), 11, 12, 15, 22, 30–33, 36, 127–29, 132, 134, 137, 139, 141; Cobb as quoted in McCash, *Thomas R. R. Cobb*, 244.

9. Eric Walther, *William Lowndes Yancey and the Coming of the Civil War* (Chapel Hill: University of North Carolina Press, 2008), 150–51, 295, 296, 298, 330, 332; Craig L. Symonds, *Joseph E. Johnston: A Civil War Biography* (New York: Norton & Company, 1992), 179.

10. Nuermberger, *The Clays of Alabama*, 147, 184–85, 312; William C. Davis, *Jefferson Davis*, 293, 312, 443.

11. Nuermberger, *The Clays of Alabama*, 191.

12. Harrison A. Trexler, "The Davis Administration and the Richmond Press, 1861–1865," *Journal of Southern History* 16 (May 1950): 179, 183–84, 187, 188; *Examiner*, February 24, 1862; *Southern Literary Messenger* 34 (February-March 1862), 194.

13. Rowland, ed., *JDC*, 5:226.

14. Warner and Yearns, *BRCC*, 89; "Proceedings of the Confederate Congress," *SHSP*, 44:55.

15. Thomas Bragg Diary, February 27, 1862, March 3, 4, 1862, SHC.

16. *OR*, 10(2):917. Perhaps 2,500, including Nathan Bedford Forrest's regiment, escaped.

17. Judah Benjamin to Davis, March 8, 1862, Jefferson Davis Papers, DU; Rowland, ed., *JDC*, 5:214; *Whig*, February 22, 1862; *Dispatch*, February 21, 26,

March 17, 1862; Thomas C. DeLeon, *Four Years in Rebel Capitals: An Inside View of Life in the Southern Confederacy, from Birth to Death* (Mobile: Chronicle Publishing Company, 1874), 164; Crist et al., eds., *PJD*, 8:150.

18. *Dispatch*, April 19, 1862; *Enquirer*, April 15, 1862. For the full minority report, see "Proceedings of the Confederate Congress," *SHSP* 45 (May 1925):135–37.

19. Scarborough, ed., *DER*, 2:248; Hughes, *Liddell's Record*, 59–60.

20. Hughes, ed., *Liddell's Record*, 60; Ferguson, *Ashes of Glory*, 119; Jones, *Rebel War Clerk's Diary*, 133; Woodworth, *Davis & Lee at War*, 103; *Dispatch*, March 11, 1862.

21. *Dispatch*, March 6, 1862; *OR*, 10(2):302.

22. Ada Sterling, *Belle of the Fifties: Memoirs of Mrs. Clay of Alabama, Covering Social and Political Life and the South, 1855–1866* (New York: Doubleday, Paige & Company, 1905), 172, 182.

23. Scarborough, ed., *DER*, 2:248.

24. "Proceedings of the Confederate Congress," *SHSP*, 44:133–34.

25. Robert K. Krick, *Civil War Weather in Virginia* (Tuscaloosa: University of Alabama Press, 2007), 52; "Proceedings of the Confederate Congress," *SHSP*, 44:130–35; *Dispatch*, March 11, 1862; civilwartalk.com/threads/currin-sr-david-maney-cs-congressman-tn.190206, accessed February 2, 2022; Davis, *Recollections of Mississippi*, 436–37; Davis, *Rise and Fall*, 2:40; Warner and Yearns, *BRCC*, 119–20. Foote was incorrect that Nashvillians supplied all the slaves requested of them; indeed, not more than 200 of the requested 1,500 were ever sent. Johnston, *Life of Gen. Albert Sidney Johnston*, 418. Foote's reference to criticism of the citizens of Nashville may have been in reference to an editorial in the *Examiner*, reprinted in the *Enquirer* of March 11, in which the citizens were denounced for "disgraceful and despicable cowardice" and for their "painful and dastardly exhibition."

26. Scarborough, ed., *DER*, 2:254; Thomas Bragg Diary, March 12, 1862, SHC.

27. William C. Davis, *Jefferson Davis*, 263–64; Thomas Bragg Diary, March 7, 19, 1862, SHC; Judah Benjamin to Davis, March 8, 1862, Jefferson Davis Papers, DU; Rowland, ed., *JDC*, 5:214.

28. *Dispatch*, February 20, 24 (12,000), 1862; *Whig*, February 27, 1862 (7,000); Robertson, "Diary of a Southern Refugee," 171; *DER*, 2:258; Wynne, *The Man Who Punched Jefferson Davis*, 224.

29. Davis to Hammond, March 17, 1862, Taylor, "Boyce-Hammond Correspondence," 349–50.

30. "Proceedings of the Confederate Congress," *SHSP*, 44:187; *Whig*, March 20, 1862, Warner and Yearns, *BRCC*, 70.

31. Ferguson, *Ashes of Glory*, 111, 119; Evans, *Judah P. Benjamin*, 155; McCash, *Thomas R. R. Cobb*, 283–84; Daniel, "'The Assaults of the Demagogues in Congress,'" 333; Jones, *Rebel War Clerk's Diary*, 1:118.

32. Welsh, *Medical Histories of Confederate Generals*, 181; McPherson,

Embattled Rebel, 3, 16; Murray and Hsieh, *A Savage War*, 103–04. William C. Davis (*Jefferson Davis*, 480) suspicioned that there was a more sinister reason for Davis's selection of Randolph. "Sick men could be dominated," he wrote. Randolph was one of several advisors who rarely ever challenged, criticized, or complained. In a word—"they did what they were told."

33. Woodworth, *Davis & Lee at War*, 14, 16–18, 102–03; Eicher, *Dixie Betrayed*, 102; *Southern Literary Messenger* (February–March 1862), 197.

34. George G. Shackelford, *George Wythe Randolph and the Confederate Elite* (Athens: University of Georgia Press, 1988), 73–75, 105, 116, 148, 184–85.

35. *Dispatch*, March 6, 1862. The mention of a 50,000-man Federal army facing Columbus was an apparent reference to Frederick Steele's 6,200-man division at Cairo.

36. *Whig*, March 5, 1862; *Dispatch*, March 6, 1862, Rowland, ed., *PJD*, 8:107; Bryan Steele Wills, *The Confederacy's Greatest Cavalryman: Nathan Bedford Forrest* (Lawrence: University Press of Kansas, 1992), 379.

37. See findagrave.com/memorial/131952747/thomas-mckinney-jack (accessed March 20, 2021); Johnston, *Life of Gen. Albert Sidney Johnston*, 519–20; Christ et al., eds., *PJD*, 8:117.

38. *Dispatch*, March 21, 26, 28, 31, 1862; *Whig*, March 19, 22, 27, 1862.

39. *Dispatch*, March 22, 25, 1862; *OR*, 10(2):376; Thomas Bragg Diary, March 17, 14, 1862.

40. Rowland, ed., *JDC*, 5:225.

41. *OR*, 10(2):387, 394.

42. Varina Davis, *Jefferson Davis*, 2:230; 10(1):384.

43. *Whig*, April 7, 8, 1862; *Dispatch*, April 7, 1862; Preston to Davis, April 7, 1862, as quoted in William C. Davis, *Jefferson Davis*, 404; John Wither's Diary, April 7, 1862, Adjutant General's Office, NARG 109; Robertson, "Diary of a Southern Refugee," 177; John F. Henry, CMSF; findagrave.com/memorial/15212403/john-f-henry, accessed April 3, 2021.

44. J. L. Burrows, "Shiloh," mss 4849, SHC.

45. *Whig*, April 8, 9, 1862; *Enquirer*, April 10, 29, 1862; Wiggins, ed., *Journals of Josiah Gorgas*, 43.

46. Krick, *Civil War Weather in Virginia*, 54; *Dispatch*, April 9, 1862.

47. *Dispatch*, April 9, 1862.

48. *Dispatch*, April 8, 1862.

49. Thomas Bragg Diary, April 8, 1862, SHC; Daniel, *Richmond Examiner During the War*, 48; *Enquirer*, April 11, 1862; *Enquirer*, April 11, 1862.

50. DeLeon, *Four Years in Rebel Capitals*, 169–70; Scarborough, *ed.*, *DER*, 2:276–77.

51. *Whig*, April 17, 1862; Andrews, *South Reports the Civil War* (Mobile: Chronicle Publishing Company, 1874), 28; *Enquirer*, April 19, 1862.

52. Krick, *Civil War Weather in Virginia*, 54; Thomas Bragg Diary, April 9, 1862, SHC.

53. *Whig*, April 14, 1862; *Dispatch*, April 9, 1862.

54. Scarborough, ed., *DER*, 2:279, 282–83, 285, 286.

55. *Dispatch*, April 23, 1862; *Examiner*, April 25, 1862. Johnston's body would not be removed to Texas for nearly five years. Roland, *Albert Sidney Johnston*, 353.

56. Roland, *Albert Sidney Johnston*, 145–50, 261; Davis, *Jefferson Davis*, 397–98, 405; Shaw, *William Preston Johnston* (Baton Rouge: Louisiana State University Press 1943), 18, 52, 71–72; Johnston to wife, May 4, 13, 1862; William Preston Johnston Papers, TU.

Chapter 6

1. *Whig*, March 21, 1862; *Dispatch*, March 6, 1862; Jones, *Rebel War Clerk's Diary*, 1:112.

2. *Dispatch*, March 10, 14, 1862; *DER*, 2:249.

3. Roman, *Military Operations of General Beauregard*, 2:356; Dispatch, March 3, 4, 19, 1862; *Whig*, March 11, 1862; *Enquirer*, March 21, 1862; *OR*, 8:132; *PJD*, 8:117. Following the loss of New Madrid, McCown was reassigned and Brigadier General William Mackall assumed command. The garrison strength was reduced from 7,500 to about 4,400, with the transferred troops being sent to Corinth, where they subsequently fought at Shiloh. See Larry J. Daniel and Lynn N. Bock, *Island No. 10: Struggle for the Mississippi Valley* (Tuscaloosa: University of Alabama Press, 1996), 156, 157.

4. *OR*, 8:125; *Whig*, April 1, 7, 1862; *Enquirer*, April 8, 11, 14, 1862; *Dispatch*, April 1, 8, 9, 1862; Thomas Bragg Diary, March 26, 1862, SHC.

5. *Dispatch*, April 14, 17, 1862; Jones, *Rebel War Clerk's Diary*, 1:119–20; Thomas Bragg Diary, April 11, 25, 1862, SHC; *Dispatch*, April 17, 18, 19, 22; Putman, *Richmond During the War*, 131; Jewitt, ed., *Rise and Fall of the Confederacy*, 142. The actual number of prisoners was 4,400, with 1,000 escaping. See Daniel and Bock, *Island No. 10*, 159–60.

6. *Southern Literary Messenger* 34 (February-March 1862), 192, 194; John Withers Diary, April 19–21, 1862, Adjutant General's Office, NARG 109.

7. *Whig*, June 14, 17, 1862; *Enquirer*, June 18, 1862.

8. *OR*, 6:827, 828, 832, 836, 837, 839, 841, 847; Larry J. Daniel, *Shiloh: The Battle That Changed the Civil War* (New York: Simon & Schuster, 1997), 312–13.

9. *Dispatch*, September 21, 1861, January 14, 1862; *Whig*, December 23, 1861; *Enquirer*, December 20, 1861.

10. Bragg Diary, January 6, 1862, Thomas Bragg Diary, SHC; John H. Eicher and Davis J. Eicher, *Civil War High Commands* (Stanford, CA: Stanford University Press, 2002), 464–65; Woodworth, *Jefferson Davis*, 93; Grady McWhiney, *Braxton*

Bragg and Confederate Defeat (Tuscaloosa: University of Alabama Press, 1969), 152–54; Jones, *Rebel War Clerk's Diary*, 108.

11. Thomas E. Redard, "The Port of New Orleans: An Economic History, 1821–1860," PhD diss., Louisiana State University and Agricultural and Mechanical College, 1985, 423; Scarborough, ed., *DER*, 2:290.

12. *Dispatch*, January 14, 1862; *OR*, 6:875, 870–71.

13. *OR*, 6:865; *Enquirer*, March 25, 1862; *Dispatch*, March 13, 1862; *Whig*, April 8, 1862.

14. *OR*, 6:865, 867, 869, 870, 871, 872; Rowland, ed., *JDC*, 5:231.

15. *OR*, 6:872, 873, 53:802; Rowland, ed., *JDC*, 5:232–33; *Official Records of the Union and Confederate Navies in the War of the Rebellion* (Washington, DC: Government Printing Office, 1894–1922), series 2, 1:641 [hereafter cited as *ONR*].

16. Thomas Bragg Diary, April 15, 24, 1862, SHC; *OR*, 6:877, 878, 883, 884; John Withers Diary, April 18, 1862; *Whig*, April 23, 1862; *Dispatch*, April 24, 1862; *Enquirer*, April 25, 1862.

17. Scarborough, ed., *DER*, 2:288; *New York Herald*, August 8, 1862; McGuire, *Diary of a Southern Refugee*, 108; Thomas Bragg Diary, April 26 [28], 1862, SHC.

18. Constance Cary Harrison, "Richmond Scenes in '62," in *Battles and Leaders of the Civil War*, 4 vols. (New York: Thomas Yoseloff, 1956), 2:229; Wiggins, ed., *Journals of Josiah Gorgas*, 47.

19. *OR*, 6:746; Davis, *Jefferson Davis*, 407–08; Neal P. Chatelain, *Defending the Arteries of the Rebellion: Confederate Naval Operations in the Mississippi Valley* (El Dorado Hills, CA: Savas Beatie, 2020), 155–60, 169; Stephen Mallory Diary, May 15, 1862, SHC. See Thomas Bragg Diary, February 21, 1862, SHC for mention of one of Foote's tirades against Mallory.

20. *Enquirer*, April 28, 1862; Yancey to Davis, May 5, 1862, Crist et al., eds., *PJD*, 8:184–85.

21. Hess, *Civil War in the West*, 87–88; *Dispatch*, May 21, 1862; *Whig*, June 4, 6, 1862; Walther, *William Lowndes Yancey*, 347–48. See also Scarborough, ed., *DER*, 2:354.

22. *Enquirer*, June 20, 1862; *Dispatch*, June 20, 30, 1862; Jones, *Union in Peril*, 119–20.

23. *Enquirer*, May 2, 1862; Woodworth, *Jefferson Davis*, 110; Stoker, *The Grand Design*, 233; Murray and Hsieh, *A Savage War*, 547.

24. *Enquirer*, April 29, 30, May 2, 3, 16, 1862; *Dispatch*, April 29, May 7, 14, 1862; *Whig*, November 8, 1861, May 19, 1862; George C. Cable, "New Orleans Before the Capture," in *Battles and Leaders of the Civil War*, 4 vols. (New York: Thomas Yoseloff, 1956), 2:18; Arthur W. Bergeron, Jr., "Mansfield Lovell," in *Confederate Generals in the Western Theater*, ed. Lawrence W. Hewitt and Arthur W. Bergeron, Jr., 4 vols. (Knoxville: University of Tennessee Press, 2010–18): 1:49–50; Scarborough, ed., *DER*, 2:290–91; Jones, *Rebel War Clerk's Diary*, 1:135; *OR*, 6:657–58.

25. Daniel E. Sutherland, "Mansfield Lovell's Quest for Justice: Another Look at the Fall of New Orleans," *Louisiana History* 24 (Summer 1983): 235, 239–40, 244–46; Bergeron, "Mansfield Lovell," 56; Scarborough, ed., *PJD*, 8:197. An 1863 court of inquiry later exonerated Lovell. Davis refused to release the findings, until ordered to do so by Congress.

26. McMurry, *Joseph E. Johnston*, 46–47; Woodworth, *Davis & Lee at War*, 173; Eicher, *Dixie Betrayed*, 134.

27. "Proceedings of the Confederate Congress," *SHSP*, 45:197, 257, 259, 261–62. In Lovell's after-action-report, he listed several failures for the fall of the city—the inability of the forts to withstand the 9- and 11-inch Dahlgrens of the enemy, an insufficient number of heavy guns, the high water that swept away all river obstructions, the failure to complete the *Louisiana*, and the "very poor show" of the six-boat river defense fleet. *OR*, 6:510–517.

28. *OR*, 6:746; Woodworth, *Jefferson Davis*, 112; *Dispatch*, June 2, 1862; Rowland, ed., *JDC*, 5:266; *Whig*, June 2, 1862. For Lovell's units that originally formed the garrison of Vicksburg, see S. H. Lockett, "The Defense of Vicksburg,"In *Battles and Leaders of the Civil War*, 4 vols. (New York: Thomas Yoseloff, 1956), 3:482 and *OR*, 15:7.

29. McGuire, *Diary of a Southern Refugee*, 121; *Dispatch*, June 7, 1862.

30. Rowland, ed., *JDC*, 5:294; Van Dorn to Davis, June 22, 24, 1862, Samuel Richey Collection of the Southern Confederacy, MU.

31. *Dispatch*, July 18, 21, 1862.

32. Van Dorn to Davis, July 15, 1862, Samuel Richey Collection of the Southern Confederacy, MU; *Dispatch*, July 18, 1862; *Enquirer*, July 25, 26, 29, August 1, 1862; *Whig*, July 17, 25, 1862; McGuire, *Diary of a Southern Refugee*, 127.

33. Van Dorn to Davis, July 22, 24, 1862, Samuel Richey Collection of the Southern Confederacy, MU; Jones, *Rebel War Clerk's Diary*, 1:147.

Chapter 7

1. Arthur B. Carter, *The Tarnished Cavalier; Major General Earl Van Dorn, C. S. A.* (Knoxville: University of Tennessee Press), 32–33; Welsh, *Medical Histories of Confederate Generals*, 22; Crist et al., eds., *PJD*, 7:32–33; Castel, *General Sterling Price*, 67; *Dispatch*, January 20, 24, 1862; Emily Van Dorn Miller, *A Soldier's Honor with Reminiscences of Major General Earl Van Dorn* (New York: The Abbey Press, 1902), 62; Peter Cozzens, *The Darkest Days of the War: The Battles of Iuka and Corinth* (Chapel Hill: University of North Carolina Press, 1997), 7.

2. Thomas Bragg Diary, January 16, 1862, SHC.

3. George Bagby Diary, March 12, 1862, VHS; *Dispatch*, March 13, April 19, 1862; *Whig*, March 19, 22, 27, April 5, 1862; *Enquirer*, April 8, 18, 1862; Withers

Diary, March 14, 1862, Adjutant General's Office, NARG 109; Thomas Bragg Diary, March 12, 1862, SHC; Scarborough, ed., *DER*, 2:261, 285; DeLeon, *Four Years in Rebel Capitals*, 167. Van Dorn had 16,000 in his army, about 13,000 of whom were engaged at Pea Ridge. He lost at least 2,000, and hundreds more deserted in the retreat. The Federals had 10,250 on the field and sustained 1,384 casualties. William H. Shea and Earl J. Hess, *Pea Ridge: Civil War Campaign in the West* (Chapel Hill: University of North Carolina Press, 1992), 270–71.

4. *Whig*, April 3, 1862; *Dispatch*, April 7, 10, 12, 1862; *OR*, 10(2):361.

5. *OR*, 13:814–16; Rowland, ed., *JDC*, 5:248–49; *Enquirer*, February 28, 1862.

6. Welsh, *Medical Histories of Confederate Generals*, 102; Bobby L. Roberts, "General T. C. Hindman and the Trans-Mississippi District," *Arkansas Historical Quarterly* 32 (Winter 1973): 302; Diane Neal and Thomas W. Kremm, *The Lion of the South: General Thomas C. Hindman* (Macon, GA: Mercer University Press, 1993), 114, 117–18; Daniel, *Conquered*, 58–59; Charles Edward Nash, *Biographical Sketches of Gen. Pat Cleburne and Gen. T. C. Hindman* (Little Rock: by author, 1898), 59, 73, 74, 77–78, 154, 217–18.

7. *Whig*, July 16, 1, 25, August 2, 5, 8, 1862; *Dispatch*, July 3, 7, 21, 26, 1862; *Enquirer*, July 18,

28, 1862; Van Dorn to Davis, June 9, 1862, *OR*, 13:832, 836–37, 874–75; Robertson, "Diary of a Southern Refugee, January–July 1862," 144. Curtis brushed aside the blocking units under the inept Brigadier General Albert Rust at the Cache River. See Thomas L. Snead, "The Conquest of Arkansas," in *Battles and Leaders of the Civil War*, 4 vols. (New York: Thomas Yoseloff, 1956), 3:445.

8. William C. Davis, *Jefferson Davis*, 461; *OR*, 13:867, 846–47; *Enquirer*, September 2, 1862; Thomas M. Settles, *John Bankhead Magruder: A Military Reappraisal* (Baton Rouge: Louisiana State University Press, 2009), 1, 11, 238–41; Cutrer, *Theater of a Separate War*, 139.

9. Mallory Diary, June 21, 1862, SHC; *OR*, 13, 832; William C. Davis, *Jefferson Davis*, 410; *OR*, 17(2):653.

10. Walter C. Halderman, *Theopilus Hunter Holmes: A North Carolina General in the Civil War* (Jefferson, NC: McFarland & Co., Inc., 2014), 97; Jewett, ed., *Rise and Fall of the Confederacy*, 242; *OR*, 53:816–17.

11. Shackelford, *George Wythe Randolph*, 97, 98, 127, 129, 136, 139.

12. *Dispatch*, July 14, 1862; *Whig*, August 26, 1862; Jones, *Rebel War Clerk's Diary*, 1:149.

13. *OR*, 53:818, 891; Welsh, *Medical Histories of Confederate Generals*, 210–11; Richard Taylor, *Destruction and Reconstruction: Personal Experiences in the Late War* (New York: D. Appleton, 1879), 98; Geise, *Confederate Military Forces in the Trans-Mississippi*, 68; Jeffrey S. Prushankin, *A Crisis in Confederate Command: Edmund Kirby Smith, Richard Taylor, and the Army of the Trans-Mississippi* (Baton Rouge: Louisiana State University Press, 2005), 5.

14. *Whig*, January 10, 1862; Crist et al., eds., *PJD*, 8:237.

15. *Whig*, May 24, 1862; Castel, *General Sterling Price*, 281; Cozzens, *The Darkest Days of the War*, 24.

16. *Dispatch*, February 5, 6, 1862; *Enquirer*, February 4, March 7, 1862; *Whig*, April 10, 1862; *OR*, 8:736–37, 744–45, 747–48. Woodworth (*Jefferson Davis*, 151) wrote: "All in all, Jefferson Davis had to conclude, Price would be more trouble outside the army than in."

17. Thomas L. Snead, "With Price East of the Mississippi," in *Battles and Leaders of the Civil War*, 4 vols. (New York: Thomas Yoseloff, 1956), 3:723–24; Castel, *General Sterling Price*, 82, 87, 89–91; Rable, *The Confederate Republic*, 134. Castel (*General Sterling Price*, 82) wrote: "Few of the approximately 8,000 soldiers who followed Price across the Mississippi ever saw their Missouri homes again." The papers did not comment on Price's arrival, but according to a Davis dispatch the general had not arrived by June 13. The visit therefore had to have occurred during the last two weeks of June. *JDC*, 5:276.

18. Snead, "With Price East of the Mississippi," 724–25; Castel, *General Sterling Price*, 87–89.

19. Castel, *General Sterling Price*, 89; Snead, "With Price East of the Mississippi," 725–26; Davis, *Jefferson Davis*, 276, 278–79; Florence Elizabeth Holladay, "The Powers of the Confederate Commander of the Confederate Trans-Mississippi Department, 1863 to 1865" *Southwestern Historical Quarterly* 21 (January 1918): 280; *Enquirer*, August 27, 1862; *OR*, 8:841.

20. *OR*, 13:833–34; Warner and Yearns, *BRCC*, 109–10.

21. Jewett, *Rise and Fall of the Confederacy*, 5; *Enquirer*, April 8, 1862; *Dispatch*, July 12, 1862; Northrop to W. A. Broadwell, July 26, 1862, J. T. Ward to Broadwell, August 4, 1862, and Broadwell to Crothers, September 24, 1862, William A. Broadwell, CMSF, NARG 109; *OR*, 10(1):776.

22. Phelan to Davis, June 18, 1862, James Phelan Letter, LSU.

23. *OR*, 53:825; *OR*, 13:881–82, 912.

Chapter 8

1. *Whig*, May 9, 10, June 10, 1862; Putnam, *Richmond During the War*, 124; Jones, *Rebel War Clerk's Diary*, 1:118.

2. *Whig*, April 24, 1862; *OR*, 10(2):403.

3. *Whig*, May 23, 1862; *Dispatch*, May 14, 21, 23, 1862; Harriette Cary Diary, College of William and Mary; Scarborough, ed., *DER*, 2:294, 299, 323–34, 331.

4. *Dispatch*, April 18, May 7, 1862; Henry W. Smart to sister, May 26, 1862, Henry W. Smart Letter, William and Mary.

5. Thomas Bragg Diary, April 7, 1862, SHC; Johnston to wife, May 19, 1862, William Preston Johnston Papers, TU.

6. Beauregard-Bragg as quoted in Woodward, *Jefferson Davis*, 104; Williams, *P. G. T. Beauregard*, 152–53. Williams interpreted this letter as indirectly asking for a free hand. "At the same time he was attempting to protect himself against criticism in Richmond if he had to yield Corinth."

7. *Whig*, June 6, 9, 13, 1862; *Dispatch*, June 10, 16, 1862; *Enquirer*, June 10, 1862; Scarborough, ed., *DER*, 2:333; Phelan to Davis, June 18, 1862, James Phelan Letter, LSU.

8. Phelan to Davis, June 18, 1862, James Phelan Letter, LSU.

9. Rowland, ed., *JDC*, 5:277; Mallory Diary, June 21, 1862, SHC.

10. William C. Davis, *Jefferson Davis*, 406; Preston to William Preston Johnston, May 30, 1862, William Preston Johnston Papers, TU; *OR*, 10(2):780–86; Williams, *P. G. T. Beauregard*, 157.

11. Williams, *P. G. T. Beauregard*, 157–59.

12. Wiggins, ed., *Journals of Josiah Gorgas*, 46; Crist et al., eds., *PJD*, 8:254, 262; Stephen Mallory Diary, June 21, 1862, SHC.

13. Jones, *Rebel War Clerk's Diary*, 1:135; *Dispatch*, June 27, 28, 30, 1862; *Whig*, June 28, August 22, 1862.

14. *Dispatch*, June 10, October 2, November 20, 1861; *Enquirer*, May 3, June 11, 1861, April 11, May 6, 1862; *Whig*, September 12, 1861; Thomas Bragg Diary, June 8, 1862, SHC; Pugh to Bragg, March 16, 1862, and Curry to Bragg, May 14, 1862, Braxton Bragg Papers, WRHS.

15. Curry to Bragg, May 14, 1862, Braxton Bragg Papers, WRHS; Jesse Pearl Rice, *J. L. M. Curry: Southerner, Statesman, and Educator* (New York: King's Crown Press, 1949), 40–41; Hess, *Braxton Bragg*, 51; Wiggins, ed., *Journals of Josiah Gorgas*, 50; Crist et al., eds., *PJD*, 8:258.

16. Crist et al., eds., *PJD*, 8:256–58, 259–60.

17. *Whig*, August 5, 1862; Davis to Bragg, Braxton Bragg Papers, Samuel Richey Collection of the Southern Confederacy, Miami University. See also Crist et al., eds., *PJD*, 8:258–59, 269. The newspaper clipping in question is unfortunately not extant.

18. Phelan to Davis, June 18, 1862, James Phelan Letter, LSU; *Whig*, September 18, 1862. For the most detailed explanation of the incident, see Hess, *Braxton Bragg*, 44–45.

19. *Enquirer*, September 9, 16, 1862; *Whig*, September 13, 1862; "Proceedings of the Confederate Congress," *SHSP*, 46:113–19, 127–28; Thomas Bragg Diary, September 12, 1862, SHC; Phelan to Bragg, December 4, 1862, Braxton Bragg Papers, WRHS.

20. Roman, *Military Operations of General Beauregard*, 1:415–17; Williams, *P. G. T. Beauregard*, 163–64. In Roman's biography, which Beauregard essentially wrote himself, he conveniently left out his letters to Villere.

21. John Withers Diary, September 13, 1863, NARG 109.

22. Roman, *Military Operations of General Beauregard*, 1:417–18.

23. Mary S. Estill, ed., "Diary of a Confederate Congressman, 1862–1863," *Southwestern Historical Quarterly* 38 (April 1935): 276, 278–79.

24. Johnston as quoted in William C. Davis, *Jefferson Davis*, 449–50; Warner and Years, *BRCC*, 83, 179, 235–36.

25. *Whig*, July 25, 1861, June 23, 24, 1862; *Dispatch*, June 25, 1861; Prushankin, *A Crisis in Confederate Command*, 10; Groce, *Mountain Rebels*, 84–86; *OR*, 16(2):679–80, 683, 685, 695–96, 701. The Cumberland Gap Federal column was George W. Morgan's division, which did in fact include two brigades of Tennessee and Kentucky volunteers.

26. *OR*, 53:246; 16(2):701–02, 706, 707, 708, 710, 711, 713.

27. *Enquirer*, August 1, 1862; *Dispatch*, July 18, 23, 25, 26, 28–30; *Whig*, June 22, July 18, 1862; McGuire, *Diary of a Southern Refugee*, 128; *OR*, 16(2):732. McCown's Division arrived in Chattanooga on July 16, 1862.

28. *OR*, 17(2):655–56, 656–57, 635; Earl J. Hess, *Banners to the Breeze: The Kentucky Campaign, Corinth, & Stones River* (Lincoln: University of Nebraska Press, 2000), 20. Van Dorn's Division had been bolstered by several exchanged regiments from Fort Donelson and Island No. 10, plus some newly recruited regiments of volunteers who flocked to join to avoid the onus of being drafted. Grant did in fact have only a single 9,000-man division at Corinth, but there were at least five other divisions within supporting distance, exclusive of two divisions at Memphis. Grant and Rosecrans thus had a present-for-duty strength of 42,305 compared to Bragg's 45,393.

29. Jones, *Rebel War Clerk's Diary*, 1:142; *Dispatch*, June 14, August 5, 13, 1862; *Whig*, August 11, 1862; *OR*, 17(2):148.

30. *Whig*, August 5, 11, 23, 1862; *Enquirer*, August 26, 1862; *Dispatch*, August 28, 1862.

31. *OR*, 16(2):741.

32. *OR*, 16(2):771, 739–40, 292; *OR*, 52(2):366; Christ et al., eds., *PJD*, 8:417.

33. John Withers Diary, September 8, 1862, NARG 109; *Whig*, September 8, 1862; Johnston to wife, August 15, 1862, William Preston Johnston Papers, TU; Scarborough, ed., *DER*, 2:429; *OR*, 16(2):740–41.

34. Woodworth, *Davis & Lee at War*, 174–85; *Dispatch*, September 9, 1862. At the Battle of Richmond, both sides had about 6,500 troops engaged. The Federals lost 5,353 (mostly captured) and the Confederates 451. Hess (*Civil War in the West*, 451) wrote: "The Battle of Richmond led to Confederate seizure of the entire Bluegrass and the fall of Lexington and Frankfort."

35. Jones, *Rebel War Clerk's Diary*, 1:153–54.

36. *Enquirer*, September 11, 26, 1862; *Whig*, September 9, 10, 23, 24, 1862; *Dispatch*, September 9, 10, 23, 1862; Jones, *Rebel War Clerk's Diary*, 1:163.

37. *Enquirer*, September 13, 1862; Jones, *Rebel War Clerk's Diary*, 1:153–54; Rowland, ed., *JDC*, 5:345–46; William C. Davis, *Jefferson Davis*, 470; Report

of the Select Committee, appointed by the Senate of the Confederate States to examine the condition of hospitals, 13. Jackson's Harper Ferry's captures included 12,000 prisoners, 73 guns, and 13,000 small arms.

38. Scarborough, ed., *DER*, 2:455–56.

39. *Dispatch*, October 16, 17, 1862; *Enquirer*, October 18, 1862; *Central Presbyterian*, October 16, 1862; Scarborough, ed., *DER*, 2:464. See also *OR*, 16(2):952.

40. Scarborough, ed., *DER*, 2:464; Younger, ed., *Inside the Confederate Government*, 28; Jones, *Rebel War Clerk's Diary*, 1:171; Wiggins, ed., *Journals of Josiah Gorgas*, 54.

41. *Dispatch*, October 18, 1862; Jones, *Rebel War Clerk's Diary*, 1:174.

42. *OR*, 52(2):369; Jones, *Rebel War Clerk's Diary*, 163.

43. *Whig*, October 20, 1862; Jones, *Rebel War Clerk's Diary*, 1:184; *Enquirer* as quoted in *Appeal*, October 30, 1862.

44. *Dispatch*, October 22, 24, 1862; Jones, *Rebel War Clerk's Diary*, 1:174; Gilmer to wife, October 22, 1862, Jeremy Gilmer Papers, SHC; Scarborough, ed., *DER*, 2:469–70.

45. Johnston as quoted in William C. Davis, *Jefferson Davis*, 472; Warner and Yearns, *BRCC*, 159; Crist et al., eds., *PJD*, 8:452.

46. Seitz, *Braxton Bragg*, 206; *Examiner*, November 21, 1862; *Charleston Mercury*, October 25, November 18, 1862; *Enquirer*, November 28, 1862; *Dispatch*, February 13, 1862.

47. McWhiney, *Braxton Bragg*, 324; Thomas Bragg Diary, September 12, 1862, SHC; Crist et al., eds., *PJD*, 8:464, 483; *American Citizen*, May 24, 1873; Lyon to Bragg, January 22, 1863. Braxton Bragg Papers, WRHS.

48. *OR*, 16(2):982–83; *Central Presbyterian*, November 6, 1862; Jones, *Rebel War Clerk's Diary*, 1:176; Thomas Bragg Diary, October 27, 1862, SHC; *Charleston Mercury*, November 4, 5, 1862.

49. McWhiney, *Braxton Bragg*, 327–28; William C. Davis, *Jefferson Davis*, 473. Woodworth (*Jefferson Davis*, 308) believed that the greater sin of Davis was at the beginning of the campaign. He "hesitated and failed to take decisive action to ensure vitality needed cooperation between Bragg and Kirby Smith."

50. Daniel, *Conquered*, 45–46; William C. Davis, *Jefferson Davis*, 473–74; Bagby articles as quoted in *Columbus Sun*, November 6, 11, 18, 1862; John Withers Diary, November 8, 1862, NARG 109; Jones, *Rebel War Clerk's Diary*, 1:186; Connelly and Jones, *Politics of Command*, 63; Hess, *Braxton Bragg*, 83; Horn, *Leonidas Polk*, 278; Hardee to Johnston, November 19, 1862, William Preston Johnston Papers, TU; Younger, ed., *Inside the Confederate Government*, 30–31.

51. *OR*, 17(2):376–77.

52. *OR*, 17(1):441, 425, 449(2):713.

53. *OR*, 17(2):704, 707; Van Dorn to Davis, September 10, 1862, Samuel Richey Collection of the Southern Confederacy, MU. Woodworth (*Jefferson Davis*, 153) concluded that Price was "unwilling to share the glory with Van Dorn"

and used Bragg's orders as "an excuse to undertake independent command." While not discounting Price's ego, the Missourian had little choice but to follow Bragg's directive. Failure to do so would have set him up as a scapegoat in the event of Bragg's defeat, something that surely must have crossed Price's mind.

54. *Whig*, September 29, 1862; *Dispatch*, September 29, 1862; *Enquirer*, October 7, 1862; *OR*, 17(1):126(2):707, 715; Snead, "With Price East of the Mississippi," 731.

55. Crist et al., eds., *PJD*, 8:417; *OR*, 52(2):876.

56. *Dispatch*, October 7, 8, 9, 1862; *Enquirer*, October 7, 1862; Scarborough, ed., *DER*, 2:458, 459; Jones, *Rebel War Clerk's Diary*, 1:164, 165; Crist et al, eds., *PJD*, 8:412.

57. McGuire, *Diary of a Southern Refugee*, 166; Scarborough, ed., *DER*, 2:461. Confederate perceptions to the contrary, the opposing forces at Corinth were about equal.

58. Michael B. Ballard, *Pemberton: A Biography* (Jackson: University of Mississippi Press, 1991), 106, 107, 111; Michael B. Ballard, "Misused Merit: The Tragedy of John C. Pemberton," in *Confederate Generals of the West*, 4 vols. (Knoxville: University of Tennessee Press, 2010), 1:106, 108; *OR*, 17(2):724, 726.

59. *OR*, 17(1):381–82, (2):733.

60. *Whig*, October 27, 1862; *Examiner*, October 31, 1862.

61. William C. Davis, *Jefferson Davis*, 474; Phelan to Davis, June 18, 1862, James Phelan Letter, LSU; Crist et al., eds., *PJD*, 8:433, 537–38; Van Dorn to Davis, October 12, 1862, Samuel Richey Collection of the Southern Confederacy, MU.

62. *OR*, 17(2):788–89.

63. *OR*, 17(1):415–16; Thomas Bragg Diary, October 17, 1862, SHC.

Chapter 9

1. *Dispatch*, November 19, 1862. The number of killed and wounded during November and December did not total 25,000, as Alexander feared, but was closer to 15,000. However, he failed to consider the number of prisoners who took the Oath of Allegiance, which included fully 10 percent of the Fort Donelson prisoners, and the number of prisoner parolees who were disabled and no longer fit for duty, which included over one-fourth of the Island No. 10 and Fort Donelson parolees. See Daniel, *Conquered*, 6; and Larry J. Daniel, *Battle of Stones River: The Forgotten Conflict Between the Confederate Army of Tennessee and the Union Army of the Cumberland* (Baton Rouge: Louisiana State University Press, 2012), 3–4.

2. Castel, *Decision in the West*, 29; Arthur James L. Fremantle, *Three Months in the Southern States, April–June 1863* (New York: J. Bradburn, 1864), 117; Symonds, *Joseph E. Johnston*, 140, 150; McMurry, *Civil Wars of Joseph E. Johnston*,

8, 19, 26, 29, 30–31, 35–37, 53, 142; Woodworth, *Jefferson Davis*, 176; Craig L. Symonds, "No Margin for Error: Civil War in the Confederate Government" in Steven E. Woodworth, ed., *The Art of Command in the Civil War* (Lincoln: University of Nebraska Press, 1998), 7; Thomas C. DeLeon, *Belles, Beaux, and Brains of the 60's* (New York: G. W. Dillingham Company, 1907), 402.

3. Welsh, *Medical Histories of Confederate Generals*, 120; McMurry, *Civil Wars of Joseph E. Johnston*, 139–42. McMurry (1–41) has the most complete explanation of the complex Johnston–Davis seniority issue. Symonds ("No Margin for Error," 5) concluded that Johnston's recuperating at Wigfall's home was "[t]he decisive turning point in their [Davis–Johnston] relationship."

4. Symonds, *Johnston*, 183; Mrs. D. Wright, *A Southern Girl in '61* (New York: Doubleday, Page & Co., 1905), 100; McMurry, *Civil Wars of Joseph E. Johnston*, 163–65; *OR*, 17(2):758. Joseph E. Johnston, "Jefferson Davis and the Mississippi Campaign," in *Battles and Leaders of the Civil War*, 4 vols. (New York: Thomas Yoselfff, 1956), 3:473. McMurry (177) argues that there were only three possible assignments for Johnston: the West, the coast (Charleston-Savannah), and the trans-Mississippi. Beauregard had just been assigned to the coast, and Johnston and his allies would have seen the trans-Mississippi as banishment. The West was thus his only option. I see another possibility: Davis could have given Johnston both theater *and* army command (Army of Tennessee) and recalled Bragg to Richmond, making him inspector general (as Polk had already suggested) or make him adviser to the president. In other words, he could have done in 1862 what he subsequently did in late 1863. It seems clear that Davis at this juncture would not have accepted either of these options, but they were available.

5. *Examiner*, December 12, 19, 1862; *Whig*, November 22, 1862.

6. Woodworth, *Davis & Lee at War*, 112–20; McMurry, *Civil Wars of Joseph E. Johnston*, 178.

7. McMurry, *Civil Wars of Joseph E. Johnston*, 178–79, 181–82; King, *Louis T. Wigfall*, 163; *Columbus Sun*, December 5, 1862.

8. Scarborough, ed., *DER*, 2:483; *OR*, 16(2):974, 20(2):386.

9. *OR*, 20(2):421–23; *Dispatch*, November 20, 1862; *Examiner*, December 2, 1862; Scarborough, ed., *DER*, 2:501.

10. Edward G. Longacre, *Cavalry in the Heartland: The Mounted Forces of the Army of Tennessee* (Yardley, PA: Westholme, 2009), 14–15; James A. Ramage, *Rebel Raider: The Life of General John Hunt Morgan* (Lexington: University Press of Kentucky, 1986), 38–39, 43, 138, 147; *Dispatch*, November 3, December 17, 19, 24, 29, 30, 1862; *Whig*, December 10, 17, 24, 1862, January 28, 1863; *Enquirer*, December 27, 1862; *OR*, 20(1):64, 20(2):445, 17(2):592.

11. *Dispatch*, December 20, 1862; Rable, *The Confederate Republic*, 174.

12. William C. Davis, *Jefferson Davis*, 482; *Dispatch*, December 12, 1862; *Whig*, December 12, 17, 1862; Jones, *A Rebel War Clerk's Diary*, 1:210; Younger, ed., *Inside the Confederate Government*, 33.

13. *OR*, 20(2):492 (three *dispatch*es), 459; Jones, *Rebel War Clerk's Diary*, 232; Hess, *Braxton Bragg*, 93. Rosecrans knew of the transfer of Stevenson's Division by the evening of December 24, 1862. Johnston argued that to take more troops from Bragg would enable Rosecrans to send reinforcements to either Virginia or Mississippi.

14. John Wihters Diary, December 25, 1862, NARG 109; *Whig*, December 27, 1862; *Dispatch*, December 16, 1862; *Enquirer*, December 23, 1862; civilwarpoetry.org/authors/mccarthy.html, accessed May 28, 2023.

15. *OR*, 20(2):463, 466, 467, 468; *Dispatch*, December 29, 30, 31, 1862; *Enquirer*, December 30, 1862.

16. *OR*, 20(1):662; Jones, *Rebel War Clerk's Diary*, 1:228–29; Younger, ed., *Inside the Confederate Government*, 36; Scarborough, ed., *DER*, 530.

17. Jones, *Rebel War Clerk's Diary*, 229; *Enquirer*, January 7, 1863; *Whig*, January 3, 1863; *Dispatch*, January 5, 1863.

18. *OR*, 20(1):662; Jones, *Rebel War Clerk's Diary*, 1:231.

19. *Dispatch*, January 7, 1863; *Whig*, January 6, 7, 1863; Scarborough, ed., *DER*, 232.

20. Jones, *Rebel War Clerk's Diary*, 1:231–32, 234, 235; Preston to Johnston, January 26, 1863, and Johnston to wife, January 28, 1863, William Preston Johnston Papers, TU.

21. *Whig*, January 7, 9, 10, 12, 13; *OR*, 20(1):670.

22. McMurry, *Civil Wars of Joseph E. Johnston*, 192, 201; William Preston Johnston to wife, January 6, 1862, William Preston Johnston Papers, TU; Johnston to Wigfall, January 8, 1863, Wright, *A Southern Girl in '61*, 101; McGuire, *Diary of a Southern Refugee*, 183.

23. *Examiner*, November 21, 1862, January 6, 1863; *Dispatch*, January 6, 7, 1863; *Southern Literary Messenger*, January 1863, 57; Hess, *Braxton Bragg*, 113.

24. Hess, *Braxton Bragg*, 42; *Enquirer*, January 23, 1863; Younger, ed., *Inside the Confederate Government*, 83.

25. King, *Louis T. Wigfall*, 165–66; Crist et al., eds., *PJD*, 8:464, 483, 467; Jones, *Rebel War Clerk's Diary*, 1:208.

26. *Whig*, January 26, February 16; *OR*, 20(2):493.

27. "Proceedings of the Confederate Congress," *SHSP*, 48:209–18; Estill, ed., "Diary of a Confederate Congressman," 299; Pugh to Bragg, March 5, 1863, Bragg Papers, WRHS.

28. Don Carolos Seitz, *Braxton Bragg: General of the Confederacy* (Columbia, SC: State, 1924), 284–85; Phelan to Bragg, March 6, 1862, and Pugh to Bragg, March 5, 1863, Bragg Papers, WRHS; Thomas Bragg Diary, September 12, 1862, SHC; Jewett, ed., *Rise and Fall of the Confederacy*, 177; Hess, *Braxton Bragg*, 134.

29. findagrave.com/memorial/112568964/john-burris-sale; Larry J. Daniel,

Cannoneers in Gray: The Field Artillery of the Army of Tennessee, 1861–1865 (Tuscaloosa: University of Alabama Press, 1984), 79; Daniel, *Conquered*, 86.

30. Johnston to Jordan, March 28, 1863, William Preston Johnston Papers, TU; Daniel, *Conquered*, 87; Johnston to "My dear General," May 18, 1863, William Preston Johnston, CMSF.

31. Younger, ed., *Inside the Confederate Government*, 38, 42; William C. Davis, *Jefferson Davis*, 490; *Examiner*, January 20, 1863; *JDC*, 5:420–21.

32. *OR*, 20(1):698–99; *Whig*, January 15, 1863.

33. McMurry, *Civil Wars of Joseph E. Johnston*, 221–22; *Examiner*, January 30, 1863.

34. Crist et al., eds., *PJD*, 9:48–49; *OR*, 23(2):632–33, 52(2):426. McMurry (*Civil Wars of Joseph E. Johnston*, 222) believed that Johnston's reports represented his "honest convictions" and was not merely attempting to deflect army command.

35. *OR*, 20(2):640, 659; Symonds, *Johnston*, 199; *PJD*, 9:86–87; McMurry, *Civil Wars of Joseph E. Johnston*, 224. McMurry deduced that Davis had three options. First, place Johnston in command of the Army of Tennessee and Beauregard in command in Mississippi. Second, give Bragg some other position, place Johnston over the Army of Tennessee, and let theater command simply "dissolve away." Third, which he considered the best option, simply replace Polk and Hardee and retain Bragg. There were, of course, other options. Polk and Pemberton could be swapped and Johnston given command of the Vicksburg army.

36. Younger, ed., *Inside the Confederate Government*, 46, 50. See also McMurry, *Civil Wars of Joseph E. Johnston*, 209.

37. Wigfall as quoted in Hess, *Braxton Bragg*, 134–35.

38. *Courier* store as reported in *Appeal*, April 3, 1863. See also *Appeal*, March 26, April 4, 1863.

39. *OR*, 23(2):745; Daniel, *Conquered*, 99–100; McMurry, *Civil Wars of Joseph E. Johnston*, 223, 226. McMurry surmised that Davis hoped that Johnston would assume army command, thereby satisfying "Bragg's many critics without, so it would appear, having given in to pressure or soiling their own bureaucratic hands."

Chapter 10

1. *Whig*, December 4, 1862; *PJD*, 8:561. For additional statistics, see Hess, *Civil War in the West*, 3–4.

2. Jones, *Rebel War Clerk's Diary*, 1:266.

3. Jones, *Rebel War Clerk's Diary*, 1:184, 186; *OR*, 17(2):745; *Dispatch*, November 11, 1862.

4. *OR*, 17(2):771.

5. Crist et al., eds., *PJD*, 8:525; Jones, *Rebel War Clerk's Diary*, 1:208, 208.

6. *OR*, 17(2):779, 801; *Whig*, December 10, 11, 1862.

7. *OR*, 17(2):788–89.

8. *OR*, 17(2):812; *Dispatch*, January 15, 1862. Northern newspapers also admitted the loss of a locomotive, 40 boxcars, 225 wagons, and 4,000 bales of cotton. The *Mobile Advertiser & Register* claimed 1,000 pistols, 5,000 arms, 500 horses and mules, and several spiked cannon.

9. *Enquirer*, December 27, 1862; *Whig*, December 30, 1862, January 10, 17, 1863; *Dispatch*, December 31, 1862, January 10, 17, 1863; Jones, *Rebel War Clerk's Diary*, 1:226–27, 230. For the particulars of the Battle of Chickasaw Bayou, see Timothy B. Smith, *Early Struggles for Vicksburg: The Mississippi Campaign and Chickasaw Bayou, October 25–December 31, 1862* (Lawrence: University Press of Kansas, 2022), chapters 11–13. Casualties in the engagement totaled 187 for the Confederates, 1,776 for the Federals.

10. *Dispatch*, February 2, 4, 1863; Scarborough, ed., *DER*, 563; *OR*., 23(2):599, 600, 605.

11. *OR*, 24(2):646, 656; *Enquirer*, March 17, 1863; *Whig*, March 17, 30, 1863; *Dispatch*, March 13, 1863; Rowland, ed., *JDC*, 5:427, 444.

12. Krick, *Civil War Weather in Virginia*, 92, 94; *OR*, 24(3):751, 767, 778; Jones, *Rebel War Clerk's Diary*, 1: 292, 295, 297.

13. Jones, *Rebel War Clerk's Diary*, 1:298–99; *OR*, 23(2):778; *Whig*, May 5, 1863. The Benjamin Grierson raid successfully made it to Baton Rouge.

14. Crist et al, eds., *PJD*, 9:161; *OR*, 24(3):807, 815; *Whig*, May 6, 1863; *Dispatch*, May 6, 13, 15, 1863; Younger, ed., *Inside the Confederate Government*, 54.

15. Ferguson, *Ashes of Glory*, 201–10; Wiggins, ed., *Journals of Josiah Gorgas*, 64; Younger, ed., *Inside the Confederate Government*, 56; Woodworth, *Davis & Lee at War*, 223.

16. *OR*, 52(2):461, 462–63, 467–69; Crist et al., eds., *PJD*, 9:173–75.

17. *OR*, 14:923, 925, 926, 932, 934, 936–37, 940, 942, 947, 24(1):224.

18. John H. Reagan, *Memoirs, with Special Reference to Secession and the Civil War* (New York: Neale, 1906), 23.

19. Woodworth, *Davis & Lee*, 228–29; James Longstreet, *From Manassas to Appomattox* (Philadelphia: J. P. Lipponcott Co., 1896), 331.

20. It was Richard McMurry who theorized the West to East reinforcement.

21. *OR*, 52(2):468–69; *Whig*, May 20, 23, 1863.

22. Reagan, *Memoirs*, 121–22, 150–51.

23. William C. Davis, ed., *A Fire-Eater Remembers: The Confederate Memoir of Robert Barnwell Rhett* (Columbia: University of South Carolina Press, 2000), 82.

24. Daniel, *Conquered*, 160–61.

25. Younger, ed., *Inside the Confederate Government*, 62; Wiggins, ed., *Journals of Josiah Gorgas*, 67.

26. *OR*, 23(1):218, 219; Jones, *Rebel War Clerk's Diary*, 1:327, 328, 329, 863; McGuire, *Diary of a Southern Refugee*, 216; Scarborough, ed., *DER*, 2:661–62; *Whig*, May 20, 21, 23, 28, 1863; Wiggins, ed., *Journals of Josiah Gorgas*, 67–68; Younger, ed., *Inside the Confederate Government*, 66. See also *Dispatch*, May 20, 21, 1863. The Battle of Champion Hill was fought on May 16, 1863. The Confederates sustained losses of 2,181 killed and wounded and 671 captured, for a total of 3,851. Total Federal loss was 2,441. At the Battle of Big Black River Bridge, fought the next day, Pemberton lost 1,750, for a total loss of 5,601.

27. Younger, ed., *Inside the Confederate Government*, 64; *Dispatch*, May 25, 1863; *Whig*, May 25, 1863; Scarborough, ed., *DER*, 2:666; McGuire, *Diary of a Southern Refugee*, 216. The accounts were referring to the assault of May 22, 1863. The Federals sustained losses of 3,199, the Confederates around 500. The Federal assault on May 19 was not reported in the Richmond press. Federal losses were 942, the Rebels about 200. See Earl J. Hess, *Storming Vicksburg: Grant, Pemberton, and the Battles of May 19–22, 1863* (Chapel Hill: University of North Carolina Press, 2020), 68, 250–51.

28. *Dispatch*, June 8, 1863; *Whig*, June 2, 15, 1863; *Enquirer*, July 28, 1863; Scarborough, ed., *DER*, 2:675; Jones, *Rebel War Clerk's Diary*, 1:338, 340; Emma A. Tyler to "My Dear Friend," June 30, 1863, in Richard Holloway to Daniel, June 21, 1863.

29. Younger, ed., *Inside the Confederate Government*, 66; *Whig*, July 1, 1863; Jones, *Rebel War Clerk's Diary*, 1:344.

30. *OR*, 24(1):194. For additional examples of the squabbling between Davis and Johnston, see *OR*, 24(1):194–98. McMurry (*Civil Wars of Joseph E. Johnston*, 265) wrote: "By this time (Grant's campaign) Johnston had concluded that events of the past two weeks had stripped Vicksburg of its value to the Confederacy and that the Rebels could not hold the town once Grant reestablished contact with the Union fleet in the Yazoo and Mississippi rivers. Realizing that a siege would ultimately end up with the loss of both Pemberton's army and Vicksburg, Johnston rushed off a message to his subordinate to evacuate the town and march to the northeast 'if it is not too late.'" For Johnston's estimate of Grant's strength, see *OR*, 24(1):222–23.

31. Younger, ed., *Inside the Confederate Government*, 71–72; *Dispatch*, July 1, 1863.

32. *OR*, 24(1):227, 228; *Louis T. Wigfall* to Clay, June 12, 1863, Clement Clay Papers, DU.

33. Fremantle, *Three Months in the Southern States*, 105, 111.

34. McGuire, *Diary of a Southern Refugee*, 229; Wiggins, ed., *Journals of Josiah Gorgas*, 73. Beginning July 6, 1863, numerous articles about the Battle of Gettysburg appeared in the *Dispatch*, *Whig*, *Sentinel*, *Examiner*, and *Enquirer*.

35. Andrews, *South Reports the Civil War*, 279–80; McMurry, *Civil Wars of Joseph E. Johnston*, 291–93; *OR*, 24(1):230.

36. Putnam, *Richmond During the War*, 229; Jones, *Rebel War Clerk's Diary*, 1:374; Neal E. Wixson, ed., *From Civility to Survival: Richmond Ladies During the Civil War* (Bloomington, IN: iUniverse, 2011).

51; Scarborough, ed., *DER*, 3:53; Wiggins, ed., *Journals of Josiah Gorgas*, 73.

37. *OR*, 24(1):199; Michael Bedout and Leslie Jean Roberts, eds., *Exile in Richmond: The Confederate Journal of Henri Garidel* (Charlottesville: University of Virginia Press, 2001), 44; *OR*, ser. 4, 2:991; Mary A. DeCredico, ed., *Confederate Citadel: Richmond and Its People at War* (Lexington: University Press of Kentucky, 2020), 94; Jones, *Rebel War Clerk's Diary*, 1:374; Rowland, ed., *JDC*, 8:352.

38. *Sentinel*, July 13, 1863; *Whig*, July 9, 1863; Scarborough, ed., *DER*, 54–55; Jones, *Rebel War Clerk's Diary*, 1:374–375.

39. Scarborough, ed., *DER*, 3:53; *Enquirer*, July 28, 1863; Jones, *Rebel War Clerk's Diary*, 378. Grant's report of 30,000 prisoners represented "aggregate present." Doubtless thousands in that number, Pemberton claimed one-third, were either sick or wounded.

40. *Enquirer*, July 10, 1863; Crist et al., eds., *PJD*, 9:324,339, 343, 378; *OR*, 52(2):514–15. See also Crist et al., eds., *PJD*, 9:315, 333, 336, 341, 342, 346, 365; Rowland, ed., *JDC*, 5:580–82; *Whig*, November 9, 1863.

41. *Whig*, July 11, 1863; Scarborough, ed., *DER*, 3:53.

42. Daniel, *Richmond Examiner During the War*, 108–09.

43. *Sentinel*, July 9, 1863.

44. *OR*, 52(2):508.

45. Wiggins, ed., *Journals of Josiah Gorgas*, 74–75; Younger, ed., *Inside the Confederate Government*, 76; McMurry, *Civil Wars of Joseph E. Johnston*, 295–97. McMurry concluded that Davis's response was "in large part something of an emotional catharsis for a sick, sad chief executive, suffering in body, mind, and spirit." Chesnut as quoted in Symonds, *Joseph E. Johnston*, 226; Wigfall as quoted in McMurry, *Civil Wars of Joseph E. Johnston*, 298.

46. Symonds, *Joseph E. Johnston*, 225–26. William C. Davis (*Jefferson Davis*, 511) concluded that Johnston grasped the theater concept, but resisted it, "by finding flaws, dragging his feet, and refusing to comprehend, in effect using staling and deliberate confusion to demonstrate the impracticality of it all."

47. King, *Louis T. Wigfall*, 173, 176, 179.

48. King, *Louis T. Wigfall*, 180.

49. William C. Davis, *Jefferson Davis*, 509.

50. William C. Davis, *Jefferson Davis*, 509; Younger, ed., *Inside the Confederate Government*, 83; *OR*, 24(1):232, 234.

51. Jones, *Rebel War Clerk's Diary*, 1:391, 335; Crist et al., eds., *PJD*, 9:315, 353, 335, 356, 312, 319; Eicher, *Dixie Betrayed*, 203.

52. Crist et al., eds., *PJD*, 9:321; Jones, *Rebel War Clerk's Diary*, 1:382.

53. Rowland, ed., *JDC*, 5:498, 528–30; Walther, *William Lowndes Yancey*, 367–68, 371; Jones, *Rebel War Clerk's Diary*, 1:391; Eicher, *Dixie Betrayed*, 178.

54. *Dispatch*, July 24, 1863; Warner and Yearns, *BRCC*, 35.

55. King, *Louis T. Wigfall*, 177; Neurmberger, *The Clays of Alabama*, 224–25; Rice, *J. L. M. Curry*, 43–44; *Whig*, November 30, 1863 (Walker).

56. Rable, *The Confederate Republic*, 231, 234; Warner and Yearns, *BRCC*, 96–97, 194–95, 250; Wilfred Buck Yearns, *Confederate Congress* (Athens: University of Georgia Press, 1960), 49–52; *Whig*, November 16, 19, 1863; Johnston as quoted in William C. Davis, *Jefferson Davis*, 441.

57. Jones, *Rebel War Clerk's Diary*, 2:16.

58. Younger, ed., *Inside the Confederate Government*, 78.

Chapter 11

1. Shackelford, *George Wythe Randolph*, 143–45, 149; Younger, ed., *Inside the Confederate Government*, 30–31.

2. Rowland, ed., *JDC*, 5:356–57.

3. *OR*, 13:900, 906–07; Jones, *Rebel War Clerk's Diary*, 188.

4. Shackleford, *George Wythe Randolph*, 144–47; Johnston as quoted in William C. Davis, *Jefferson Davis*, 477.

5. Younger, ed., *Inside the Confederate Government*, 34; Shackelford, *George Wythe Randolph*, 147; Jones, *Rebel War Clerk's Diary*, 190–91; Benjamin H. Trask, ed., *Two Months in the Confederate States: An Englishman's Travels Through the South* (Baton Rouge: Louisiana State University Press, 1996), 99.

6. William C. Davis, *Jefferson Davis*, 480; Roy Watson Curry, "James A. Seddon: A Southern Prototype," *Virginia Magazine of History* 63 (April 1955): 138–39; Jones, *Rebel War Clerk's Diary*, 1:191–92; Younger, ed., *Inside the Confederate Government*, 33; Foote, *War of the Rebellion: or Scylla and Charybdis*, 365.

7. King, *Louis T. Wigfall*, 162; Wright, *A Southern Girl in '61*, 102. Benjamin strongly opposed the appointment of Johnston, but Seddon's advocacy carried the argument. See Rembert W. Patrick, *Jefferson Davis and His Cabinet* (Baton Rouge: Louisiana State University Press, 1944), 135.

8. Crist et al., eds., *PJD*, 8:561, 585.

9. *Enquirer*, January 5, 1863; *Whig*, January 6, 7, 1863; *OR*, 22(1):138; *PJD*, 9:91.

10. *Dispatch*, January 20, 21, February 3, 13, 1863; *Examiner*, January 21, 22, 26, February 5, 10, 25, 1863; *Enquirer*, January 27, 1863; *Whig*, February 7, 23, 1863; *PJD*, 9:43. See also Jones, *Rebel War Clerk's Diary*, 1:242, 243, 247. Most Southern accounts placed the number of prisoners at 4,000.

11. Crist et al., eds., *PJD*, 9:10, 38.

12. Crist et al., eds., *PJD*., 9:36, 38, 42–43, 47, 64, 70, 74–75; *OR*, 53:848.

13. Rowland, ed., *JDC*, 5:457–59.

14. Crist et al., eds., *PJD*, 9:100, 104; Rowland, ed., *JDC*, 5:457–59.

15. Younger, ed., *Inside the Confederate Government*, 38, 45.

16. McMurry, *The Civil Wars of Joseph E. Johnston*, 169, 173–74. Wrote McMurry: "The clear possibility of politically losing a state by its secession from the Confederacy . . . and the political crisis that such a development might well engender explain, if they do not justify, the President's concern for Arkansas and Missouri. This concern also accounts for his unwillingness to place Holmes and Pemberton under one command."

17. Johnston, "Jefferson Davis and the Mississippi Campaign," 473; Crist et al., eds., *PJD*, 8:585; *OR*, 22(2):802; Jones, *Rebel War Clerk's Diary*, 1:292.

18. *OR*, 22(2):802; "Proceedings of the Confederate Congress," *SHSP*, 49:142, 158; *Whig*, December 11, 1863; Scarborough, ed., *DER*, 3:123.

19. *Examiner*, August 5, 1863.

20. Joseph H. Parks, *General Edmund Kirby Smith, C. S. A.* (Baton Rouge: Louisiana State University Press, 1954), 251–52; *Whig*, January 12, 1863; Crist et al., eds., *PJD*, 9:221; *OR*, 22(2):786, 788.

21. *Whig*, December 23, 1862, and January 5, 1863; Castel, *General Sterling Price*, 133–34.

22. Castel, *General Sterling Price*, 134–35, 38.

23. *Whig*, June 29, 1863. Price asked Tucker to modify his anti-Davis rhetoric, but he declined.

See Castel, *General Sterling Price*, 135.

24. *OR*, 22(2):871–73, 913; Prushankin, *A Crisis in Confederate Command*, 24; Castel, *General Sterling Price*, 142; Parks, *General Edmund Kirby Smith*, 258–59.

25. *OR*, 15:386–87; Parks, *General Edmund Kirby Smith*, 260–64; Prushankin, *A Crisis in Confederate Command*, 24–33.

26. Parks, *General Edmund Kirby Smith*, 255–56; Stoker, *The Grand Design*, 269–70; *Whig*, March 16, May 29, June 12, 15, 18, 22, 23; July 18, 1863; *Dispatch*, June 6, 10, 12, 18, 1863; *Enquirer*, June 23, July 10, 1863; Snead, "The Conquest of Arkansas," 3:456; Prushankin, *A Crisis in Confederate Command*, 24–25; *PJD*, 9:280.

27. *OR*, 41(2):1058–59.

28. *OR*, 53:879–80.

29. *Enquirer*, July 10, 1863; Jones, *Rebel War Clerk's Diary*, 382.

30. *OR*, 22(2):925–27.

31. *OR*, 22(2):1003–10; Jones, *Rebel War Clerk's Diary*, 2:14; Jewett, ed., *Rise and Fall of the Confederacy*, 233–35; *Whig*, September 23, 1863; *OR*, 53:894–95.

32. Welsh, *Medical Histories of Confederate Generals*, 104; Snead, "The Conquest of Arkansas," 456–57; *Whig*, September 7, 15, 1863; *Enquirer*, August 19, September 7, 11, 1863; *Dispatch*, September 7, 1863; *OR*, 53:897–98.

33. *OR*, 22(2):925–26, 931–32; Crist et al., eds., *PJD*, 9:323.

34. *Enquirer*, October 8, 10, 1863; *Dispatch*, October 10, 12, 1863; *Whig*, September 24, October 6, 14, 1863.

35. Crist et al., eds., *PJD*, 9:412–13; *OR*, 22(2):1029–30.

36. Jones, *Rebel War Clerk's Diary*, 2:74–75; *Dispatch*, March 2, October 27, 1863.

Chapter 12

1. *OR*, 52(2):817–19; *PJD*, 9:171, 180; *Enquirer*, May 8, 21, 1863; *Dispatch*, May 25, 1863; *Whig*, May 9, 1863; Younger, ed., *Inside the Confederate Government*, 58; Wiggins, ed., *Journals of Josiah Gorgas*, 65.

2. *OR*, 23(1):583–84; Crist et al., eds., *PJD*, 9:247; *Whig*, June 27, 1863; Younger, ed., *Inside the Confederate Government*, 79; Jones, *Rebel War Clerk's Diary*, 2:6.

3. *Whig*, July 4, 7, 11, 17, 1863; *Dispatch*, July 7, 1863; Scarborough, ed., *DER*, 3:51. For a brief recap of the Tullahoma Campaign, see Daniel, *Conquered*, 162–71. Confederate losses, which were never fully reported, amounted to about 2,500, mostly prisoners.

4. *Enquirer*, June 22, 26, 17, 1863; *Whig*, June 5, 24, 1863; *Dispatch*, July 28, August 1, 1863; *Enquirer*, July 10, 22, 28, August 1, 5, 12, 1863; *Whig*, July 7, 15, 20, 1863; Younger, ed., *Inside the Confederate Government*, 85; Scarborough, ed., *DER*, 3:94; Jones, *Rebel War Clerk's Diary*, 1:384.

5. *OR*, 23(2):932–33, 948, 952; Jones, *Rebel War Clerk's Diary*, 2:19. Such a concentration would have left only Forrest's 3,800-man division in Mississippi. *OR*, 23(2):945, 957, 24(3):1039.

6. Crist et al., eds., *PJD*, 9:361; *Dispatch*, August 24, 1863; *Whig*, August 29, 31, September 3, 1863; *OR*, 30(4):531, 583–84, 540; Scarborough, ed., *DER*, 3:127; Connelly, *Autumn of Glory*, 149; Jones, *Rebel War Clerk's Diary*, 2:23.

7. William C. Davis, *Jefferson Davis*, 517.

8. *OR*, 30(4):583–84, 599; *Dispatch*, September 3, 4, 14, 1863; *Enquirer*, August 25, 29, September 8, 1863; *Whig*, August 31, September 4, 5, 14, 1863.

9. *OR*, 30(4):599, 608; Rowland, ed., *JDC*, 6:23, 30, 25–26.

10. *Whig*, September 14, 1863; *Enquirer*, September 18, 1863; *OR*, 51(2):760; Wiggins, ed., *Journals of Josiah Gorgas*, 81.

11. Woodworth, *Davis & Lee at War*, 255–56.

12. John E. Clark, Jr., *Railroads in the Civil War: The Impact of Management on Victory and Defeat* (Baton Rouge: Louisiana State University Press, 2004), 88–95; Younger, ed., *Inside the Confederate Government*, 103; Jones, *Rebel War Clerk's Diary*, 2:32, 33, 36, 37; Scarborough, ed., *DER*, 3:138; *Whig*, September 22, 1863. Somehow the news leaked out, and by September 9 the *New York Herald* reported that some of Lee's troops were going southward, but it was not certain whether to Charleston or Chattanooga. David A. Powell, *The Chickamauga Campaign*, 3 vols. (El Dorado Hills, CA: Savas Beatie, 2014–16), 1:205.

13. *OR*, 52(2):522; Bragg to Davis, September 18, 1863, Braxton Bragg Papers, DU; Jones, *Rebel War Clerk's Diary*, 2:49; *Dispatch*, September 24, 25, 1863; *Whig*, September 25, 1863; Larry J. Daniel, *Engineering in the Confederate Heartland* (Baton Rouge: Louisiana State University Press, 2022), 58–60.

14. Jones, *Rebel War Clerk's Diary*, 2:49; *Dispatch*, September 23, 1863.

15. *Dispatch*, September 29, 1863; *Sentinel*, September 24, 1863; Christ et al., eds., *PJD*, 9:414; Jones, *Rebel War Clerk's Diary*, 2:50, 59; Bragg to Cooper, September 24, 1863, Braxton Bragg Papers, DU. The loss at Chickamauga totaled 16,170 for the North and 18,454 for the South.

16. Thomas J. Semmes to Bragg, October 6, 1863, and James L. Pugh to Bragg, October 11, 1863, Braxton Bragg Papers, WRHS; *Enquirer*, November 20, 1863; *Sentinel*, October 31, 1863; *Dispatch*, November 19, 1863.

17. Younger, ed., *Inside the Confederate Government*, 122; Wiggins, ed., *Journals of Josiah Gorgas*, 81, 82; *Dispatch*, September 29, 1863; *Whig*, October 29, 1863.

18. *OR*, 30(4):707, 711–12, 749; *Dispatch*, October 2, 8, 26, 1863; Jones, *Rebel War Clerk's Diary*, 2:55, 57, 60.

19. Crist et al., eds., *PJD*, 9:405.

20. *Dispatch*, October 24, November 28, 1863; Hal Bridges, *Lee's Maverick General: Daniel Harvey Hill* (Lincoln: University of Nebraska Press, 1991), 240–41; *OR*, 30(4):727; *PJD*, 9:410; Jones, *Rebel War Clerk's Diary*, 2:20, 27.

21. *OR*, 52(2):538; Younger, ed. *Inside the Confederate Government*, 109. I have not mentioned the petition, signed by a dozen of Bragg's generals, requesting his removal from command because it was never submitted to Davis, or at least he claimed that he never saw it. For details, see Bridges, *Lee's Maverick General*, 234–38.

22. *Dispatch*, October 15, 19, 24, 1863; *Whig*, October 26, November 4, 1863; *Enquirer*, October 30, 1863; Jones, *Rebel War Clerk's Diary*, 2:70.

23. Younger, ed., *Inside the Confederate Government*, 111; Orr as quoted in Grady McWhiney, *Southerners and Other Americans* (New York: Basic Books, 1973), 93.

24. *OR*, 30(4):751; *OR*, 31(3):586; *Enquirer*, October 30, 1863; Jones, *Rebel War Clerk's Diary*, 88; Younger, ed., *Inside the Confederate Government*, 115. The document in question feigned concern for Bragg's health as the reason for their desire to have him removed. Several months after the incident, Davis claimed that he never asked the generals for their opinion. Woodworth (*Jefferson Davis*, 242) concluded: "Davis was in an impossible situation. He had allowed Polk and his band of malcontents to undermine Bragg so completely that to support Bragg properly would now require sacking half the officers corps of the Army of Tennessee."

25. *Enquirer*, November 10, 1863; William C. Davis, *Jefferson Davis*, 527; Jones, *Rebel War Clerk's Diary*, 2:74.

26. *Whig*, November 4, 1863; *Sentinel*, November 13, 1863.

27. Jones, *Rebel War Clerk's Diary*, 2:95–94; *Whig*, October 9, 1863; Younger, ed., *Inside the Confederate Government*, 115.

28. Jones, *Rebel War Clerk's Diary*, 2:80; *Whig*, October 27, November 2, 1863; Younger, ed., *Inside the Confederate Government*, 115.

29. *Whig*, November 9, 1863; *OR*, 52(2):558, 554–55.

30. *OR*, 31(4):586, 31(3):684.

31. Earl J. Hess, *The Knoxville Campaign: Burnside and Longstreet in East Tennessee* (Knoxville: University of Tennessee Press, 2012), 30–31; Hess, *Braxton Bragg*, 192–93. There was a significant shifting of units in November 1863, leaving Bragg with a net loss of 7,200 troops. See Daniel, *Conquered*, 232–34.

32. *Whig*, November 28, 1863; G. A. Henry to Davis, November 17, 1863, G. A. Henry Letters, Civil War Collection, box 9, folder 22, TSLA.

33. Jones, *Rebel War Clerk's Diary*, 2:104, 106; *Whig*, October 26, November 5, 10, 1863; *Dispatch*, November 5, 26, 1863. The Confederates placed their losses in the Battle of Lookout Mountain at 1,251. *OR*, 31(2):690.

34. *OR*, 31(2):679, 681; *Whig*, November 27, 1863; Jones, *Rebel War Clerk's Diary*, 106.

35. *OR*, 31(2):682; *Whig*, November 27, 30, December 1, 10, 11, 1863; *Dispatch*, December 3, 1863; Jones, *Rebel War Clerk's Diary*, 2:106, 110, 111; Scarborough, ed., *DER*, 3:249; Younger, ed., *Inside the Confederate Government*, 124; Wiggins, ed., *Journals of Josiah Gorgas*, 87.

36. *Whig*, November 27, 28, 30, 1863; Daniel, *Richmond Examiner During the War*, 146–48, 152.

37. *Whig*, December 15, 1863; "Proceedings of the Confederate Congress," *SHSP*, 50:15–23.

38. *Dispatch*, December 9, 1863; *Whig*, December 16, 1863.

39. Jones, *Rebel War Clerk's Diary*, 2:106; *OR*, 31(2):682; *Dispatch*, December 4, 1863; *Whig*, December 2, 1863; Woodward, ed., *Mary Chesnut's Civil War*, 259.

40. Younger, ed., *Inside the Confederate Government*, 126; Rable, *The Confederate Republic*, 249–50; King, *Louis T. Wigfall*, 187.

41. Warner and Yearns, *BRCC*, 262; Bell I Wiley, ed., *Letters of Warren Aiken: Confederate Congressman* (Athens: University of Georgia Press, 1959), 27; *Enquirer*, February 5, 1864.

42. *Whig*, November 20, 23, December 5, 1863; Scarborough, ed., *DER*, 3:239, 245.

43. *Whig*, November 27, December 2, 1863; Jones, *Rebel War Clerk's Diary*, 2:110, 112; Younger, ed., *Inside the Confederate Government*, 124; *Dispatch*, December 5, 7, 1863; Scarborough, ed., *DER*, 3.

44. *OR*, 31(1):475, (3):817–19; Hess, *The Knoxville Campaign*, 171.

45. *Whig*, December 25, 1863; Jones, *Rebel War Clerk's Diary*, 1:122; Daniel, *Richmond Examiner During the War*, 155.

Chapter 13

1. Younger, ed., *Inside the Confederate Government*, 88, 128; Wiggins, ed., *Journals of Josiah Gorgas*, 89; *Whig*, December 17, 1863, January 4, 1864; Hess, *Braxton Bragg*, 217.

2. *Sentinel*, February 20, 1864; Jones, *Rebel War Clerk's Diary*, 154; *OR*, 52(2):607; *JCCS*, 6:825; Wiggins, ed., *Journals of Josiah Gorgas*, 93; *Enquirer*, February 23, 1864.

3. Younger, ed., *Inside the Confederate Government*, 138; *Examiner* as quoted in William C. Davis, *Jefferson Davis*, 542; *Examiner*, June 8, 1864; *Whig*, May 27, 1864; *OR*, 32(2):799; Jones, *Rebel War Clerk's Diary*, 2:220; Hess, *Braxton Bragg*, 218.

4. *Dispatch*, June 22, 1864; *Enquirer*, February 25, 26, 1864; Jones, *Rebel War Clerk's Diary*, 2:158–59.

5. *Whig*, May 26, 1864; Jones, *Rebel War Clerk's Diary*, 2:220, 221.

6. *Whig*, December 8, 1863; Woodworth, *Davis & Lee at War*, 262–63.

7. Beauregard quoted in Williams, *P. G. T. Beauregard*, 201; Jones, *Rebel War Clerk's Diary*, 2:110; *Dispatch*, December 16, 1863; King, *Louis T. Wigfall*, 188–89.

8. Hudson Strode, *Jefferson Davis: American Patriot* (New York: Harcourt, Brace, 1955), 510; William C. Davis, *Jefferson Davis*, 530; *OR*, 31(3):835–36; Rowland, ed., *JDC*, 8:349, 351; King, *Louis T. Wigfall*, 188–89; Woodward, ed., *Mary Chesnut's Civil War*, 265.

9. Stephen Davis, *Texas Brigadier: To the Fall of Atlanta* (Macon, GA: Mercer University Press, 2019), 99–106; Mrs. Burton Harrison, *Recollections Grave and Gray* (New York: C. Scribner's sons, 1911), 172; McMurry, *John Bell Hood*, 91.

10. *OR*, 31(3):856–57, 878.

11. Woodward, ed., *Mary Chesnut's Civil War*, 259; Crist et al., eds., *PJD*, 10:136.

12. *OR*, 31(3):510–11, 873–74.

13. Bruce Levine, *Confederate Emancipation: Southern Plans to Free and Arm Slaves During the Civil War* (New York: Oxford University Press, 2006), 25–26, 38; Daniel, *Conquered*, 269.

14. Quotes from Levine, *Confederate Emancipation*, 28.

15. "General Cleburne's Views on Slavery," *Annals of the Army of Tennessee and Early Western History* 1 (May 1878): 50–52; Reagan, *Memoirs*, 148; quote from Hallock, *Braxton Bragg*, 180.

16. *Dispatch*, February 5, 27, 1864; Connelly, *Autumn of Glory*, 295–303.

17. *OR*, 38(3):613–15, 618–19, 627–28, 649, 653–54.

18. Stephen M. Hood, *The Lost Papers of Confederate General John Bell Hood* (El Dorado Hills, CA: Savas Beatie, 2015), 145.

19. Castel, *Decision in the West*, 76–77, 99–100; Richard M. McMurry, *John Bell Hood and the War for Southern Independence* (Lexington: University Press of

Kentucky, 1982), 97–97; Davis, *Texas Brigadier*, 113, 115. In a rare instance of disagreement with my longtime friend Richard McMurry, he is much more generous in the intentions ascribed to Hood for writing these letters than I am.

20. Jones, *Rebel War Clerk's Diary*, 2:185; Bruce S. Allardice, *Confederate Colonels: A Biographical Register* (Columbia: University of Missouri Press, 2008), 141; Anne W. Chapman, "Benjamin Stoddert Ewell: A Biography" (1984), Dissertations, Thesis, and Masters Projects 1539623748, College of William and Mary, 34–42, 52–61.

21. *Whig*, April 12, 1864.

22. *Dispatch*, April 12, 1864; *Whig*, April 12, 1864.

23. *OR*, 38(3):839–42, 781; 52(2):657; Chapman, "Benjamin Stoddert Ewell," 163–64; Castel, *Decision in the West*, 103–04. The evidence that Bragg did in fact read Johnston's reply telegram comes in Hood's letter to Wigfall. He wrote: "So Bragg replied that as he had failed to accept the plan to move forward, nothing could be done and no troops furnished." Hood as quoted in Davis, *Texas Brigadier*, 120.

24. Johnston, *Narrative of Military Operations*, 301; Johnston as quoted in Castel, *Decision in the West*, 104; Connelly, *Autumn of Glory*, 311–12.

25. Jones, *Rebel War Clerk's Diary*, 2:188; *OR*, 32(3):622–23.

26. *OR*, 32(3):624–25.

27. *OR*, 32(3):824.

28. *OR*, 32(3):792, 793, 797, 788, 838, 767, 748, 838, 801, 866, 817, 790–91, 811–12; *OR*, 38(3):627, 866.

29. William C. Davis, *Jefferson Davis*, 552; Jones, *Rebel War Clerk's Diary*, 2:285; *Dispatch*, May 2, 1864; Wiggins, ed., *Journals of Josiah Gorgas*, 101–02.

30. Woodworth, *Davis & Lee at War*, 271–76 (Lee quote); Ferguson, *Ashes of Glory*, 264–66; Joseph T. Glatthaar, *General Lee's Army: From Victory to Collapse* (New York: Free Press, 2008), 364–74; Jones, *Rebel War Clerk's Diary*, 2:209.

31. *Dispatch*, May 6, 7, 1864; *OR*, 38(4):650–60, 661, 684, 733–37, 672, 691. Polk's actual present for duty strength was 9,341 infantry and 2,756 cavalry.

32. *OR*, 38(4):692, 698, 705, 712; *Dispatch*, May 13, 16, 1864.

33. *OR* 38(4):716, 725, 736; Younger, ed., *Inside the Confederate Government*, 150.

34. *OR*, 38(4):728, 736; *Dispatch*, May 20, 23, 1864.

35. *OR*, 38(4):745; *Dispatch*, June 1, 4, 6, 7, 1864.

36. Davis, *Rise and Fall*, 2:556; Wiggins, ed., *Journals of Josiah Gorgas*, 109; Younger, ed., *Inside the Confederate Government*, 150; *OR*, 38(4):780, 792, 795–96.

37. *Dispatch*, May 28, June 3, 1864; *Enquirer*, May 31, 1864; Wiggins, ed., *Journals of Josiah Gorgas*, 109; Younger, ed., *Inside the Confederate Government*, 151.

38. Castel, *Decision in the West*, 252; William C. Davis, *Jefferson Davis*, 559.

39. *OR*, 38(4):762, 753, 759, 775; *Whig*, June 3, 7, 1864; *Dispatch*, June 15, 17, 1864; Davis, *Rise and Fall*, 2:554–55; Jones, *Rebel War Clerk's Diary*, 2:554–55.

40. *OR*, 38(4):780, 796; *Dispatch*, July 7, 1864. Castel (*Decision in the West*, 319–20) places Union losses at Kennesaw Mountain of "nearly 3,000" and "about 700" for the Confederates.

41. William C. Davis, *Jefferson Davis*, 571–73; Younger, ed., *Inside the Confederate Government*, 161, 152.

42. Crist et al., eds., *PJD*, 10:491–92; Chesnut as quoted in McMurry, *John Bell Hood*, 143; Rowland, ed., *JDC*, 8:352. See also McMurry, "The Enemy at Richmond: Joseph E. Johnston and the Confederate Government," *Civil War History* 27 (March 1981), 5–31.

43. *OR*, 47(2):1311; *OR*, 38(4):792, 795–96. Hood, in postwar years, placed Johnston's losses at 9,972 killed and wounded and 9,918 captured, for a total of 19,890. If 5,000 or so sick were added, the number would be close to that of Davis. See John Bell Hood, *Advance and Retreat: Personal Experiences in the United States & Confederate States Armies* (Bloomington: Indiana University Press, 1959), 222–23.

44. King, *Louis T. Wigfall*, 196; *OR*, 38(5):860, 867, 865; *Dispatch*, July 8, 1864; Jones, *Rebel War Clerk's Diary*, 2:247; Connelly, *Autumn of Glory*, 363–64. Johnston later presented several "plans" for defeating Sherman, all of which amounted to no more than thoughts and possible options.

45. Warner and Yearns, *BRCC*, 247; *OR*, 52(2):685–86; Wiggins, ed., *Journals of Josiah Gorgas*, 120–21.

46. *Whig*, June 14, 15, 20, July 11, 1864; *Enquirer*, May 17, 1864. The Brice's Crossroads National Battlefield Site places Forrest's strength as 3,500 and Sturgis's at 8,500. Confederate losses were 495 and Union casualties were 2,610.

47. *Whig*, June 16, 18, 1864; *Dispatch*, June 15, 1864.

48. Crist et al., eds., *PJD*, 10:492; Johnston, *Narrative of Military Operations*, 359; *OR*, 38(4):777. Sherman acknowledged that there was "great danger" that "Forrest would collect a heavy cavalry command in Mississippi . . . and break up our railroad below Nashville." He also wrote his wife that "I expect to hear every day of Forrest breaking into Tennessee." Quotes in James Lee McDonough, *William Tecumseh Sherman: In the Service of My Country, A Life* (New York: W. W. Norton & Company, 2016), 499.

49. Younger, ed., *Inside the Confederate Government*, 166; *Whig*, July 23, 1864; *Sentinel*, July 22, 1864; Crist et al., eds., *PJD*, 10:525; Ulrich B. Phillips, ed., *The Correspondence of Robert Toombs, Alexander H. Stevens, and Howell Cobb* (Washington, DC: American Historical Association, 1913), 632, 642.

50. Johnston, *Narrative of Military Operations*, 860–62; Crist et al., eds., *PJD*, 498–500.

51. Warner and Yearns, *BRCC*, 118–19; Haywood J. Pearce, Jr., *Secession and*

Reconstruction (New York: Negro Universities Press, 1928), 62, 69, 78–79; Walther, *William Lowndes Yancey*, 359–60.

52. *OR*, 52(2):704–07; Davis, *Rise and Fall*, 2:558–59. Johnston, in his "Opposing Sherman's Advance to Atlanta," in *Battles and Leaders of the Civil War*, 4 vols., ed. Robert U. Johnson and Clarence C. Buel (New York: Thomas Yoseloff, 1956), 4:277 denied that he was "a party to no such conversations as those given by Mr. Hill." The statement represented yet one more absurdity in Johnston's self-serving memoirs.

53. *OR*, 52(2):685–86; Jones, *Rebel War Clerk's Diary*, 219.

54. Davis, *Rise and Fall*, 2:558–59; *OR*, 38(5):875–76; Crist et al., eds., *PJD*, 10:497.

55. Davis, *Rise and Fall*, 2:559; Younger, ed., *Inside the Confederate Government*, 166; *OR*, 38(5):878, 879; Benjamin H. Hill, *Senator Benjamin H. Hill of Georgia: His Life, Speeches, and Writings* (Atlanta: H. C. Hudgins & Co., 1891), 90; *Dispatch*, July 23, 1864.

56. *OR*, 39(2):648; Crist et al., eds., *PJD*, 10:482; Edwin C. Bearss, *Outwitting Forrest: The Tupelo Campaign in Mississippi, June 22–July 23, 1864* (El Dorado Hills, CA: Savas Beatie, 2023), 34, 106; Thomas E. Parson, *Work for Giants: The Campaign and Battle of Tupelo/Harrisburg, Mississippi, June–July, 1864* (Kent, OH: Kent State University Press, 2014), 186–87; Richard M. McMurry, *Atlanta 1864: Last Chance for the Confederacy* (Lincoln: University of Nebraska Press, 2000), 198–203.

57. Younger, ed., *Inside the Confederate Government*, 166; *OR*, 38(5):875; *OR*, 52(2):692; Earl J. Hess, *Civil War Supply and Strategy: Feeding and Moving Armies* (Baton Rouge: Louisiana State University Press, 2020), 156–57.

58. *OR*, 41(2):1016.

59. *Dispatch*, July 15, 1864; *Whig*, July 14, 1864; *Sentinel*, July 22, 1864; Wiggins, ed., *Journals of Josiah Gorgas*, 121; Davis, *Texas Brigadier*, 220–21.

60. Davis, *Texas Brigadier*, 222–23; *OR*, 52(2):704, 707.

61. Younger, ed., *Inside the Confederate Government*, 165.

62. *OR*, 39(2):712–14; Wiggins, ed., *Journals of Josiah Gorgas*, 115.

63. *OR*, 38(5):881–882.

64. Rowland, ed., *JDC*, 8:353; *OR*, 47(2):1310. Castel (*Decision in the West*, 358) concluded: "Either Johnston does not think that Davis will dare remove him, or else he does not care if he does." Perhaps so, but a Johnston staff officer noted that "old Joe looks uneasy." See Hallock, *Braxton Bragg*, 192. McMurry, in *Atlanta 1864*, 138, described Johnston's answer as "a mind-boggling document."

65. Rowland, ed., *JDC*, 8:353, 356; Mallory Diary, December 8, 1865, SHC; Younger, ed., *Inside the Confederate Government*, 165; Davis, *Rise and Fall*, 2:561; Younger, ed., *Inside the Confederate Government*, 167; Davis as quoted in Stephen Davis, *Texas Brigadier*, 255. Even Leroy Walker, the first secretary of war, wrote of his approval of the removal of Johnston. See Jones, *Rebel War Clerk's Diary*, 2:288.

66. *OR*, 38(5):885, 888; Jones, *Rebel War Clerk's Diary*, 2:250; *Dispatch*, July 20, 1864; *Whig*, July 19, 1864; *Examiner* as quoted in *Weekly Chronicle & Sentinel* (Augusta), August 3, 1864.

67. *Dispatch*, July 21, 1864; *Whig*, July 20, 22, 1864; *Sentinel*, July 23, 1864.

68. Scarborough, ed., *DER*, 3:503–04; Crist et al., eds., *PJD*, 10:552; Rable, *The Confederate Republic*, 265; Wiggins, ed., *Journals of Josiah Gorgas*, 123.

69. Crist et al., eds., *PJD*, 11:50.

70. *OR*, 38(5):894; *Dispatch*, July 22, 1864; Jones, *Rebel War Clerk's Diary*, 2:252–53; *Whig*, July 20, 1864.

71. *OR*, 38(5):908, 917; *Dispatch*, August 1, 2, 3, 4, 1864; *Enquirer*, August 30, 1864; *Whig*, July 25, August 3, 1864.

72. *OR*, 38(5): Stephen Davis, *Texas Brigadier*, 349–50; *Dispatch*, August 2, 3, 1864; *Whig*, August 10, 1864; Castel (*Decision in the West*, 381, 412, 434) placed Southern casualties as follows: Peachtree Creek-2,500; Atlanta-5,500; Ezra Church, 3,000, for a total of 11,000. McMurry (*Atlanta 1864*, 132, 155, 157) accepts these figures. The tabulations of the Army of Tennessee, which the War Department almost certainly had access to, were not a true indication of casualties. The July 31 return revealed 51,793 present for duty, a reduction of only 7,403 from the July 10 return. Hood, however, placed 1,000–2,000 blacks as teamsters, thus freeing that number of enlisted men into the ranks. He also replaced hospital attendants with woman, sent cooks into the ranks, placed 150 cannoneers into the infantry, and began stripping quartermaster depots and arsenals of badly needed artisans. See Stephen Davis, *Texas Brigadier*, 393.

73. Krick, *Civil War Weather in Virginia*, 133; Crist et al., eds., *PJD*, 10:569–74.

74. *OR*, 38(5):987–88; *Dispatch*, September 8, 1864.

75. Younger, ed., *Inside the Confederate Government*, 168; Jones, *Rebel War Clerk's Diary*, 2:261; *Dispatch*, August 8, 12, 15, 17, 19, 1864.

76. Jones, *Rebel War Clerk's Diary*, 2:277; *OR*, 38(5):1016. The initial rumor was based on Hardee's September 1 telegraph to Davis stating that Hood's army was divided and that Atlanta should be evacuated; Davis disagreed. See *OR* 38(5):1011.

77. *OR*, 38(5):1016, 1021; *Whig*, September 5, 8, 20, October 19, 1864; *Dispatch*, September 5, 6, 7, 1864; Crist et al., eds., *PJD*, 11:71.

78. *Whig*, September 8, 9, 1864; Jones, *Rebel War Clerk's Diary*, 2:277; Younger, ed., *Inside the Confederate Government*, 173; *Whig*, September 8, 9. 1864.

79. *Dispatch*, September 5, 1864; Daniel, *Richmond Examiner During the War*, 211–12. See my view of the 1864 election and the effect of the Atlanta Campaign on it: "The South Almost Won by Not Losing: A Rebuttal," *North & South*, 1 (February 1998), 44–48, 50–51.

80. McGuire, *Diary of a Southern Refugee*, 303; Wiggins, ed., *Journals of Josiah Gorgas*, 132, 133.

81. Phillips, ed., *Correspondence of Toombs, Stevens, and Cobb*, 651.

Chapter 14

1. "Proceedings and Speeches on the announcement of the death of Hon. William M. Cooke of Missouri, in House of Representatives" (Richmond: Smith, Bailey & Co., 1863), 1–19; *Dispatch*, April 16, 1863; *Whig*, April 18, September 17, 1863; "Proceedings and Speeches on the Announcement of Hon. R. L. Y. Peyton, of Missouri" (Richmond: Sentinel Job Office, 1864), 1–22; Warner and Yearns, *BRCC*, 193–94; Castel, *General Sterling Price*, 168–70.

2. Crist et al., eds., *PJD*, 10:226; Castel, *General Sterling Price*, 188.

3. Price, *General Sterling Price*, 188–96. Castel concluded that Reynolds "suspicions of Price probably were not justified," although he could "not be blamed for entertaining them."

4. Warner and Yearns, eds., *BRCC*, 177; *Dispatch*, November 5, 1864; Crist et al., eds., *PJD*, 11:106.

5. *OR*, 34(2):895; *Enquirer*, March 29, 1864; Prushankin, *A Crisis in Confederate Command*, 64–70.

6. Jones, *Rebel War Clerk's Diary*, 2:186; *OR*, 34(1):476, 477; *Whig*, April 15, 1864. Although Bank's force numbered 31,000, after detaching two divisions he fought the two battles in question with 25,736. Casualties were officially listed as 5,245 for the Union and 3,976 for the Confederates.

7. Wiggins, ed., *Journals of Josiah Gorgas*, 100, 113; *Whig*, May 14, 1864; *Enquirer*, May 10, 1864; Jones, *Rebel War Clerk's Diary*, 2:165; Younger, ed., *Inside the Confederate Government*, 154.

8. *OR*, 34(1):478, 531, 537, 476; Prushankin, *A Crisis in Confederate Command*, 114–15; Castel, *General Sterling Price*, 173; Michael Parrish, *Richard Taylor: Soldier Prince of Dixie* (Chapel Hill: University of North Carolina Press, 1992), 398.

9. *Dispatch*, May 17, 1864; Castel, *General Sterling Price*, 177, 178. Castel placed Union losses at 1,401 in the two incidents.

10. *Whig*, May 11, 1864; *Enquirer*, May 20, 1864; *Dispatch*, May 13, 1864; Younger, ed., *Inside the Confederate Government*, 150–51.

11. Prushankin, *A Crisis in Confederate Command*, 150–53.

12. *Whig*, April 22, June 7, 1864; *Dispatch*, June 7, 1864.

13. *New York Times*, July 4, 1887; *Lake Charles Echo*, July 9, 1887; Parrish, *Richard Taylor*, 42–43, 65; *OR*, 34(1):513, 519.

14. Prushankin, *A Crisis in Confederate Command*, 177–78; *OR*, 41(2):1017, 1042.

15. *OR*, 34(1):482, 540–48; Prushankin, *A Crisis in Confederate Command*, 173–74, 198.

16. Jones, *Rebel War Clerk's Diary*, 2:208; *OR*, 41(2):1017; *OR*, 34(1):597.

17. *Dispatch*, May 13, 1864; Castel, *General Sterling Price*, 196–97, 201; *OR*, 41(1):478.

18. *OR*, 41(1):92–93, 102.

19. Parrish, *Richard Taylor*, 406; *OR*, 41(1):90, 92–93, 103, 108, 110–13, 120–22; Wiggins, ed., *Journals of Josiah Gorgas*, 129; Parrish, *Richard Taylor*, 406; Jones, *Rebel War Clerk's Diary*, 2:302. Taylor crossed by the use of a canoe. See Taylor, *Destruction and Reconstruction*, 198. Taylor never mentioned in his memoir the embarrassing incident of the near rebellion to cross the Mississippi River.

20. *Whig*, October 8, 1864; *Dispatch*, October 13, 1864; *OR*, 41(3):966. Price's after-action report, filed in December 1864, placed his beginning strength at 12,000, 4,000 of whom were unarmed, and fourteen guns. See *OR*, 41(1):627.

21. Castel, *General Sterling Price*, 209–16; *Whig*, October 10, 1864; *Dispatch*, October 31, 1864. Castel placed Confederate strength at 8,700 and the Federals at 900. Cutrer (*Theater of a Separate War*, 410) states Union strength was 1,201. Castel places Confederate losses at "over a thousand" and the Federals at seventy-three.

22. *Dispatch*, October 5, 8, 10, 13, 17, 18, 1864.

23. *Dispatch*, October 27, 28, 31, 1864; *Whig*, October 25, 1864; Wiggins, ed., *Journals of Josiah Gorgas*, 147. Castel (*General Sterling Price*, 256 [Reynolds quote], 236, 252) places Southern casualties at about a thousand. Price managed to escape, but his army largely disintegrated in the retreat. Price, in his after-action report, pronounced his campaign a remarkable success, but Castel evaluates that he actually lost two-thirds of his original fighting force and by December 15 counted only 3,500 troops, only a third of whom were armed.

24. *Whig*, December 14, 20, 1864; Parks, *General Edmund Kirby Smith*, 446.

25. *OR*, 48(1):1417; *OR*, 41(1):123–24.

26. Prushankin, *A Crisis in Confederate Command*, 216; Cutrer, *Theater of a Separate War*, 447–48; Oldham, *Rise and Fall of the Confederacy*, 233–34; William C. Davis, *Jefferson Davis*, 461.

Chapter 15

1. Rable, *The Confederate Republic*, 271, 287–88.

2. Jones, *Rebel War Clerk's Diary*, 2:287; *OR*, 39(2):836; Crist et al., eds., *PJD*, 11:36, 57.

3. Jones, *Rebel War Clerk's Diary*, 2:287, 290; *Dispatch*, September 20, 29, October 4, 19, 1864; *Whig*, September 24, October 11, 1864; Crist et al., eds., *PJD*. 11:41; Rable, *The Confederate Republic*, 245, 264, 274. The *Dispatch* of October 11, 1864, made is clear that it considered Alexander Stephens one of the "peace delusion" advocates.

4. Davis as quoted in Stephen Davis, *Into Tennessee & Failure: John Bell Hood* (Macon, GA: Mercer University Press, 2020), 38–39; Crist et al., eds., *PJD*, 11:73–74.

5. *Dispatch*, October 12, 1864; *Enquirer*, October 22, 1864; Castel, *Decision in the West*, 551 ("thin, care-worn, and angry"), 551. The stories of soldiers shouting out "Give us Johnston!" were in fact true; Hood even wrote about the incident in postwar years. On September 27 Davis privately interviewed the corps commanders. Before the president's departure, Hood related to him that he was "aware of the outcry against me, through the press," and that he would not hesitate to be relieved, or be placed in a corps command, if a more competent leader was found. At 6 p.m., as the president mounted his horse, he told Hood that "he might find it necessary to assign another to the command of the Army." The decision had not been finalized. See Hood, *Advance and Retreat*, 253–55. Stephen Davis (*Into Tennessee & Failure*, 45–49) discusses the confusion as to when exactly Davis made his comment about moving into Tennessee, suggesting that it could not possibly have been made (as stated by some) on his arrival of September 25. The article in the *Columbus Enquirer* clearly states that the speech was made on September 26. The more important issue, whether or not Davis later denial that he approved a move into Tennessee while at Palmetto, is thoroughly discussed by Stephen Davis.

6. Stephen Davis, *Into Tennessee & Failure*, 32–35; Williams, *P. G. T. Beauregard*, 236, 239–40; *Whig*, September 29, 1864; *Enquirer*, October 4, 1864; Woodworth, *Davis & Lee at War*, 275–82; *OR*, 39(2):880; Jones, *Rebel War Clerk's Diary*, 2:300.

7. Nathaniel C. Hughes, Jr., *General William J. Hardee: Old Reliable* (Wilmington, NC: Broadfoot Publishing Company, 1987), 247–48; *Dispatch*, October 7, 15, 1864; *Enquirer*, October 4, 5, 11, 21, 1864.

8. *Dispatch*, October 2, 12, 1864; *OR*, 39(2):850–51, 829; *OR*, 38(3):676–77; Hood, *Advance and Retreat*, 257.

9. *Dispatch*, October 4, 15, 1864; *Whig*, October 19, 1864; *OR*, 39(2):862, 870.

10. *OR*, 39(2):864; *Enquirer*, October 8, 1864.

11. McMurry, *John Bell Hood*, 156, 158; Castel, *Decision in the West*, 551 ("thin, care-worn, and angry"); Younger, ed., *Inside the Confederate Government*, 175.

12. *OR*, 39(2):790, 801, 805, 820; *Dispatch*, October 12, 14, 15, 17, 18, 1864; *Whig*, October 18, 19, 21, 1864; Jones, *Rebel War Clerk's Diary*, 2:300–301.

13. Jones, *Rebel War Clerk's Diary*, 2:302–303, 304, 307; *OR*, 39(3):796, 828; *Whig*, October 21, 27, 1864; *Dispatch*, October 19, 21, 27, 1864.

14. *Dispatch*, October 28, 26 (*Tribune* quote), 1864.

15. *OR*, 39(3):831, 841, 858.

16. *OR*, 39(3):858; Rowland, ed., *JDC*, 6:398–99; *Dispatch*, November 23, 1864.

17. Jones, *Rebel War Clerk's Diary*, 2:309, 324, 327; *Whig*, October 19, November 10, 1864; *Dispatch*, November 5, 16, 1864.

18. Jones, *Rebel War Clerk's Diary*, 2:294–95; Wynne, *The Man Who Punched Jefferson Davis*, 232.

19. *Whig*, November 24, 1864; *Dispatch*, November 23, 24, 1864; *Sentinel*, November 24, 1864; *Enquirer*, November 9, 1864; Wynne, *The Man who Punched Jefferson Davis*, 232–34.

20. *OR*, 38(3):620; William C. Davis, *Jefferson Davis*, 587; Symonds, *Joseph E. Johnston*, 340.

21. *Dispatch*, December 3, 1864; Wiggins, ed., *Journals of Josiah Gorgas*, 142.

22. *Dispatch*, December 5, 1864.

23. *Dispatch*, December 1, 6, 14, 24, 1864; Scarborough, ed., *DER*, 3:667; Jones, *Rebel War Clerk's Diary*, 2:348; *OR*, 45(2):643–44.

24. *Sentinel*, December 19, 1864; *Dispatch*, December 19–23, 1864; Wiggins, ed., *Journals of Josiah Gorgas*, 144. Gorgas wrote this on December 19, but he must have mistaken his date. No Richmond paper offered any news of the two-day Battle of Nashville until December 20. Hood lost over 6,000 at Franklin, bringing his army to 25,000. If the present-for-duty total at the end of the campaign (18,708) is subtracted from the present for duty total at the beginning, the loss would equal 16,825. See Daniel, *Conquered*, 392n36.

25. Wiley, ed., *Letters of Warren Aiken*, 43, 48–49; Jones, *Rebel War Clerk's Diary*, 2:346–47, 359, 361–62; *Whig*, December 24, 1864.

26. *Dispatch*, December 12, 13, 15, 22, 1864; *Whig*, December 13, 20, 1864; Wiggins, ed., *Journals of Josiah Gorgas*, 144; Johnston to William W. Mackall, December 31, 1864, William W. Mackall Papers, SHC; Younger, ed., *Inside the Confederate Government*, 181. Davis did in fact write a lengthy refutation of Johnston's report but thought better about delivering before Congress. See William C. Davis, *Jefferson Davis*, 587.

27. *Dispatch*, December 24, 1864; Jones, *Rebel War Clerk's Diary*, 2:364–65.

28. Wynne, *The Man Who Punched Jefferson Davis*, 233–38; *Enquirer*, September 13, 1864 *Dispatch*, January 14, 19, 25, 26, February 6, 11, April 14, 1865; *Whig*, September 5, 1864, January 19, 20, 25, February 20, 24, April 14, 17, May 18, 1865; Wiley, ed., *Letters of Warren Aiken*, 94, 96; Wiggins, ed., *Journals of Josiah Gorgas*, 153; Wiley, ed., *Letters of Warren Aiken*, 94.

29. Wiley, ed., *Letters of Warren Aiken*, 74–75; Wiggins, ed., *Journals of Josiah Gorgas*, 153.

30. Hoge as quoted in Ferguson, *Ashes of Glory*, 320; Decredico, *Confederate Citadel*, 136–41; Evans, *Judah P. Benjamin*, 294–96.

31. Jewitt, ed., *Rise and Fall of the Confederacy*, 177–81.

BIBLIOGRAPHY

Manuscripts

Duke University, Rare Books, Manuscripts, and Special Collections, Durham, North Carolina
- Braxton Bragg Papers
- Clement Clay Papers

Louisiana State University, Special Collections, Memorial Library, Baton Rouge
- James Phelan Letter, Mss. 2844

Miami University, Oxford, Ohio
- Samuel Richey Collection of the Southern Confederacy

National Archives, Washington, DC
- Compiled Military Service Files, NARG 109
- John Withers Diary, Adjutant General's Office, NARG 109

Southern Historical Collection, University of North Carolina, Chapel Hill
- Gustavus A. Henry Papers, coll. 01431
- James T. Harrison Papers, coll. 02441, folder 9 (1862 letters)
- Jeremy Gilmer Papers, coll. 00276
- Stephen Mallory Diary, coll. 02229
- Thomas Bragg Diary, coll. 033304-z, folder 1
- William W. Mackall Papers, coll. 01299

Tennessee State Library and Archives, Nashville
- Gustavus A. Henry Letters, Civil War Collection, box 9, folder 22

Tulane University, New Orleans, Louisiana
- William Preston Johnston Papers

University of Georgia, Athens
- Howell Cobb Papers

Virginia Historical Society, Richmond
- George Bagby Diary, George William Bagby Papers

Western Reserve Historical Society, Cleveland, Ohio
Braxton Bragg Papers, William Palmer Collection
William and Mary University, Earl Gregg Swem Library, Special Collections, Williamsburg, Virginia
Hariette Cary Diary
Cary Constance Letter
Henry W. Smart Letters

Newspapers

American Citizen (Canton, MS)
Charleston Mercury
Columbus (GA) *Sun*
Iron County (MO) *Register*
Lake Charles (LA) *Echo*
Memphis Appeal
Mobile Advertiser & Register
New York Dispatch
New York Times
New York Tribune
Pulaski (TN) *Citizen*
Richmond Dispatch
Richmond Enquirer
Richmond Examiner
Richmond Whig
Sedalia (MO) *Weekly Bazoo*
Weekly Chronicle & Sentinel (Augusta, GA)

Official Documents

The City Intelligencer, or, Stranger's Guide. Richmond: Macfarland & Ferguson, 1862.

Crist, Lynda L., et al., eds. *The Papers of Jefferson Davis*. 14 vols. Baton Rouge: Louisiana State University Press, 1971–2015.

Journal of the Congress of the Confederate States of America, 1861–1865. 10 vols. Washington, DC: Government Printing Office, 1905.

The Official Records of the Union and Confederate Navies in the War of the Rebellion. 30 vols. Washington, DC: Government Printing Office, 1894–1922.

Rowland, Dunbar, ed. *Jefferson Davis, Constitutionalist: His Letters, Papers, and Speeches*. 10 vols. Jackson, MS: Department of Archives and History, 1923.

U. S. War Department. The War of the Rebellion: A Compilation of the Official Records of the Union and Confederate Armies. 128 vols. Washington, DC: Government Printing Office, 1880–1901.

Published Primary and Secondary Sources

Alexander, Thomas B., and Richard E. Berninger. *The Anatomy of the Confederate Congress: The Study of the Influences of Member Characteristics on Legislative Voting Behavior, 1861–1865*. Nashville: Vanderbilt University Press, 1972.

Allardice, Bruce S. *Confederate Colonels: A Biographical Register*. Columbia: University of Missouri Press, 2008.

Andrews, J. Cutler. *The South Reports the Civil War*. Pittsburgh: University of Pittsburgh Press, 1985.

Ballard, Michael B. "Misused Merit: The Tragedy of John C. Pemberton." In *Confederate Generals of the West*. 4 vols. Knoxville: University of Tennessee Press, 2010, 1:103–21.

Ballard, Michael B. *Pemberton: A Biography*. Jackson: University of Mississippi Press, 1991.

Bearss, Edwin C. *Outwitting Forrest: The Tupelo Campaign in Mississippi, June 22–July 23, 1864*. El Dorado, CA: Savas Beatie, 2023.

Bedout, Michael, and Leslie Jean Roberts, eds. *Exile in Richmond: The Confederate Journal of Henri Garidel*. Charlottesville: University of Virginia Press, 2001.

Bergeron, Arthur W., Jr. "Mansfield Lovell." In *Confederate Generals in the Western Theater*. 4 vols. Ed. Lawrence L. Hewitt and Arthur W. Bergeron, Jr. Knoxville: University of Tennessee Press, 2010, 1:45–68.

Bledsoe, Andrew S., and Andrew F. Lang. "Military History and the American Civil War." In *Upon the Field of Battle: Essays on the Military History of America's Civil War*. Ed. Andrew S. Bledsoe and Andrew F. Lang. Baton Rouge: Louisiana State University Press, 2018, 3–19.

Bonds, Russell. "Leonidas Polk: Southern Civil War General." *Civil War Times Illustrated* 45 (May 2006): 46–58.

Bridges, Hal. *Lee's Maverick General: Daniel Harvey Hill*. Lincoln: University of Nebraska Press, 1991.

Cable, George C. "New Orleans Before the Capture." In *Battles and Leaders of the Civil War*. 4 vols. New York: Thomas Yoseloff, 1956, 2:14–21.

Carter, Arthur B. *The Tarnished Cavalier: Major General Earl Van Dorn, C. S. A.* Knoxville: University of Tennessee Press, 1999.

Cashin, Joan. *First Lady of the Confederacy: Varina Davis's Civil War*. Cambridge: Belknap Press of Harvard University Press, 2006.

Castel, Albert. *Decision in the West: The Atlanta Campaign of 1864*. Lawrence: University Press of Kansas, 1992.

Castel, Albert. *General Sterling Price and the War in the West*. Baton Rouge: Louisiana State University Press, 1968.

Castel, Albert. *Victors in Blue: How Union Generals Fought the Confederates, Battled Each Other, and Won the Civil War*. Lawrence: University Press of Kansas, 2011.

Chatelain, Neal P. *Defending the Arteries of the Rebellion: Confederate Naval Operations in the Mississippi Valley*. El Dorado Hills, CA: Savas Beatie, 2020.

Clark, John E., Jr. *Railroads in the Civil War: The Impact of Management on Victory and Defeat*. Baton Rouge: Louisiana State University Press, 2004.

Connelly, Thomas L. *Army of the Heartland: The Army of Tennessee, 1861–1862*. Baton Rouge: Louisiana State University Press, 1967.

Connelly, Thomas L. *Autumn of Glory: The Army of Tennessee, 1862–1865*. Baton Rouge: Louisiana State University Press, 1971.

Connelly, Thomas L., and Archer Jones. *The Politics of Command: Factions and Ideas in Confederate Strategy*. Baton Rouge: Louisiana State University Press, 1973.

Cooling, Benjamin F. *Fort Donelson's Legacy: War and Society in Kentucky and Tennessee, 1862–1863*. Knoxville: University of Tennessee Press, 1997.

Cooper, William J. *Jefferson Davis, American*. New York: Vintage, 2000.

Coulter, E. Merton. *The Civil War and Readjustment in Kentucky*. Gloucester, MA: P. Smith, 1966.

Cozzens, Peter. *The Darkest Days of the War: The Battles of Iuka and Corinth*. Chapel Hill: University of North Carolina Press, 1997.

Curry, J. L. M. *Civil History of the Government of the Confederate States, with Some Personal Reminiscences*. Richmond, VA: Johnson Publishing Company, 1901.

Curry, Roy Watson. "James A. Seddon, A Southern Prototype," *Virginia Magazine of History* 63 (April 1955): 123–50.

Cutrer, Thomas W. *Theater of a Separate War: The Civil War West of the Mississippi River, 1861–1865*. Chapel Hill: University of North Carolina Press, 2017.

Dalton, C. David. "He Died on the Field of Glory: Felix Zollicoffer and the Confederate Defeat at Mill Springs." In *Confederate Generals in the Western Theater*. 4 vols. Ed. Lawrence C. Hewitt and Thomas E. Schott. Knoxville: University of Tennessee Press, 2018, 4:1–31.

Daniel, John M. *The Richmond Examiner During the War*. New York: Arno, 1972.

Daniel, Larry J. "'The Assaults of the Demagogues in Congress': General Albert Sidney Johnston and the Politics of Command." *Civil War History* 37 (December 1991): 328–35.

Daniel, Larry J. *Battle of Stones River: The Forgotten Conflict Between the Confederate Army of Tennessee and the Union Army of the Cumberland*. Baton Rouge: Louisiana State University Press, 2012.

Daniel, Larry J. *Cannoneers in Gray: The Field Artillery of the Army of Tennessee, 1861–1865*. Tuscaloosa: University of Alabama Press, 1984.

Daniel, Larry J. *Conquered: Why the Army of Tennessee Failed*. Chapel Hill: University of North Carolina Press, 2019.

Daniel, Larry J. *Engineering in the Confederate Heartland*. Baton Rouge: Louisiana State University Press, 2022.

Daniel, Larry J. *Shiloh: The Battle That Changed the Civil War*. New York: Simon & Schuster, 1997.

Daniel, Larry J. *Soldiering in the Army of Tennessee: A Portrait of Life in a Confederate Army*. Chapel Hill: University of North Carolina Press, 1991.

Daniel, Larry J., and Lynn N. Bock. *Island No. 10: Struggle for the Mississippi Valley*. Tuscaloosa: University of Alabama Press, 1996.

Davis, Jefferson. *Rise and Fall of the Confederate Government*. 2 vols. New York: D. Appleton and Company, 1881.

Davis, Reuben. *Recollections of Mississippi and Mississippians*. Boston: Houghton, Mifflin and Company, 1889.

Davis, Stephen. *Into Tennessee & Failure: John Bell Hood*. Macon, GA: Mercer University Press, 2020.

Davis, Stephen. *Texas Brigadier: To the Fall of Atlanta*. Macon, GA: Mercer University Press, 2019.

Davis, Varina. *Jefferson Davis: Ex-President of the Confederate States*. 2 vols. New York: Belford Company, 1890.

Davis, William C. *Breckinridge: Statesman, Soldier, Symbol*. Baton Rouge: Louisiana State University Press, 1974.

Davis, William C. "General Samuel Cooper." In *Leaders of the Lost Cause: New Perspectives on the Confederate High Command*. Ed. Gary W. Gallagher and Joseph T. Glatthaar. Mechanicsburg, PA: Stackpole Books, 2004, 101–31.

Davis, William C. *Jefferson Davis: The Man and His Hour*. New York: Harper Collins, 1991.

Davis, William C. "Richmond Becomes the Confederate Capital." In *Virginia at War 1861*. Ed. William C. Davis and James I. Robertson, Jr., Lexington: University Press of Kentucky, 2005, 113–29.

Davis, William C., ed. *A Fire-eater Remembers: The Confederate Memoir of Robert Barnwell Rhett*. Columbia: University of South Carolina Press, 2000.

De Credico, Mary A. *Confederate Citadel: Richmond and Its People at War*. Lexington: University Press of Kentucky, 2020.

DeLeon, Thomas C. *Belles, Beaux, and Brains of the 60's*. New York: G. W. Dillingham Company, 1907.

DeLeon, Thomas C. *Four Years in Rebel Capitals: An Inside View of Life in the Southern Confederacy, from Birth to Death*. Mobile, AL: Chronicle Publishing Company, 1874.

Eicher, David J. *Dixie Betrayed: How the South Really Lost the Civil War*. New York: Little, Brown & Company, 2006.

Eicher, David J., and John H. Eicher. *Civil War High Commands*. Stanford: Stanford University Press, 2002.

Escott, Paul D. *After Secession: Jefferson Davis and the Failure of Confederate Nationalism*. Baton Rouge: Louisiana State University Press, 1978.

Estill, Mary S., ed. "Diary of a Confederate Congressman, 1862–1863." *Southwestern Historical Quarterly* 38 (April 1935): 270–301.

Evans, Eli N. *Judah P. Benjamin: The Jewish Confederate*. New York: The Free Press, 1988.

Ferguson, Ernest B. *Ashes of Glory: Richmond at War*. New York: Vintage Books, 1996.

Fisher, Noel C. *War at Every Door: Partisan Politics & Guerrilla Violence in East Tennessee, 1860–1869*. Chapel Hill: University of North Carolina Press, 1997.

Foote, Henry S. *Casket of Reminiscences*. Washington, DC: Chronicle Publishing Company, 1874.

Foote, Henry S. *War of the Rebellion: or Scylla and Charybdis*. New York: Harper & Brother, 1866.

Freehling, William F. *The South vs. The South: How Anti-Confederate Southerners Shaped the Course of the Civil War*. Oxford and New York: Oxford University Press, 2001.

Freeman, Joanne B. *The Field of Blood: Violence in Congress and the Road to the Civil War*. New York: Picador Farrar, Strauss and Giroux, 2018.

Fremantle, Arthur James L. *Three Months in the Southern States, April–June 1863*. New York: J. Bradburn, 1864.

Geise, William R. *The Confederate Military Forces in the Trans-Mississippi West, 1861–1865: A Study in Command*. El Dorado Hills, CA: Savas Beatie, 2022.

"General Cleburne's Views on Slavery." *Annals of the Army of Tennessee and Early Western History* 1 (May 1878): 50–52.

Glatthaar, Joseph T. *General Lee's Army: From Victory to Collapse*. New York: Free Press, 2008.

Goodwin, Doris Kearns. *Team of Rivals: The Political Genius of Abraham Lincoln*. New York: Simon & Schuster, 2005.

Groce, W. Todd. *Mountain Rebels: East Tennessee Confederates and the Civil War, 1860–1870*. Knoxville: University of Tennessee Press, 1999.

Hafendorfer, Kenneth A. *Mill Springs: Campaign and Battle of Mill Springs*. Louisville: KH Press, 2001.

Halderman, Walter C. *Theophilus Hunter Holmes: A North Carolina General in the Civil War*. Jefferson, NC: McFarland & Co., Inc., 2014.

Harrison, Constance Cary. "Richmond Scenes in '62." In *Battles and Leaders of the Civil War*. 4 vols. New York: Thomas Yoseloff, 1956, 2:439–48.

Harrison, Lowell H. "The Government of Confederate Kentucky." In *The Civil War in Kentucky: Battle for the Bluegrass State*. Ed. Kent Masterson Brown. Mason City, IA: Savas Publishing Company, 2000, 79–101.

Hartje, Robert J. *Van Dorn: The Life and Times of a Confederate General*. Nashville: Vanderbilt University Press, 1967.

Hess, Earl J. *Banners to the Breeze: The Kentucky Campaign, Corinth, & Stones River*. Lincoln: University of Nebraska Press, 2000.

Hess, Earl J. *Braxton Bragg: The Most Hated Man of the Confederacy*. Chapel Hill: University of North Carolina Press, 2016.

Hess, Earl J. *The Civil War in the West: Victory and Defeat from the Appalachians to the Mississippi*. Chapel Hill: University of North Carolina Press, 2012.

Hess, Earl J. *Civil War Supply and Strategy: Feeding and Moving Armies*. Baton Rouge: Louisiana State University Press, 2020.

Hess, Earl J. *The Knoxville Campaign: Burnside and Longstreet in East Tennessee*. Knoxville: University of Tennessee Press, 2012.

Hess, Earl J. "Revitalizing Traditional Military History." In *Upon the Fields of Battle: Essays on the Military History of America's Civil War*. Ed. Andrew S. Bledsoe and Andrew F. Lang. Baton Rouge: Louisiana State University Press, 2018, 20–42.

Hess, Earl J. *Storming Vicksburg: Grant, Pemberton, and the Battles of May 19–22, 1863*. Chapel Hill: University of North Carolina Press, 2020.

Hess, Earl J. *Supply and Strategy: Feeding Men and Moving Armies*. Baton Rouge: Louisiana State University Press, 2020.

Hill, Benjamin H. *Senator Benjamin H. Hill of Georgia: His Life, Speeches, and Writings*. Atlanta: H. C. Hudgins & Co., 1891.

Holladay, Florence Elizabeth. "The Powers of the Confederate Commander of the Confederate Trans- Mississippi Department, 1863 to 1865." *Southwestern Historical Quarterly* 21 (January 1918): 279–98.

Hood, John Bell. *Advance and Retreat: Personal Experiences in the United States & Confederate States Armies*. Bloomington: Indiana University Press, 1959.

Hood, Stephen M. *The Lost Papers of Confederate General John Bell Hood*. El Dorado Hills, CA: Savas Beatie, 2015.

Horn, Huston. *Leonidas Polk: Warrior Bishop of the Confederacy*. Lawrence: University Press of Kansas, 2019.

Hughes, Nathaniel C., Jr., ed. *General William J. Hardee: Old Reliable*. Wilmington, DE: Broadfoot Publishing Company, 1987.

Hughes, Nathaniel C., Jr., ed. *Liddell's Record: St. John Liddell: Brigadier General CSA, Staff Officer and Brigade Commander in the Army of Tennessee*. Dayton, OH: Morningside, 1983.

Hughes, Nathaniel C., Jr., and Roy P. Stonesipher, Jr. *The Life and Wars of Gideon J. Pillow*. Chapel Hill: University of North Carolina Press, 1993.

Jewitt, Clayton C., ed. *Rise and Fall of the Confederacy: The Memoir of Senator Williamson B. Oldham*. Columbia: University of Missouri Press, 1986.

Johnston, Joseph E. "Jefferson Davis in the Mississippi Campaign." In *Battles and Leaders of the Civil War*. 4 vols. New York: Thomas Yoseloff, 1956, 3:472–82.

Johnston, Joseph E. *Narrative of Military Operations During the Civil War*. New York: Da Capo Press, 1959.

Johnston, Joseph E. "Opposing Sherman's Advance to Atlanta." In *Battles and Leaders of the Civil War*. 4 vols. New York: Thomas Yoseloff, 1956, 4:260–77.

Johnston, William Preston. *The Life of Gen. Albert Sidney Johnston, Embracing His Services in the Armies of the United States, the Republic of Texas, and the Confederate States*. New York: D. Appleton, 1879.

Jones, Archer. *Confederate Strategy from Shiloh to Vicksburg*. Baton Rouge: Louisiana State University Press, 1991.

Jones, Howard. *Union in Peril: The Crisis Over British Intervention in the Civil War*. Chapel Hill: University of North Carolina Press, 1992.

Jones, John B. *A Rebel War Clerk's Diary of the Confederate States*. 2 vols. Philadelphia: J. P. Lippincott, 1866.

Kimball, Greg D. *American City, Southern Place: A Cultural History of Antebellum Richmond*. Athens: University of Georgia Press, 2000.

King, Alvy T. *Louis T. Wigfall: Southern Fire-eater*. Baton Rouge: Louisiana State University Press, 1970.

Kirkpatrick, Arthur J. "Missouri Delegation in the Confederate Congress." *Civil War History* 5 (June 1959): 188–98.

Krick, Robert K. *Civil War Weather in Virginia*. Tuscaloosa: University of Alabama Press, 2007.

Levine, Bruce. *Confederate Emancipation: Southern Plans to Free and Arm Slaves During the Civil War*. New York: Oxford University Press, 2006.

Link, William A. *The Last Fire-eater: Roger A. Pryor and the Search for a Southern Identity*. Baton Rouge: Louisiana State University Press, 2023.

Lockett, S. H. "The Defense of Vicksburg." In *Battles and Leaders of the Civil War*. 4 vols. New York: Thomas Yoseloff, 1956, 3:482–92.

Longacre, Edward G. *Cavalry in the Heartland: The Mounted Forces of the Army of Tennessee*. Yardley, PA: Westholme, 2009.

Longstreet, James. *From Manassas to Appomattox*. Philadelphia: J. P. Lippincott Co., 1896.

Mackey, Thomas C. "Not a Pariah, but a Keystone: Kentucky and Secession." In *Sister States, Enemy States: The Civil War in Kentucky and Tennessee* (Lexington: University Press of Kentucky, 2011). Ed. Kent T. Dollar, Larry H. Whitaker, and W. Calvin Dickinson. Lexington: University Press of Kentucky, 2011, 25–45.

McCash, William B. *Thomas R. R. Cobb: The Making of a Southern Nationalist*. Macon, GA: Mercer University Press, 1983.

McDonough, James Lee. *William Tecumseh Sherman: In the Service of My Country, A Life*. New York: W. W. Norton & Company, 2016.

McGuire, Judith. *Diary of a Southern Refugee During the War*. New York: E. J. Hale & Son, 1867.

McKenzie, Robert. *Lincolnites and Rebels: A Divided Town in the American Civil War*. New York: Oxford University Press, 2007.

McMurry, Richard M. *Atlanta 1864: Last Chance for the Confederacy*. Lincoln: University of Nebraska Press, 2000.

McMurry, Richard M. *The Civil Wars of General Joseph E. Johnston, Confederate States Army*. El Dorado, CA: Savas Beatie, 2023.

McMurry, Richard M. "The Enemy at Richmond: Joseph E. Johnston and the Confederate Government." *Civil War History* 27 (March 1981): 5–31.

McMurry, Richard M. *John Bell Hood and the War for Southern Independence*. Lexington: University Press of Kentucky, 1982.

McMurry, Richard M. *Two Great Rebel Armies: An Essay in Confederate Military History*. Chapel Hill: University of North Carolina Press, 1989.

McPherson, James M. *Embattled Rebel: Jefferson Davis and the Confederate Civil War*. New York: Penguin Books, 2015.

McWhiney, Grady. *Braxton Bragg and Confederate Defeat*. Tuscaloosa: University of Alabama Press, 1969.

McWhiney, Grady. *Southerners and Other Americans*. New York: Basic Books, 1973.

Miller, Emily Van Dorn. *A Soldier's Honor with Reminiscences of Major General Earl Van Dorn*. New York: The Abbey Press, 1902.

Morrison, James I., ed. *The Memoirs of Henry Heth*. Westport, Conn.: Greenwood Press, 1974.

Murray, Williamson, and Wayne Wei-siang. *A Savage War: A Military History of the Civil War*. Princeton: Princeton University Press, 2016.

Nash, Charles Edward. *Biographical Sketches of Gen. Pat Cleburne and Gen. T. C. Hindman*. Little Rock: By author, 1898.

Neal, Diane, and Thomas W. Kremm. *The Lion of the South: General Thomas C. Hindman*. Macon: Mercer University Press, 1993.

Nuemberger, Ruth Anna. *The Clays of Alabama: A Planter-Lawyer-Politician Family*. Lexington: University Press of Kentucky, 1958.

Parish, Michael. *Richard Taylor: Soldier Prince of Dixie*. Chapel Hill: University of North Carolina Press, 1992.

Parks, Joseph H. *General Edmund Kirby Smith, C. S. A.* Baton Rouge: Louisiana State University Press, 1954.

Parson, Thomas E. *Work for Giants: The Campaign and Battle of Tupelo/Harrisburg, Mississippi, June–July 1864*. Kent, OH: Kent State University Press, 2014.

Patrick, Rembert W. *Jefferson Davis and His Cabinet*. Baton Rouge: Louisiana State University Press, 1944.

Peace, Haywood, Jr. *Secession and Reconstruction*. New York: Negro Universities Press, 1928.

Phillips, Ulrich B., ed. *The Correspondence of Robert Toombs, Alexander H. Stevens, and Howell Cobb*. Washington, DC: American Historical Association, 1913.

Polk, William K. *Leonidas Polk: Bishop and General*. 2 vols. New York: Longmans, Green, 1915.

Powell, David A. *The Chickamauga Campaign*. 3 vols. El Dorado Hills, CA: 2014–2016.

Pritchard, James M. "Glory Denied: The Hard Fate of George B. Crittenden." In *Confederate Generals in the Western Theater*. Ed. Lawrence B. Hewitt and Arthur W. Bergeron, Jr. Knoxville: University of Tennessee Press, 2010, 1–22.

"Proceedings and Speeches of the Announcement of Hon. R. L. Y. Peyton, of Missouri." Richmond, VA: Sentinel Job Office, 1864.

"Proceedings and Speeches of the Death of Hon. William M. Cooke of Missouri, in House of Representatives." Richmond, VA: Smith, Bailey & Co., 1863.

"Proceedings of the Confederate Congress." *Southern Historical Society Papers*. Vols. 44–49, Richmond: William Ellis Jones, 1876–1957; and vols. 50–52, Richmond: Virginia Historical Society, 1958–1959.

Prushankin, Jeffrey S. *A Crisis in Confederate Command: Edmund Kirby Smith, Richard Taylor, and the Army of the Trans-Mississippi*. Baton Rouge: Louisiana State University Press, 2005.

Putnam, Sallie Brock. *Richmond During the War: Four Years of Personal Observation*. New York: G. W. Carleton & Co., 1867.

Rable, George. *The Confederate Republic: A Revolution Against Politics*. Chapel Hill: University of North Carolina Press, 1994.

Rable, George. *God's Almost Chosen People: A Religious History of the American Civil War*. Chapel Hill: University of North Carolina Press, 2010.

Ranck, James B. *Albert Gallatin Brown: Radical Southern Nationalist*. Philadelphia: Porcupine Press, 1974.

Rawley, John A. *Turning Points of the Civil War*. Lincoln: University of Nebraska Press, 1966.

Reagan, John H. *Memoirs, with Special Reference to Secession and the Civil War*. New York: Neale, 1906.

Rice, Jessie Pearl. *J. L. M. Curry: Southerner, Statesman, and Educator*. New York: King's Crown Press, 1949.

Roberts, Bobby L. "General T. C. Hindman and the Trans-Mississippi District." *Arkansas Historical Quarterly* 32 (Winter 1973): 297–311.

Robertson, James I., Jr. "Diary of a Southern Refugee During the War, January–July 1862." In *Virginia at War 1862*. Ed. William C. Davis and James I. Robertson, Jr. Lexington: University Press of Kentucky, 2007, 155–227.

Robertson, James I., Jr. "Diary of a Southern Refugee in 1861: Judith Brockenbrough" In *Virginia at War 1861*. Ed. William C. Davis and James I. Robertson, Jr. Lexington: University Press of Kentucky, 1972, 159–223.

Robins, Glenn. *The Bishop of the Old South: The Ministry and Civil War Legacy of Leonidas Polk*. Macon, GA: Mercer University Press, 2006.

Roland, Charles P. *Albert Sidney Johnston: Soldier of Three Republics*. Austin: University of Texas Press, 1964.

Roman, Alfred. *The Military Operations of General Beauregard in the War Between the States, 1861– 1865: Including a Brief Personal Sketch of His Service in the War with Mexico, 1846–48*. 2 vols. New York: Harper & Row, 1883.

Rose, Victor M. *The Life and Services of Gen. Ben McCulloch*. 1958 reprint. Philadelphia: Pictorial Bureau of the Press, 1888.

Rowland, Dunbar, ed. *Jefferson Davis, Constitutionalist: His Letters, Papers and Speeches*. 10 vols. Jackson: Mississippi History Department of Archives and History, 1923.

Russell, William H. *My Diary North and South*. London: T. O. P. H. Burnham, 1861.

Scarborough, William K, ed. *The Diary of Edmund Ruffin*. 3 vols. Baton Rouge: Louisiana State University Press, 1972.

Schott, Thomas E. *Alexander H. Stephens of Georgia: A Biography*. Baton Rouge: Louisiana State University Press, 1988.

Sears, Stephen W. *Lincoln's Lieutenants: The High Command of the Army of the Potomac*. New York: Houghton Mifflin Harcourt, 2017.

Seitz, Don Carlos. *Braxton Bragg: General of the Confederacy*. Columbia, SC: State, 1924.

Settles, Thomas M. *John Bankhead Magruder: A Military Reappraisal*. Baton Rouge: Louisiana State University Press, 2009.

Shackelford, George G. *George Wythe Randolph and the Confederate Elite*. Athens: University of Georgia Press, 1988.

Shaw, Arthur Marion. *William Preston Johnston*. Baton Rouge: Louisiana State University Press, 1943.

Shea, William L., and Earl J. Hess. *Pea Ridge: Civil War Campaign in the West*. Chapel Hill: University of North Carolina Press, 1992.

Simon, John W. "Lincoln, Grant, and Kentucky in 1861." In *The Civil War in Kentucky: Battle for the Bluegrass State*. Ed. Kent Masterson Brown. Mason City, IA: Savas Publishing Company, 2000, 1–21.

Smith, Timothy B. *Early Struggles for Vicksburg: The Mississippi Campaign and Chickasaw Bayou, October 25–December 31, 1862*. Lawrence: University Press of Kansas, 2022.

Smith, Timothy B. *Grant Invades Tennessee: The 1862 Battles for Forts Henry and Donelson*. Lawrence: University Press of Kansas, 2016.

Snead, Thomas L. "The Conquest of Arkansas." In *Battles and Leaders of the Civil War*. 4 vols. New York: Thomas Yoseloff, 1956, 3:441–59.

Snead, Thomas L. *The Fight for Missouri: From the Election of Lincoln to the Death of Lyon*. New York: Charles Scribner's Sons, 1886.

Snead, Thomas L. "With Price East of the Mississippi." In *Battles and Leaders of the Civil War*. 4 vols. New York: Thomas Yoseloff, 1956, 717–34.

Southern Literary Messenger 34 (February–March 1862).

Sterling, Ada. *Belle of the Fifties: Memoirs of Mrs. Clay of Alabama, Covering Social and Political Life and the South, 1855–1866*. New York: Doubleday, Paige & Company, 1905.

Stevenson, William G. *Thirteen Months in the Rebel Army by an Impressed New Yorker*. New York: A. S. Barns & Burr, 1862.

Strode, Hudson. *Jefferson Davis: American Patriot*. New York: Harcourt, Brace, 1955.

Stoker, Donald. *The Grand Design: Strategy and the U.S. Civil War*. New York: Oxford University Press, 2010.

Sutherland, Daniel E. "Mansfield Lovell's Quest for Justice: Another Look at the Fall of New Orleans." *Louisiana History* 24 (Summer 1983): 233–59.

Symonds, Craig L. *Joseph E. Johnston: A Civil War Biography*. New York: Norton & Company, 1992.

Symonds, Craig L. "No Margin for Error: Civil War in the Confederate Government." In *The Art of Command in the Civil War*. Ed. Steven E. Woodworth. Lincoln: University of Nebraska Press, 1998, 1–16.

Tate, Allen. *Jefferson Davis: His Rise and Fall*. Nashville: J. S. Sanders & Company, 1998.

Taylor, Richard. *Destruction and Reconstruction: Personal Experiences in the Late War*. New York: D. Appleton, 1879.

Taylor, Thomas H. "Boyce-Hammond Correspondence." *Journal of Southern History* 31 (May 1937): 384–58.

Temple, Oliver Perry. *East Tennessee in the Civil War*. Cincinnati: R. Clarke Company, 1899.

Thomas, Emory M. *The Confederate State of Richmond: A Biography of a Capital*. Baton Rouge: Louisiana State University Press, 1971.

Trask, Benjamin H. *Two Months in the Confederate States: An Englishman's Travels Through the South*. Baton Rouge: Louisiana State University Press, 1996.

Trexler, Harrison A. "The Davis Administration and the Richmond Press, 1861–1865." *Journal of Southern History* 16 (May 1950): 177–95.

Underwood, Rodman L. *Stephen Russell Mallory: A Biography of the Confederate Navy Secretary and United States Senator*. Jefferson, NC: McFarland & Co., 2005.

Vandiver, Frank F. *Ploughshares into Swords: Josiah Gorgas and Confederate Ordnance*. College Station: Texas A&M University, 1980.

Vandiver, W. D. "Reminiscences of General John B. Clark." *Missouri Historical Review* 20 (January 1926): 223–35.

Walther, Eric. *William Lowndes Yancey and the Coming of the Civil War*. Chapel Hill: University of North Carolina Press, 2008.

Warner, Ezra J. *Generals in Gray: Lives of the Confederate Commanders*. Baton Rouge: Louisiana State University Press, 1959.

Warner, Ezra J., and W. Buck Yearns. *Biographical Register of the Confederate Congress*. Baton Rouge: Louisiana State University Press, 1975.

Welsh, Jack D. *Medical Histories of Confederate Generals*. Kent, OH: Kent State University Press, 1995.

Wiggins, Sarah L., ed. *The Journals of Josiah Gorgas, 1857–1878*. Tuscaloosa: University of Alabama Press, 1995.

Wiley, Bell I., ed. *Letters of Warren Aiken: Confederate Congressman*. Athens: University of Georgia Press, 1959.

Williams, T. Harry. *P. G. T. Beauregard: Napoleon in Gray*. 1995 reprint. Baton Rouge: Louisiana State University Press, 2011.

Wills, Brian Steel. *The Confederacy's Greatest Cavalryman: Nathan Bedford Forrest*. Lawrence: University of Press of Kansas, 1992.

Wixson, Neal E., ed. *From Civility to Survival: Richmond Ladies During the Civil War*. Bloomington, IN: iUniverse, 2011.

Woods, Earl C. *The Diary of Edmund Enoul Livaudais*. New Orleans: Archdiocese of New Orleans, 1982.

Woodward, C. Van, ed. *Mary Chesnut's Civil War*. New York: Princeton University Press, 1981.

Woodworth, Steven E. *Davis & Lee at War*. Lawrence: University Press of Kansas, 1998.

Woodworth, Steven E. "Davis, Polk, and the End of Kentucky Neutrality." In *No Band of Brothers: Problems of the Rebel High Command*. Ed. Steven E. Woodworth. Columbia: University of Missouri Press, 1999, 12–18.

Woodworth, Steven E. *Jefferson Davis and His Generals: The Failure of Confederate Command in the West*. Lawrence: University Press of Kansas, 1990.

Woodworth, Steven E. *This Great Struggle: America's Civil War*. New York: Rowman & Littlefield, 2011.

Wright, Mrs. D. Giraud. *A Southern Girl in '61*. New York: Doubleday, Page & Co., 1905.

Wynne, Ben. *The Man Who Punched Jefferson Davis: The Political Life of Henry S. Foote, Southern Unionist*. Baton Rouge: Louisiana State University Press, 2018.

Yearns, Wilfred Buck. *The Confederate Congress*. Athens: University of Georgia Press, 1960.

Younger, Edward, ed. *Inside the Confederate Government: The Diary of Robert Garlick Kill Kean*. New York: Oxford University Press, 1967.

Dissertations and Thesis

Bellamy, James W. "The Political Career of Landon Carter Haynes." Master's thesis, University of Tennessee, 1952.

Bryan, Charles F., Jr. "The Civil War in East Tennessee: A Social, Political, and Economic Study." PhD diss., University of Tennessee, 1978.

Chapman, Anne W. "Benjamin Stoddard Ewell: A Biography." Dissertations, Thesis, and Master's Projects 1539623748, College of William and Mary.

Redard, Thomas E. "The Port of New Orleans: An Economic History, 1821–1860." PhD diss., Louisiana State University and Agricultural and Mechanical College, 1985.

INDEX